Supporting and Educating

Traumatized Students

Supporting and Educating Traumatized Students

A Guide for School-Based Professionals

EDITED BY

ERIC ROSSEN

AND

ROBERT HULL

OXFORD
UNIVERSITY PRESS

Oxford University Press is a department of the University of Oxford. It furthers the
University's objective of excellence in research, scholarship, and education by publishing
worldwide.

Oxford   New York
Auckland   Cape Town   Dar es Salaam   Hong Kong   Karachi
Kuala Lumpur   Madrid   Melbourne   Mexico City   Nairobi
New Delhi   Shanghai   Taipei   Toronto

With offices in
Argentina   Austria   Brazil   Chile   Czech Republic   France   Greece
Guatemala   Hungary   Italy   Japan   Poland   Portugal   Singapore
South Korea   Switzerland   Thailand   Turkey   Ukraine   Vietnam

Oxford is a registered trademark of Oxford University Press in the UK and certain other
countries.

Published in the United States of America by
Oxford University Press
198 Madison Avenue, New York, NY 10016

Library of Congress Cataloging-in-Publication Data
    Supporting and educating traumatized students: a guide for school-based professionals/
    edited by Eric Rossen, Robert Hull.
        p. cm.
    ISBN 978-0-19-976652-9
    1. Students—Mental health.   2. Students—Mental health services.
    3. Psychic trauma in children.   4. Psychic trauma—Treatment.
    5. Educational psychology.   I. Rossen, Eric A.   II. Hull, Robert (Robert V.)
    LB3430.S87 2013
    371.4'04—dc23
    2012005614

Printed in the United States of America on acid-free paper

CONTENTS

SECTION THREE Administrative and Policy Considerations: Fostering Resiliency

Numerous students in our schools have been exposed to traumatic and other adverse circumstances. To illustrate, a recent epidemiological study[1] revealed that approximately 71% of children aged 2 to 17 were exposed to at least one victimization event in the past year (e.g., assault, theft, criminal victimization, maltreatment), with the majority of those students exposed to multiple victimizations. Other studies have also projected similar statistics, with the prevalence of at least one exposure to trauma over the lifetime as high as 61% in males and 51% in females.[2] Even more alarming, those rates increase among urban youth (87% in males, 78% in females).[3] These experiences often undermine students' ability to learn, form relationships, and manage their feelings and behavior. Unfortunately, many educators and other professionals working with this population are often unaware of these children's complex needs or how to meet those needs within the hours of the typical school day.

Knowledge of these factors has become increasingly important given issues related to natural disasters, terrorism, economic instability, military deployment, and immigration, as well as continued concerns such as homelessness, community violence, abuse, and neglect.

PURPOSE OF THE BOOK

Given this context, the purpose of this book is to provide a thorough look at the impacts of numerous traumatic experiences (both general and specific) on school-aged children and adolescents and provide a variety of strategies to help improve their educational and social outcomes in school. Some interventions are more school-wide policy driven, whereas others are directed at individual educators who know and work with students personally. The goal is to empower all educators with practical ways to support traumatized students in schools, regardless of the amount of specific training in mental health interventions.

WHY THE BOOK WAS DEVELOPED

We (the editors) spent a large part of our careers responding to the needs of traumatized students. Several years ago, in response to the need of increasing the capacity of educators to respond effectively to these students, we developed a graduate course designed for master's-level teachers and counselors on this topic. In searching for an appropriate text, we found that few books comprehensively addressed the unique educational needs of students who had experienced various sources of trauma. Most books tend to focus on single-event trauma (e.g., Hurricane Katrina, grief following loss) or clinical interventions that require either outpatient clinic services or highly specialized treatment programs that could not reach a large number of students due to time constraints and ongoing reductions in force. Further, as stated by Wong,[4] "...there are few, if any, preservice teacher preparation programs that help educators to develop skills and coping strategies to detect and teach traumatized, depressed, or anxious students." Similarly, most educators, in our experience, viewed the implementation of evidence-based clinical protocols as unrealistic within many schools, particularly those in districts that have limited resources and multiple sources of community stressors, where such services are needed the most.

Though many psychological texts address the impact of trauma on children and adolescents, this book is designed specifically for busy educators who work with traumatized students daily. Aside from improving awareness of multiple trauma sources and their unique impacts on learning and behavior, this book will focus on practical, implementable, and effective strategies for supporting traumatized students in school, many of which do not require an advanced degree in mental health. Its aim is to present effective strategies for creating a classroom climate of mutual respect and empathy and, most important, to foster positive self-esteem and competency building for traumatized students.

Notably, the strategies contained within this volume are not meant to supplant existing, evidence-based clinical treatment programs provided by trained practitioners, nor are they intended to replace comprehensive, integrated school-wide policies that improve conditions for learning. In fact, a toolkit on existing school-based programs designed to help support traumatized students was compiled by RAND and the Gulf States Policy Institute,[5] and we encourage readers to examine these options. In this vein, our goal is to supplement such policies and interventions with a school workforce equipped to provide supports throughout the school day. To meet this goal, we used an approach that combined knowledge of the cognitive and behavioral effects of trauma, research-based clinical interventions, educational practices, and the experiences of veteran educators to create a new framework for assisting students with a history of trauma. Nevertheless, it remains critical that schools provide a range of school-based mental health support professionals in the school building who have the knowledge and training to provide more intensive individual and school-wide supports.

LIMITATIONS—WHAT THE BOOK IS AND WHAT IT IS NOT

The book contains many chapters targeting specific populations of students based on a potential source of trauma (e.g., being homeless, being immigrants and refugees, having incarcerated parents), although the editors recognize and acknowledge that not all sources of trauma are included, and not all available strategies or resources could be included. Other sources of trauma not directly addressed in the book include chronic illnesses, commercial sexual exploitation and human trafficking, chronic bullying, frequent mobility through the foster care system, and parents with severe mental illness, to name a few. Our hope is that some of the strategies presented may also apply to these other sources of trauma or at least stir creative thinking and allow educators to develop a framework for how to support all traumatized students. Taken further, we hope that readers will consider that many students will experience more than one stressor at a given time, potentially complicating their symptoms and needs.

Many chapters contain specific sections titled "Cultural Considerations." These chapters do not offer a full review of the complex interactions of cultural contexts and trauma; instead, they are intended to generate thought and increase awareness about this interaction. These same chapters also include specific sections titled "Developmental Considerations," with the intent to help educators navigate the complexities of working with students from various age groups and developmental stages. The scope of reactions, and effective strategies to support students, will vary based on developmental level and thus is an important consideration. Chapter 3 offers additional perspectives into understanding the impact of trauma within a developmental context.

Again, the strategies contained within this book are intended to support and supplement empirically based interventions for traumatized students, for which there are several. The intent is to *empower* educators who typically do not have the skills, training, or time in a school day to provide clinically oriented interventions, yet remain frustrated with their lack of ability to support and educate these students. This book will enable educators to support the work of mental health professionals.

WHO SHOULD USE THIS BOOK?

We believe this book will be a useful resource for all practicing school-based professionals. This will also be an excellent text or supplement for courses that address crisis, trauma, and education for a broad spectrum of specializations, including teachers, school social workers, school psychologists, special educators, school counselors, school administrators, and other school-based professionals.

HOW SHOULD THIS BOOK BE USED?

The book will most likely serve as a reference guide for busy educators. Given the layout of the book, educators can raise their awareness about targeted groups of students who have experienced a specific source of trauma; search for specific, practical strategies aimed at those groups; and locate available web-based resources. The first three chapters offer a broader introduction to trauma and its impacts on cognitive and social functioning, behavior, learning, and development. The final three chapters provide a broad sense of how to build trauma-sensitive school systems and develop resiliency among students.

Some chapters may offer suggestions or recommendations that appear in more than one chapter or reference another chapter. In some cases, recommendations that are somewhat implicit (e.g., providing a safe, caring, nonjudgmental environment for students) were not explicitly stated in the interest of space. In other cases, recommendations were omitted from chapters if they were already noted in some other chapters (e.g., sexual abuse, physical abuse, neglect, sudden death and anticipated death); however, readers are directed throughout the book on appropriate chapters to cross-reference and review. For these chapters, the experiences were distinct enough, in our opinion, to warrant separate chapters, despite the fact that some of the same recommendations could apply.

Teachers may utilize the book by raising personal awareness of trauma and directly implementing the strategies provided. School instructional support personnel may decide to use the book to also raise awareness and help develop ideas to share with other stakeholders in team meetings or through consultative relationships. Administrators and others may benefit from gaining insight on how to support a potentially large subset of students and use these guidelines to improve school/district policies. Parents may also find this resource useful as well, although school-based professionals compose the primary audience. Importantly, all those utilizing this resource should employ personal and professional judgment as each student's experiences, and the context in which they occur, are unique.

NOTES

1. Finkelhor, Ormrod, Turner, & Hamby, 2005.
2. Kessler, Sonnega, & Bromet, 1995.
3. Breslau, Wilcox, Storr, Lucia, & Anthony, 2004.
4. Wong, 2008, p. 399.
5. Jaycox, Morse, Tanielian, & Stein, 2006.

REFERENCES

Breslau, N., Wilcox, H. C., Storr, C. L., Lucia, V. C., & Anthony, J. C. (2004). Trauma exposure and posttraumatic stress disorder: A study of youths in urban America. *Journal of Urban Health: Bulletin of the New York Academy of Medicine, 81,* 530–544.

Finkelhor, D., Ormrod, R. K., Turner, H. A., & Hamby, S. L. (2005). The victimization of children and youth: A comprehensive, national survey. *Child Maltreatment, 10,* 5–25.

Jaycox, L. H., Morse, L. K., Tanielian, T., & Stein, B. D. (2006). *How schools can help students recover from traumatic experiences: A toolkit for supporting long-term recovery.* Santa Monica, CA: RAND Corporation. Retrieved from http://www.rand.org/content/dam/rand/pubs/technical_reports/2006/RAND_TR413.pdf

Kessler, R. C., Sonnega, A., & Bromet, E. (1995). Posttraumatic stress disorder in the national comorbidity survey. *Archives of General Psychiatry, 52*, 1048–1060.

Wong, M. (2008). Interventions to reduce psychological harm from traumatic events among children and adolescents: A commentary on the application of findings to the real world of schools. *American Journal of Preventive Medicine, 35*, 398–400.

ACKNOWLEDGMENTS

I would like to thank my wonderful, brilliant, beautiful, and supportive wife, Lauren, whose calming effect had a positive influence on this book, as well as all other aspects of my life. I'd also like to thank my daughter, Emily—while she remained the number one reason for my procrastination during work on this book, she also continued to remind me of the most important things in life. Emily, you are just the best. Finally, I'd like to thank the rest of my family for their unwavering encouragement, love, and support.
—E. Rossen

I want to thank my parents and brothers and sisters for always providing me with the belief that anything can be overcome and better things are always just around the next bend in the road. I also want to acknowledge my wife and children for their constant support and all the others who are too many to list that have provided support and encouragement. Finally, working with the various authors of this volume has changed the meaning of what I do with my daily work and has transformed my ability to support teachers and families.
—R. Hull

In 2009, Dr. Karen Weston, with the University of Missouri at Columbia, asked us to create a graduate-level course that could assist school-based professionals in educating students with a trauma history. Along with Jennifer MacLaughlin and Amanda Mercer, both school psychologists, we worked diligently to create this course and first offered it in the fall of 2009. We were surprised at the overwhelming interest and enthusiasm that the course generated. As the course went on, we were inspired by our students' efforts to assist their students. This inspiration led us to consider creating a book that provided practical strategies for educators. Thus, a special thank you goes to Dr. Weston and those graduate students for helping inspire this book.

We would like to thank Sarah Harrington, our editor with Oxford University Press, for her positive, responsive, and supportive role throughout the development of the book.

We would like to acknowledge the many school-based professionals that dedicate their time, lives, and hearts to educating all students and providing the conditions for learning in schools across the globe. Your work is inspirational, and incredibly important. Thank you for all you do.

And finally, this book is dedicated to the students we have worked with throughout our careers, and the youth who will continue to rely on the support of schools to learn, develop, and grow. When all is said and done, this book is for you.

—E. Rossen & R. Hull

Eric Rossen, PhD

Dr. Rossen received his doctorate in School Psychology from the University of Florida and is a Nationally Certified School Psychologist and licensed psychologist in the state of Maryland. He has experience working in public schools as well as independent practice and is currently the Director of Professional Development and Standards for the National Association of School Psychologists. Aside from his interests in trauma, Dr. Rossen has published several manuscripts and presented nationally on issues related to bullying, crisis response, behavior management, emotional intelligence, social-emotional functioning, and psychological assessment. He also has served as a college instructor and adjunct faculty at the University of Missouri and Prince George's Community College.

Robert Hull, EdS, MHS

With over 30 years of experience in education, Hull has been nationally recognized for his work with serving students and improving school psychology services. He has worked in high school, middle school, and elementary settings and with students with cognitive, behavioral, and emotional disabilities. His vast experience includes working in overseas Department of Defense schools and rural, suburban, urban, and highly diverse schools and school systems. In addition, Hull has worked as a special education administrator and state-level administrator of school psychology, working to improve the impact of mental health practices from an administrative perspective. Hull provided intensive crisis intervention services to the Baltimore City School System for several years and has presented on trauma issues at multiple national conferences. He teaches graduate classes at the University of Missouri at Columbia.

Howard S. Adelman, PhD
Professor of Psychology
Co-director, School Mental Health
　Project, Center for Mental Health
　in Schools
Department of Psychology, University
　of California at Los Angeles

Myrna Ann Adkins, MA
President and Chief Executive Officer
Spring Institute for Intercultural
　Learning

Mardi Bernard, RN, BScN, MEd
School Mental Health Nurse
Edmonton Public School District

Dina Birman, PhD
Associate Professor
Department of Psychology
University of Illinois at Chicago

Margaret E. Blaustein, PhD
Director of Training and Education
The Trauma Center at the Justice
　Resource Institute

Diana Bowman, MA
Director, National Center for
　Homeless Education
The SERVE Center at the University
　of North Carolina-Greensboro

**Jennifer K. Buxton-McClendon,
　MEd, EdS**
Regional Admissions Representative
University of Missouri

Courtney D. Carter, MEd
Middle School Teacher
Waterford Public Schools

Delphine Collin-Vézina, PhD
Tier II Canadian Research Chair
Assistant Professor
School of Social Work, McGill
　University

Susan A. Craft, MEd
School Psychology Doctoral
　Candidate
University of Florida

Brian R. Devine, EdS
Alternative Education Teacher
Parker High School, Janesville School
　District

Burna L. Dunn, MS
Project Director
Spring Institute for Intercultural
　Learning

George S. Everly, Jr., PhD
Professor of Psychology, Loyola
    University, Maryland
Associate Professor of Psychiatry, The
    Johns Hopkins University School of
    Medicine

Rachel M. Firestone, MA
Graduate Student in Loyola
    University's (Maryland) Clinical
    Psychology Program

Jarena G. Fleischman, EdS
School Counselor
Rolla Public Schools

Laura Gardner, MSW
Education Technical Assistance
    Specialist
Bridging Refugee Youth & Children's
    Services

Virginia Gil-Rivas, PhD
Associate Professor of Psychology
Director, Interdisciplinary Health
    Psychology Program
University of North Carolina at
    Charlotte

Steven J. Hardy, MA
Doctoral Candidate
Health Psychology PhD Program
University of North Carolina at
    Charlotte

Ron Hertel, BSEd

Mona M. Johnson, MA
Director, School Behavioral Health
Office of Child, Adolescent and
    Family Behavioral Health
U.S. Army Medical Command

Ryan P. Kilmer, PhD
Associate Professor of Psychology
University of North Carolina at
    Charlotte

Deseri A. Burgess, MS
School Counselor
Republic R-III School District

Lyn Morland, MSW, MA
Director, Bridging Refugee Youth &
    Children's Services

A. Michelle O'Banion, MA
High School Teacher
Webb City R-7 School District

Elizabeth Popard Newell, MA
Licensed Professional Counselor
Comprehensive Psychological
    Services

Patricia A. Popp, PhD
State Coordinator for the Education of
    Homeless Children and Youth
Project HOPE—Virginia

Joel M. Ristuccia, EdM, MBA
School Psychologist
Consultant to the Trauma and
    Learning Policy Initiative

Dorothy Rohde-Collins, BS
High School Teacher
Saint Louis Public Schools

Linda Taylor, PhD
Co-Director, Center for Mental
    Health in Schools
Department of Psychology,
    University of California at
    Los Angeles

Lisa Weed Phifer, MEd
National Certified School
  Psychologist
Prince George's County Public
  Schools

Lisa Wegman, BS
Supervisor of the Foster Care
  Department
Missouri Alliance for Children and
  Families

LaDona R. Wiebler, MS, BCBA
Manager, ABA Services
Easter Seals Central Illinois

Robert J. Wingfield, MA
Nationally Certified School
  Psychologist
School Psychology Doctoral
  Candidate, University of Florida

Introduction to Trauma and Its Impact on School Functioning

Childhood Trauma and a Framework for Intervention

MARGARET E. BLAUSTEIN ■

INTRODUCTION

Imagine a virus spreading across your community. The virus is far-reaching, affecting more than 20% of the population. This virus has the potential to rob the health of all those it touches—impacting nutrition, brain development, emotional well-being, risk for other illnesses, and, ultimately, longevity. The virus is complex and expresses itself in different ways. In some people, its influences may be subtle, nearly invisible, while in others its effects may be powerful and readily apparent. Some people may resist the virus naturally; others will be particularly vulnerable. Importantly, the impact of the virus is also influenced by the environment. With timely and effective intervention, its influences may be minimized and even healed; in the absence of care, however, the negative effects will build and worsen over time, leading to deep illness, great financial cost, and eventually the risk of serious disability or death.

Now imagine that your task is to address this virus by preventing it from spreading, minimizing its influences, and, ultimately, bringing the greatest health to the greatest number of people. Where do you begin? Simply targeting the most obviously impacted is not enough. Because its influences may be subtle or difficult to detect, you may not know who has been exposed, who is most in need of support, and who might regain health with no intervention.

An epidemic is defined as an illness "affecting or tending to affect a disproportionately large number of individuals within a population, community, or region at the same time."[1] The world of public health has taught us that, in the face of an epidemic, the best lines of defense are large-scale, community-wide efforts. With a far-reaching illness, there can be no assumption that any individual has not been exposed or is not at risk; therefore, good intervention should have the longest "reach" possible. In a scenario such as that described here, given the immense personal and societal costs and the responsiveness of this virus to treatment and environmental changes, it is likely that intervention efforts would and should go toward building healthy environments that counteract the virus's influence and that eventually lead to positive outcomes.

Now, reread the opening paragraphs, and replace the words *a virus* with *childhood trauma*. The validity of the statements continues to hold true. By all standards, childhood trauma is an epidemic. It is widespread, affecting far more than 20% of the population. The influences of trauma are vast, and though some children may be able to draw on innate strengths to overcome these experiences, for many children the effects of early trauma will be far-reaching. Like our hypothetical virus, the influences of childhood trauma are impacted by the environment; a sensitive, caring, and supportive environment has great potential to support resilient outcomes, whereas an unsupportive and unstable environment can worsen the influence of trauma, or be the very source of it.

It is difficult to imagine a psychosocial factor more relevant to the educational world than childhood trauma. The numbers of children who have or who will experience significant adversity are staggering, and the implications of this adversity are immense. It is the rare classroom that will not contain at least one child who has experienced significant stress. In communities more touched by poverty, community violence, homelessness, racism, and/or other layers of social vulnerability, it is conceivable that the majority of students in a school will have experienced significant stress.

THE FAR-REACHING IMPACT OF TRAUMA HISTORIES

Trauma, like all salient childhood experiences, shapes the course of development and influences outcomes across numerous domains of functioning. Children who have experienced trauma may struggle with a multitude of competencies that influence school performance and engagement, including concentration and attention, managing behavior, negotiating relationships, regulating emotions, executive functions and goal-oriented actions, a belief in the capacity to build a future, and faith in having the potential to work toward one.

Trauma is not solely a burden of childhood: Given the statistics, it is reasonable to assume that in any given school, there are a proportion of teachers, administrators, support staff, and other professionals who have themselves experienced (or are currently experiencing) significant stress. In the case of school or community violence, entire systems may experience traumatic stress, which likely takes a toll on the functioning of classrooms, schools, and larger educational structures.

Addressing this trauma is no easy task. It is often difficult to separate the influences of trauma from other factors. Trauma does not discriminate—it touches the lives of children who might otherwise have had no difficulties, and it touches the lives of children who simultaneously struggle with learning and developmental challenges, environmental stressors, and physical illnesses. It touches children in communities that have ready access to resources, and it touches those communities who struggle with limited funds and community-wide exposures. The effects of trauma, the challenges it brings, and the needed intervention intertwine and build in complexity.

Trauma, like our hypothetical virus, has a long reach, potentially affecting children, professionals, and communities. Therefore, the building of educational systems that are able to sensitively and effectively address the needs of those who have been exposed must be a task of whole communities, rather than simply a task of alternative or specialized schools or programs. School engagement, experience, and success are among the most predictive variables of adult healthy outcomes and of resilience in highly stressed populations. An investment in healthy schools is therefore an investment in a society's future.

WHAT IS TRAUMA? THE NATURE OF TRAUMATIC EXPERIENCE IN CHILDHOOD

Debate exists over the proper definition of the term *trauma*, but it is generally agreed upon that traumatic experiences are those that are *overwhelming*; lead to *strong negative emotions* such as shame, helplessness, and fear; and involve some degree of *experienced or witnessed threat to self*, whether that threat is physical, mental, or emotional. Traumatic experience is, in many ways, subjective, developmentally bound, and individual. Consider, for instance, the term *overwhelming*; whether an event is experienced as overwhelming may depend on age (i.e., separation from caregivers may be overwhelming for a 3-year-old, but less so for an adolescent), external resources (i.e., a child with a supportive caregiving system may tolerate a distressing event more easily than a child who lacks love and support), perception of coping capacity (i.e., a child who feels able to manage a difficult experience versus a child who feels incapable of coping), and previous experiences (i.e., a child who has repeatedly experienced rejection may perceive a subsequent rejection as overwhelming, whereas a child with strong connections may be able to perceive the rejection as less meaningful).

It is an unfortunate truth that there are far too many potentially traumatic experiences that may touch the lives of children and families. These exposures may be acute or chronic. An *acute* stressor is one that is typically sudden and of relatively brief duration (i.e., a terrorist act or a motor vehicle accident). *Chronic* stressors are those that occur over a period of time and involve layers of experience or repeated exposure (i.e., ongoing physical abuse, homelessness), rather than a single event. Importantly, trauma is not just about overt events such as violence or accidents; it also incorporates experiences such as neglect or impacted caregiving due to parental mental or physical health issues or substance use, as well as the chain of *resulting personal impacts* that may occur following this range of experiences—for instance, the ongoing ripples from a death in the family and other attachment losses, or the layering impact of multiple school placements and housing instability.

Trauma is complex, consisting of numerous dimensions on which traumatic experiences may vary. For instance, trauma may be interpersonal (e.g., an act committed by a specific individual, such as an assault) or noninterpersonal (e.g., an act of nature, such as a tornado). Acts may be perpetrated by family members, by trusted others, or by strangers. They may be publicly known, or they may occur in secrecy and be known solely by the child or the family. They may have long-lasting physical and environmental repercussions (e.g., the hurricane that leads to the loss of a house or the car accident that leads to disfigurement) or the impact may be relatively limited. They may occur in the context of immense social support (consider, for instance, the outpouring of empathy and support for victims of large-scale disasters), or they may occur in the context of shame, blame, and disapproval (consider the child victim who discloses abuse by a beloved and trusted member of the community and who is disbelieved). Trauma may start early in life, from conception for children in chronically stressed households, or may impact a later developmental period. Each of these nuances, along with the myriad individual differences in children and families, will impact the way the trauma is experienced and the potential outcomes. It is no wonder that trauma and its effects are so difficult to define.

PREVALENCE OF TRAUMA

Exposure to trauma impacts all subgroups, and across demographics, youth are exposed to violence and other stressors on a startlingly large scale. In a national survey of youth younger than the age of 17, more than half (60.6%) reported exposure to violence in the past year.[2] Nearly a quarter of these children and adolescents reported being victims of crimes such as robbery, and nearly half were assaulted at least once in the past year. In a classroom of 25 students, this would mean that 15 were exposed to violence in the last year, and 6 were victims of crime. See chapters 6 and 9 for more information on exposure to community and domestic violence.

Youth experience proportionally high rates of exposure to violent crime, with victimization rates higher than all adult age groups and more than two times higher than that of adults older than the age of 35.[3] This is particularly problematic given the increased likelihood of negative outcomes as a result of childhood trauma.

Violence in the home accounts for a substantial proportion of youth trauma. In 2008, 3.7 million children in the United States were investigated as potential victims of child maltreatment, and approximately 20% of victims of maltreatment were removed from their homes (e.g., placed in foster care) as a result of that investigation.[4] In total, it is estimated that well over 400,000 youth in this country were living in alternative care in 2008.[5] Children removed from their homes often face continuing stress, disruption, and instability, with an average length of stay of over 2 years in out-of-home placements. Over 25,000 children "age out" of the child welfare system each year, having never achieved reunification or permanent placement.

Environmental stressors affect millions of children, which can be a chronic source of trauma or exacerbate the effects of preexisting trauma. For example, nearly one in five (19%) children in the United States lives in poverty, and a similar number (22%) lives in a household considered "food insecure." Further, nearly half of U.S. households with children (43%) have significant housing problems, including homes that are overcrowded and physically inadequate or unsafe.[6] Children represent a disproportionate share of the poor in the United States; they are 25% of the total population, but 35% of the poor population.[7] The poverty rate for children varies substantially by race and Hispanic origin; approximately 1 in 10 White (non-Hispanic) children (11.9%) live in poverty, whereas nearly 1 in 3 Black children (35.4%) and Hispanic children (33.1%) experience this same stressor.[8]

Unfortunately, schools do not currently represent a safe "haven" from trauma exposure. In the 2007–2008 school year, 75% of all public schools reported at least one violent crime; this rate climbs to 94% when examining middle and high schools.[9] In fact, youth ages 12 to 17 are victims of violent crime at higher rates within the school setting than away from it.[10]

Across studies, estimates of lifetime exposure to potentially traumatic experiences range from half to nearly all of the population. In one large-scale study, 74.4% of adults report lifetime exposure to one or more adversities, and 34.6% report exposure to three or more adversities; notably, the rates of exposure were highest at the youngest ages.[11] Trauma and adversity, too often, are part of the daily fabric for youth in our society.

IMPACT OF TRAUMA ON CHILD AND ADOLESCENT DEVELOPMENT

Trauma, and particularly chronic trauma, appears to play a qualitatively different role in the lives of children than in the lives of adults, with differing diagnostic profiles and more wide-reaching influences.[12] Adversities occurring during early childhood or adversities of a chronic nature routinely result in more complex presentations and more significant challenges in daily functioning (e.g., difficulty managing and organizing emotions, body sensations, thoughts, behaviors, and relationships) when compared to acute trauma or adversities occurring later in life.[13] Given a heightened vulnerability in early childhood, children may meet criteria for posttraumatic stress disorder (PTSD)[14] or a host of other psychological or psychiatric diagnoses; however, rarely does a single definitive diagnosis capture these impacts.[15] Therefore, it may be more useful to shift away from thinking diagnostically and shift toward thinking developmentally when considering the influence of childhood trauma.

Childhood development is shaped by many different factors, including biology and the range of human experiences, including nutrition and environment, caregiving and relationships, and experiences of success and failure. Development is dynamic and purposeful—children's course of development changes as their experiences change, and in turn children actively respond to their worlds in ways that help them cope and be successful. Development builds in layers—for instance, children learn basic communication skills in their early relationships with parents, siblings, and other family members, and these skills (or lack of skill) then translate into how they eventually communicate with others in the school setting.

The influence of trauma may be thought of as twofold: first, the prioritization of developmental factors that support the child's successful adaptation to his or her world—in this case, those factors that support safety and/or need fulfillment—and second, the de-emphasis of those developmental competencies that are less immediately relevant to survival.

All skills become more efficient as they are repeated, and the response to perceived danger is no different. Children who have experienced chronic adversity have brains that have learned to prioritize those skills that support survival. Survival skills may include *heightened awareness of danger* in the environment, *rapid mobilization* in the face of perceived threat, and *self-protective behaviors* including aggression, withdrawal, and freezing. For these children, there may be a hypervigilance and a rapid (and often inaccurate) identification of potential threats in the environment. Notably, identification of danger requires not just the presence of threat, but merely the suggestion of it. For example, a child or adolescent with exposure to multiple and/or chronic adversities may perceive threat in simple facial expressions, a tone of voice, a rapid movement, criticism/correction, or a smell. In the face of this threat, children's bodies rapidly mobilize to respond to the potential danger, setting off a chain of responses that include surges of arousal, selective attention to the source of potential danger, and de-emphasis of nonessential functions, including higher order thought. Subsequent behaviors represent the triad of the human danger response: fighting, fleeing, and freezing; and the arousal response that drives these behaviors may also lead to more diffuse behaviors such as clinginess, silliness, or agitation. For a child with a heightened alarm system, this cycle may repeat itself many times within a day, and all may occur outside of the child's conscious awareness.

Consider, for instance, the child who has learned from repeated early experience that a frustrated adult facial expression is associated with imminent risk—that is, physical violence or verbal abuse—and who has learned that "freezing," or attempting to remain "unseen," will minimize the risk of the child being the direct target of that anger. Upon registering the perceived frustration of any adult in the school setting, the child's brain will rapidly initiate a sequence of responses—often outside of the child's conscious awareness—that may include a surge in arousal, freezing, and emotionally shutting down. Visually, the child may appear suddenly inattentive, noncompliant, and belligerent; in fact, the child is—consciously or unconsciously—engaging in what has been an adaptive and protective response. This is described in more detail in chapter 2.

Also heightened in these children may be *need-fulfilling* behaviors—those adaptations that children have learned in order to fill physiological, emotional, or relational needs in the absence of these needs having been reliably met. For instance, the child who has experienced significant early neglect may learn to steal and hoard food and other objects; the child who has received inadequate early care and soothing may learn to engage in sexualized behaviors to meet intimacy needs. Needs may substitute for each other over time, and it is not uncommon, for instance, for a child who lacks emotional nurturance to seek comfort through food, or for a child who has previously gone hungry to hoard unrelated objects. Emotionally and physically neglected children who are attempting to fill needs may seem particularly demanding and difficult, pulling for adult attention, and lacking awareness of peer and adult physical and emotional boundaries. Without previous knowledge of these patterns, educators may falsely perceive these children as deceitful and manipulative.

At the same time that these children develop a heightened and adaptive, though often undesirable, danger response to perceived threat, other developmental tasks that contribute to school success are often underdeveloped. Research has consistently proven that these experiences take their toll on *regulatory capacities, interpersonal skills, intrapersonal development,* and *cognitive development,* leading to a reduced capacity to manage the demands of the school environment (see Table 1.1).

CHALLENGES IN IDENTIFYING AND ADDRESSING THIS IMPACT

The reality of childhood trauma is that it affects a significant proportion of the school-aged population, and its influences are considerable within the school setting. As with the hypothetical virus described at the start of this chapter, trauma is far-reaching, and its influences are both broad and subtle. However—also as with the hypothetical virus—the influences of trauma are strongly moderated by the environment in which development takes place. As such, schools offer a remarkable opportunity to address the needs of the substantial youth population whose lives have been affected by traumatic stress. Unfortunately, there are significant challenges to sensitively and effectively addressing the influence of trauma in the school setting.

Mental Health Viewed as Secondary and Unrelated to Academic Success

Rightfully, the primary goal of schools is the education of youth. Increasingly, there is an understandable emphasis on the meeting of "benchmarks" that demonstrate

Table 1.1[a] IMPACT OF TRAUMA ON CHILDREN

Domain of Impact	Potential Impact on Traumatized Children	What Educators May See
Regulatory capacities	• Surges of arousal and/or numbing (shutting down of arousal) • Disconnection from internal states, particularly when feeling overwhelmed • Inadequate coping skills • Difficulty sharing feelings with others	• Children may appear shut down, inattentive and bored, or listless; others may present as hyperactive, impulsive, aggressive, reactive, and/or silly. Some children go back and forth between these two response styles in an unpredictable manner. • Facial expression and "emotional communication" may range from guarded/constricted to intense and quickly changing. • May be easily overwhelmed (upset, angry, worried) by even mild stressors
Interpersonal skills	• Difficulty forming and maintaining safe connections; may include: • Feelings of helplessness or vulnerability in relationship(s) • Distrust of others • Social skills deficits	• Social withdrawal or isolation • Difficulty developing close or lasting friendships. • Bullying, aggression, or opposition ("talking back") to maintain control or at risk for victimization by others • Vulnerable to entering into negative peer relationships
Intrapersonal skills	• Confused, fragmented, and/or negative sense of self • Feelings of helplessness or lack of control • Loss of (or failure to develop) future orientation	• Hesitant in approaching new tasks; unwilling to take risks (e.g., not raising hand to avoid risk of getting the wrong answer; not turning in challenging homework) • Easily frustrated or "give up" in the face of failure • Trouble setting and working toward goals, both short and long term

Cognitive	• Difficulty reflecting upon and acting on information	• Apparent difficulty understanding information and following directions, particularly when information is challenging or child is overwhelmed
	• Impaired executive functions	• Appearing bored, inattentive, and/or impulsive
	• Information processing that is impacted by emotions and/or environmental stimuli	• Trouble asking for or accepting help from others or overly dependent in approaching tasks
	• Trouble with those factors that support cognitive abilities (i.e., frustration tolerance, self-sufficiency)	• Trouble generating ideas and solving problems
		• Difficulty understanding the consequences of their actions

[a] Cahill, Kaminer, & Johnson, 1999; Eckenrode, Laird, & Doris, 1993; Kendall-Tackett & Eckenrode, 1996; Kurtz, Gaudin, Wodarski, & Howing, 1993; Leiter & Johnson, 1994; Shonk & Cicchetti, 2001; Trickett, McBride-Chang, & Putnam, 1994.

that a school is adequately addressing this primary goal; these often include objective criteria such as test scores, discipline rates, attendance rates, and success standards such as graduation rates or college enrollment. Pressure to meet these standards flows downward, from federal standards to states to districts to school administrators to individual teachers. In an effort to meet these benchmarks—often in situations that are stressed by overcrowding, limited support, lack of professional development, and underfunding—teachers and administrators may view additional demands of developing trauma-informed systems as burdensome and superfluous to the institution's primary goal. See chapter 18 for more on this.

Difficulty Identifying Traumatized Youth

A second challenge with addressing the needs of trauma-impacted youth within the school setting is one of identification: It is often not known *which* youth have experienced trauma. Although some trauma is public and generally known, many stressors occur within a context of silence and secrecy. Identification of trauma exposure may be perceived as stigmatizing by families or individuals, and schools may wish to stay away from knowledge that is perceived as highly personal. Further, families and/or youth may not identify their experiences as "traumatic": Stress and adversity are part of the daily fabric for many families and even whole communities and thus become normalized.

The Many "Faces" of Trauma

A challenge that further complicates service delivery is the varying presentation of those who have experienced trauma: Some children who have been impacted by stress present as "difficult" and come quickly to the attention of teachers and administrators; others, who may be more constricted or emotionally shut down, fly under the radar. Children who have experienced trauma may excel academically or may struggle with attention, concentration, learning issues, or task completion. Children may get along with peers or may avoid them; they may be leaders or they may be bullies. Given the complexity of traumatic experience and ensuing response, there is no single face of childhood trauma, even among children experiencing the same adversity in the same households.

Lack of Resources

Lack of adequate resources may play a significant role in the challenge of addressing the needs of this population. School systems often lack adequate access to clinical services or sufficient resources for training and support of nonclinical personnel. As a result, schools may be hesitant to address the mental health and behavioral needs of children and adolescents affected by adversity that they perceive themselves as ill-equipped to handle. The intention of this book is to offer strategies that effectively help to support trauma-impacted youth and reduce the need for limited and expensive resources that do not necessarily lead to positive outcomes (e.g., special education, discipline procedures, and alternative education).

A FRAMEWORK FOR INTERVENTION

Despite these significant challenges, it is a tenet of this chapter—and of this text—that the addressing of trauma within school settings is not only feasible but also fully consistent with and supportive of the primary goals of academic programs. A trauma-sensitive environment is one that is, to the degree possible, safe and attuned to the needs of students, families, staff, and the community. Such an environment supports the academic competence of all students, whether trauma impacted or not; provides tools to support students and staff with managing emotional and behavioral challenges; supports teachers and other staff in negotiating difficult situations, often reducing stress and burnout among teaching staff; and, ultimately, has the potential to increase positive outcomes among youth across domains. Although the needs of individual students will vary, whole-school approaches (see chapter 17) incorporate core principles that support the healthy functioning of all of those who function within a community without necessarily placing a significant strain on funding resources or clinically trained personnel. Importantly, many of these principles associated with whole-school approaches can be applied to individual classrooms.

One evidence-based approach to building a trauma-sensitive environment may be found in the Attachment, Self-Regulation, and Competency (ARC)[16] intervention framework. Developed to be applicable across the range of settings that provide services to youth and families, ARC is a flexible framework for intervention with children and adolescents who have experienced traumatic stress. Drawing from the foundational literatures on child development, attachment, and traumatic stress, as well as research on resilient outcomes among stress-exposed youth, ARC identifies 3 core domains and 10 primary "building blocks," or targets for intervention (see Figure 1.1). These domains and targets, along with applications within a school setting, are briefly discussed in the following sections.

Attachment

The first domain targeted by the ARC framework is *Attachment*. The overarching goals of this domain include the creation of a safe environment (trauma-informed

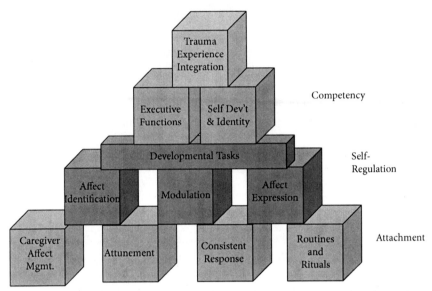

Figure 1.1 Ten primary building blocks, or targets for intervention, within the ARC framework.

system) that is able to support youth in meeting developmental, emotional, and relational needs and, in parallel, to support caregivers in addressing those needs. The ARC framework defines caregivers broadly and may be applied to parents, teachers, clinicians, legal personnel, case managers, and whole systems such as residential programs. For the purposes of this book, the focus is on applications with teachers and other academic staff. There are four primary building blocks used to reach the goal of building a safe environment:

1. *Caregiver affect management* involves supporting teachers, administrators, and other school staff in understanding, managing, and coping with their own emotional responses, so that they are better able to support the students in their care. School-based application includes development of a system that acknowledges and supports the very real emotional responses that professionals have when working with challenging students. Strategies may include professional support forums (i.e., access to consultation and supervision); training on vicarious trauma; establishment of collaborative "teams"; initiatives that support self-care; and creation of an environment that supports competency and positive experiences such as team-building activities, staff retreats, and social activities.

2. *Attunement* involves increasing the capacity of caregivers to accurately and empathically understand and respond to children's actions, needs, and feelings. A primary tenet of this goal is the understanding that *all* behaviors (whether those of students, parents, staff, etc.) are functional and meaningful; in the face of difficult or confusing behaviors, then, the role of the attuned adult is to be curious and ultimately responsive,

rather than reactive. This is achieved through training and education about the effects of trauma and other psychosocial stressors on behavior and functioning, and ideally supported through ongoing consultation and concrete application (for instance, routine identification of individual students' triggers or cues that lead to distress, typical resulting behaviors, and helpful adult responses).

3. *Consistent response* highlights the importance of building predictable, safe, and appropriate responses to behaviors that acknowledge and are sensitive to why the behavior occurred. The first two targets identified within this domain—caregiver affect management and attunement—are crucial in achieving this third goal. Trauma-sensitive application of consistent response requires the capacity of adults, first, to manage their own emotional response to youth behaviors, and second, to attempt to sensitively understand where those behaviors come from. For instance, a child who refuses to complete homework may be a child who is not working hard enough but may also be a child who is overwhelmed or has no safe place to actually sit, think, and complete homework. A child who becomes oppositional when asked to complete a task may be viewed as noncompliant or aggressive but may also be understood as anxious, triggered, and attempting to self-protect based on a learned response to a perceived attack. Here, it is important for educators to recognize that the *student's* perception drives the behavior, regardless of its accuracy or basis in reality. Increased awareness of children's behavioral patterns and training in how to respond to them (e.g., emphasizing the importance of positive response and reinforcement) will generally increase the success of both the adult and the youth in the interaction.

4. *Routines and rituals* address the role of predictability in establishing a sense of safety. Because trauma is often associated with unpredictability, trauma-exposed youth (and adults) learn to be vigilant to potential danger in the face of uncertainty. In contrast, environments and situations that are familiar, predictable, and consistent allow these youth to "let down their guard" and focus their energy on more positive developmental tasks such as learning. Incorporating an understanding of the importance of routine allows adults to be mindful of building rhythm into the day. This may include attention to how the day starts and ends, to classroom activities, and to larger school rituals. Particular attention should be paid to times that are often difficult for trauma-impacted students, such as transitions from one activity to another and management of unstructured time.

Self-Regulation

The second primary domain targeted by this framework is *Self-Regulation*. The primary goal of this domain is to support children and adolescents in building the capacity to safely and effectively manage their responses across various areas: emotional, physiological, cognitive, and behavioral. In parallel, this domain highlights the importance of building a system (i.e., school and educational staff) that is also able to regulate its own policies and responses, rather than being reactive. There are three primary building blocks within the Self-Regulation domain:

1. *Affect identification* involves supporting children and adolescents in building an awareness of their own internal emotions and physical experience. Trauma-impacted youth frequently disconnect from or are unaware of their emotions and physiological reactions to experiences; as a result, these reactions may "play out" in certain behaviors and interactions. In normative development, adults play a primary role in the support of this capacity, and in a school setting, adults may support this skill through curiosity about and observation of youth experience. Strategies as simple as routinely checking in with youth ("How are you today?"), inviting students to monitor their own energy level using charts or other tools, and observing identifiable affect ("I can see how proud you are of that score; I know how hard you worked for that") will play a significant role in supporting youth in developing an awareness of experience and a rich emotional vocabulary.

2. *Modulation* involves the capability to use safe and effective strategies for managing and regulating physiological and emotional experiences. Surges of arousal or emotional numbing interfere with trauma-impacted children's ability to maintain a state of arousal that allows for learning and appropriate peer interactions. Schools may support this capacity by incorporating modulation strategies into daily routines (i.e., engaging in classroom relaxation exercises or activities used to adaptively expend energy); by utilizing small modulation tools, such as handheld manipulatives (clay, stress balls, etc.); and by learning to read, cue, and support trauma-impacted children by identifying and using regulation strategies as needed.

3. *Affect expression* involves supporting youth in building skills in and tolerance for sharing of internal experience with others. Due to the potential for a lack of trust and heightened vulnerability brought on by insecure relationships, as well as inadequate skills in effective communication, trauma-affected youth may have difficulty appropriately connecting to others and expressing their thoughts and feelings. Schools offer rich opportunities to support children and adolescents in building appropriate social communication skills. These may be built and practiced in whole-classroom activities and reinforced through regular opportunities for students to express themselves in supported environments (i.e., student journals, "open-mic day," wall collages, etc.). Individualized communication plans can support the needs of individual students, and staff can work to develop alternatives to purely verbal communication (i.e., hand gestures, desk signs, or "code" phrases).

Because safe expression requires having safe resources with whom to communicate, the availability of a safe and receptive adult—whether teacher, administrator, or other professional staff—is crucial to supporting this skill.

Competency

The third primary domain, *Competency*, targets the range of developmental capacities that have been found to be predictive of healthy youth development and ultimately of resiliency and personal growth. These skills support youth in negotiating the world in goal-directed ways, building a coherent and positive sense of self, and developing the ability to anticipate and create a future. In parallel, this domain highlights the importance of building a system that is active, effective, and goal oriented, rather than reactive and crisis driven. The primary targets within this domain include the following:

1. *Executive functions* include delaying impulses, setting goals, considering alternatives, and problem solving. Individuals who have experienced significant trauma often learn to react quickly to their worlds, as their brains prioritize rapid response—and perceived associated survival—over thoughtful and planned-out decisions. Not surprisingly, then, children, adolescents, and adults who have experienced significant stress may demonstrate challenges with higher order cognitive processes and executive functions. These challenges are particularly apparent in moments of emotional distress. Development of this capacity is strongly predictive of resilience and is also a highly desirable ability for all youth, regardless of trauma history. School-based personnel can support youth in considering their goals, generating possible solutions, and thinking through those solutions, rather than simply naming the "correct" choice or stating what "should" have been done. For instance, in moments when a youth expresses frustration with a situation, teachers or counselors may support youth in validating the experience ("I can see that you're frustrated"), identifying goals ("What do you think you would like to happen next/instead?"), identifying possible solutions ("Let's think about all the things you could do"), considering outcomes ("What do you think might happen if you did that?"), and trying out possible solutions. These skills can be built into multiple classroom scenarios (e.g., considering the behaviors of characters in books or historical figures), conflict situations, and problem solving in classrooms.

2. *Self and identity* involves supporting youth in the development of a positive and coherent sense of self and supporting the capacity to consider the future. The understanding of self begins to develop from a very young age and is layered and expanded over time. Although

trauma-impacted youth are vulnerable to multiple disturbances of self, including internalization of negative messages and difficulty imagining future possibilities, schools offer a strong opportunity to provide both corrective and positive messages and experiences, as well as concrete support in anticipating and developing future plans. There are numerous ways schools can create opportunities for success and help students to identify and celebrate them. Schools can also support children in understanding and linking the past, present, and future through self-exploration, individual "life plans," and building awareness and access to resources such as job placement, college planning, and housing. The latter is particularly important for transitional-age youth, who may lack these supports at home or in other settings for a variety of reasons.

3. *Developmental tasks* highlights the importance of recognizing the range of developmental skills that normally develop at each stage when targeting interventions, particularly given the diffuse impact of traumatic stress on childhood development. Schools may consider ways to target, for instance, gross motor skills and learning readiness in young children; social skills development and competency building in later-elementary-school-aged children; peer negotiation and emerging independence skills in middle-school children; and independent functioning, leadership and responsibility, and community involvement in adolescents.

CONCLUSION

It is an unfortunate truth that exposure to traumatic stress is part of the experience of a significant proportion of our children and adolescents. Like a virus that sweeps through a community, childhood trauma is complex, pervasive in its effects, and significant in its potential impacts. Too often, response to trauma is delegated: It is the problem of families, child welfare systems, courts, or mental health specialists. It is the problem and the responsibility of somebody *else*. The reality is, trauma is the problem of a society, and the larger scale and more community based our intervention efforts are, the greater the likelihood of addressing, ameliorating, and potentially preventing negative effects.

Schools represent the front line of primary prevention efforts. School experiences are salient and remembered on both conscious and unconscious levels long after they are complete. It is the rare adult who is unable to remember a meaningful and positive school experience—the teacher who made a difference, the strength of attaining success, the pride of a challenge overcome. It is also the rare adult who is unable to remember a more difficult school experience—the feeling of shame, embarrassment, or distress from a negative encounter, or the vulnerability brought by a moment of failure.

Schools are the core environment in which we address the academic competence of our youth, but they are far more than that. As with all caregiving environments, they are a significant and long-lasting social environment. They are a forum in which youth learn about themselves, about others, and about the world. They are where children and adolescents succeed or fail, gain competency or internalize vulnerability. They are the context in which youth experiment with self, with ideas, and with possible future roles. Without question, our school experiences help shape who we ultimately become.

Whole-school efforts to become trauma informed have the potential to build positive outcomes, not just for trauma-impacted youth, but for all students, as well as for the professionals whose task is to guide, teach, and care for them. As school systems approach this effort, a starting question is often, understandably, "Is the effort worth it? Will the investment—in time, in money, in personnel, in resources—ultimately pay off in benefits for our students?" As a response, imagine your task is to combat a virus, one that affects well over 20% of your student population. Even among those only subtly impacted, it may affect brain development, nutrition, sleep, physiological regulation, and socio-emotional development. At its most significant level, it may be fatal. By shifting your environment, by creating a space that is nurturing, safe, and responsive, you can minimize its effects, almost to the point that the virus never existed; by ignoring it, its costs grow and multiply.

Is it worth it?

NOTES

1. Merriam-Webster, 2012.
2. Finkelhor, Turner, Ormrod, & Hamby, 2009.
3. U.S. Department of Justice, 2009.
4. U.S. Department of Health and Human Services, Administration for Children and Families, Administration on Children, Youth and Families, Children's Bureau, 2010.
5. U.S. Department of Health and Human Services, Adoption and Foster Care Analysis and Reporting System (AFCARS), 2009.
6. Federal Interagency Forum on Child and Family Statistics, 2010.
7. Federal Interagency Forum on Child and Family Statistics, 2010.
8. DeNavas-Walt, Proctor, & Smith, 2010.
9. Dinkes, Kemp, & Baum, 2009.
10. U.S. Department of Justice, 2009.
11. Kessler, 1995.
12. van der Kolk et al., 2009; van der Kolk, Roth, Pelcovitz, Sunday, & Spinazzola, 2005.
13. van der Kolk et al., 1996.

14. American Psychiatric Association, 1994.
15. van der Kolk, 2005.
16. Arvidson et al., 2011; Blaustein & Kinniburgh, 2010; Kinniburgh & Blaustein, 2005.

REFERENCES

American Psychiatric Association (APA). (1994). *Diagnostic and statistical manual of mental disorders* (4th ed.). Washington, DC: Author.

Arvidson, J., Kinniburgh, K., Howard, K., Spinnazola, J., Strothers, H., Evans, M., et al. (2011). Treatment of complex trauma in young children: Developmental and cultural considerations in application of the ARC model. *Journal of Child and Adolescent Trauma, 4,* 34–51.

Blaustein, M., & Kinniburgh, K. (2010). *Treating traumatic stress in children and adolescents: How to foster resilience through attachment, self-regulation, and competency.* New York, NY: Guilford Press.

Cahill, L., Kaminer, R., & Johnson, P. (1999). Developmental, cognitive, and behavioral sequelae of child abuse. *Child & Adolescent Psychiatric Clinics of North America, 8,* 827–843.

DeNavas-Walt, C., Proctor, B. D., & Smith, J. C. (2010). *Income, poverty, and health insurance coverage in the United States: 2009.* In U.S. Census Bureau, *Current population reports* (pp. 60–238). Washington, DC: U.S. Government Printing Office.

Dinkes, R., Kemp, J., & Baum, K. (2009). *Indicators of school crime and safety: 2009* (NCES 2010–012/NCJ 228478). Washington, DC: National Center for Education Statistics, Institute of Education Sciences, U.S. Department of Education, and Bureau of Justice Statistics, Office of Justice Programs, U.S. Department of Justice.

Eckenrode, J., Laird, M., & Doris, J. (1993). School performance and disciplinary problems among abused and neglected children. *Developmental Psychology, 29,* 53–62.

Merriam-Webster. (2012). Epidemic. In *Merriam-Webster online.* Retrieved June 20, 2012, from http://www.merriam-webster.com/dictionary/epidemic

Federal Interagency Forum on Child and Family Statistics. (2010). *America's children: Key national indicators of well-being, 2010.* Washington, DC: U.S. Government Printing Office. Retrieved from http://childstats.gov

Finkelhor, D., Turner, H., Ormrod, R., & Hamby, S. (2009). Violence, abuse, and crime exposure in a national sample of youth. *Pediatrics, 124,* 1411–1423.

Kendall-Tackett, K. A., & Eckenrode, J. (1996). The effects of neglect on academic achievement and disciplinary problems: A developmental approach. *Child Abuse & Neglect, 20,* 161–169.

Kessler, R. (1995). The national comorbidity survey: Preliminary results and future directions. *International Journal of Methods in Psychiatric Research, 5,* 139–151.

Kinniburgh, K., & Blaustein, M. (2005). *Attachment, Self-Regulation, and Competency: A comprehensive framework for intervention with complexly traumatized youth. A treatment manual.* Boston, MA: Author.

Kurtz, P., Gaudin, J., Wodarski, J., & Howing, P. (1993). Maltreatment and the school-aged child: School performance consequences. *Child Abuse and Neglect, 17,* 581–589.

Leiter, J., & Johnson, M. (1994). Child maltreatment and school performance. *American Journal of Education, 102,* 154–189.

Shonk, S. M., & Cicchetti, D. (2001). Maltreatment, competency deficits, and risk for academic and behavioral maladjustment. *Developmental Psychology, 37,* 3–17.

Trickett, P., McBride-Chang, C., & Putnam, F. (1994). The classroom performance and behavior of sexually abused females. *Development & Psychopathology, 6,* 183–194.

U.S. Department of Health and Human Services, Administration for Children and Families, Administration on Children, Youth and Families, Children's Bureau. (2010). *Child maltreatment 2008.* Retrieved from http://www.acf.hhs.gov/programs/cb/pubs/cm09/cm09.pdf

U.S. Department of Health and Human Services, Adoption and Foster Care Analysis and Reporting System (AFCARS). (2009). *FY 2008 data (October 1, 2007 through September 30, 2008).* Retrieved from http://www.acf.hhs.gov/programs/cb/stats_research/afcars/tar/report16.htm

U.S. Department of Justice. (2009). *National Crime Victimization Survey.* Retrieved from http://bjs.ojp.usdoj.gov/index.cfm?ty=pbdetail&iid=1975

van der Kolk, B. (2005). Developmental trauma disorder: Toward a rational diagnosis for children with complex trauma histories. *Psychiatric Annals, 35*(5), 401–408.

van der Kolk, B., Pelcovitz, D., Roth, S., Mandel, F., McFarlane, A., & Herman, J. (1996). Dissociation, somatization, and affect dysregulation: The complexity of adaptation to trauma. *American Journal of Psychiatry, 153,* (Suppl. 7), 83–93.

van der Kolk, B., Pynoos, R., Cicchetti, D., Cloitre, M., D'Andrea, W., Ford, J., et al. (2009, February). *Proposal to include a developmental trauma disorder diagnosis for children and adolescents in DSM-V.* Unpublished manuscript. Retrieved from http://www.traumacenter.org/announcements/DTD_papers_Oct_09.pdf

van der Kolk, B., Roth, S., Pelcovitz, D., Sunday, S., & Spinazzola, J. (2005). Disorders of extreme stress: The empirical foundation of a complex adaptation to trauma. *Journal of Traumatic Stress, 18,* 389–399.

2

How the Traumatic Experiences of Students Manifest in School Settings

RON HERTEL AND MONA M. JOHNSON ∎

INTRODUCTION

Every day, students arrive in classrooms feeling hungry, tired, frustrated, and alone—students who are impacted by serious family issues, alcohol and drugs, homelessness, maltreatment, physical or mental health–related issues, loss of a loved one, or a family member's military deployment. These can be stressful and often traumatic experiences for many students.

Trauma is not an event; rather, it is the response to an adverse experience that can negatively impact physical, mental, and emotional functioning. Trauma may also occur as a series of experiences where overlapping reactions add complexity to the response. This is known as complex trauma and may lead to increasingly pervasive and harmful effects on functioning for students, including cognitive, academic, and social/emotional functioning.

Trauma affects school performance for many students. Unfortunately, trauma is not always immediately detectable as it may include a wide variety of expressions from overt acting-out behavior to covert withdrawal or depression, or even a student who constantly strives for perfection in his or her work. As a means of survival, many students impacted by trauma may seem to blend in to expected school behaviors while experiencing emotional distress.

Often, children impacted by trauma come from homes where emotional reactions are unpredictable, illogical, disorganized, inconsistent, and volatile. Such inconsistency and unpredictability prevent a child from learning how to effectively deal with stress from adult modeling and create a chronic sense of hardship. Interestingly, children seem to be able to adjust more skillfully to a consistent situation of abuse or neglect than a situation that is inconsistent, volatile, and unpredictable—loving one moment, abusive the next—never being able to predict a logical reaction. In severe cases, a child can eventually shut down completely and become an emotional "failure to thrive." These children tend to give up hope as they wait for the next traumatic event to occur and remain in a state of learned helplessness, which can be defined as a sense of helpless loss of control through the expectation that trauma will continue in their lives and there is little they can do to mitigate it. Therefore, they are not able to practice the higher order skills of executive function that are essential for learning; thus, they struggle academically.

The Adverse Childhood Experiences (ACE) study[1] highlighted how trauma affects individuals over time. The ACE study examined health outcomes among 17,421 adults who had exposure to childhood adversities earlier in life. Most study participants were college graduates and had health coverage. In the study, nine adversities were identified and categorized (see Table 2.1). The researchers developed an understanding of how these nine ACEs affected the health outcomes of the study participants as they reached adulthood.

This study implied that those who had experienced ACEs had various negative health outcomes as adults, including alcoholism and alcohol abuse, chronic obstructive pulmonary disease and ischemic heart disease, depression, high-risk sexual behavior, illicit drug use, intimate partner violence, liver disease, obesity, sexually transmitted diseases, smoking, unintended pregnancy, suicide attempts, depression, and other mental health and emotional issues. These outcomes were often indicated in compromised job performance and relationship instability. Further, a dose/response relationship between the number of ACEs that each person reported and negative outcomes suggests that the higher the number of ACEs reported (even more important than the actual severity of an individual ACE), the more profound the negative outcomes became.

Table 2.1 ADVERSE CHILDHOOD EXPERIENCES (ACEs)

1. Child physical abuse
2. Child sexual abuse
3. Child emotional abuse
4. Neglect
5. Mentally ill, depressed, or suicidal person in the home
6. Drug-addicted or alcoholic family member
7. Witnessing domestic violence against the mother
8. Loss of a parent to death or abandonment, including abandonment by parental divorce
9. Incarceration of a family member for a crime

It is assumed that these outcomes for adults can also be translated into the lives of students where the indicator is learning and academic achievement. This was confirmed by Grevstad,[2] who found that students exposed to three or more ACEs were two and a half times more likely to fail a grade, score lower on standardized achievement tests, have more receptive and expressive language difficulties, or be suspended or expelled, and were more often referred to special education services. Further, a recent study[3] that incorporated information from Washington State's Healthy Youth Survey for middle and high school revealed that almost half of the students surveyed experienced three or more adversities, and 10% reported six or more adversities.

Given the wide-ranging impacts of trauma on students, which are described in more detail later in this chapter, teachers must develop new and improved ways for understanding how trauma can affect learning and overall functioning. They must also employ compassionate and creative responses and strategies to help students and their families develop healthy habits of resiliency in order to see successful results in school engagement and student learning.

IMPACT OF TRAUMA ON NEUROBIOLOGY AND BRAIN DEVELOPMENT

Neurobiology refers to the study of brain functioning from a neurological and biological perspective, including how various parts of the brain function independently and interdependently, and how external experiences and physical responses affect healthy neurological development.

From conception to adulthood, the brain progressively develops through a process of maturing and adjustment to the experiences of daily life. It develops and organizes itself in response to the stimulation it receives, both positive and negative. In this regard, the brain is exceptionally adaptive in terms of ensuring its survival. Exposure to trauma, however, can lead to terror, fear, perceived threat, unpredictability, instability, frustration, cognitive impairments, chaos, or pain, thus impacting one's perception of the world. As an example, two areas of the brain are critical for developing and maintaining cognitive competence: (1) the cerebellar vermis, which helps regulate cognitive functioning, and (2) the hippocampus, where short-term memory is converted into long-term memory. When children are repeatedly exposed to high levels of stress, these two areas of the brain can be impacted by a flush of hormones that can become toxic to the brain, which negatively affects cognitive capabilities and academic performance.

The complete effects of trauma on the brain are not fully understood, although we have learned it can produce lasting alterations in the structure (e.g., reduced size) and function (e.g., irritability, excitability, reduced function of sections responsible for learning and behavior) of the brain.[4] Trauma overstimulates the brain and causes the body to produce hormones, including adrenaline and cortisol, which impacts a student's neurobiology. While these hormones are beneficial in times of threat to quickly engage a physical response into a fight-or-flight mode, chronic and overexposure to them can damage and destroy brain cells and impede normal development.[5] Along these lines, "survival" often becomes paramount to students impacted by trauma, which can further undermine learning.

The survival mode is governed by pathways in the brain that appraise threat, prepare the body for a speedy response, make decisions outside of consciousness, and mobilize the body for the fight, flight, or freeze response. When in the survival mode, students' higher order brain functions that are typically required for learning are temporarily suspended. Instead, actions and responses are generated in the limbic system of the brain, which is responsible for fear and anger. Heart rate and blood pressure increase and pain is suppressed. The outward expressions of such physical changes can be anything from a student who emotionally loses control to one who sits quietly internalizing his or her circumstance—in either case, the ability to learn from instruction is reduced. Therefore, for these students, survival often supersedes learning.

Recommendations for Educators

Human brains, particularly those in the process of developing, are not well equipped to handle long-term stress. Therefore, it is easy to understand that some educators may feel hopeless and overwhelmed with students who are responding to chaos and dysfunction while the school's mission is to engage them in learning. For students to achieve academically, schools must do what they can to soothe the survival mode by instilling a sense of safety, hope, compassion, and resilience for all students, especially those impacted by trauma. A diminished need to activate survival strategies provides access to improved cognitive functioning and the availability for learning.

Encourage physical activity. Physical exercise significantly boosts brain functioning and is integral to learning. When we exercise, the body produces a protein called BDNF (brain-derived neurotrophic factor) that mitigates the amount of damaging hormones introduced into the brain. Therefore, recess and other physical activity before, during, or after school hours take on a renewed importance when it comes to supporting students impacted by trauma in our schools. One particular elementary school of 600 students in Washington State, as part of the Washington State Compassionate School Initiative, instituted Calming Yoga as part of the curriculum for all students along with other physical activities and compassionate school strategies. After 2 years of implementation, test scores rose dramatically, referrals to special education decreased, and discipline referrals dropped precipitously.

Given that many physical activities become competitive, which can lead to additional stress, schools may wish to offer noncompetitive opportunities for physical activity, such as walking or gardening clubs. In addition to physical exercise, students can be taught calming mind and body exercises to assist them in becoming more reflective thinkers, rather than reflexive, and to reduce impulsive, reactive behaviors.

Similarly, schools would be well advised to consider redesigning, maintaining, and supporting physical education programs for students. Unfortunately, due to increased demand to achieve academic outcomes, many schools have greatly reduced such opportunities. Only 8% of middle schools and 2% of high schools offer daily physical education classes, and only 78% require physical education at all.[6] In addition, many educators continually limit access to recess as a means of discipline, which may in fact exacerbate the disciplinary concern.

Support the development of routines at home to ensure adequate sleep and rest. Sleep is also a critical component for optimal brain functioning, including long-term memory, reaction time, processing speed, and self-regulation. Unfortunately, many students who are impacted by trauma often do not get sufficient sleep for optimal brain functioning, therefore adding an additional challenge to learning and retaining information. For younger children, educators would be well advised to encourage parents to develop routines and sufficient sleep schedules for their children. For adolescents, it may be more a matter of supporting them in developing healthy routines.

IMPACT OF TRAUMA ON ACADEMIC AND COGNITIVE SKILLS

Academic and cognitive skills are necessary to read, write, listen, speak, compute, think abstractly, process information, and solve problems. Further, to acquire learning of academic material, a student must possess the ability to focus, pay attention, comprehend, organize thoughts, and integrate/assimilate the material being presented.

Trauma can interfere with the healthy and normal development of the academic and cognitive skills needed for students to succeed in school. Students impacted by trauma often have difficulty processing verbal, nonverbal, or written instruction; thus, in many cases, short circuiting their ability to learn. Further, trauma often results in diminished concentration and memory, loss of focus or perspective, confusion, rigidity, self-doubt, perfectionism, difficulty in making decisions, hypervigilance, and impaired thinking. Therefore, prolonged periods of trauma can impair the ability to learn for months or even years, creating a barrier to academic success. Dr. Kenneth Fox, veteran high school teacher from Mount Vernon, Washington, explains that "Focusing on academics while struggling with trauma is like trying to play chess in a hurricane."[7]

Trauma also interferes with *executive functioning,* which occurs in the prefrontal lobe of the cerebral cortex and describes the ability to set and follow through on goals, develop plans, make decisions, anticipate consequences, evaluate outcomes, generate alternatives, and maintain attention. These abilities are crucial in promoting academic success. Unfortunately, children who experience chronic trauma lag behind their peers in the development of age-appropriate executive function skills.[8] Students impacted by trauma tend to react, rather than plan in a thoughtful way, and are driven by the need for survival. This is likely why some students frequently misbehave and feel remorseful later. When many actions are perceived as threats or viewed as distracting stimuli, learning becomes secondary.

Recommendations for Educators

Maintain high academic expectations for all students. Relaxing academic expectations for traumatized students can send the message that they are being discarded or that we are giving up on them. Conversely, many of these students may benefit from increased expectations. However, educators can offer flexibility and understanding while still maintaining high expectations for learning. Additional ways to bolster students' achievement and to help them meet expectations can be gained by creating calm zones or peaceful areas in the classroom and in the school to help them successfully carry out academic tasks without the perceived need for hypervigilance. Educators should also consider creating transition plans for students, especially if the transition from class to class may cause stress in the final minutes of instruction.

Provide opportunities for success. Quite often, the classroom behavior of students with trauma histories cause educators to view them as disengaged, disinterested, and unwilling to cooperate. However, these students are often reacting both to their experiences outside the classroom and to their frustration with the content. Like anyone else, these students prefer not to participate in activities when they believe they will repeatedly experience failure. Therefore, provide differentiated instruction and at least one activity each day that will always lead to success. This can simply be a warm-up word search or a reading activity borrowed from a teacher several grade levels below that of the student. Success increases motivation.

Find ways to monitor and reward student progress. Students benefit from being able to see their gains, such as through visual charts or tangible rewards for progress. In addition, rewarding progress serves as a catalyst for further gains and increased self-worth.

IMPACT OF TRAUMA ON BEHAVIORAL FUNCTIONING

Behavioral functioning describes a student's ability to act and respond verbally and physically in a manner that demonstrates skill acquisition and is socially acceptable to peers as well as authority figures. Nearly every student behaves inappropriately at one time or another—expecting otherwise will set students up for failure. Inappropriate behaviors may be the result of many factors, including stress in their daily lives or the desire to get attention, task avoidance, or fatigue. Other times misbehavior may be the result of a lack of awareness of expectations.

As previously indicated, trauma changes brain chemistry and neurology and can therefore create behaviors that are outside normal functioning, including perfectionism, self-harm, high-risk behavior (e.g., substance abuse), sleep disturbances, aggression, withdrawal, elevated startle response, impatience, impulsivity, irritability, moodiness, and reduced problem-solving abilities. When educators review the reasons that children are not behaving or learning, particularly when considering a referral for special education eligibility, exposure to trauma should definitely be considered as a possible contributing factor. As noted by Tishelman, Haney, O'Brien, and Blaustein,[9] differentiating adverse reactions to trauma from other disturbances in students can be incredibly challenging given a great deal of overlapping symptoms; thus, they encourage assessment that utilizes a "trauma lens" when evaluating a student's needs.

Trauma and subsequent activation of stress hormones can excite the limbic system, which plays an important role in the control of emotional behavior, management of fear and panic, and assessment of danger before we respond to a situation. Overstimulation of the amygdala (part of the limbic system) activates fear centers in the brain and results in behaviors that can produce anxiety, hyperarousal, and hypervigilance. It can result in the inability to calm down or lead to overreactions, impulsivity, and poor judgment. These are some of the same behaviors frequently cited when teachers make referrals for special education eligibility or disciplinary action.

Recommendations for Educators

Recognize that behaviors may be a response to students experiencing trauma in their lives. There may also be links between the trauma and the classroom environment, which can trigger certain behaviors. Responding to trauma-influenced behavior with patience, care, compassion, and consistency will allow the student to respond without feeling and acting in defensive ways. Compassion does not infer that one dismisses responsible behavior for a student; instead, it implies empathy while holding the student to high behavioral and academic expectations. Those expectations help students to understand that they have abilities and talents that can transcend their traumatic experience and that they have the capacity not only to survive but also to thrive.

Acknowledge and respect boundaries when discovering that a student is responding to trauma in his or her life. If a child discloses a family issue, for example, school staff would do best to focus on safety for the child and how the child feels about what's happening in the home, rather than asking for more details about the incident, which could potentially retraumatize the child. Asking children, in an age-appropriate way, how they feel about a situation lets them know someone cares for them and provides a sense of safety and well-being. Certainly, asking some detailed questions about the trauma may be necessary to gauge student safety and document the concern, although careful attention should be given to which questions are essential.

Provide opportunities to practice self-regulation. Guide students in developing various self-regulation skills through introspection, thoughtful reflection, self-monitoring, and being allowed to set appropriate consequences for their own behavior.

Use prudent judgment in reporting behavioral problems. Sometimes what may be seen as acting-out behavior in school may actually be a survival strategy for a child who comes from a home that is fraught with stress and chaos. A casual call to the home to report a behavioral problem in the school may be upsetting to the parent, who may, in turn, take it out on the child and exacerbate the stress and chaos in the home and could result in the situation becoming more harmful for the student. In these cases, consider whether the school has exhausted all resources in addressing the problem behavior.

IMPACT OF TRAUMA ON SOCIAL-EMOTIONAL FUNCTIONING

Social-emotional functioning refers to attributes and skills related to emotional well-being, the ability to manage and regulate emotions, social competence, quality of peer relationships and interactions, and self-esteem, among others. Students cannot learn academics and profit from instruction without first mitigating the impact of social and emotional conditions that interfere with learning. After all, emotions affect how and what we learn, and schools are social places where relationships provide a foundation for learning. Unfortunately, decreased social-emotional functioning frequently interferes with academic functioning. For example, the 2008 Washington State Healthy Schools Survey[10] revealed that 25% to 30% of youth (8th, 10th, and 12th grades) felt so sad and hopeless for 2 or more weeks in a row that they stopped their usual activities; 16% to 32% (6th, 8th, 10th, and 12th grades) had been bullied in the past 30 days; 8% to 12% (8th, 10th, and 12th grades) attempted or made a plan for suicide; and 9% to 26% of youth ages 13 to 17 engaged in binge drinking.

Since schools are clearly part of the student's community and are often the first responders to a struggling student, it is here that social and emotional skills must be developed for the student while providing a sense of safety, well-being, belonging, and achievement. And yet, some schools seem to struggle most in terms of creating a supportive learning environment for all, including students impacted by trauma.

Recommendations for Educators

Help students differentiate the skills they have developed at home from the skills it takes to navigate the school setting. The social skills that enable a student to survive at home or in the community, particularly in violent or abusive environments, are most often not the same social skills needed to thrive in a classroom. By learning to differentiate behaviors between environments, students learn how to engage appropriately in small and large group work, get the attention of an adult in an appropriate way, or argue constructively with a peer. This requires a great deal of patience from educators.

Help students develop an emotional vocabulary. Students with a rich emotional vocabulary can better identify and understand their emotions. The earlier this vocabulary can be developed in the lives of children, the better chance they will have to understand and express their emotions as they mature. Evidence-based programs, such as Second Step,[11] are designed to help children develop the language of feelings as a way of identifying and understanding them. Through this learning they can increase empathy and listening skills, become appropriately assertive in meeting their own needs and the needs of others, and, importantly, learn conflict resolution skills. Adding feeling words to spelling lists or to other language-related activities is an easy way for teachers to improve students' feeling-word vocabulary. Additionally, there is an array of other evidence-based materials available for social-emotional learning available through the Collaborative for Academic, Social, and Emotional Learning (http://casel.org) that are designed for and can be incorporated into classroom curricula for students from pre-K through grade 12.

Further, consider these six principles that guide how we teach and support social, emotional, and academic learning[12]:

1. *Always empower, never disempower.* Students who are impacted by trauma often compete with teachers and other adults for power and control. For most students, boundaries with adults are tested, which is considered normal development in solidifying their own personality. For students impacted by trauma, this competition is often experienced as a way to control their environment and as a means to feel safe and secure in an environment they perceive as unpredictable and unsafe. Consider offering students options when placing demands to give them a greater sense of control and autonomy.

2. *Provide unconditional positive regard.* Children impacted by trauma sometimes have a difficult time feeling worthy, taking initiative, and forming relationships. As educators, we can help them in these areas with simple sustained kindness, empathy, and creating a positive school climate that feels safe and academically supportive. See chapter 17 for more on safe and supportive schools.

3. *Maintain high expectations.* Educators can often be so concerned about their students that they may be hesitant to set limits; thus, expectations for achievement are lowered. Doing so can send a negative message such as "You are too damaged to behave and I am giving up on you." Instead, send the message that students can work up to expectations with support and good instruction.

4. *Check assumptions, observe, and question.* Making quick and potentially unfounded assumptions about who is impacted by trauma based on preconceived ideas may stop us from seeing students for who they really are. Pay special attention to students' gifts and talents, as well as their challenges. Observe students closely, ask questions, and listen to what students are really saying, which sometimes is only communicated through behavior.

5. *Be a relationship coach.* As educators, we also serve as relationship coaches for our students. The relationships we establish with and among students influence the tone and demeanor in our classrooms. But even more than that, many students are keen observers of how adults relate to others in their world, so we become role models in terms of how we interact with others. Take advantage of opportunities to provide meaningful feedback when helping a student reframe an interaction that has not gone well. In many circumstances, the school may be the only opportunity for shaping healthy interactions with others.

6. *Provide opportunities for meaningful participation.* When we make meaningful contributions to the welfare of others, we improve our own feelings of self-worth. Helping others strengthens resiliency, and providing guided opportunities for participation in activities that support the welfare of others is an important principle of compassionate teaching for educators. Such supervised opportunities can provide solace, create mutual trust, and affirm the self-worth of those involved. Participation can also be meaningful if extended to families and others throughout the school and community. Simple things like being a crossing guard, assisting with beautification of the grounds on earth day, having students read to the lower grades, or being a volunteer during after-school activities can give students a feeling of engagement, connectedness, and self-worth.

SECONDARY TRAUMA AND SELF-CARE

Educators, because of their access to children and their tremendous capacity to care, are often first responders when dealing with children and trauma. This capacity to care for others is critical, particularly when it comes to working in schools. However, caring takes energy, and the more we care for others, the more energy we expend in our day-to-day work. Perhaps the greatest challenge for educators is to make sure that while simultaneously caring for others we abso-lutely make time each and every day to also practice self-care to stay energized, positive, and motivated. Otherwise, our energy decreases and the constant demands of our daily jobs may cause apathy, fatigue, or emotional stress, which may lead to burnout. In fact, approximately 9% of public school teachers with 1 to 3 years of experience left the teaching profession during the 2008–2009 school year.[13] Once educators realize that they are manifesting symptoms of sec-ondary trauma, they have an ethical and personal responsibility to address their own needs and, in some cases, the residual effects of their own constellation of ACEs. Consider visiting the Child Trauma Academy website[14] to self-assess the possibility of secondary trauma.

Why is self-care so important? If we as educators do not take time to care for ourselves on a regular basis, we deplete our capacity to be helpful and ulti-mately become vulnerable to secondary traumatic stress, which is the stress that results from helping or wanting to help a suffering or traumatized person, or compassion fatigue, which is the weariness that results from caring. Secondary traumatic stress and compassion fatigue can lead to sleep problems, relation-ship difficulties, frequent irritability and moodiness, feeling overwhelmed, and depression. It also impacts our ability to teach and motivate students.

Therefore, much like we are instructed to do while flying in a commercial airplane, we must first put our own oxygen masks on before we attempt to put them on those for whom we have assumed responsibility. Taking care of your-self first is the only way that you will be able to provide care and assistance to those who need it. Practicing self-care for educators is not only important; it is vital.

Some suggested strategies for practicing professional wellness and self-care include:

1. *Physical self-care*—taking care of your body in healthy ways including exercise, nutrition, sleep, and regular doctor visits
2. *Emotional self-care*—dealing with feelings in a healthy way including talking about feelings, journaling, counseling, or therapy
3. *Psychological self-care*—improving your mind and understanding yourself better through reading for pleasure, working, or continuing education
4. *Social self-care*—improving relationships with others; spending time with family, friends, and colleagues; and belonging to groups, communities, and organizations that promote positive social connections
5. *Financial self-care*—spending and saving responsibly
6. *Spiritual self-care*—gaining perspective on your life through such activities as prayer, meditation, working a 12-step program, contact with nature, and self-reflection

CONCLUSION

Stress and trauma can exist anywhere at any time in the lives of children as well as adults. Teachers see it every day. Often, the effects of the stresses that occur at home and in the lives of family members resonate in the classroom. The impact can cause impaired ability to learn as well as challenging and inappropriate behavior at school. By taking the time to understand the impact of trauma on learning and behavior, educators can begin to change their approach to students by changing an accusingly toned "What's wrong with you?" to a soft, inquisitive "Tell me about what happened, and how I can help." This offers an opening to a real conversation with a student, rather than a potential reaction that will likely have a detrimental outcome.

Through ongoing research, we now know that brains that have been negatively impacted due to trauma have the ability to regenerate and rewire themselves. Schools have the ability to create an environment that can nurture students who have been impacted by trauma. We also know that by getting the correct amount of sleep, eating nutritiously, and engaging in mental and physical activity, we can assist the brain in developing and, when necessary, even healing itself. The good news is, there is hope to provide improved learning outcomes for students impacted by trauma. To that end, it is our hope that those reading this chapter will improve their ability to:

- Exemplify practical and applicable compassionate approaches to education that may be of benefit to all members of the school community
- Provide a new lens through which members of our educational communities may better understand events and consequent behaviors that interfere with the attainment of educational goals
- Foster resilience and create supportive learning environments for students through a cadre of school and community-based resources
- Provide tools and resources to members of school communities wishing to revise policies, procedures, curricula, and instruction that will enhance strategies for students who have been impacted by trauma
- Take good care of yourselves because we can only give to others what we have attained ourselves

NOTES

1. Felitti et al., 1998.
2. Grevstad, 2007.
3. Anda & Brown, 2010.
4. Teicher et al., 2003.
5. Medina, 2009.
6. Kann, Brener, & Wechsler, 2007.
7. Wolpow, Johnson, Hertel, & Kincaid, 2009, p. 3.

8. Kinniburgh, Blaustein, & Spinazzola, 2005.
9. Tishelman, Haney, O'Brien, & Blaustein, 2010.
10. Washington State Department of Health, n.d.
11. Committee for Children, n.d.
12. Wolpow et al., 2009.
13. Keigher & Cross, 2010.
14. http://www.childtraumaacademy.com/cost_of_caring/lesson02/page01.html

REFERENCES

Anda, R. F., & Brown, D. W. (2010). *Adverse childhood experiences and population health in Washington: The face of a chronic public health disaster.* Washington State Family Policy Council. Retrieved from http://www.casey.org/resources/events/earlylearning/wa/pdf/AdverseChildhoodExp.pdf

Committee for Children. (n.d.). *Second Step: Social-emotional skills for early learning.* Seattle, WA: Author. Retrieved from http://www.cfchildren.org/programs/ssp/early-learning/.

Felitti, V. J., Anda, R. F., Nordenberg, D., Williamson, D. F., Spitz, A. M., Edwards, V., et al. (1998). The relationship of childhood abuse and household dysfunction to many of the leading causes of death in adults: The adverse childhood experiences (ACE) study. *American Journal of Preventive Medicine, 14,* 245–258.

Grevstad, J. (2007). *Adverse childhood experiences in juvenile justice—Pierce County, WA.* Paper presented at the Family Policy Council Partners Summit, Seattle, WA.

Kann, L., Brener, N. D., & Wechsler, H. (2007). Overview and summary: School Health Policies and Programs Study 2006. *Journal of School Health, 77,* 385–397.

Keigher, A., & Cross, F. (2010). *Teacher attrition and mobility: Results from the 2008–09 Teacher Follow-up Survey* (NCES 2010-353). U.S. Department of Education. Washington, DC: National Center for Education Statistics. Retrieved from http://nces.ed.gov/pubsearch

Kinniburgh, K. J., Blaustein, M., and Spinazzola, J. (2005). Attachment, self-regulation, and competency: A comprehensive intervention framework for children with complex trauma. *Psychiatric Annals, 35,* 424–430.

Medina, J. (2009). *Brain rules: 12 principles for surviving and thriving at work, home, and school.* Seattle, WA: Pear Press.

Teicher, M. H., Anderson, S. L., Polcari, A., Anderson, C. M., Navalta, C. P., & Kim, D. M. (2003). The neurobiological consequences of early stress and childhood maltreatment. *Neuroscience and Biobehavioral Reviews, 27,* 33–44.

Tishelman, A. C., Haney, P., O'Brien, J. G., & Blaustein, M. E. (2010). A framework for school-based psychological evaluations: Utilizing a "trauma lens." *Journal of Child & Adolescent Trauma, 3,* 279–302.

Washington State Department of Health. (n.d.). *Healthy youth survey.* Retrieved from http://www.doh.wa.gov/healthyyouth/default.htm

Wolpow, R., Johnson, M. M., Hertel, R., & Kincaid, S. O. (2009). *The heart of learning and teaching: Compassion, resiliency, and academic success.* Olympia, WA: Washington Office of Superintendent of Public Instruction (OSPI) Compassionate Schools.

Developmental Differences in Response to Trauma

LADONA R. WIEBLER ■

INTRODUCTION

A child's cognitive, social, behavioral, and even physical developmental levels directly impact both the *perceived* and *real* ability to prevent, influence, understand, and recover from traumatic experiences. Children from the same family can develop completely unique patterns despite being exposed to identical environments and events. It is important for all educators to be aware of these differences; likewise, interventions for children of any age must be adapted with a child's developmental level in mind.

Factors Impacting Response to Trauma

Event factors. How a child responds to trauma is often dependent on the source of trauma itself. Exposure to violence, for example, may be viewed as more traumatic than a natural disaster[1]; however, if the natural disaster destroyed a child's home, school, or community, then that may lead to more severe trauma. Thus, the events and the personal outcomes of those events often dictate a child's response.

Risk and protective factors. A risk factor is a variable or characteristic that makes a person more vulnerable to the adverse effects of physical and psychological hazards. External factors that may increase risk of trauma often include factors that increase individual or family stress, such as single-parent households; poverty; previous exposure to trauma; lack of family, school, or social support; and parental depression or other illness. Internal risk factors may include deficits in communication, problem solving, executive functioning, social-emotional functioning, and cognitive ability. Understandably, children at different stages of development vary significantly in the existence of many of these internal risk factors.

Conversely, protective factors are those variables within the person or within his or her environment that help lessen the adverse effects of stress-ful life events, increase the ability to avoid risks in the future, and foster an adaptive response to environmental hazards.[2] Protective factors may include communication, problem solving, and cognitive and physical skills, along with supportive relationships and connectedness. All of these factors contribute to a child's response to a potentially traumatic event and are largely dependent on a child's stage of development.

Environmental, family, and social influences and individual differences. Children's responses to adverse experiences are impacted by their own risk and protective factors *as well as* the risk and protective factors of their parents.[3] This is especially true of young children, whose primary sources of support are their parents; these children count on their parents having built their own systems of competency and resilience. With only limited access to the outside world and a high level of dependency on adults, a young child looks to the parent as a role model as to how to handle the potentially traumatic events of life. Those parents who have little competency of their own cannot teach their child to access external protective factors (e.g., social supports) or to build internal protective factors. In addition, parents who carry personal risk factors (e.g., substance abuse or depression) may have no means of supporting their child during or after trauma. Thus, the child is left to learn how to cope on his or her own.

As children get older, language skills increase, social circles expand, and peers become more than playmates; they also become role models of academic and behavioral standards. The role of peers continues to increase given the emerging quest for independence apart from the nuclear family. Children also begin to learn that there is a world outside their home; that world is largely contained within the school community.

Older children in elementary school incorporate their own and their parents' competencies and resilience, although they may also begin benefiting (or suffering) from the risk and protective factors of peers, and even peers' families.[4] Older children are more likely to spend the night at a friend's house or accompany the friend to church or family gatherings. As children engage in prosocial activities with their own family or a peer's family, they develop personal competency. Conversely, children with few opportunities for healthy and prosocial activities with different people in the community may exhibit maladaptive behaviors that turn peers away from them, resulting in fewer healthy relationships.

When children reach adolescence, they continue to explore their growing independence through peer groups, school activities, and employment opportunities. No longer is their world just home and school; it has expanded into the community at large. High school usually involves a teacher per subject, increasing the opportunity of developing relationships with other adults. Experiences through school sports and activities or through worksites also increase exposure to a variety of adult protective and risk factors alike.[5]

Chronological age and developmental level. Just as children's bodies begin growing and changing from birth, their ability to think and to get along with others is a growth process that must be nurtured along the way if they are to be successful as adults. Chronological age is often used as a metric to help estimate developmental level; however, in the case of a developmental delay, chronological age is no longer a relevant measure of ability. Further, even in the absence of a developmental delay, normal developmental trajectories vary considerably from child to child. Therefore, while there is a general sequence of developmental capacities that progress as children age (which is described throughout this chapter), the assumption that *all* students in the same grade or age group are developmentally alike or would respond to trauma similarly is misguided. Teachers must look at the developmental stage of each child individually to accurately gauge the child's capability to process, understand, and rebound from traumatic experiences.

DEVELOPMENTAL DIFFERENCES IN RESPONSE TO TRAUMA

Preschool

During the first years of life, children learn through inborn reflexes to create more complex combinations of cause-and-effect relationships. They learn to pretend, to recall from memory, and to imitate. In a nurturing household, the child learns to trust others, to gain some autonomy and self-confidence for exploration, and the ability for imaginative, active play with others, leading to the beginnings of cooperation. On the opposite end, if the child's environment is not as responsive, supportive, or healthy, the child will have difficulty learning cause-and-effect relationships, which can lead to mistrust, insecurity, fearfulness of others, isolation from peers, and dependence on adults to navigate his or her world.

When a young child experiences trauma during the first few years of life, that child relies on other individuals in the environment to understand what is happening. This lack of understanding may serve as a protective factor in some ways, particularly when the child's family provides a stable and relatively unchanged home environment.[6] On the other hand, for some young children general fears may emerge that are seemingly not connected to the traumatic experience, in part due to confusion and difficulty making sense of the situation. In other cases, younger children may be more likely to dissociate given the inability to fight or flee from threatening situations.[7]

Children who can trust their caregivers (and educators) and who are secure in their ability to be cared for can explore their full range of emotions, knowing the adults will continue to care for them. This trust is often built from an environment that provides consistency, predictability, structure, and the opportunity to develop caring relationships. On the other hand, children who do not trust adults due to environmental risk factors or a lack of an established relationship with those adults may be unable to regulate any response at all. A child may withdraw completely from participating in any activity or may blow up at the most innocent act or comment. The child's lack of trust may be reinforced by the trauma itself; the adult's inability to keep the child safe was just proven again.

When exposed to trauma, very young children often have no other reality against which to compare their own life circumstances. What they see is their only reality. They may accept blame or responsibility in an attempt to regain a sense of control or explain the experience(s) (e.g., if they were just a little less clumsy or a better behaved student, the adverse experience may not have occurred).[8] This is also known as *magical thinking* and can be attributed to their developmental stage given the egocentric thinking that makes them feel responsible for what happens. Without the verbal skills to question circumstances or express feelings, their internal anger or fear may also be directed at adults because they did not protect them or prevent the trauma from happening.

Preschool children exposed to trauma may also protest when being left by either parent, whether at school, at childcare, or even when someone tries to leave the child alone in a room (i.e., separation anxiety). Without having established trust of others or autonomy, these children may cling to a parent in fear of something happening to that parent or themselves. They may lash out at teachers or peers with no clear reason behind the anger, other than distrust, when faced with a change in routine or expectation. It is not uncommon to see regression in toileting, dressing, or feeding skills following adverse experiences. The preschool child may also learn to remain in a hyperaroused state of mind in an effort to pick up nonverbal environmental cues that may help predict an adverse experience.[9] This child cannot "relax" and is often unavailable for learning.

While most children at this age are still going through developmentally appropriate stages of temper tantrums in response to frustration and anger, children with chronic trauma exposure run the risk of being unable to learn to handle stress in less impulsive, more integrated ways. While some traumatized children may withdraw or avoid challenging tasks, other children's attempts to come to terms with a home situation that they cannot explain in words could be exhibited by destroying materials, being aggressive to peers, or cursing. Some other symptoms may include disturbed sleep (e.g., difficulty falling asleep, nightmares, excessive sleep), a constant state of fear, crying frequently, or playing out a traumatic event repeatedly.[10]

Elementary School

During elementary school, children begin learning there are definite rules for games and play and that working together as a team is often required for play and sports. On the other hand, children who have not developed the trust of others and confidence in themselves as a result of a traumatic experience may lack the ability to successfully join in group activities, and thus not experience the feelings of competency that result from those endeavors. Inability to work cooperatively in groups can significantly impact school functioning given the social nature of learning in the classroom.

As children begin to understand a set of rules that apply either in play or in the classroom, any discrepancy between rules at home and at school can become confusing. For example, some children may be asked to follow rules of respect in the classroom, whereas such rules may not exist at home. Reconciling these differences in rules may be particularly difficult for elementary school-aged children.

Friends are becoming an important part of the child's world and an important base of modeling, support, and acceptance. Peers can become protective or risk factors, and as such, can either help a child adapt after a trauma or contribute to the child's adverse reaction. Educators who have built an environment of trust, safety, connectedness, and community in school have already built the environment to provide the kind of peer support needed for a child who has experienced trauma.

Traumatized elementary school-aged children may show an increase in somatic complaints, such as headaches or stomachaches. Children may use these complaints as a reason to stay home from school, having learned that somatic complaints are safer to report than the source of trauma in some cases (e.g., reporting abuse, which may lead to anger from the parent or separation from the home, or reporting a parent's incarceration, which may lead to shame or embarrassment). Avoiding school reduces others' scrutiny of the child's physical states and security issues and also avoids the accusations of inattention and impulsivity that come with a constant state of hyperarousal. While increased social contacts at school can provide children with more opportunities to form typical relationships, it brings with it the pressure to conceal the atypical nature of their traumatic experience. The more examples of typical relationships that are encountered, the more atypical their own relationships may appear. At a stage when blending in is of utmost importance, children may choose to withdraw completely or keep their experiences to themselves rather than stand out to peers. Research suggests that some children and adolescents do not report maltreatment, for example, due to factors such as embarrassment, a desire to avoid discussing the experience, or wanting to protect the parent.[11]

While elementary school children can begin to verbally communicate better than preschool children, behavioral expression of distress also remains common.[12] Some children may not be able to handle their feelings of anger or fear and become physically aggressive in response to even the slightest frustration. They may aim their anger or fear at the perceived source of the trauma, adults who failed to protect them, or they may feel anger toward themselves for not being able to avoid the trauma in the first place. Some children might identify situations in which they believe they can express their anger without potential consequences, which may even lead to bullying other children. In cases where perceived failure or misbehavior has led to negative consequences at home (e.g., maltreatment), a child may become noncompliant with teachers in order to avoid taking the same risk of failure at school.[13] Some additional responses to trauma among elementary school-aged students may include excessive worry, anxiety, perseverating on a traumatic experience or their response to the experience, emotional numbing, withdrawal and isolation from others, restlessness, and learning difficulties.[14]

Secondary School

As children reach adolescence, they begin developing their identity of self and their role in society. It is the exploration of "Who am I?" and "Where do I fit?" that can lead to bouts of rebellion and experimentation until the right fit is found. Some adolescents find their fit readily, whereas others spend years searching. Experiencing trauma at this age can blur the role the adolescent is trying to find; for example, some adolescents may feel compelled to take on the role of an adult or caretaker following trauma, whereas others may regress to a level of increased dependency on their parents.

In high school, the focus turns toward becoming an adult, and the future looms large on the horizon. There is much less tolerance by adults for impulsive, inappropriate behavior because the child should have "learned better" by that point. Traumatized children, however, may not have had the opportunities to acquire these skills by typical standards. What they *have* learned is to survive their situation by alternately laying low, moving fast, scanning constantly, striking first, giving up, or avoiding potentially damaging relationships. While they may have adapted these survival skills in response to their home situations, these behaviors become a hindrance in learning, sporting, and work environments.

With adolescents at the stage of looking for justice in life and beginning to understand that what happens now affects the future, their feelings of injustice about their home situation may spill over into an all-inclusive "life isn't fair" attitude. This perceived lack of control over an adverse set of circumstances may then lead to a series of reckless or self-destructive behaviors in efforts to regain control, encouraged by those peers who are also seeking their own sense of autonomy. At a time when even typical adolescents begin to question authority and look for a place to belong among peer groups, traumatized children's maladaptive behaviors tend to lead them into associations with other children with similar behaviors.[15] Older teens may have more life skills at their disposal, such as driving, employment (money), or a wider circle of friends, which reduces their dependence on adults and opens them up to a wider range of risk-laden situations.

Given that adolescents are generally more cognitively aware and verbally adept at expressing emotions and feelings, they are more likely to process events through discussion or writing activities. However, they also will likely react with other behaviors including self-consciousness about feelings of shame, guilt, or worry; preoccupation with an event, a topic related to the trauma (e.g., a parent's cancer), or death; fantasies of revenge or retribution; withdrawal; internalizing feelings out of fear of reaction from peers; depression and anxiety; and hypervigilance.[16]

Across the Lifespan

It was previously believed that children do not experience trauma as adults do and instead experience brief, temporary adjustment reactions.[17] We now know that exposure to stress during childhood can lead to traumatic stress, increased reactivity to adverse experiences, and cognitive deficits through adolescence and adulthood. In fact, the long-lasting effects of early exposure to trauma typically become most evident during adolescence. Even prenatal exposure to stress leads to changes in developmental trajectories of children, including lower birth weight, attention problems, sleep disturbances, and an increased prevalence of psychiatric disorders. Importantly, exposure to stress and trauma leads to ongoing and often long-term effects on brain development. Given that different developmental periods are associated with the development of different structures of the brain (e.g., hippocampus during childhood, frontal cortex during adolescence), trauma at any given time has the greatest impact on that particular developing brain structure.[18]

INTERVENING ACROSS DEVELOPMENTAL LEVELS

Intervening and providing supports to any traumatized child should take developmental level into consideration and is a component of each of the chapters in the next section of this book. What may work with children at one level could have no effect, or worse, disastrous effects on children at another level.[19] For example, young children may not have the vocabulary to describe what they have endured or how they feel about it, and being asked to do so may lead to more frustration. Conversely, asking some older students to draw or role-play may lead to resistance, despite being an effective communication strategy for young children. The developmental level of the student is a prime determinant of what interventions and supports should be provided.

Preschool and Elementary School

Return to normal routines as soon as possible. Routines help everyone function, including adults. Without routines, life seems somewhat unpredictable and frustrating and does not allow us to focus on other things, such as learning. Routines are particularly important for younger children, making a return to routines following a trauma critical for recovery.

Provide opportunities to feel empowered. Children often feel helpless in controlling their surroundings. This is particularly evident during traumatic experiences. Educators can support students by giving them a chance to take positive action or feel empowered in some way. This can include writing letters to others, making cards, helping organize a fundraiser, donating to others in need, volunteering, or attending funerals/memorials when appropriate. Empowering children can also come in the form of providing choices in the classroom and acknowledging any successes in the classroom.

Utilize peer partners rather than groups. Consider pairing trauma-impacted children with children who possess strong empathy and social skills. This can give the trauma-impacted child a chance to experience and practice social competency without the added anxiety of waiting long periods for a turn or adding to his or her sensory overstimulation with a group of active children.

Allow expression without having to speak. Despite some beliefs that some young children are too young to recall traumatic experiences, even preverbal children are still capable of recalling events.[20] Children who cannot express themselves through words can often draw what they feel or what they have endured. Trauma often is a physiological experience; drawing is a motor response that taps into the sensory aspects of a traumatic memory.[21] Art is great a way to draw out any existing verbal skills. Young children hesitant to discuss their experience or feelings may be more willing to discuss the picture than an experience from memory—especially a traumatic one. Adults may also consider drawing *with* the child; as the adult draws and verbalizes his or her own thoughts, the child may slowly begin to take over the direction of the work, adding his or her feelings and interpretations to the art. This partnership may help the child feel less anxious about the activity and actually be able to recall more from his or her memory.[22] Teachers should always encourage drawing as a means of expression, especially for emotions.

Since children at this age may also try to re-enact a traumatic experience through play, using toys and materials may also help children express their thoughts and feelings and explain how they interpreted the event. Cars can crash, dolls can fall, and fire engines may come to the rescue. Having an adult verbalize what the "doll" can do the next time around can be very helpful for young children trying to make sense of their world.

Be careful not to overanalyze. Educators should be cautious when trying to "interpret" art or expressive play in any way. Play therapy is considered a direct intervention,[23] and care must be taken in who conducts the play session. While an experienced professional (e.g., school psychologist, mental health therapist, school counselor) is better suited to interpreting a child's behavior in response to structured play scenarios, teachers and parents are often the first to notice changes in tone and manner of play when a child may be suffering from trauma. Alerting families or school support service personnel to the change in play behavior can be a first step in helping a traumatized child.

Use visual supports for schedules, rules, and communication. Pictures can help adults communicate with children. Pictures are constant and consistent and do not vary from one situation to the next. Having rules and expectations visually represented not only helps individual children understand but also helps reinforce the rules in the classroom. It also helps to ensure consistency across adults, as substitutes and volunteers will know what is expected at any given time.

Provide reassurances. When possible, reassure young children that they will be safe, treated fairly, and taken care of in the educational setting. Identify any continuing misperceptions that a child may display and address them as necessary with clear and simple explanations.

Be flexible and understanding Some children may regress, have difficulty focusing, be less inclined to talk about feelings, or become anxious or oppositional. Many of these behaviors will subside when provided with an empathic, caring environment that offers structure, consistency, predictability, and flexibility.

Secondary School

Engage peer groups with students from similar backgrounds or experiences. Peer groups can be powerful tools for older children and adolescents who have experienced or are experiencing similar stressful situations. Talking about what happened, the feelings and reactions, and how to possibly change those reactions in the future can be extremely helpful to adolescents, especially when suggestions for change come from a peer who has "been there, done that." Such peer groups further serve to normalize an adolescent's feelings and help develop a sense of connectedness with others.

Provide a venue for discussion. Within limits, educators have the opportunity to create an environment where adolescents can openly discuss their lives outside the classroom. In this role, educators can provide encouragement for prosocial activities (e.g., after-school sports or community volunteering), discourage antisocial activities (ideas for revenge, substance abuse, risk-taking behavior), and provide an outlet for a range of emotions and feelings. This environment is built from the first day a student walks into a classroom.

Acknowledge the distress. Adults often underestimate students' distress and overestimate their ability to rebound from distress on their own. Therefore, if educators see a change in behavior or become aware of an adverse experience in a student's life, acknowledge it or simply pull the student aside and say, "I've noticed you have _____ this week. Do you want to talk?"

Use a strength-based approach to intervention. Rather than relying on a problem-focused, deficit perspective when intervening with students, consider focusing on the strengths of those who have experienced trauma.[24]

Concentrating on the positive qualities not only helps the adult tune into what the student *can* do instead of *can't* do but also bolsters the student's own sense of competency and resilience. Using this approach pulls in the strengths of the student's family, friends, and community. This approach can lay a better foundation for continued success by providing assurances to traumatized students that they have what it takes to be successful. This can be incorporated into classroom discussions by asking students and their peers to help identify the strengths in historical figures or characters in literature and relate them to their own coping styles.

CONCLUSION

This chapter reviewed some of the typical developmental differences seen in children's responses to trauma and what that means for educators. Importantly, various factors impact a child's or adolescent's response to trauma, although the stage of development has significant implications for both the response and appropriate intervention. Educators who develop a general understanding of these developmental factors are better prepared to support all students following a traumatic experience.

NOTES

1. Kanan & Plog, 2010.
2. Centers for Disease Control and Prevention, 2009.
3. Calhoun & Tedeschi, 2006.
4. Masten & Coatsworth, 1998.
5. Masten & Coatsworth, 1998.
6. Osofsky, 2004.
7. van der Kolk, Roth, Pelcovitz, Sunday, & Spinazzola, 2005.
8. Craig, 2008.
9. Perry, 2001.
10. Kanan & Plog, 2010.
11. Fergusson, Horwood, & Woodward, 2000.
12. Kanan & Plog, 2010.
13. Craig, 2008.
14. Kanan & Plog, 2010.
15. Masten & Coatsworth, 1998.
16. Kanan & Plog, 2010.
17. Davis & Siegel, 2000.
18. Lupien, McEwen, Gunnar, & Heim, 2009.
19. Calhoun & Tedeschi, 2006.
20. Kaplow, Saxe, Putnam, Pynoos, & Lieberman, 2006.
21. Malchiodi, 2001.
22. Malchiodi, 2001.

23. Luby, 2006.
24. O'Connell, 2006.

REFERENCES

Calhoun, L. G., & Tedeschi, R. G. (2006). *Handbook of posttraumatic growth: Research and practice.* New York, NY: Lawrence Erlbaum Associates.

Centers for Disease Control and Prevention. (2009). *School connectedness: Strategies for increasing protective factors among youth.* Atlanta, GA: U.S. Department of Health and Human Services.

Craig, S. E. (2008). *Reaching and teaching children who hurt: Strategies for your class room.* Baltimore, MD: Brookes Publishing.

Davis, L., & Siegel, L. J. (2000). Posttraumatic stress disorder in children and adolescents: A review and analysis. *Clinical Child and Family Psychology Review, 3,* 135–154.

Fergusson, D. M., Horwood, L. J., & Woodward, L. J. (2000). The stability of child abuse reports: A longitudinal study of the reporting behavior of young adults. *Psychological Medicine, 30,* 529–544.

Kanan, L. M., & Plog, A. E. (2010). Trauma reactions in children: Information for parents and caregivers. In A. Canter, L. Paige, & S. Shaw (Eds.), *Helping children at home and school III: Handouts for families and educators* (S9H22-1–4). Bethesda, MD: National Association of School Psychologists.

Kaplow, J. B., Saxe, G. N., Putnam, F. W., Pynoos, R. S., & Lieberman, A. F. (2006). The long-term consequences of early childhood trauma: A case study and discussion. *Psychiatry: Interpersonal and Biological Processes, 69,* 362–375.

Luby, J. L. (Ed). (2006). *Handbook of preschool mental health: Development, disorders, and treatment.* New York, NY: Guilford Press.

Lupien, S. J., McEwen, B. S., Gunnar, M. R., & Heim, C. (2009). Effects of stress throughout the lifespan on brain, behaviour, and cognition. *Nature Reviews Neuroscience, 10,* 434–445.

Malchiodi, C. (2001). Using drawing as intervention with traumatized children. *Trauma and Loss: Research and Intervention, 1,* 21–28.

Masten, A. S., & Coatsworth, J. D. (1998). The development of competence in favorable and unfavorable environments. *American Psychologist, 53*(2), 205–220.

O'Connell, D. (2006). *Brief literature review on strength-based teaching and counseling.* Research and draft prepared for the Metropolitan Action Committee on Violence Against Women and Children (METRAC). Osofsky, J. D. (Ed.). (2004). *Young children and trauma: Interventions and treatment.* New York: Guilford Press.

Perry, B. D. (2001). The neurodevelopmental impact of violence in childhood. In D. Schetky & E. Benedek (Eds.), *Textbook of child and adolescent forensic psychiatry* (pp. 221–238). Washington, DC: American Psychiatric Press.

van der Kolk, B. A., Roth, S., Pelcovitz, D., Sunday, S., & Spinazzola, J. (2005). Disorders of extreme stress: The empirical foundation of a complex adaptation to trauma. *Journal of Traumatic Stress, 18,* 389–399.

Potential Sources of Trauma and Implications for Classroom Instruction and School-Based Interventions

4

Immigrant Students

LYN MORLAND, DINA BIRMAN, BURNA L. DUNN,
MYRNA ANN ADKINS, AND LAURA GARDNER ■

INTRODUCTION

Immigrants residing in the United States are more diverse than ever before, arriving from almost every country in the world and speaking hundreds of languages. The majority of today's 40.2 million immigrants arrived legally with a number of different visas, as family members of U.S. citizens and legal permanent residents, as professionals and workers in a number of designated fields, and as refugees who were approved for immigration by the U.S. Department of Homeland Security due to a "well-founded fear of persecution."[1] The majority of immigrants in the United States without legal documentation are students and workers who overstay their visas. Other undocumented immigrants include workers and children who crossed the U.S. southern border and those who seek political asylum (refugee status) after arrival in this country.

In this chapter we offer a *social ecological* perspective on educating the most vulnerable immigrant children, emphasizing the interaction between a child and the environment, including the family, school, peer group, community, larger society, and country of origin.[2] Viewing immigrant children through this ecological prism can help educators better understand them and provide them with more tools to address issues that affect learning and behavior in the classroom. This approach is especially important for immigrants, since they and their families may have endured experiences that are different from those of most Americans and, at the same time, are adjusting to life in a new country. Following the social ecological perspective, we also focus on the strengths of the immigrant child as well as those within the child's family and community. Together, these various strengths or protective factors can help promote children's resilience, success in school, and developmental growth despite significant adversity.[3] The schools play a particularly critical role in helping promote such outcomes.

Diversity of Today's Immigrants

Numbering 40.2 million in 2010, immigrants differ according to legal status, race, ethnicity, religion, education, income, and where they settle.[4] The majority of children of immigrants (85%) today are U.S.-born citizens with immigrant parents. Ten percent of children of immigrants arrived in the United States with an immigrant visa, while only 6% entered the United States without documentation, including those crossing the southern U.S. border with family or alone, as victims of human trafficking, or as asylum seekers (see Figure 4.1). In addition to recognizing these differences among immigrants, it is important to note that these categories do not break down neatly for most families. Many children of immigrants live in mixed-status families where, for example, one parent may be undocumented, the other may be a legal permanent resident, and the children may be U.S.-born citizens.

Today's immigrants also differ by race and ethnicity. At the beginning of the 20th century the majority of immigrants came from Europe. However, the reform of U.S. immigration laws in the 1960s resulted in unanticipated changes in the backgrounds of those arriving in the United States.[5] More than half of today's immigrants are from Latin America, particularly Mexico (the source of one-third of all immigrants), and more than one-quarter are from Asia (see Figure 4.2). Refugees arrive in fewer numbers than other immigrants (75,000 in 2009, over 28,000 of which were classified as dependent children), but they are also more diverse today, coming from more than 70 different countries. The highest numbers are currently from Asia (Bhutan and Burma), the Middle East (Iraq and Iran), and Africa (Somalia and the Democratic Republic of Congo).[6]

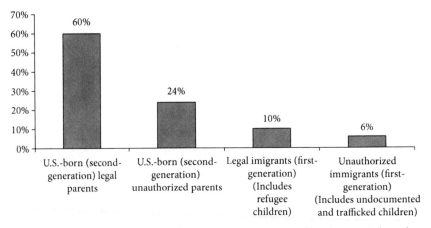

Figure 4.1 Children of immigrants by generation and parental legal status (adapted from Passel, 2011, compiled from March 2009 current population survey).

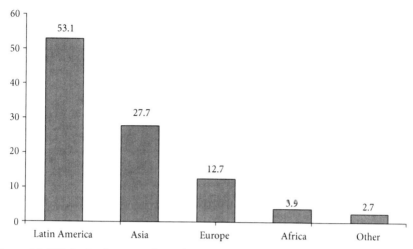

Figure 4.2 U.S. foreign-born population by region of birth 2009 (U.S. Census Bureau, 2010).

Although still relatively small in number at 2.6 million, or 0.8% of the U.S. population, a larger proportion of the population today is Muslim than at any other time in our history. In particular, the majority of refugees today from Southeast Asia, Africa, the Middle East, and Eastern Europe (Bosnians, Kosovars, etc.) are Muslim.[7]

Changes in Settlement Patterns

Although many immigrants still settle in the traditional immigration gateway states, such as California and New York, immigrants are now residing in almost every community, rural and urban, across the United States. In fact, the current "top 10" gateway states include such new destinations as Massachusetts, Georgia, and Washington (see Table 4.1), and between 2000 and 2009, the states with the fastest growing immigrant populations were South Carolina, Alabama, and Tennessee (see Table 4.2).[8] Thus, it is reasonable for educators to expect that children of immigrants are enrolled in their schools.

Serving immigrants in these newer destination states can prove particularly challenging since they tend to have fewer existing resources for immigrants. For example, areas with historically high immigration often have well-established ethnic communities that are important sources of support for newly arrived families and children. Schools in such areas may have long-standing connections with ethnic community organizations that provide interpretation and translation, assist with parental engagement, and offer an array of support services to immigrant families. Such schools also frequently have a better infrastructure for serving the foreign born, such as established English as a second language (ESL)

Table 4.1 Top 10 Destination States for U.S. Immigrants in 2009[a]

State	Estimate	Rank
California	9,946,758	1
New York	4,178,170	2
Texas	3,985,239	3
Florida	3,484,141	4
New Jersey	1,759,467	5
Illinois	1,740,763	6
Massachusetts	943,335	7
Arizona	925,376	8
Georgia	920,381	9
Washington	810,637	10

[a] Migration Policy Institute Data Hub, 2009.

programs and "newcomer" programs that can provide orientation to those with limited formal education to help ease their transition. Since it takes time to build this type of community support and infrastructure, schools in states with historically lower immigration often have fewer resources available.

In summary, this country's demographics have changed dramatically over the past 40 to 50 years. Educators in virtually every school system today are finding not only that their classrooms are more ethnically diverse but also that these

Table 4.2 States Ranked by Percent Change in the Foreign-Born Population: 1990–2000 and 2000–2009[a]

State	Change 1990 to 2000		Change 2000 to 2009	
	Percent change	Rank	Percent change	Rank
South Carolina	132.1%	11	76.9%	1
Alabama	101.6%	17	67.5%	2
Tennessee	169.0%	6	67.1%	3
Delaware	101.6%	18	64.9%	4
Arkansas	196.3%	4	63.2%	5
South Dakota	74.6%	27	61.3%	6
Nevada	202.0%	3	60.0%	7
Georgia	233.4%	2	59.4%	8
Kentucky	135.3%	10	59.4%	9
North Carolina	273.7%	1	54.7%	10

[a] Migration Policy Institute Data Hub, 2009.

children come from a broader range of backgrounds and experiences. It is therefore essential to understand the challenges that the most vulnerable immigrant children share as well as how to support the specific strengths that promote their successful adjustment.

Challenges Faced by Immigrant Children

It is important to keep in mind that there is tremendous diversity among immigrant children and their families. However, despite this diversity, most immigrant children will experience stress related to cultural adjustment in addition to the challenges of resettling in a new community, and a great number will live in poverty.[9] A number of immigrant children will have experienced physically and emotionally traumatic migration journeys, including separation from parents and other key family members. Others may be exposed to trauma indirectly due to the experiences of their parents or other family members. Many children may also have difficulty adjusting to U.S. schools, particularly those with limited formal education prior to immigration. Further, immigrant children from racial, ethnic, and minority groups often face some kind of discrimination in school, such as bullying.[10]

Traumatic stress. Perhaps the most vulnerable children are those that migrate to the United States to escape harsh conditions of poverty, violence, and political persecution in their countries. Some children take the often-harrowing journey across the southern border alone to join parents or other relatives living in the United States, either to work or as a result of fraud or coercion as victims of human trafficking. Traveling without the safety and security of their families, these undocumented and trafficked children are likely to have experienced severe forms of physical and emotional trauma during their journeys.[11]

By definition, *refugees* are immigrants who are fleeing persecution and have been granted political asylum in the United States.[12] Rather than experiencing a discrete incident of violence, refugees often endure events that occur over months or even many years. These events include being forced to leave their homes, suffering bombing raids and attacks by soldiers, surviving on limited food and water without medical attention, staying for extended periods in makeshift refugee camps, and seeing loved ones harmed. Such constellations of events can be particularly difficult for children because caretakers, who are generally a source of comfort in traumatic situations, are themselves being threatened. These immigrants are also susceptible to harm after arrival in the United States, since they often resettle in high-poverty and high-crime areas where they may experience continued victimization or exposure to crimes.[13] In these circumstances, learning and educational development are frequently pushed to the side and undermined during particularly critical periods of a child's development.

Resettlement stress. Immigrants must deal with past and ongoing challenges within the context of adjusting to their new lives. Resettlement can be particularly challenging for adults who must learn English and secure employment, creating an additionally stressful environment for children. It is not uncommon for immigrants to discount the problems of children, whom they see as capable of picking up the new language and making the cultural adjustment fairly quickly. Often parents feel that they have sacrificed a great deal to bring their children to this new country, and they may believe that in contrast to the difficulties experienced by adults, children will find their way in the new country with relative ease. For the adults the demands of resettlement are acute, and many families feel the need to attend to survival needs rather than the full span of emotional or educational needs of the children in the family. In this context, children's concerns—particularly psychological concerns—may be overlooked or marginalized.[14]

Acculturative stress. Most immigrant children acculturate more quickly than their parents, and therefore may experience conflict caused by both the intergenerational differences that virtually all children experience in the United States and an acculturation gap.[15] Since parents grew up very differently from their children, they may find it difficult to understand the pressures and demands children face at school and with their peers. At the same time, children may no longer fully share their parents' beliefs and customs and often do not understand the pressures parents are under. This gap may result in children receiving less of the support and guidance they need to negotiate the stresses of adaptation and success in their new country. Intergenerational conflict in immigrant families has been consistently associated with poor adjustment in children.[16]

Students with interrupted formal education and low literacy. A number of children arrive in this country with their education interrupted by war and migration, or who may never have had access to formal education for economic or cultural reasons.[17] For example, children may be less likely to attend school beyond primary grades in countries when families are poor, education is expensive, and children may not need a formal education for the work available to them. In some societies, girls in particular may traditionally have less access to formal education. Refugee children may have had their educations interrupted due to flight or escape, long migration journeys, and years spent in refugee camps. These children will have the additional burden of needing to make up for lost years of schooling. This can be particularly difficult for older youth who may be years behind their peers, may be under some pressure to help their families by working, and may find it particularly difficult to adjust to structured learning in a new language and culture.

Discrimination. Immigrant students often become ethnic and racial minorities when they arrive in this country and experience discrimination here that may exacerbate other traumas they have endured.[18] For example, some immigrants may have left their countries of origin to escape ethnic discrimination and violence (e.g., indigenous Guatemalans), assuming they are safe in this country, only to experience discrimination once again. Others may come from a majority Black and Muslim country (e.g., Somalia) and suddenly find themselves considered minorities and facing racial and religious discrimination for the first time in their lives. As a result, many immigrant children find themselves the victims of bullying in school.[19] Recent research has documented the impact of perceived discrimination on the mental health of immigrant children. For example, a study of Somali refugee youth found that the perception of discrimination was related to greater symptoms of posttraumatic stress disorder (PTSD) as well as depression.[20]

CULTURAL CONSIDERATIONS

Immigrant children face many of the same challenges as other children affected by trauma. However, the majority of immigrant children today come from cultures that may place less emphasis on each person as an individual and more on each person as part of an intricate web of family, community, and ancestral relationships. Moreover, they may interpret traumatic experiences more in terms of human suffering and religion, with mind and body integrated, rather than separating mind and body as Western thought does. Furthermore, immigrants may have different interpretations of the symptoms associated with psychological trauma, based on their own cultural belief systems.[21]

Complicating matters is the fact that mental health treatment is often associated with severe stigma in many cultures. This, combined with the different interpretations of mental health symptoms based on cultural frames of reference, results in immigrant families very rarely seeking mental health treatment for their children in the United States, even if it may be indicated.[22] It is also likely that available treatments and interventions supporting trauma-affected students are not as effective for immigrant families due to language and cultural differences, creating additional barriers to children's education.

In a recent edited volume, Marsella and colleagues[23] provide an overview of the central role of culture in the experience and interpretation of symptoms often associated with trauma. For example, *ataque de nervios*, an illness common in most parts of Latin America and frequently interpreted as a combination of anxiety and depression, collapses the mind–body dichotomy and provides a culturally meaningful interpretation of distress.[24] Beliefs related to health and healing differ by culture and degree of acculturation, and it is important to be aware of the larger cultural context when working with immigrant children.

VIGNETTES—MARIELENA

Following is a brief description of the experience of an immigrant child served by the first author in a school-based mental health program. The child's name and some details have been changed to protect confidentiality.

At age 15 Marielena decided to leave her rural town in El Salvador to look for her mother, who had left her in the care of her grandmother 6 years earlier to find work in the United States to support her children. She met other teens on the way, and together they made their way through Mexico to the U.S. border. There they met a coyote (term used to describe those who smuggle immigrants), who promised to help them across the border. Once there they would have to work and pay him back. In the United States the coyote attempted to force Marielena and her teenage friends into prostitution. However, she was able to escape, made her way to Georgia, and found her mother, who had remarried and started a new family there. Marielena is having difficulty getting along with her new stepfather and siblings and is worried about her friends who could not escape. Now enrolled in school, she is a quiet and well-behaved student but is having difficulty concentrating and is falling behind in her classes.

VIGNETTES—AHMED

Following is a brief description of the experience of an immigrant child served by the first author in a school-based mental health program. The child's name and some details have been changed to protect confidentiality.

Ahmed, 11, is originally from Somalia, where he saw his father and older brother murdered. He fled with his mother and two younger sisters, leaving behind his grandparents and aunts' families, to whom he was very close. After spending time in Kenya in a refugee camp, the family was admitted to the United States with refugee status. Although successfully resettled in the Midwest, his mother is having difficulty making ends meet, and they live in a low-income, high-crime, inner-city neighborhood. Kids at school sometimes call him "Osama" because he is Muslim, and they tease him for being so thin and not knowing much English. After missing critical years of formal schooling, he is excited about being able to attend school and works very hard at his studies. However, after 1 year he often seems frustrated and angry, and recently got into a fight with two other students.

Strength-Based Approach: Recognizing Student Strengths

In addition to recognizing the extreme difficulties that the children in the vignettes experienced before, during, and after migration, we must point out that they survived their journeys as a result of their strengths, their own resourcefulness, and, often, sheer luck. Typical immigrant strengths include deep and broad family ties, an abiding faith in the value of education, and "immigrant optimism"—or the confidence that life will be better in the United States.[25] In addition, many immigrants are motivated by strong religious beliefs and sociocentric values. These values prioritize family or community welfare over the individual's, keeping their lives focused on larger goals and helping them endure and adapt to ongoing and often quite dramatic changes in their lives. For example, one study[26] found that most undocumented children left their country to reunify with family members or support their families by working—decisions driven by family connections and social values—and they demonstrated remarkable resilience in doing so. Some of these strengths are reflected in the immigrant paradox, which characterizes first-generation immigrant children as healthier and performing better in school than subsequent generations. Researchers have found that immigrant children are less likely to engage in health-risk behaviors such as smoking, drinking, and drug use; tend to eat a healthier diet; and out-perform their U.S.-born peers in school.[27] However, researchers are beginning to distinguish variations among ethnicities and backgrounds. For example, immigrant children who arrive with low literacy and interrupted formal education are at a greater disadvantage in school and may be more likely to drop out than other immigrant children due to the additional challenge of making up for years of lost schooling.[28] At the same time, there is growing evidence that protective factors and processes such as supportive relationships with teachers, peers, family, and the community can help mediate these risks, resulting in improved academic performance of even the most vulnerable immigrant children over time.[29]

Other strengths of immigrant children include the cognitive benefits of bilingualism, such as increased capacity for conflict resolution.[30] Bilingual children who provide language brokering (interpretation and translation) for family members have also demonstrated improved academic performance and social self-efficacy.[31] Some researchers have documented disadvantages for children who broker for their parents, particularly when such brokering leads to role reversal with parents, missing school, or interpretation of such sensitive matters as parental medical or financial problems, child disciplinary issues at school, or possible child abuse.[32] However, recent research suggests that many of the disadvantages originally assumed to result from brokering may be associated with poverty instead, and that children and families with fewer resources may need children to broker more often.[33] This means that, despite the perception that brokering may negatively affect the mental health of immigrant children, in certain circumstances, it may actually help build their resilience by increasing self-efficacy.

The strengths outlined previously relate strongly to the current literature on protective factors and resilience in children exposed to trauma. In fact, when children have a combination of internal and external strengths or *protective factors*, such as those discussed earlier, they are most likely to be *resilient*.[34] Schools provide crucial opportunities for promoting resilience among immigrant children who have faced adversity, whether due to their traumatic journeys, resettlement stress, academic and cultural challenges, or discrimination. A focus on the potential for recovery and learning can provide a framework for helping foster resilience in these children.[35] Table 4.3 provides a summary of this framework, including approaches that educators can take to help children recognize and build on their strengths.

Table 4.3 Summary Table of Risk and Protective Factors for Immigrant Children

Risk Factors for Immigrant Children	Protective Factors	Suggestions for Promoting Resilience in School
Traumatic migration journeys	• Successfully overcoming migration stress and transition to a new country can increase sense of self-efficacy, self-confidence, autonomy	• Establish safety and predictability in the classroom • Share stories (within limits of comfort, in supportive context) • Focus on strengths, successes
Separation from immediate and extended family members; loss of friends, community support	• Supportive relationships with adults and peers • School belonging/connectedness	• Build sense of community in classroom • Use mentoring programs • Engage ethnic community leaders in school activities
Resettlement stress	• Cohesive family and co-ethnic community • Language/cultural services of local school system • Limited language brokering for family	• Know community service systems for immigrants • Work with school social workers, school psychologists, and school counselors to ensure the entire family is linked with services that will benefit the child's learning
Language and cultural differences/transition; acculturative stress	• Cognitive flexibility and problem-solving skills • Language and cultural competency skills can increase sense of self-efficacy	• Ensure accurate assessment • Support maintaining both languages, biculturalism • Engage families in school
Low literacy/interrupted formal education	• Highly value education as path to success; sacrifice by parents and students to prioritize school	Use transitional programs: • English as a second language • Newcomer centers • Family literacy
Discrimination due to race, religion, language, other differences	• Conflict resolution skills • Ethnic pride • Grounding in family, culture, religion, larger sense of purpose	• Teach and celebrate different cultures, languages, religions • Promote tolerance, social justice • Use antibullying strategies • Promote positive school climate

Promoting Resilience in Immigrant Children

Every day, educators face the challenge of distinguishing normal stress and adjustment to a new country and language from symptoms of serious mental health problems in immigrant children. So what can a teacher do? The good news is that simply trying to understand and engage a child on his or her own terms helps relieve distress. In a recent study of Somali refugee students, their sense of school belonging and connectedness was most strongly related to healthy adjustment and academic success, despite past exposure to trauma.[36] Thus, educators can have a positive effect on immigrant students' mental health simply by nurturing this sense of belonging. Related to the concept of school belonging, other studies point to discrimination and alienation as key factors in refugee youth adjustment difficulties.[37] In addition, research has shown that for many forms of posttrauma reactions, it is most effective to provide general support and opportunities for success.[38] While educators should always consult with other support personnel in the school (e.g., school psychologists, school social workers, parent liaison) when in doubt, it is clear that what happens in the classroom plays a key role in the adjustment of children. The recommendations that follow suggest ways that educators can recognize vulnerabilities, focus on strengths, and promote the resilience of immigrant children in their classrooms.

STRATEGIES TO SUPPORT STUDENTS

Learn about your immigrant students and their countries of origin and incorporate this information into classroom activities and routines. Researching students' countries, including history, culture, religion,[39] and educational systems,[40] can help educators understand the larger contexts of their behaviors and provide ideas for ways to ease immigrant children's adjustment to school. Once you have gathered this information, regularly incorporate students' histories and cultures into lesson plans, activities, and field trips. Teachers can turn to their immigrant students as resources on their own countries; students can prepare presentations for the class on history, foods, music, religion, and other interesting facts. Sharing experiences from their cultures in an atmosphere of acceptance and celebration can help immigrant students feel fully accepted at school and, at the same time, support a positive identification with their heritage. Further, the more educators know about student backgrounds, the more they can make accommodations that can increase students' sense of school connectedness.[41] For example, some schools have set aside a classroom where Muslim students can pray during the day, which has been helpful to these students' adjustment.[42]

Collaborate with local immigrant community organizations. Learning about your local immigrant communities can expand the resources and supports available to the school and to students.[43] For example, refugee resettlement agencies and ethnic community-based organizations, including religious institutions, can assist schools in a number of ways, including helping engage parents, providing information and background on newly arriving students, providing interpretation and translation services, and linking students and their families to culturally appropriate community agencies. Just one effective contact in an immigrant-serving organization can provide access to a broad array of information and services to educators. Inviting ethnic community leaders to be part of an advisory committee, to act as mentors, or to speak at special events can help bridge the school and immigrant communities. State Refugee Coordinators can be excellent sources of information and can often provide contacts at local immigrant organizations.[44]

Establish a sense of safety through routines. All children can benefit from being in a predictable environment with clear rules. For immigrant children, structure can be especially reassuring and comforting, particularly if their migration occurred as a crisis and resulted in frequently changing and unpredictable experiences for extended periods of time. On the other hand, some children may find adapting to a structured environment and rules stressful at first, such as those who have survived on the streets or lived in refugee camps for years. These children may also exhibit survival behaviors, such as hoarding food or readily defending themselves.[45] Despite the additional time and patience such students may require from teachers, helping them learn to function in a structured environment will benefit them in school as well as outside of the classroom. At the same time, it is important to keep in mind that children who have endured difficult migration experiences and loss may also seem unusually mature for their age and demonstrate positive behaviors, such as empathy and compassion for the troubles of other children.[46]

Focus on students' strengths. A premise of the strengths approach is that it tends to build and enhance strengths and resilience in children who have experienced adversity.[47] Those students who have endured tremendous loss and stressful migration experiences have survived these journeys in part due to their strengths. Think about particular positive characteristics of these children and how these may have helped them survive. Was it a strong sense of connection to a particular family member or to their religion? Do they have a strong drive to succeed in school, natural leadership skills, an ability to make friends quickly, a love of music or animals, or facility for learning new languages, math, or science? What support do their families, cultures, and communities provide?[48] Although difficulties need to be recognized and addressed, it can help students who have been through difficult experiences and who may be different in some ways from their U.S.-born peers to focus on such strengths. For example, the high value that Ahmed (see vignettes) and his family place on education can be nurtured and used to help him succeed in school.

Support maintaining the home culture and language. While it is crucial to help students learn English, it is also important to support the maintenance of students' home languages and cultures. Maintaining knowledge of their cultural roots and languages helps children remain connected with parents and other relatives, express themselves fully at home, and develop a positive bicultural identity—all important to their immediate and long-term adjustment.[49] Recommendations include placing books and posters in students' native languages around the classroom, offering language classes or bilingual education, and hiring staff that speak students' native languages and understand their cultures.[50] Engaging immigrant community organizations in the schools can also support this goal.

Engage immigrant parents and families as a part of the school community. Children need the support of their parents to succeed, and the more that families feel connected to and understand the U.S. school system, the better they can support their child and the more engaged they will become. However, immigrant parents may face daunting barriers to engaging with schools. In many cultures, parents leave the responsibility of education at the school to the teacher, and therefore may feel that they are impinging on the teacher's role by becoming too involved. In addition, parents may not be proficient in English or may have limited formal education themselves, and so may not feel comfortable interacting with school staff. Practical barriers include working long hours and not owning a car. It is important that teachers not assume that parents who do not participate in school activities are not interested. Most immigrant parents are very interested in their children's education and may well be very involved with their children's education at home.[51]

Empower and educate parents. Family literacy programs can help facilitate immigrant parents' involvement in their children's education by increasing their confidence in their own intellectual abilities and giving them the skills to read to their children or help them with their homework. Build on families' strengths and interests and help them recognize that reading or telling stories in the native language greatly benefits children, too.[52]

Recruit mentors. Mentors can provide support and serve as positive role models for immigrant children and youth as they adjust to their new home, school, and friends. For newly arrived immigrants to this culture, U.S.-born children, children of immigrants, or immigrants here for some time can be ideal mentors to assist with orientation to this new country. Bicultural mentors can also help youth as they explore how to adopt the strengths of both their native and new cultures. Some schools use group mentoring models that have proven to be both efficient for the schools and effective for immigrant students.[53]

Address discrimination, promote tolerance, and teach conflict resolution. Unfortunately, bullying is a common problem for many immigrant children and youth. Being different in some way can make a child more vulnerable to bullying, and attitudes among children often reflect current issues in the larger culture.[54] In Ahmed's case, just being Muslim and new to the United States made him a target of bullies. These experiences can be particularly frightening for children who have experienced discrimination or violence due to their ethnicity or religion in their previous countries or a refugee camp, or whose parents or other family members were targeted for political violence, as were Ahmed's. In addition, immigrant youth may need assistance in developing appropriate skills for dealing with conflicts with their peers or others. Refugee students, for example, often spend years in refugee camps where they develop strong survival skills and may need to be taught skills for responding appropriately to threats in their new school environment. It is not unusual to hear about conflicts between students from different countries, particularly if these countries have a history of conflict; between newly arrived and more acculturated students from the same country; and between U.S.-born and immigrant students.[55] Intervening and teaching such skills early on can help promote a safer and more positive school environment and build capacity for positive mental health among all students.[56]

Ensure civil rights are protected. Be aware that some children's rights may have been violated and that they may have access to legal relief and a range of services due to these experiences. From our vignettes, Marielena qualifies as a victim of human trafficking due to her treatment by the *coyote*. There are laws and services in place that protect her and can help her get the health and mental health care that she needs. For example, qualified victims of human trafficking are eligible for services through the Office of Refugee Resettlement.[57] In addition, all immigrant students have the right to attend school in the United States regardless of immigration status, and in many instances, immigrant students and their families have the right to interpretation or translation services. Ensuring basic protection and rights for vulnerable students can help support their sense of security, school belonging, and learning and can help them access additional services they may need.

Support students with interrupted formal education. Students who missed years of schooling due to war or other situations will need extra assistance to help them adjust socially and academically.[58] Consider developing a "newcomer program" for students with interrupted formal education. These transitional programs help develop immigrant students' English language skills and provide cultural orientation to the schools to help them prepare to enter ESL, bilingual, or mainstream classrooms. Newcomer programs are a relatively recent development for schools with students who need more support due to limited formal education and a larger cultural and language gap than the usual language resources can bridge. These programs generally provide transitional assistance to students for their first year in school, although some programs serve students for several years.[59] The children highlighted in both vignettes needed additional support to help them address language and cultural barriers to success in school. Ahmed, in particular, may have benefited from a newcomer program, where he could learn basic English and begin to make up for some of the years of schooling that he missed. It is particularly important to begin these services early on to prevent additional stress and loss of self-confidence for particularly vulnerable students.

CONCLUSION

This chapter discussed a broad range of circumstances that shape the experiences of immigrant children. Many of these children will have endured trauma and loss, whether a result of arduous journeys, resettlement stress, adjustment to a new culture and language, academic challenges, or discrimination. As one of the main influences in children's lives, schools can provide a safe space for healing, learning a new language and culture, and keeping a child on a positive developmental track. By learning about the cultures and backgrounds of immigrant students, engaging their families and communities, identifying and focusing on student strengths, providing transitional academic support, encouraging tolerance, and celebrating cultures, educators can help promote immigrant children's resilience. Finally, we direct readers to a growing number of resources and tools that educators can use to help the most vulnerable immigrant children succeed in today's increasingly diverse classrooms.

NOTES

1. United States Immigration and Nationality Act § 101(a)(42) (1996).
2. Bronfenbrenner, 1979.
3. Betancourt & Khan, 2008; Masten, Herbers, Cutuli, & Lafavor, 2008.
4. Passel, 2011.
5. Frum, 2000.
6. U.S. Department of Homeland Security, 2010.
7. Lugo, Cooperman, O'Connell, & Stencel, 2011.
8. U.S. Census Bureau, 2010.
9. Borjas, 2011.
10. Bridging Refugee Youth and Children's Services (BRYCS), 2010a.
11. Catholic Relief Services, 2010; Gozdziak, Bump, Duncan, MacDonnell, & Loiselle, 2006; Jaycox, 2002.
12. BRYCS, 2011a.
13. American Psychological Association, 2010; Lustig et al., 2003.
14. Birman, 2002; Birman & Chang, 2008.
15. Ho & Birman, 2010.
16. Birman, 2006.
17. Birman, n.d.
18. García Coll & Szalacha, 2004.
19. BRYCS, 2010a.
20. Ellis, MacDonald, Lincoln, & Cabral, 2008.
21. Jenkins, 1996.
22. Chow, Jaffee, & Snowden, 2003.
23. Marsella, Johnson, Watson, & Gryczynski, 2008.
24. Arredondo, Bordes, & Paniagua, 2008.
25. Portes & Rumbaut, 2001.

26. Scott, 2008.
27. Crosnoe & Lopez Turley, 2011; Perreira & Ornelas, 2011.
28. DeCapua & Marshall, 2011.
29. Suarez-Orozco, C., Rhodes, J., & Milburn, M., 2009.
30. Bialystok, 2001; Carlson & Meltzoff, 2008.
31. Buriel, Perez, DeMent, Chavez, & Moran, 1998.
32. Hall & Sham, 2007; Trickett & Jones, 2007.
33. Jones, Trickett, & Birman, 2012.
34. Betancourt & Khan, 2008; Masten, 2001; Ungar, 2008.
35. Masten et al., 2008.
36. Kia-Keating & Ellis, 2007.
37. Ellis et al., 2008.
38. Marsella et al., 2008.
39. BRYCS, 2011a.
40. Flaitz, 2006.
41. BRYCS, 2008.
42. Shepard, 2008.
43. BRYCS, 2010b.
44. U.S. Department of Health and Human Services, Administration for Children and Families, Office of Refugee Resettlement, n.d.
45. Birman, 2002.
46. Portes & Rumbaut, 2001.
47. Masten et al., 2008.
48. Morland, 2007.
49. Suarez-Orozco, Suarez-Orozco, & Todorova, 2008.
50. BRYCS, 2011b.
51. BRYCS, 2007.
52. Weinstein, 1998.
53. Birman & Morland, in press.
54. BRYCS, 2010a.
55. Washington State Office of the Education Ombudsman, 2009.
56. BRYCS, 2010a.
57. Polaris Project website, http://www.polarisproject.org/
58. Birman, n.d.
59. Robertson & Lafond, 2008; Short & Boyson, 2003.

REFERENCES

American Psychological Association. (2010). *Resilience and recovery after war: Refugee children and families in the United States*. Washington, DC: Author. Retrieved from http://www.apa.org/pubs/info/reports/refugees-full-report.pdf

Arredondo, P., Bordes, V., & Paniagua, F. A. (2008). Mexicans, Mexican Americans, Caribbean, and other Latin Americans. In A. J. Marsella, J. L. Johnson, P. Watson, & J. Gryczynski (Eds.), *Ethnocultural perspectives on disaster and trauma: Foundations, issues, and applications* (pp. 299–320). New York, NY: Springer Science + Business Media.

Betancourt, T. S., & Khan, K. T. (2008). The mental health of children affected by armed conflict: Protective processes and pathways to resilience. *International Review of Psychiatry, 20,* 317–328.

Bialystok E. (2001). *Bilingualism in development: Language, literacy, and cognition.* New York, NY: Cambridge University Press.

Birman, D. (2002). *Mental health of refugee children: A guide for the ESL teacher.* Denver, CO: Spring Institute for Intercultural Learning.

Birman, D. (2006). Measurement of the "acculturation gap" in immigrant families and implications for parent-child relationships. In M. Bornstein and L. Cotes (Eds.), *Acculturation and parent child relationships: Measurement and development* (pp. 113–134). Mahwah, NJ: Lawrence Erlbaum Associates, Publishers.

Birman, D. (n.d.). *Refugee children with low literacy skills or interrupted education: Identifying challenges and strategies.* Denver, CO: Spring Institute. Retrieved from http://www.springinstitute.org/Files/refugeechildrenbehavior3.pdf

Birman, D., & Chang, W. Y. (2008). *Screening and assessing immigrant and refugee youth in school-based mental health programs.* Washington, DC: Center for Health and Health Care in Schools. Retrieved from http://www.rwjf.org/files/research/332 0.32211.0508issuebriefno.1.pdf

Birman, D., & Morland, L. (in press). Immigrant and refugee youth. In M. Karcher and D. Dubois, Eds., *The handbook of youth mentoring,* Los Angeles, CA: Sage Publications.

Borjas, G. J. (2011). Poverty and program participation among immigrant children. *The Future of Children, 21*(1), 247–266.

Bridging Refugee Youth & Children's Services (BRYCS). (2007). *Involving refugee parents in their children's education.* Retrieved from http://www.brycs.org/documents/upload/brycs_spotspring2007-2.pdf

Bridging Refugee Youth & Children's Services (BRYCS). (2008). *Welcoming and orienting newcomer students to U.S. schools.* Retrieved from http://www.brycs.org/documents/upload/brycs_spotspring2008-2.pdf

Bridging Refugee Youth & Children's Services (BRYCS). (2010a). *Refugee and immigrant youth and bullying in school: Frequently asked questions.* Retrieved from http://www.brycs.org/documents/upload/bullying.pdf

Bridging Refugee Youth & Children's Services (BRYCS). (2010b). *Schools and refugee-serving agencies: How to start or strengthen collaboration.* Retrieved from http://www.brycs.org/publications/schools-toolkit.cfm

Bridging Refugee Youth & Children's Services (BRYCS). (2011a). *About refugees.* Retrieved from http://www.brycs.org/aboutRefugees/index.cfm

Bridging Refugee Youth & Children's Services (BRYCS). (2011b). *Resource lists for the schools.* Retrieved from http://www.brycs.org/schools.cfm

Bronfenbrenner, U. (1979). *The ecology of human development: Experiments by nature and design.* Cambridge, MA: Harvard University Press.

Buriel, R., Perez, W., DeMent, T. L., Chavez D. V., & Moran, V. R. (1998). The relationship of language brokering to academic performance, biculturalism, and self-efficacy among Latino adolescents. *Hispanic Journal of Behavioral Sciences, 20*(3), 283–296.

Carlson, S.M., & Meltzoff, A.N. (2008). Bilingual experience and executive functioning in young children. *Developmental Science, 11,* 279–295.

Catholic Relief Services. (2010). *Child migration: The detention and repatriation of unaccompanied Central American children from Mexico.* Baltimore, MD: Author.

Center for Applied Linguistics. (2009). *Newcomer database for secondary school programs*. Washington, DC: Author. Retrieved from http://www.cal.org/CALWebDB/Newcomer/

Center for Health and Healthcare in Schools. (2009). *Partnering with parents and families to support immigrant and refugee children at school*. Retrieved from http://www.rwjf.org/files/research/partneringwithparentsandfamiliesimmigrants.pdf

Chow, J. C-C., Jaffee, K., & Snowden, L. (2003). Racial/ethnic disparities in the use of mental health services in poverty areas. *American Journal of Public Health, 93*(5), 792–797.

Crosnoe, R., & Lopez Turley, R. N. (2011). K–12 educational outcomes of immigrant youth. *The Future of Children, 21*(1), 129–152.

DeCapua, A., & Marshall, H. (2011). *Breaking new ground: Teaching students with limited or interrupted formal education in U.S. secondary schools*. Ann Arbor, MI: University of Michigan Press/ELT.

Ellis, B. H., MacDonald, H. Z., Lincoln, A. K., & Cabral, H. J. (2008). Mental health of Somali adolescent refugees: The role of trauma, stress, and perceived discrimination. *Journal of Consulting and Clinical Psychology, 76*(2), 184–193.

Flaitz, J. (2006). *Understanding your refugee and immigrant students: An educational, cultural, and linguistic guide*. Ann Arbor, MI: University of Michigan Press.

Frum, D. (2000). *How we got here: The '70s*. New York, NY: Basic Books.

García Coll, C., & Szalacha, L. A. (2004). The multiple contexts of middle childhood. *The Future of Children, 14*(2), 80–97.

Gozdziak, E., Bump, M., Duncan, J., MacDonnell, M., & Loiselle, M. B. (2006). The trafficked child: Trauma and resilience. *Forced Migration Review, 25*, 14–15.

Hall, N., & Sham, S. (2007). Language brokering as young people's work: Evidence from Chinese adolescents in England. *Language and Education, 21*, 16–30.

Ho, J., & Birman, D. (2010). Acculturation gap in Vietnamese refugee families: Impact on family adjustment. *International Journal of Intercultural Relations, 34*, 22–33.

Jaycox, L. H., Stein, B. D., Kataoka, S. H., Wong, M., Fink, A., Escudero, P., et al. (2002). Violence exposure, posttraumatic stress disorder, and depressive symptoms among recent immigrant schoolchildren. *Journal of the American Academy of Adolescent Psychiatry, 41*, 1104–1110.

Jenkins, J. H. (1996). Culture, emotion, and post-traumatic stress disorder. In A. Marsella and N. Freedman (Eds.), *Ethnocultural aspects of post-traumatic stress disorder* (pp. 165–182). Washington, DC: American Psychological Association Press.

Jones, C., Trickett, E., & Birman, D. (2012). Neighborhood and familial determinants of the child culture broker role, child distress, and family disagreements in families from the former Soviet Union. *American Journal of Community Psychology*. doi:10.1007/s10464-012-9488-8

Kia-Keating, M., & Ellis, H. (2007). Belonging and connection to school in resettlement: Young refugees, school belonging, and psychosocial adjustment. *Clinical Child Psychology and Psychiatry, 12*, 29–43.

Lugo, L., Cooperman, A., O'Connell, E., & Stencel, S. (2011). *The future of the global Muslim population: Projections for 2010–2013*. Retrieved from http://pewforum.org/uploadedFiles/Topics/Religious_Affiliation/Muslim/FutureGlobalMuslimPopulation-WebPDF-Feb10.pdf

Lustig, S., Kia-Keating, M., Grant-Knight, W., Geltman, P., Ellis, H., Birman, D., et al. (2003). *Review of child and adolescent refugee mental health*. White paper from the National Child Traumatic Stress Network Refugee Trauma Task Force, Boston, MA.

Marsella, A. J., Johnson, J. L., Watson, P., & Gryczynski, J. (2008). Essential concepts and foundations. In A. J. Marsella, J. L. Johnson, P. Watson, & J. Gryczynski (Eds.), *Ethnocultural perspectives on disaster and trauma: Foundations, issues, and applications* (pp. 3–13). International and Cultural Psychology Series. New York, NY: Springer Science + Business Media.

Masten, A. S. (2001). Ordinary magic: Resilience processes in development. *American Psychologist, 56*, 227–238.

Masten, A. S., Herbers, J. E., Cutuli, J. J., & Lafavor, T. L. (2008). Promoting competence and resilience in the school context. *Professional School Counseling, 12*, 76–84,

Migration Policy Institute Data Hub, using U.S. Census Bureau (2009). *American Community Survey data*. Retrieved from http://www.migrationinformation.org/datahub/acscensus.cfm

Morland, L. (2007). Promising practices in positive youth development with immigrants and refugees. *The Prevention Researcher, 14*(4), 18–20.

National Child Traumatic Stress Network, Refugee Trauma Task Force, Children of War Production Committee. (2005). *Children of war: A video for educators*. Retrieved from http://www.nctsnet.org/nccts/asset.do?video=true&id=1054

Nazario, S. (2006). *Enrique's journey: The story of a boy's dangerous odyssey to reunite with his mother. Teacher's Guide*. New York, NY: Random House. Retrieved from http://www.randomhouse.com/catalog/teachers_guides/9780812971781.pdf

Passel, J. S. (2011). Demography of immigrant youth: Past, present, and future. *The Future of Children, 21*(1), 19–41.

Perreira, K. M., & Ornelas, I. J. (2011). The physical and psychological well-being of immigrant children. *The Future of Children, 21*(1), 195–218.

Portes, A., & Rumbaut, R. G. (Eds.). (2001). *Legacies: The story of the immigrant second generation*. Berkeley, CA: University of California Press.

Robertson, K., & Lafond, S. (2008). *How to support ELL students with interrupted formal education (SIFEs)*. Colorín Colorado, an initiative of WETA public television and radio, Washington, DC. Retrieved from http://www.colorincolorado.org/article/27483/

Scott, S. (2008). *Resilience in undocumented, unaccompanied children*. Unpublished doctoral dissertation. The Catholic University of America.

Shepard, R. M. (2008). *Cultural adaptation of Somali refugee youth*. New York, NY: LFB Scholarly Publishing.

Short, D. J., & Boyson, B. A (2003). *Establishing an effective newcomer program* (ERIC Digest). Washington, DC: Center for Applied Linguistics. Retrieved from http://www.cal.org/resources/digest/digest_pdfs/0312short.pdf

Suarez-Orozco, C., Rhodes, J., & Milburn, M. (2009). Unraveling the immigrant paradox: Academic engagement and disengagement among recently arrived immigrant youth. *Youth & Society, 41*(2), 151–185.

Suarez-Orozco, C., Suarez-Orozco, M., & Todorova, I. (2008). *Learning a new land: Immigrant students in American society*. Cambridge, MA: Harvard University Press.

Trickett, E., & Jones, C. (2007). Adolescent culture brokering and family functioning: A study of families from Vietnam. *Cultural Diversity and Ethnic Minority Psychology, 13*, 143–150.

U.S. Census Bureau. (2010). Place of birth of the foreign-born population: 2009. *American Community Survey Briefs*. Retrieved from http://www.census.gov/ prod/2010pubs/acsbr09-15.pdf

U.S. Department of Health and Human Services, Administration for Children and Families, Office of Refugee Resettlement. (n.d.). Office of Refugee Resettlement website, Partners, State Refugee Coordinators. Retrieved from http://www.acf.hhs. gov/programs/orr/partners/state_coordina.htm

U.S. Department of Homeland Security. (2010). *Yearbook of immigration statistics: 2009*. Washington, DC: U.S. Department of Homeland Security, Office of Immigration Statistics.Retrievedfromhttp://www.dhs.gov/xlibrary/assets/statistics/yearbook/2009/ ois_yb_2009.pdf

Ungar, M. (2008). Resilience across cultures. *British Journal of Social Work, 38*(2), 218–235.

Washington State Office of the Education Ombudsman. (2009). *Resolving conflict at school: A guide for families* (in English, Cambodian, Chinese, Korean, Russian, Somali, Spanish, and Vietnamese). Retrieved from http://www.governor.wa.gov/ oeo/publications/#resources

Weinstein, G. (1998). *Family and intergenerational literacy in multilingual communities*. Center for Applied Linguistics. Retrieved from http://www.cal.org/caela/esl_ resources/digests/Famlit2.html

WEB RESOURCES

- Bridging Refugee Youth and Children's Services (BRYCS) (http://www. brycs.org) has thousands of resources on refugee and immigrant children and youth in a searchable online clearinghouse. Two particularly valuable resources include:
  - *Refugee Children in U.S. Schools: A Toolkit for Teachers and School Personnel*: http://www.brycs.org/publications/schools-toolkit.cfm
  - *Resource Lists for the Schools*: http://www.brycs.org/schools.cfm, including:
    - Selected children's literature about the refugee and immigrant experience: http://www.brycs.org/clearinghouse/Highlighted-Resources-Children-Books-about-the-Refugee-Immigrant-Experience.cfm
    - Instructional materials for increasing awareness about refugees and immigrants: http://www.brycs.org/clearinghouse/Highlighted-Resources-Immigrant-Refugee-Awareness-Instructional-Materials.cfm
- The Center for Applied Linguistics (CAL) (http://www.cal.org) includes backgrounds on different refugee populations, cultural orientation materials, and a Database of Secondary Newcomer Programs in the U.S. (http://www. cal.org/CALWebDB/Newcomer/).
- The Center for Health and Healthcare in Schools (http://www. healthinschools.org/Immigrant-and-Refugee-Children.aspx), particularly:
  - *Partnering With Parents and Families to Support Immigrant and Refugee Children at School*: www.rwjf.org/files/research/ partneringwithparentsandfamiliesimmigrants.pdf

- *Screening and Assessing Immigrant and Refugee Youth in School-Based Mental Health Programs*: http://www.rwjf.org/files/research/3320.32211.0508issuebriefno.1.pdf
- The Children's Hospital Center for Refugee Trauma and Resilience: http://www.chcrtr.org
  - *Refugee Services Toolkit:* http://www.chcrtr.org/toolkit/
- Locating local resources for immigrant students
  - U.S. government's official web portal for new immigrants: http://www.welcometousa.gov/
    - Federal Office of Refugee Resettlement (ORR) website, which includes a list of state refugee coordinators that can help schools locate and connect with local immigrant resources. http://www.act.hhs.gov/programs/orr/partners/state_coordina.htm
- The National Child Traumatic Stress Network has produced a number of resources on culture and trauma (http://nctsnet.org/resources/topics/culture-and-trauma/resources), including the resource "Children of War: A Video for Educators." This instructional video is of a theater production of children telling very personal stories about their experiences of war and migration.
- Sonia Nazario's book, *Enrique's Journey: The Story of a Boy's Dangerous Odyssey to Reunite With His Mother,* has developed a *Teacher's Guide* to support classroom discussion about the experiences of immigrant children, including separation from family and adjustment to the United States (http://www.randomhouse.com/catalog/teachers_guides/9780812971781.pdf).
- The MENTOR National Mentoring Partnership created a toolkit for developing mentoring programs for immigrant children: http://www.mentoring.org/downloads/mentoring_1197.pdf.
- Spring Institute for Intercultural Learning (http://www.spring-institute.org) has produced two key resources, authored by Dina Birman, PhD:
  - *Mental Health of Refugee Children: A Guide for the ESL Teacher*[1]
  - *Refugee Children With Low Literacy Skills or Interrupted Education: Identifying Challenges and Strategies*[2]

---

[1] Birman, 2002.

[2] Birman, n.d.

5

Students Experiencing Homelessness

DIANA BOWMAN AND PATRICIA A. POPP ■

INTRODUCTION

Children and youth who experience homelessness face many challenges to educational success. They are among the most vulnerable and invisible of our at-risk students. How schools define homelessness is broad and includes children, youth, and families who live doubled up with family or friends due to the loss of their housing. Appendix A describes other types of living situations that meet the education definition of homelessness. This broad definition allows schools to be a safety net for students facing residential instability.

Approximately 1 in 50 children in the United States experiences homelessness each year.[1] Further, during the 2008–2009 academic year, schools across the United States identified 956,914 students who were homeless, a 41% increase over 2 years.[2] Despite these numbers, many communities and school districts are unaware that homelessness exists in their localities and that these children and their families struggle daily to meet basic needs for food, shelter, and clothing. Moreover, this lack of awareness may lead to misattributions for the various academic challenges faced by children of poverty and homeless families, such as thinking the student is lazy, unmotivated, oppositional, or has a disability. The following two vignettes offer a peek into the ways unstable housing affects a student's education.

VIGNETTE—MARLENA

Marlena is 9 years old. Her brother, Todd, is 2, and her sister, Dana, is 6. Last year, their father lost his job and fell behind on the mortgage, leading to a foreclosure in January. The family moved in with Marlena's uncle and his family, 10 miles from Marlena's and Dana's school. The parents were driving them to this school instead of enrolling them near the uncle's home. However, their car broke down and they could not afford to get it fixed. The girls were out of school for 1 week. The parents thought they would be able to get a friend to fix the car or arrange a ride with someone else, but that did not happen.

As a result, the parents enrolled Marlena and Dana in the school closest to where they were staying. The girls were sad to leave their friends and teachers in their former school. Getting used to the new school was hard. Marlena, who struggled with reading, was having a particularly difficult time catching up with her class academically and adjusting to a different routine. Her teachers believed that her difficulties were the result of an adjustment to the new setting.

Marlena and her family stayed with her uncle for 4 weeks, and then one day the uncle told them they would have to leave. He said his house just wasn't big enough for all of them to live comfortably, and this arrangement was putting a strain on his own family. He said they would have to be out of his house by the end of the week.

Marlena's family moved into an emergency homeless shelter in the town where they had lived before losing their house, which consisted of a single room for the entire family with a communal dining room, kitchen, and bathroom. Moreover, since space was limited, they could not bring many of their belongings. Marlena's parents had no way to get the girls to the school near their uncle's house, so the girls transferred to the school closest to the shelter.

A school bus took Marlena and Dana, along with several other children at the shelter, to school and back. Since the bus arrived at the school at the same time every day, the other children at the school knew that these were the "shelter kids" and sometimes teased them. Marlena was falling further behind in math and reading and needed some extra help. However, the school district did not provide transportation home from the after-school tutoring program, so Marlena was not able to participate.

The shelter had a 30-day limit; at the end of the month, Marlena's family had to move again. Her father had not been able to find a job, so renting an apartment or house was not feasible. A friend with a one-room apartment over his garage with a kitchenette and bathroom allowed them to stay there until they found something permanent, provided they could help with utilities. Marlena's mother had a part-time job at the local grocery store and could pay a little toward utilities, but the parents worried how long their friend's offer would stand since they could not help very much. Once again, the family was living in one room, but at least they had some privacy.

This new arrangement was across the school district line from the school near the shelter where Marlena and Dana were last enrolled, so they transferred schools once again, now the fourth school they attended this school year.

The experience of homelessness and frustration with not being able to provide for the family took a toll on the parents. They argued frequently and seemed too consumed by their own problems to notice those of their children.

Marlena was spending a lot of time taking care of Dana and Todd. She rarely completed her homework.

Marlena's teacher noticed Marlena came to school stressed and tired and occasionally acted aggressively toward the other children. She was failing most subjects, and her attendance was poor. She complained of stomachaches a lot, so her mother would let her stay home from school. It was almost the end of the school year, and the likelihood of Marlena passing the end-of-grade tests was very slim.[a]

---

[a] Marlena's scenario is a composite based on several students assisted by the National Center for Homeless Education Helpline.

Vignette—Jerome

Jerome is a 17-year-old junior in high school. Jerome's father died after a long illness when Jerome was 13. The stack of medical bills left him and his mother with no choice but to move in with his grandmother in a neighboring state. Jerome was a track star at his middle school but was unable to participate in sports when he changed schools so late in eighth grade.

Jerome's mother suffered with depression since his father's death, and her conflicts resulted in multiple moves with aunts and uncles and even family friends. Jerome lived at six addresses and attended three different schools between his freshman and sophomore years of high school. He was able to join the track team in his sophomore year and made it to the state championship.

When Jerome was 16, his mother remarried. Jerome and his stepfather did not get along and Jerome was sent to live with his 80-year-old grandfather in the town where he grew up prior to his father's death. The change in high school curriculum affected Jerome's credit accrual and he lost a half year of credits. Seeing graduation delayed and feeling abandoned by family, Jerome was often truant and became a discipline problem at school and with his grandfather. Jerome was sent back to his mother but was unable to get along with his stepfather, leading to a physical altercation.

For the past 6 months, Jerome has stayed with various friends, sleeping on couches, on porches, and in garages. Most recently, he stayed on a friend's porch. The temperature fell below freezing and the only warmth besides an old comforter was his friend's Labrador that would curl up with him as he tried to sleep. Jerome has lost weight and his coach asked him about his diet. Jerome explained that he had eaten only rice for the past week. When asked why, Jerome explained that he figured the family he was staying with would let him stay longer if he didn't eat too much.

Jerome will be 18 in July. He is working with his school counselor on a schedule for his senior year. His coach believes he has the potential of getting

a track scholarship, but his multiple moves and schools and erratic atten-
dance have affected his grade point average. Just getting to school has been
a hassle since he is not always living near a bus stop that goes to his school and
he has no car; Jerome has been tardy frequently and is at risk of failing his
first-period class, English III. If he fails, he may not have senior status in the
fall. Jerome dreams of a career in sports medicine but is starting to consider
dropping out and getting a full-time job in town.[b]

---

[b] Jerome's scenario is based on a number of actual essays written by LeTendre
Scholars recognized by the National Association for the Education of Homeless
Children and Youth.

Educational Challenges Faced by Children and Youth Experiencing Homelessness

As the vignettes illustrate, the complicated lives of children and youth experiencing homelessness impact their ability to attend and succeed in school. Maslow's Hierarchy of Need[3] offers insight into how school success may become secondary, and perhaps irrelevant, for many students with unstable housing. Maslow theorized that physiological needs (e.g., food, shelter, clothing, and medical attention) and social-emotional needs (e.g., safety, security, belonging) must be met before the potential exists for fulfilling needs at higher levels (e.g., academic success, learning). Children experiencing homelessness face barriers in having all these needs met; and without these needs met, success in school can be undermined.

Lack of basic needs. Many homeless children and youth are living in temporary situations in which they are unable to bathe and change clothes. Frequently, the only clothes they have are the ones they are wearing. In addition, many homeless children are unable to eat regularly or nutritiously and only have balanced meals when they come to school. Having a safe place to rest and get enough sleep may not exist. Imagine a child falling asleep in your classroom because it is the only place the child feels safe enough or warm enough. Finally, school supplies and a quiet space to do homework or school projects may not be available outside of school, making it extremely difficult to come to school well prepared.[4]

High mobility. Many families lose their housing due to economic or health crises and discover that their communities lack affordable housing or shelters, resulting in temporary stays with friends or relatives, in hotels or motels, or in cars, parks, or abandoned buildings. If a homeless shelter exists, most limit the time in which a family may stay. Changing environments often mean new schedules and patterns of behavior, making it difficult for infants, toddlers, and preschoolers to develop routines and self-regulate. Maternal depression is observed more frequently among homeless women, lessening the likelihood that they will be able to provide the rich language and social interaction needed for cognitive and affective growth. Transience further affects emotional development as the child may learn to build walls that cut off relationships to prevent feelings of loss when another move occurs. Without these relationships, students face greater risk of dropping out of school, particularly given the social nature of learning in a school environment.

As families are forced to move frequently, children's attendance in school and learning continuity are disrupted. It is not uncommon to see children in families experiencing homelessness attending three to five schools during one academic year,[5] leading to missed academic content or repeated content covered in a previous class. One might compare the learning experience of a homeless student who changes schools several times to reading a book with several pages missing out of each chapter. In fact, changing schools more than three times within a 6-year period can lead to a 1-year lag in academic performance when compared to stable students.[6]

High mobility creates even greater educational challenges for homeless students in need of special education evaluations or services. Students' teachers may begin to suspect a disability is affecting performance, but the children are gone before eligibility processes are completed. New classrooms may not receive timely records and new teachers may assume students need time to acclimate to new environments, not realizing the difficulty is more serious until another move is imminent. While special education records should follow students quickly, delays happen, individualized education plans (IEPs) expire, and appropriate placements and services may not be implemented in timely ways. For older youth, mobility can impede credit accrual for graduation when school transfers lead to shifts between traditional and block scheduling or courses are not analogous from one school to another.

Poor health. Children and youth who are homeless frequently lack sufficient nutrition and rest, and they experience a much higher incidence and prevalence of illness than housed children.[7] As with other children experiencing poverty, their families often lack adequate insurance and resources to obtain medical attention and needed medicines. Stomach disorders, ear infections, and asthma occur at least twice as frequently among children who lack a stable home. It should not be surprising to find that these children experience higher absenteeism. Homeless students are frequently unprepared to learn when they come to school due to health problems that may be undiagnosed or untreated.[8]

Lack of transportation. School attendance is impacted when families do not have a way to transport their children to a new school in areas where there is no pupil or public transportation, or when parents are unable to transport their children to the school they were attending before they became homeless. Removing barriers to transportation for homeless students is consistently reported as the most frequently identified need among school districts.[9]

Academic barriers. Homeless children and youth often enroll in new schools without records. As schools seek to obtain records and enroll children, valuable time may be lost trying to identify academic needs and maintain educational continuity. As a result, students who are highly mobile can take up to half a year to adjust academically to moving to a new school, with a larger cumulative effect on achievement accruing with each additional move.[10] Older youth frequently lose credits as they enroll in new schools where policies require minimum days of attendance before awarding credit or when credit accrual systems differ greatly from formerly attended schools. Consequently, homeless children and youth are twice as likely as housed students to repeat a grade,[11] and their high mobility is related to lower achievement and increased dropout rates.[12] In 2008–2009, school districts across the nation that receive subgrants to serve students experiencing homelessness reported that the proficiency rate for homeless children and youth taking state assessments in grades 3 through 12 was 48% in math and 49% in reading, well below state targets for adequate yearly progress.[13]

Mental health and exposure to violence and trauma. Children and youth experiencing homelessness exhibit a high level of stress due to living in crisis. Children often take on caretaker roles in the family and bear the stress of worrying about finances, where they will live, and how they will eat. Moreover, they experience the loss of their home, belongings, and friends—all that they consider familiar and comfortable. These young people are at greater risk for behavioral problems[14] and mental disorders (e.g., disruptive behavioral disorders, social phobias, and major depression)[15] than housed peers, even when compared to low-income peers living in stable homes.

Living in vulnerable situations, such as overcrowded or unsafe buildings or on the street, may lead to increased exposure to violence (see chapter 6).[16] Given that homelessness includes runaways and youth abandoned by their parents, older youth on their own are also at increased risk for physical and sexual victimization. One study found that more than one-third of its sample of runaway and homeless youth on the streets or in shelters was diagnosed as suffering from posttraumatic stress disorder (PTSD).[17] Furthermore, substance abuse and suicide attempts are significantly higher for youth on their own.[18]

Invisibility and stigma. For many, the word *homeless* conjures images of individuals living on the streets and under bridges, begging for money or food. While some children experience homelessness in such settings, the majority identified by schools live temporarily with family or friends due to loss of housing.[19] Because they do not live in places typically considered temporary dwellings for homeless people, children and families living "doubled up" are difficult to identify. Given that signs of homelessness are not always obvious, teachers and other school staff must be aware of potential clues, including lack of preparation for class, falling asleep in class, becoming withdrawn or acting out, hoarding food, and reluctance to separate from belongings. Patterns of mobility with multiple schools and frequent absences can also suggest homelessness (see appendix B for a more comprehensive list of possible warning signs). To confound the identification process further, there is still significant stigma associated with the word *homeless*, leading many families and youth to work diligently to hide their lack of a stable home.

STRATEGIES TO SUPPORT STUDENTS

Children experiencing homelessness and other forms of high mobility enter and leave teachers' classrooms repeatedly throughout the school year. For some class-rooms with high student turnover, it is like teaching with a revolving door in your room. Such teachers are continually greeting and acclimating new students into the classroom, bidding farewell to others, and always preparing for the next new arrival and next departure. Therefore, supporting homeless students pres-ents an added challenge to educators; however, the following recommendations may help.[20]

Make every day count. Despite the many challenges and stark statistics, there are many children and youth in homeless situations who recognize the impor-tance of education and meet academic demands with success. Resilience is asso-ciated with more positive outcomes for homeless students, and teachers play critical roles in nurturing resilience.[21] It is helpful for educators to ask them-selves, "If I only had a child for [a month, a week, a day], what would I want that student to take away from my class?" It is easy for many educators to dismiss homeless/temporary students, thinking that efforts will go unnoticed or unre-warded due to another ensuing move; however, making each day as meaningful as possible is critical—there is no time to waste.

Be discreet and compassionate. As mentioned earlier, the stigma associated with the word *homeless* can make conversations with students and families uncom-fortable. Focusing on the temporary nature of the current housing arrangement and avoiding the "homeless" label or stigma is recommended when starting a conversation. Teachers should remember to ask open-ended questions and avoid loaded questions that imply a value judgment about the family's situa-tion. For example, one could ask, "I've noticed James has been having difficulty completing his homework. Would you help me figure out what we can do to help him?" rather than, "James hasn't completed his homework lately and says you are not helping him," or "It sounds like you don't make any time to work with James." Especially in national economic crises and natural disasters, home-lessness is experienced by middle-class and well-educated families who never anticipated losing their housing. Thinking, "That could just as easily be me!" rather than, "If they just made different choices…" changes your relationship with families and provides an important bridge to build trust needed for families to share their housing crises.

Become familiar with the McKinney-Vento Act. Becoming familiar with the legal requirements schools must fulfill to serve homeless students is as impor-tant for classroom teachers as educational administrators. Originally passed in 1987, and most recently reauthorized as Title X, Part C, of the Elementary and Secondary Education Act of 2001, the McKinney-Vento Act provides for rights and services that ensure homeless children and youth have access to a free, appropriate public education.[22] The act addresses access to school and educational opportunities for children and youth experiencing homelessness. The mandates for schools apply to compulsory school ages; however, the legislation also addresses younger and older children. Table 5.1 summarizes the main themes of the McKinney-Vento Act.[23] Successful implementation of the McKinney-Vento Act requires that all educators have familiarity with the law and know where to go for assistance.

Though not a silver bullet in ameliorating the severe impacts of homelessness on students, the McKinney-Vento Act addresses some of the biggest educational barriers these children and youth face. Effective implementation depends on the awareness level of a school district's educators, administrators, parents, and community service providers of both the plight of homeless families and the responsibilities of the school district outlined in the law.

Know your contacts and resources in the McKinney-Vento program. Teachers should know who to consult when the question of homelessness arises. At the federal level, the U.S. Department of Education's (ED) Education for Homeless Children and Youth Program provides guidance and oversight to states and school districts for the implementation of the McKinney-Vento Act. The ED allocates McKinney-Vento funds to states, collects state data on homelessness, and monitors states to ensure the law is implemented. The National Center for Homeless Education (NCHE)[24] is the federal technical assistance center that provides additional information and support to states and school districts.

Every state has a state coordinator[25] for the education of homeless children and youth who provides technical assistance and support for school districts, assists with dispute resolution, coordinates and collaborates with state agencies, collects data, and carries out the state's McKinney-Vento plan.

At the local level, every school district must have a local liaison responsible for ensuring that homeless children and youth are identified and linked to services, school personnel are aware of the McKinney-Vento Act, homeless parents and youth are informed of their rights, school transportation is arranged, and enrollment disputes are mediated and resolved. The local homeless liaison may be contacted through a school district's directory of staff or by contacting the state coordinator for homeless education.

Become familiar with ways other school districts and educational programs serve homeless children and youth. Other programs have responsibilities for serving homeless students. Teachers should know who oversees these initiatives in their school district so contact can be made as needed to assist students:

- Title I, Part A of the Elementary and Secondary Education Act—states homeless children and youth are automatically eligible for services. Every school district receiving Title I funds must reserve funds to serve the needs of homeless children and youth.

Table 5.1 Main Themes of the McKinney-Vento Act

Theme	Description
School stability	If at all possible and if it is in the student's best interest, a homeless student must be allowed to stay in his or her "school of origin," that is, the school of last enrollment or last attended before becoming homeless, even if the family moves out of the local school zone. School districts must ensure that homeless families and homeless unaccompanied youth know that they have this option and provide transportation when requested to keep the child in his or her school of origin.
School access	A child or youth experiencing homelessness has the right to enroll in school immediately, even if records or documents typically required for enrollment are missing. Upon identifying them as homeless, the local school in the area where children are temporarily staying must enroll immediately and contact the prior school or other sources to obtain records. During the interim, students must be enrolled and allowed to fully participate in school activities.
Support for academic success	Children and youth experiencing homelessness must be linked with programs and resources to help them succeed academically. Many homeless children and youth fall behind in school due to mobility, having undiagnosed learning problems, or suffering from stress and deprivation. Schools must identify the needs of homeless children upon enrollment and link students with programs and resources in school and in the community to ensure barriers to learning are eliminated.
Child-centered decision making	Because homeless circumstances vary widely, McKinney-Vento encourages case-by-case approaches to meet the needs of children.
Proactive identification of homeless families	School staff must be trained to identify children who may be experiencing homelessness and ensure McKinney-Vento rights and services are in place quickly.
Coordination and collaboration	School districts must identify community resources and enlist their support to provide services for families and youth that go beyond the scope of educational needs.

For more information on the McKinney-Vento Act, visit the NCHE website at http://center.serve.org/nche/briefs.php for its Law into Practice series of briefs.

- U.S. Department of Agriculture Child Nutrition Act—enables a homeless child to receive free meals immediately without documentation of family income or other paperwork.
- Individuals With Disabilities Education Act (IDEA)—includes the McKinney-Vento definition of homelessness and ensures that evaluations and services for homeless students are not disrupted during moves to new schools or districts.
- Head Start—the 2007 reauthorization of Head Start requires Head Start programs to identify homeless preschool-aged children and prioritize them for enrollment.
- The College Cost Reduction and Access Act—allows youth who have experienced homelessness or are at risk of homelessness to be declared "independent students" by local homeless liaisons, youth shelter workers, or school counselors to fill out the federal financial aid form without the parents' information.

Pay attention to signs of need or difficulty. Many homeless students are reluctant to ask for help or disclose their problems. Pay attention to changes in appearance, health, or behavior that might indicate a need for help. School social workers, school counselors, school psychologists, and local homeless liaisons are experienced in assisting students in dealing with crises and can refer students to community resources when needs are greater than what the school can provide.

Prepare with movement in mind. While the purpose of the McKinney-Vento Act includes lessening the impact of high mobility on a student's education, there will be situations in which school moves continue. Teachers can lessen the impact of these moves within their classrooms through deliberate planning. Consider maintaining a set of records or assignments to give to the parents when the student leaves the school so they can take that immediately to the next teacher should the official record transfer be delayed. Think about children entering and leaving your classroom and the effect at each stage of movement. Consider the academic, affective, and technical (i.e., correct grade placement, seeking support services, becoming familiar with relevant laws and policies) needs that can be supported by structuring activities and resources:

- before students arrive,
- when students first enter class,
- during enrollment, and
- after departure.

Table 5.2 offers teacher tips excerpted from *Classrooms With Revolving Doors*, information briefs developed for NCHE. Elementary and secondary versions are available at http://center.serve.org/nche/ibt/research.php.

Table 5.2 TEACHING TIPS FOR SERVING CHILDREN AND YOUTH EXPERIENCING HOMELESSNESS

Affective	Academic	Technical
In Advance		
• Be caring, dedicated, motivating, nurturing, supportive, and respectful.	• Have extra copies of materials for current units.	• Have extra school supplies on hand.
• Believe you can make a difference.	• Plan mini-units to be completed within limited time frames.	• Have wholesome snacks for hungry students.
• If you use community-building activities (e.g., puzzle pieces, classroom quilt), have extras ready for new students.	• Have resources on varying reading levels that address the same content.	• Identify additional supports: school counselors, school psychologists, social workers, nurses, etc.
• Consider mini-units or book studies with mobility as the theme.[a]	• Print rules and procedures for students who missed the beginning of the year.	• Familiarize yourself with local outside agencies: community/school liaisons, Boys and Girls Clubs, youth centers, afterschool programs, local shelters.
• Establish and maintain consistent routines so students know what to expect.		• Consider starting an annual clothing drive or requesting extra uniforms if your school requires them.
Upon Arrival		
• Assign classroom ambassadors (class buddies) to provide school tours, explain rules and procedures, and begin developing friendships.	• Review student records about previous learning.	• Review student records to determine school and community services to be contacted.
	• Use curriculum-based measures (CBMs)[b] to determine current skill levels.	

(continued)

Table 5.2 (Continued)

Affective	Academic	Technical
Upon Arrival • Welcome new students officially. (Department of Defense schools working with military families who move frequently conduct "Hale and Farewell" celebrations.) • Create "New Kids on the Block" clubs. The school principal, counselor, or another person who works across grades can hold meetings with newcomers to encourage a smooth transition and identify challenges early. This could be a special lunch meeting or a pullout session. • If known in advance, add student names to classroom charts and desks/cubbies. • Model respect. Call students by name. • Handle disruptive situations in a private and respectful manner. Be a "warm demander" by maintaining a calm, quiet management style coupled with high expectations for behavior and academics. **While Enrolled** • Notice when students are absent and convey they were missed. • Arrive early and/or stay late with students who need additional time.	• Assess student interests to hook them into learning. Use K-W-L (know–want to learn–learned) charts to identify student questions. • Set up class areas to accommodate different learning styles. • Use entry of new students to review rules and procedures with the whole class. • Ask the student about previous schools and classes. Questions can help you determine whether the student received special services that might require expedited records. For example: "How many students were in your class?" "How many teachers were in your class?" "Did you go to any other teachers for reading or math?" • Provide opportunities for one-on-one or small group tutoring whenever possible, which has been shown to increase student achievement. • Use varying teaching strategies.	• Make sure meals are provided—students who are homeless are automatically eligible for free meals at school. • Know the extracurricular activities at school; connect students with interests (homelessness cannot be a barrier to participating). • Watch/listen for living situations that expose students to safety concerns; know who to contact (the local liaison or school social worker).

- Be mindful that a homeless student may not have a place to store belongings. If all special belongings are in a backpack, offer a secure storage location in the classroom.
- Take time to talk with students and build relationships. If you suspect that a student might be experiencing homelessness, you might want to ask "nonthreatening" questions to find out some information about the student's circumstances. For example, "Tell me about your family," or "What do you do after school?" or "Where do you like to do your homework?"
- Incorporate community-building techniques. Classroom meetings and group problem solving give students opportunities to learn important teamwork skills. Use cooperative learning to ensure students are included; encourage appropriate social skills.
- Use quiet reminders to shape appropriate behavior—for example, proximity, hand on shoulder, eye contact.
- Reframe the situation. Students who have limited resources can be creative problem solvers. For example, one youth who slept in a park explained that every night he folded his clothes neatly and placed them under his sleeping bag so that they would look pressed in the morning.

- Include teacher–student talk and student–student talk.
- Model what students should know and be able to do.
- Be flexible with lesson plans.
- Be engaged—make frequent eye contact with students, use students' names, and encourage discussion.
- Allow students to complete homework at school, focusing on critical assignments, to foster feelings of success.
- Assign homework that is practice, not new concepts.
- Assess in small increments, providing feedback for improvement.
- Become familiar with your school's approach to response to intervention (RTI) since this may be a vehicle to provide additional support prior to/during a special education referral.

- Allow students to use school facilities for bathing and laundry if living situations affect hygiene.

(continued)

Table 5.2 (CONTINUED)

Affective	Academic	Technical
• Be sensitive to student responses. When asked where people lived, one student responded, "In a motel". Rather than saying that wasn't a home, the teacher understood the child's living arrangement and affirmed the response. • Have options for "about me" activities. Students may not have family photos or pictures of themselves as babies.		• Notify school officials and/or community agencies if highly mobile students are absent several days.

At Departure

Affective	Academic	Technical
• Create farewell "memory" books with photos, student writing, and illustrations. • Provide departing students with self-addressed, stamped stationery to write back to the class. • Send teacher letters introducing students to their new teachers. • If students know what schools they will attend next, explore school websites with the student to ease anxiety.	• Assume a move will occur. Start work portfolios when students enter your class. • Send portfolios with exiting students. Maintain duplicates to send if lost. • If students move without notice, send portfolios (and farewell packets) to the next school when records are requested.	

[a] See Appendix C of Popp et al., 2003; Project HOPE-Virginia website has a *Bibliography of Homeless Education Resources* with pages of children's literature related to homelessness and poverty at http://education.wm.edu/centers/hope/publications/documents/bibliography.pdf and young adult literature resources at http://education.wm.edu/centers/hope/resources/index.php

[b] Popp, 2007; University of Minnesota, n.d.

APPLYING WHAT YOU HAVE LEARNED

Review the vignettes for Marlena and Jerome and think about these students' academic, affective, and technical needs. Identify tips in Table 5.2 that could support Marlena or Jerome. Do these suggestions make you think of additional actions you could take?

CONCLUSION

Homelessness is not hopelessness. While the lives of homeless children and youth are fraught with poverty, crisis, and uncertainty that impact their readiness to learn, these children and youth have the same dreams for success and prosperity as their housed peers and demonstrate great resilience when provided supports to help them overcome their challenges. Educators play instrumental roles in identifying children and youth experiencing homelessness, making them feel valued, and connecting them to programs and resources. Moreover, educators can expand their capacity to meet the needs of homeless children and youth by familiarizing themselves with laws, policies, and resources available in their school district and beyond. School for children and youth experiencing homelessness can be a haven for hope. Educators are the ones who open the doors.

APPENDIX A

WHO IS CONSIDERED HOMELESS?

The McKinney-Vento Act (Section 725) contains an overall definition of homeless children that includes any child or youth who lacks a fixed, regular, and adequate nighttime residence. Several specific examples follow the overall definition:

- Children and youth who are sharing the housing of other persons due to loss of housing, economic hardship, or a similar reason (sometimes referred to as doubled up); living in motels, hotels, trailer parks, or camping grounds due to lack of alternative adequate accommodations; living in emergency or transitional shelters; abandoned in hospitals; or awaiting foster care placement
- Children and youth who have a primary nighttime residence that is a public or private place not designed for, or ordinarily used as, a regular sleeping accommodation for human beings
- Children and youth who are living in cars, parks, public spaces, abandoned buildings, substandard housing, bus or train stations, or similar settings
- Migratory children who qualify as homeless because they are living in circumstances described in previous bullets

The act also includes unaccompanied youth who live in the circumstances mentioned here and are not in the physical custody of a parent or guardian, including youth who have run away or been thrown out of their homes.

APPENDIX B

COMMON SIGNS OF HOMELESSNESS[1]

Lack of Continuity in Education

- Attendance at many different schools
- Lack of records needed to enroll
- Inability to pay fees
- Gaps in skill development
- Poor organizational skills
- Poor ability to conceptualize

Poor Health/Nutrition

- Lack of immunizations and/or immunization records
- Unmet medical and dental needs
- Respiratory problems
- Skin rashes
- Chronic hunger (may hoard food)
- Fatigue (may fall asleep in class)

Transportation and Attendance Problems

- Erratic attendance and tardiness
- Lack of participation in after-school activities
- Lack of participation in field trips
- Inability to contact parents

Poor Hygiene

- Lack of shower facilities/washers, etc.
- Wearing same clothes for several days
- Inconsistent grooming

---

[1] NCHE, 2007.

Lack of Personal Space After School

- Consistent lack of preparation for school
- Incomplete or missing homework
- Unable to complete special projects (no access to supplies)
- Lack of basic school supplies
- Loss of books and other supplies on a regular basis
- Concern for safety of belongings

Social and Behavioral Concerns

- Poor/short attention span
- Poor self-esteem
- Extreme shyness
- Unwillingness to risk forming relationships with peers and teachers
- Difficulty socializing at recess
- Difficulty trusting people
- Aggression
- "Old" beyond years
- Protective of parents
- Clinging behavior
- Developmental delays
- Fear of abandonment
- School phobia (student wants to be with parent)
- Anxiety late in the school day

Reaction/Statements by Parent, Guardian, or Child

- Exhibiting anger or embarrassment when asked about current address
- Mention of staying with grandparents, other relatives, friends, or in a motel, or comments such as:
  - "I don't remember the name of the last school."
  - "We've been moving around a lot."
  - "Our address is new; I can't remember it."
  - "We're staying with relatives until we get settled."
  - "We're going through a bad time."

NOTES

1. National Center on Family Homelessness, 2009.
2. National Center for Homeless Education (NCHE), 2010.
3. Maslow, 1968.

4. See Van Doren, 1998, for a children's story that describes the challenges of completing homework while experiencing homelessness.
5. Popp, Stronge, & Hindman, 2003; U.S. General Accounting Office, 1994.
6. Kerbow, 1996.
7. Better Homes Fund, 1999; Homes for the Homeless, 1999.
8. Bauer, Lurie, Yeh, & Grant, 1999; Huang & Menke, 2001; Kelly, 2001; Rew, 2002.
9. NCHE, 2010.
10. Kerbow, 1996.
11. Better Homes Fund, 1999.
12. Reynolds, Chen, & Herbers, 2009.
13. NCHE, 2010.
14. Buckner, Bassuk, Weinreb, & Brooks, 1999; Masten, Miliotis, Graham-Bermann, Ramirez, & Neemann, 1993; Shinn et al., 2008.
15. Anooshian, 2005; Buckner et al., 1999.
16. Anooshian, 2005; Bassuk & Friedman, 2005.
17. Whitbeck, Hoyt, Johnson, & Chen, 2007.
18. Yoder, Whitbeck, & Hoyt, 2008.
19. NCHE, 2010.
20. Grant, Stronge, and Popp (2008).
21. For more information on resilience and homeless education, visit http://center. serve.org/nche/ibt/sps_resilience.php
22. Proposed language for reauthorization is being considered by Congress at the time of this writing. Updates on legislative considerations (including the proposed changes) can be found at http://naehcy.org
23. The full text of the EHCY program in McKinney-Vento can be found at http://www2.ed.gov/programs/homeless/legislation.html
24. The website for the National Center for Homeless Education (NCHE) can be found at www.serve.org/nche
25. The list of state coordinators can be found at http://center.serve.org/nche/downloads/sccontact.pdf

REFERENCES

Anooshian, L. J. (2005). Violence and aggression in the lives of homeless children: A review. *Aggression and Violent Behavior, 10*(2), 129–152.

Bassuk, E. L., & Friedman, S. M. (2005). *Facts on trauma and homeless children.* The National Traumatic Stress Network. Retrieved from http://www.nctsnet.org/nctsn_assets/pdfs/promising_practices/Facts_on_Trauma_and_Homeless_Children.pdf

Bauer, E. J., Lurie, N., Yeh, C., & Grant, E. N. (1999). Screening for asthma in an inner city elementary school [Abstract]. *Journal of Child and Family Nursing, 2*(5), 340–341.

Better Homes Fund. (1999). *America's homeless children: New outcasts.* Newton, MA: Author.

Buckner, J. C., Bassuk, E. L., Weinreb, I. F., & Brooks, M. G. (1999). Homelessness and its relation to the mental health and behavior of low-income school-age children. *Developmental Psychology, 35*(1), 246–257.

Grant, L., Stronge, J. H., & Popp, P. A. (2008). *Effective teaching and at-risk/highly mobile students: What do award-winning teachers do? Case studies of award-winning teachers of at-risk/highly mobile students.* Retrieved from http://www.serve.org/nche/downloads/eff_teach.pdf

Homes for the Homeless. (1999). *Homeless in America: A children's story, Part 1.* New York, NY: Institute for Children and Poverty.Huang, C., & Menke, E. M. (2001). School-aged homeless sheltered children's stressors and coping behaviors. *Journal of Pediatric Nursing, 16*(2), 102–109.

Kelly, E. (2001). Assessment of dietary intake of preschool children living in a homeless shelter. *Applied Nursing Research, 14*(3), 146–154.

Kerbow, D. (1996). Patterns of urban student mobility and local school reform. *Journal of Education for Students Placed at Risk, 1*(2), 147–169.

Maslow, A. (1968). *Toward a psychology of being.* New York, NY: Van Nostrand.

Masten, A. S., Miliotis, D., Graham-Bermann, S. A., Ramirez, M., & Neemann, J. (1993). Children in homeless families: Risks to mental health and development. *Journal of Consulting and Clinical Psychology, 61*(2), 335–343.

National Center for Homeless Education (NCHE). (2007). *Local homeless education liaison toolkit (Appendix C).* Retrieved from http://center.serve.org/nche/pr/liaison_toolkit.php

National Center for Homeless Education (NCHE). (2010). *Education for homeless children and youth program SY 2008–09 CSPR data collection summary.* Retrieved from http://center.serve.org/nche/downloads/data_comp_06-08.doc

National Center on Family Homelessness.(2009).*America's youngest outcasts: State report card on child homelessness.* Retrieved from http://www.homelesschildrenamerica.org/findings.php

Popp, P. A. (2007). *Reading on the go! Volume 2: A handbook of resources.* Greensboro, NC: NCHE. Retrieved from http://www.serve.org/nche/downloads/reading_on_the_go2.pdf

Popp, P. A., Stronge, J. H., & Hindman, J. L. (2003). *Students on the move: Reaching and teaching highly mobile children and youth* (University Diversity Series 116). ERIC Clearinghouse on Urban Education. Retrieved from http://www.eric.ed.gov/PDFS/ED482661.pdf

Rew, L. (2002). Characteristics of health care needs of homeless adolescents. *Nursing Clinics of North America, 37,* 423–431.

Reynolds, A. J., Chen, C. C., & Herbers, J. E. (2009). *School mobility and educational success: A research synthesis and evidence on prevention.* Paper prepared for the Workshop on the Impact of Mobility and Change on the Lives of Young Children, Schools, and Neighborhoods, June 29–30, The National Academies, Washington, DC. Retrieved from http://fcd-us.org/sites/default/files/ReynoldsSchoolMobilityAndEducationalSuccess.pdf

Shinn, M., Schteingart, J. S., Williams, N. C., Carlin- Mathis, J., Bialo-Karagis, N., Becker Klein, R., et al. (2008). Long-term associations of homelessness with children's well-being. *American Behavioral Scientist, 51,* 789–809.

University of Minnesota. (2005). *Curriculum-based measurement (CBM): Student assessment.* Retrieved from http://www.education.umn.edu/Pubs/ResearchWorks/CBM.html

U.S. General Accounting Office. (1994). *Elementary school children: Many change schools frequently, harming their education* (GAO/HEHS-94-45). Washington, DC: U.S. Government Printing Office.

Van Doren, P. (1998). *Where can I build my volcano?* Naperville, IL: Author.

Whitbeck, L. B., Hoyt, D. R., Johnson, K. D., & Chen, X. (2007). Victimization and posttraumatic stress disorder among runaway and homeless adolescents. *Violence and Victim, 22*(6), 721–734.

Yoder, K. A., Whitbeck, L. B., & Hoyt, D. R. (2008). Dimensionality of thoughts of death and suicide: Evidence from a study of homeless adolescents. *Social Indicators Research, 86*(1), 83–100.

WEB RESOURCES

- HEAR US: http://www.hearus.us/
- National Alliance to End Homelessness: http://www.endhomelessness.org/
- National Association for the Education of Homeless Children and Youth: http://www.naehcy.org/
- National Center for Homeless Education: http://hcenter.serve.org/nche/
- National Coalition for the Homeless: http://www.nationalhomeless.org/· Project HOPE—Virginia: http://education.wm.edu/centers/hope/

SELECTED CHILDREN'S LITERATURE

- Berck, J. (1992) *No place to be: Voices of homeless children.* Boston, MA: Houghton Mifflin Books for Children.
- Bromley, A. C. (2010). *The lunch thief.* Gardiner, ME: Tilbury House Publishers.
- Kaye, C. B. (2007). *A kids' guide to hunger & homelessness: How to take action!* Minneapolis, MN: Free Spirit Publishing.
- Williams, L. E. (2010). *The can man.* New York, NY: Lee & Low Books.
- See comprehensive lists by visiting:
  - http://homelessed.net/schools/booklist.htm: developed by the Illinois State Board of Education Homeless Education Program.
  - http://education.wm.edu/centers/hope/resources/introduction.pdf: *Exploring Homelessness Through Young Adult Literature* is an annotated bibliography with a brief introduction and appropriate grade reading level for each work. Book titles marked by an asterisk have related learning activities.
  - http://education.wm.edu/centers/hope/publications/documents/bibliography. pdf: see pages B11–B17 in this bibliography for a listing of children's and young adult literature.

6

Students Exposed to Community Violence

DOROTHY ROHDE-COLLINS ■

INTRODUCTION

Chronic community violence has been defined as frequent and continual exposure to violent behaviors including the use of weapons, drugs, burglary, mugging, and physical and sexual assault.[1] While community violence is not limited to specific geographic areas or demographic groups, it disproportionately occurs (especially homicide) among minority, low-income, and urban communities. Although all members of the community are affected, chronic exposure to violence has a particularly toxic effect on children and adolescents.

Chronic community violence is very different from other forms of violence that children may witness or directly experience. Domestic, sexual, and physical abuse involves only a single individual or family unit, whereas community violence affects entire neighborhoods and communities. Chronic community violence generally occurs without warning, and its unexpected nature combined with the seemingly random nature of the attacks contributes to an overall negative worldview. Those individuals who are either directly or indirectly victimized by community violence see the world as an extremely dangerous place where bad things can happen at any time to anyone, resulting in a general distrust of outsiders.[2] This sense of distrust is frequently directed at police, social workers, and teachers,[3] leading to a reduced likelihood to seek support services.

Twenty-five percent of children in a national sample reported witnessing violence or other indirect victimization[4]; however, these figures are higher among studies concentrating on urban U.S. cities. In fact, several studies from individual urban U.S. cities documented ranges from 55% to 97% of school-aged children reporting single or repeated exposure to violence within the community. Further, in one study of children in New Orleans, LA, 98% of children had heard about some form of violence, particularly shootings, killings, gang violence, mugging, and drug and weapon use.[5]

Children are much more likely to be harmed while they are away from school and in the community; for example, children are half as likely to be the victims of serious crimes inside school when compared to outside of school, and 70 times more likely to be murdered outside of school.[6] While this exposure largely occurs outside school walls, students typically carry these experiences into the classroom each day; thus, the widespread nature of this problem implies that a large portion of teachers will be required to teach children who have been affected by chronic community violence.

It is interesting to note that children report lower levels of exposure to community violence as they get older without reporting changes in their neighborhood. This has led some to believe that continued exposure to chronic community violence leads to habituation, or a normalization and reduced conscious awareness of the violence. On the other hand, this may be explained by the tendency of younger children to exaggerate the extent of violence. It is also possible that older children have lower rates of exposure because they are less likely to spend free time playing outdoors.[7] Whatever the reason, it is likely that those who work with young children may hear about more acts of violence than those who work with older children.

Vignette—Rachel

Rachel, 17, is not very involved in school. She rarely completes homework, does not participate in classroom discussions, and requires a great deal of encouragement to join a group for cooperative learning exercises. Her grades aren't great but she's passing—it seems as though she's just doing enough to get by. Her behavior is not excessively disruptive, but she frequently sleeps in class and occasionally is disrespectful with her teachers. Rachel does not participate in any extracurricular activities and is unable to verbalize her postgraduation plans. Concerned about her lack of achievement, Rachel's teachers and guidance counselor request a parent–teacher conference with Rachel's mother, Amanda. During the conference, Amanda reveals that Rachel's cousin was killed when an unknown person fired random shots into a crowd outside a nightclub. Rachel was extremely close to her cousin and has not seemed the same since the shooting occurred over 2 years ago. Rachel has not been sleeping at night and seems overly sensitive to noises. Rachel is quick to yell and cry when she doesn't get her way and doesn't seem to enjoy her old hobbies and interests. Amanda wants to help Rachel, but she is overwhelmed by the situation since her sister is extremely distraught by the death of her daughter and is currently going through a divorce. In short, the whole family has been affected by the violent death of Rachel's cousin and everyone is too preoccupied trying to heal themselves to help anyone else.

Vignette—Marcus

Marcus, 13, is extremely disruptive at school. He does not follow established rules or show any interest in school. His attendance is sporadic, especially at the beginning and end of the school year. Marcus has trouble following instructions and is distrustful of teachers and administrators. As he walked into class one day, Marcus visibly flinched when his teacher tried to pat him on the shoulder as he greeted him "hello." Before he realized the greeting was friendly, Marcus shouted, "Don't touch me! Don't you even think about touching me!" These behaviors continued nearly every day and Marcus's teachers were running out of behavior modification strategies. In a journal entry in which students were permitted to "free write," Marcus described how he frequently heard gunshots when he was alone at home after school. While he was thankful he has not personally had any friends or family killed by violence, he is convinced that it is only a matter of time before he has to attend a friend's funeral. He mentions that he needs to protect his mother and little brother from the violence but not knowing the right way.

IMPACT ON STUDENTS

The impact of chronic community violence (e.g., Marcus) is vastly different from that of an incident of acute community violence (e.g., Rachel). While still traumatic, an isolated incident of community violence requires only a situational adjustment while the child integrates the trauma into his or her understanding of the world and society. In contrast, chronic community violence has far-reaching effects on a child's worldview. Repeated acts of violence shatter children's assumptions about the world and lead them to believe the world is an unsafe and unfriendly place. In the minds of children, chronic community violence represents the inability of adults to protect them from danger, and in the case of Marcus, a perceived obligation to take drastic measures to protect himself and his family. Further, children may experience personality changes as they struggle to accept the role of danger in their daily routine.[8] Following trauma, many children take pride in their stoicism and ability to remain unaffected.

Caregivers also frequently have trouble making sense of the violence and may feel inadequate because they are unable to shelter their children or prevent them from witnessing violence and crime. Caregivers may express a lack of trust of outsiders, including police, doctors, social service workers, and teachers, particularly in violent urban communities. From parental reports in such communities, outsiders are perceived to only be around during the good times and seem to disappear when they may be of assistance. Teachers are considered unqualified and are often involved in altercations, both physical and verbal, with the students.[9] Some of these perceptions may be accurate in certain communities; as compared to suburban schools, teachers in urban schools are much more likely to be inexperienced, a short- or long-term substitute, or less than fully certified.[10]

Unfortunately, children often pick up on this distrust and assimilate these feelings into their own views. As a result, children frequently express the same lack of confidence and feelings of distrust, in part due to feelings of betrayal and anger for not being protected.[11] Over time, the child may develop dissociation or avoidant responses or experience a range of physical, emotional, or psychological disorders.[12]

Impact on Brain Development

Exposure to chronic community violence has a significant and lasting effect on brain development. Overexposure to the stress hormones produced in the brain can actually cause permanent physical changes. These stress hormones cause the areas of the brain that respond to threat to become overactive, causing children to react to nonthreatening actions as though they are an act of violence or a threat to their safety (i.e., hypervigilance). Even small stressors like direct eye contact or an ambiguous remark or gesture from a teacher can trigger a negative reaction,[13] as when Marcus reacted to his teacher patting him on the back.

While in a state of hypervigilance or hyperarousal, the brain is physically unable to solve problems, think creatively, or even learn and absorb new information. Over time, children who have been traumatized may become increasingly avoidant and withdrawn from classroom activities, perceiving classroom lessons as irrelevant to their survival. It becomes common for children to appear ambivalent about academic achievement and make statements such as "I don't care!" Unfortunately, this ambivalence, perceived irrelevance of school, and hypervigilant response to perceived danger may be crucial to survival, but in a classroom this response is detrimental to academic and social success (see Table 6.1). Additional impacts on overall functioning are described in Table 6.2.

It is important to state that the effects of chronic community violence may also be due, at least in part, to characteristics common to families living in dangerous communities. As stated before, families living in violent communities are also often living in poverty. Family violence, overcrowding, and abuse of drugs and

Table 6.1 PRIMARY THREAT RESPONSE

Defeat/Freezing	Fight or Flight
• Nonreactive and passive	• Aggressive and impulsive
• Compliance with requests or demands	• Highly reactive to stimuli
• Dissociation from present activities or surroundings	• Hyperactive and inattentive

Table 6.2 IMPACT OF CHRONIC COMMUNITY VIOLENCE ON CHILDREN AND
ADOLESCENTS

Physical	Social-Emotional	Classroom Behavior
• Threat response areas of brain become overactive and overdeveloped • Difficulty sleeping • Regression to previous stages of development (i.e., bed-wetting, speech patterns, neediness) • Increased somatic complaints (e.g., stomachaches or headaches) • Erratic behavior • Increased aggression, viewed as a viable way to solve problems and resolve conflicts[a]	• Pessimistic and/or negative view of the world • Low locus of control[b] • Undermines the view that hard work can lead to success • Inability to trust • Difficulty making future plans • Difficulty forming relationships with peers and/or adults • Decreased social awareness[c] • Desensitized to violence • Increased substance use or other risk-taking behaviors • Depression • Impulsivity	• Avoids classroom activities and assignments • Hesitant to make friends, join groups, or participate in classroom discussions • Ambivalent about academic achievement • Difficulty focusing or concentrating on academic work • Memory impairment

[a] Ng-Mak, Salzinger, & Feldman, 2004.
[b] Craig, 2008.
[c] Farver et al., 2005.

alcohol are common. Children frequently lack medical care and suffer from poor nutrition.[14] All of these factors contribute to an increased stress level of family members, especially the primary caregiver. Since children look to their parents to learn how to respond to a situation, a parent in distress often leads to children in distress. Similarly, positive parent–child relationships serve as protective factors against the effects of exposure to violence.[15]

DEVELOPMENTAL CONSIDERATIONS

Community violence is, by its very nature, an extremely public phenomenon, which influences entire communities. The events and victims are discussed widely and openly. Even an individual who was not personally victimized or a first-hand witness to the event is able to form a complete mental image of the incident.[16] This may be particularly detrimental to young children. Not only are young children unable to control their surroundings in order to prevent exposure to violence, but also they are often unable to protect themselves from overhearing adult conversations and media reports. Adults frequently believe young children are oblivious to events and conversations, particularly given that children may be less verbal about their fears and concerns, so their distress may go unnoticed.[17]

Early exposure to chronic violence may be more damaging in some regards as children may develop a universal understanding of the world as an unpredictable, dangerous place. Given the plasticity of the brain among younger children, such early exposure may also disrupt developmental trajectories. Conversely, some children frequently exposed to violence early in life rather than later may express more resilience due to the plasticity of their developing brain. Therefore, the developmental impacts depend largely on the individual child and the contexts in which exposure to violence occur.

STRATEGIES TO SUPPORT STUDENTS

Schools and community agencies are instrumental in enabling children and adults to process the constant violence and develop a healthy worldview. These institutions have the potential to help traumatized children reform their view of the world to become more positive, trusting, and optimistic.

Do not make assumptions. Depending on developmental level and various other personal factors, students may have perceived and processed acts of violence differently. Never assume any student will react the same as another. Ask questions such as "What do you think happened?" or "Why do you think that happened?" or "How do you feel about it?" Importantly, even if you as an adult witnessed the same violence, remember that a child's perception of the violence and what he or she saw may be very different. If a student has a much different account of what happened, do not correct the student; simply listen and help him or her process the experience.

Get involved within the community. Service-learning projects are an excellent way to improve the community while educating students about the value of altruism, commitment, political involvement, civic responsibility, and increased locus of control, particularly in urban communities with a high crime or violence rate. This may also offer students a different view of the community where people support and help one another. These service-learning projects may be initiated by a single-classroom or as a school-wide initiative and may include:

- Graffiti removal
- Petitions or a campaign of handwritten letters asking for the restoration or destruction of vacant and dilapidated buildings/homes

- Tree planting and landscaping of public areas
- Drug awareness campaign
- Abuse (physical, sexual, emotional, domestic, etc.) awareness campaign
- Mentor program between high school students and elementary school students

While all of the suggestions may not directly influence the rate of violence in a community, these projects can increase a sense of investment, pride, and belonging within the community. Further, service-learning projects can provide valuable opportunities for students to develop social, leadership, and organizational skills.

Increase parental involvement and trust. In general, urban schools struggle with parental involvement even though this is one of the most effective ways to positively influence a child's life. Developing a relationship with the parent(s) of children exposed to violence is particularly important given that adult family members are also susceptible to the negative effects of living in a dangerous environment. Consider making phone calls regularly, making as many positive comments as possible, or updating the parent on the various tasks going on in your classroom. Some teachers may have difficulty in commenting positively on academic progress; in this case, the conversation can simply focus on small successes such as arriving on time regularly, which can help to build trust and an alliance.

Develop before- and after-school opportunities. Teachers and administrators can work together to develop before- and after-school programs to prevent children from being left unattended or susceptible to the effects of violence. This can also include encouraging students to participate in extracurricular activities. Some of these programs can also help children improve in areas damaged by trauma such as social skills, stress management, and academic skills.

Encourage writing and journaling. Teachers can utilize writing prompts to stimulate thinking and allow for self-reflection in response to stress or crisis. Students will often reveal significant details or strong feelings in writing that they would otherwise not share with adults. Journal prompts can be assigned to reflect on an assignment or in response to a local or national current event. Journal prompts should always be age, grade, and contextually appropriate for students. While the following list of journal prompts may seem superficial, the topics are innocuous enough to make students feel safe when responding. Journaling often leads to impromptu class discussions, especially following a local or national event. In these circumstances, listen to the students and follow their lead. Allow students to share feelings and thoughts and intervene only when asked or it becomes necessary. Guide the discussion so all students who want to speak have the opportunity, but do not force those who are quiet to share.

Possible journal prompts include the following:

- What do you do well? What do you need to work on?
- What do you like about yourself? What would you like to improve upon?

- What do you want in a friend/neighbor/parent/teacher?
- What do you value?
- How did you feel when _____ happened? How do you think the people around you felt when _____ happened?
- What are you most looking forward to right now?
- What would your first priority be if you became president of the United States?
- What would you invent to make life better?
- When do you feel angry? What do you do?
- Describe the best/worst/happiest/saddest day of your life.
- When you have a problem, who do you talk to? Why?
- If you could improve one thing about your community, what would it be?
- Quotes (students may respond to or reflect on a teacher-selected quote)
- Free writes (students may write about any topic they choose for a specified length or amount of time)

Maintain routines and high expectations. Teachers who establish a regular routine and set consistently high expectations are communicating to their students that they can succeed. Expectations should be realistic and take into consideration the student's starting point and the outcome the teacher would like to achieve. Expectations should not be so low that they are achievable with no effort but also not so high that they become a source of stress and frustration for the students. Routines should be established for common events in the classroom like entering/exiting class, coming to class late, taking notes, turning in assignments, using the restroom, and retrieving assignments after an absence. Since traumatized children are perpetually in a state of hypervigilance, it is important to reduce the need for a child to be on high alert. Clearly communicated routines allow the student's brain to focus on academics instead of trying to figure out what the teacher expects or determine if there is an ulterior motive.

Reinforce safety. Regularly remind students that your classroom and school are safe places and that you and the other adults are there to help at any time. This may include offering phone numbers that students can call when they feel unsafe outside of school. While your influence on the community may be limited, reinforcing this sense of safety may reduce hypervigilance and heightened states of arousal, allowing for more learning. Importantly, also reinforce that any violence that occurred is not their fault.

Don't force conversations. Some children and adolescents may not be able to express themselves, may be afraid to share experiences, or simply may not have developed a trust with teachers yet. Regardless, do not force the student to talk, as such reactions may lead to withdrawal, aggression, downplaying the events, ignoring you, or changing the subject. In these cases, simply letting the student know you are there if he or she needs you goes a long way. Other methods of starting conversations may include "You look down today and I'm concerned," or "You haven't seemed yourself lately. My door is always open to you if you need to talk."

Use teachable moments to demonstrate problem solving. To counteract the state of hypervigilance, teachers have to help students relearn how to interpret social cues. In the classroom, teachers and counselors can teach stress management, coping mechanisms, and relaxation techniques that can be used at school or at home when a demanding situation arises. Modeling appropriate reactions (e.g., staying calm, taking deep breaths, showing empathy, developing nonaggressive problem-solving strategies) is an ideal way to teach these skills, especially given that many traumatized children come from violent homes and are not exposed to appropriate problem-solving skills. This does not require a special counseling group and can be effectively achieved within the context of the classroom.

Be flexible. Traumatized children are in a state of persistent arousal that prevents them from focusing on the lesson. Since they are so busy trying to determine the mood and thoughts of the teacher, traumatized students often miss instruction or directions to the assignment. Instead of accusing the child of not paying attention, teachers should provide students with multiple ways of taking in information. Teachers can provide handouts or tape recordings of lectures for students to take home, give written and oral directions to assignments, and allow opportunities for makeup work. Instead of having inflexible deadlines, teachers can allow students to submit drafts of work or complete projects in small sections. Talk with the parents about possible barriers to completing work at home, and work together to come up with solutions.

Be prepared to report possible abuse. Children exposed to chronic community violence are at increased risk for child abuse and neglect. Thus, familiarize yourself with your district's policy on mandated reporting of child maltreatment. These same children may be at increased risk for exposure to domestic violence as well.

Brainstorm. If students approach you about exposure to violence, help brainstorm what they can do in the various situations. If they see something occurring on the way home from school, perhaps there is another way, or somebody can walk with them or pick them up. Perhaps they can carry an alarm with them that might help them feel safer when walking in the community. Write the ideas down.

Know when to ask for help. Students should be referred to school support personnel, such as school psychologists, counselors, or social workers, when they exhibit one or more of the following behaviors for longer than 1 month[18]:

- Difficulty sleeping
- Nightmares
- Social withdrawal
- Frequent anger outbursts

- Physical complaints
- Rapid weight gain or loss
- Intense anxiety, depression, or hopelessness
- Increased substance use or getting in trouble with the law
- Frequent worry

CONCLUSION

Chronic community violence has far-reaching effects that impact the entire community, particularly youth. Children living within communities affected by violence develop a pessimistic impression of outsiders, which prevents families from seeking and receiving the help they need to recover from the circumstances in which they live. Parents internalize feelings of inadequacy and hopelessness, which stem from their inability to provide a safer atmosphere for their child. These feelings trickle down to children, who experience significant difficulty in school due to their inability to regulate emotions, difficulty focusing on academics, and myriad outcomes that impact school functioning.

Fortunately, schools are able to help communities affected by chronic community violence at all levels by implementing interventions for each group. While targeted mental health supports exist from trained professionals to support students exposed to violence, teachers can offer various supports within the classroom context that can substantially improve the outcome for students, families, and communities. Trauma-sensitive classrooms understand the impact of chronic community violence and counter its effects with sincere relationships between staff members and students. Administrators of trauma-sensitive schools create a warm, welcoming atmosphere and establish a school environment conducive to learning through regular routines and school-wide expectations. Teachers foster resilience and encourage the development of posttraumatic growth through relevant and meaningful classroom activities and projects. Trauma-sensitive schools encourage parental involvement and participation through invitation to events and opportunities that are of interest to the parental population. Parents are welcome at trauma-sensitive schools all of the time, not only when there is a problem. By implementing some of the interventions and strategies within this chapter, schools can become a driving force in the effort to counteract the effects of chronic community violence on youth.

NOTES

1. Osofsky, 1995.
2. Hamblen & Goguen, 2007.
3. Horowitz, McKay, & Marshall, 2005.

4. Finkelhor, Turner, Ormrod, & Hamby, 2009.
5. Osofsky, Wewers, Hann, & Fick, 1993.
6. DeVoe, Peter, Noonan, Snyder, & Baum, 2005.
7. Guerra, Huesmann, & Spindler, 2003.
8. Garbarino, Kostelny, & Dubrow, 1991.
9. Horowitz et al., 2005.
10. Jacob, 2007.
11. Horowitz et al., 2005; Osofsky et al., 1993.
12. Freyd, 2008.
13. Child Trauma Academy, 2002.
14. Margolin & Gordis, 2000.
15. Hardaway & McLoyd, 2011.
16. Margolin & Gordis, 2000.
17. Farver, Xu, Eppe, Fernandez, & Schwartz, 2005.
18. Safe Start Center, n.d.

REFERENCES

Child Trauma Academy. (2002). *The amazing human brain and human development.* Retrieved from http://www.childtraumaacademy.com/amazing_brain/index.html

Craig, S. E. (2008). *Reaching and teaching children who hurt: Strategies for your classroom.* Baltimore, MD: Paul H. Brookes Publishing.

DeVoe, J. F., Peter, K., Noonan, M., Snyder, T. D., & Baum, K. (2005). *Indicators of school crime and safety: 2005 (NCES 2006–001/NCJ 210697).* U.S. Departments of Education and Justice. Washington, DC: U.S. Government Printing Office.

Farver, J. A., Xu, Y., Eppe, S., Fernandez, A., & Schwartz, D. (2005). Community violence, family conflict, and preschooler's socioemotional functioning. *Developmental Psychology, 41*, 160–170.

Finkelhor, D., Turner, H., Ormrod, R., & Hamby, S. (2009). Violence, abuse, and crime exposure in a national sample of children and youth. *Pediatrics, 124*, 1411–1423.

Freyd, J. J. (2008). *What is a betrayal trauma? What is betrayal trauma theory?* Retrieved from http://dynamic.uoregon.edu/~jjf/defineBT.html

Garbarino, J., Kostelny, K., & Dubrow, N. (1991). What children can tell us about living in danger. *American Psychologist, 46*, 376–383.

Guerra, N. G., Huesmann, L. R., & Spindler, A. (2003). Community violence exposure, social cognition, and aggression among urban elementary school children. *Child Development, 74*, 1561–1576.

Hamblen, J., & Goguen, C. (2007). *Community violence fact sheet.* National Center for Post Traumatic Stress Disorder. Retrieved from http://www.ptsd.va.gov/professional/pages/community-violence.asp

Hardaway, C. R., & McLoyd, V. C. (2011). Exposure to violence and socioemotional adjustment in low-income youth: An examination of protective factors. *American Journal of Community Psychology, 49*, 112–126.

Horowitz, K., McKay, M., & Marshall, R. (2005). Community violence and urban families: Experiences, effects, and directions for intervention. *American Journal of Orthopsychiatry, 75*, 356–368.

Jacob, B. A. (2007). The challenges of staffing urban schools with effective teachers. *The Future of Children, 17* (1), 129–153.

Margolin, G., & Gordis, E. (2000). The effects of family and community violence on children. *Annual Review of Psychology, 51,* 445–479.

Ng-Mak, D. S., Salzinger, S., & Feldman, R. S. (2004). Pathologic adaptation to community violence among inner-city youth. *American Journal of Orthopsychiatry, 74,* 196–208.

Osofsky, J. D. (1995). The effects of exposure to violence on young children. *American Psychologist, 50,* 782–788.

Osofsky, J. D., Wewers, S., Hann, D. M., & Fick, A. C. (1993). Chronic community violence: What is happening to our children? In D. Reiss, J. E. Richters, M. Radke-Yarrow, & D. Scharff (Eds.), *Children and violence* (pp. 36–45). New York, NY: Guilford Press.

Safe Start Center. (n.d.). *Healing the invisible wounds. Children's exposure to violence: A guide for families.* Retrieved from http://www.safestartcenter.org/pdf/caregiver.pdf

WEB RESOURCES

- Child Witness to Violence Project: http://www.childwitnesstoviolence.org/
- National Center for Children Exposed to Violence: http://www.nccev.org/
- Safe Start Center: http://www.safestartcenter.org/

SELECTED CHILDREN'S LITERATURE

- Cohn, J. (1994). *Why did it happen? Helping young children cope with the experience of violence.* New York, NY: Morrow Junior Books.
- Holmes, M. M., & Mudlaff, S. J. (2000). *A terrible thing happened—A story for children who have witnessed violence or trauma.* Washington, DC: Magination Press.
- Kivel, P. (2001). *I can make my world a safer place: A kid's book about stopping violence.* Alameda, CA: Hunter House.
- Myers, W. D. (2005). *Autobiography of my dead brother.* New York, NY: HarperCollins.

7

Students With Incarcerated Parents

JENNIFER K. BUXTON-MCCLENDON ■

INTRODUCTION

Approximately 8.3 million American children have parents under correctional supervision (prison, jail, parole, or on probation), and nearly half of those children are in or are approaching adolescence.[1] This striking statistic is the harsh reality of the growing number of parents in the U.S. justice system today. With the increase in households affected by parental criminality, careful attention should be given to the children of this population, with the ultimate goal of fostering student resilience and educational success.

A recent report from the Bureau of Justice Statistics[2] found that, in 2007, an estimated 809,800 state and federal prisoners were parents (744,200 fathers, 65,600 mothers) to an estimated 1,706,600 children younger than the age of 18. This represents a 79% increase in the total number of parents in prison since 1991. In fact, over half of all inmates reported having at least one child younger than 18 years of age. Many of these parents have limited contact with their child(ren), which may be partly due to the sometimes large geographical distances between the child's home and the parent's prison.

Previous data suggest that parents expected to serve an average of 80 months in state prison and 103 months in federal prison.[3] These long sentences leave parents absent for many important developmental milestones in the life of a child or adolescent, and a large number of adolescents will reach age 18 before their incarcerated parent is released.[4] Previous data also reveal that the majority of incarcerated parents reported a criminal history, including previous incarceration,[5] thus contributing to a lifestyle of instability and unpredictability for their children. Unfortunately, given that many parents and caregivers do not report to the school that a parent is in jail or prison, educators may often be unaware that parental incarceration is a stressor for a particular child.

Stressors Associated With Parental Incarceration

Data from the Bureau of Statistics Special Report on Parents in Prison[6] suggest that in addition to parental incarceration, there may be other concurrent stressors in the home related to exposure to violence, substance abuse, poverty, and instable housing. These data clearly establish that children of parents in prison often have a long history of familial or environmental stressors at the time of, or immediately following, their parent's arrest. Table 7.1 illustrates the types and prevalence of stressors that children of incarcerated parents experience.

Some children may have witnessed their parent's arrest, which may include a physical struggle, handcuffing, drawing of weapons, and the parent being taken away in a patrol car. Witnessing a parent's arrest can lead to prolonged periods of nightmares and flashbacks, difficulty sleeping, and elevated symptoms of posttraumatic stress.[7]

Forty-eight percent of incarcerated parents in state prison reported living with their children within the month before arrest or just prior to incarceration.[8] When a resident parent becomes incarcerated, most children end up living with the nonincarcerated parent (84%), other family members (21%), or friends (2.9%), with foster homes or agencies supporting only 2.9% of the children of incarcerated parents.[9] Regardless of where children live after the imprisonment of a parent, though, there is a drastic change in their home life that often results in a lack of consistency as they've had to move from caregiver to caregiver, school to school, and into home environments where there is little structure and support.[10] The hope is that in an unpredictable and unstable home environment, consistency can be maintained at school and in the community.

Table 7.1 FAMILY STRESSORS OF PARENTS IN STATE OR FEDERAL PRISON WITH
MINOR CHILDREN

Stressor	Percent of State Prisoners	Percent of Federal Prisoners
Prior criminal history	53.2	66
Homelessness in prior year	8.9	3.9
History of abuse	19.9	10.8
Current medical problems	40.6	35.6
Mental health problems	56.5	42.6
History of substance abuse	67.4	56.4
Less than high school diploma	37.6	29.3

Re-Entry

Re-entry describes the process of prisoners being released from prison and re-entering society and returning to their families. This can often be another tumultuous time for children as they are dealing with the reintegration of their parent and the struggle of the restructured family life that has formed in their absence. The re-entry process will be different for each released prisoner based on a variety of factors, including preincarceration lifestyle (family structure and dynamic, history of substance abuse, existence of social and emotional support networks, employment history, criminal history) and his or her prison experience (GED attainment, familial contact during the prison term, length of prison term, and mental and physical health).[11] One of the greatest challenges is reestablishing a functional relationship between the parent and child, particularly when contact between the released parent and the child is limited. Recently released parents frequently fail to acknowledge the developmental changes a child has undergone during incarceration, and it is common to find that they will treat their children as if they are still the age they were upon initial incarceration.[12]

It is important for educators to recognize the re-entry of a parent as a time that could potentially be even more challenging than the actual incarceration. While radical behaviors may subside during the incarceration period for some students, they will often reappear when the parent re-enters the child's life after release. It would be helpful to increase contact with the student at this point as a way of reaching out and letting him or her know there is still consistency in the school environment while the family struggles with reintegration and an altered family structure.

DEVELOPMENTAL CONSIDERATIONS

The effects of parental arrest and incarceration on a child's development can be profound, potentially resulting in anxiety, fear, guilt, shame, distrust, dependency, decreased academic and occupational attainment, and difficulty developing relationships and personal identity.[13] Particular concerns can be noted among children of the 25% of all incarcerated women who give birth within the year of arrest or are pregnant at the time of arrest. These children are often not allowed to stay with their mothers during the period of incarceration, leading to little opportunity for forming an attachment.

Developmentally, children may experience myriad issues during a parent's incarceration, including developmental regression, cognitive delays, damaged parent–child relationships, and reduced problem-solving and coping skills. Additionally, older children may express a rejection of boundaries or limits and increases in criminal or antisocial behavior. Table 7.2 discusses the developmental progression from infancy to adolescence as it relates to parental incarceration. Suggestions are offered based on the developmental milestones that characterize each phase.[14]

Table 7.2 Developmental Impact of Parental Incarceration

Age Group	Developmental Milestones	Potential Symptoms of Parental Incarceration	How to Help
Infants and toddlers	• Trust develops between infants and caregivers • Infants learn to regulate stress • Desire for independence • Testing boundaries of authority	• Lack of emotional regulation • Inability to predict others' actions/reactions • Impaired/insecure attachments with adults • Temper tantrums • Defiance and negativity • Increased anxiety	• Provide consistency • Reduce changes in caregivers and home/daycare placements • Reassure safety and security
Preschool	• "Magical thinking" and fantasies • Transductive reasoning (relating two unrelated things)	• May blame self for incarceration • Developmental regression (resurgence in bed-wetting, nightmares, tantrums) • Internalizing problems (e.g., withdrawal, depression, somatic complaints, anxiety, shame, guilt)	• Maintain contact with incarcerated parent (if possible) • Talk about crime and punishment, and relate to child's world (e.g., prison is a long timeout) • Discuss reality of prison

Developmental stage	Developmental characteristics	Effects of parental incarceration	Interventions
Elementary school	• Focus shifts from family to peer group • Development of problem solving and reasoning • Conflict between peer affiliation and family loyalty • Learning ethical behavior • Making more independent choices	• Others may tease student about parent's incarceration, leading to stigma and conflict of affiliation vs. family loyalty • Misunderstanding of why parent was sent to prison • School avoidance • May distance self from family members or incarcerated parent • Oppositional, defiant, aggressive, or delinquent behaviors • Academic problems	• Challenge the social stigma associated with parental incarceration • Reassure student that his or her choices did not cause parent to go to jail • Equip student with appropriate strategies to deal with taunting from others • Find mentors or role models • Encourage communication • Discuss feelings and emotions
Adolescence	• Attempting to form a unique, cohesive identity • Want to assess the risks and consequences associated with exploration of risky behaviors	• Increased awareness of lack of financial stability, lack of supervision, and other aspects of parental incarceration • Risk taking (e.g., substance abuse, sexual promiscuity) • Rejection of authority	• Positive adult or peer role models should remain consistent at this phase • Maintain consistency, security, and expectations

FAMILY AND CULTURAL CONSIDERATIONS

According to the 2008 prisoners report conducted by the Bureau of Justice Statistics, more than 4 in 10 fathers in state and federal prisons were Black, about 3 in 10 were White, and 2 in 10 were Hispanic.[15] Overall, 46% of minor children who had a father in (state or federal) prison in 2007 were children of Black fathers.[16] In contrast, almost half (48%) of all mothers held in the nation's prisons in 2007 were White, followed by 28% Black and 17% Hispanic.[17] Taken together, Black children are 7.5 times more likely than White children to have an incarcerated parent, and Hispanic children are more than 2.5 times more likely than White children to have a parent in prison.

The family structure and living circumstances often change drastically following the incarceration of a parent, which can lead to a variety of negative outcomes for children.[18] Factors that contribute include the actual separation from the parent, economic hardship following lost income from the incarcerated parent, increased parental stress for the remaining caregiver, change in caregivers, harsh parenting, and increased levels of stigma and social isolation. These negative factors could be mitigated, however, by factors such as preincarceration relationships with trusted adults (particularly the relationship with the non-incarcerated parent), extended family members, and community supports including the school.

Importantly, the family's culture may impact who takes care of the child following incarceration as well as whether they pursue outside support or accept referrals to outside agencies. Teachers are often the first ones to be notified that a child's parent has been incarcerated; thus, knowing how to provide and access supports can greatly influence how a child responds.

SYMPTOMS OBSERVED IN SCHOOL

As a result of parental incarceration, many children have experienced the trauma of sudden separation from their sole caregiver, and many are at increased risk for feelings of fear, anxiety, anger, sadness, depression, and guilt.[19] Parental criminality is also associated with emotional withdrawal, social isolation, low self-esteem, inattention, acting-out or antisocial behaviors, difficulty forming relationships, delinquency, and an increased risk of intergenerational incarceration.[20] In fact, some estimates suggest that 70% of children with incarcerated parents will end up involved with the prison system themselves.[21] Not surprisingly, this also impacts academic achievement and overall functioning within the school setting, including increased suspension and dropout rates among adolescents with incarcerated parents.[22]

Some older students may experience stigma associated with having a parent in prison, which can lead to social isolation.[23] These same students will often receive less sympathy than their peers who are dealing with a parent's absence for other reasons, such as military deployment or a chronic illness. This isolation and peer rejection can be particularly distressful for adolescents given the value placed on peer relationships and their role in social development, psychosocial adjustment, and helping reduce symptoms of social anxiety and depression.[24]

It is important to acknowledge that children will vary in the degree to which they experience these problems. Many students will demonstrate characteristics of resilience, adaptability, and independence. The moderating factors that could influence how students react to parental incarceration include family configuration prior to incarceration (i.e., the role of the incarcerated parent in the child's life), relationships with parents and caregivers, and age or developmental level of the child.[25] Some youth may benefit from parental incarceration if the parent was abusive or neglectful or otherwise contributed to an unhealthy home environment for the child—in such cases, incarceration may result In being cared for in a more supportive setting. Reactions will also depend on an individual's personality and temperament. For instance, children may become increasingly aggressive or anxious after visiting a parent in prison, whereas others may experience calm and reassurance about their incarcerated parent's safety and the strength of their relationship with the parent.[26]

STRATEGIES TO SUPPORT STUDENTS

Although it is clear that parental incarceration has adverse effects on children, limited research is available on effective services to support these students in school.[27] As for many other students—trauma impacted or not—clear and consistent discipline, close monitoring and supervision, frequent positive reinforcement, and secure, responsive attachments can increase the likelihood of prosocial outcomes.[28]

In reviewing the recommendations in this section, consider this vignette:

VIGNETTE—ADRIAN

When Adrian was 8 years old, he was removed from his mother after Child Protective Services discovered she was abusing cocaine and neglectful to him and his three siblings. Adrian's older brother had met their father, although Adrian never had. Even before being removed from the home, Adrian's mother would sometimes have to go to jail for a few nights or a week at a time, leaving Adrian, his older brother, and his two younger sisters on their own. Adrian and his brother tried to stay brave for their younger sisters, although he was often angry, confused, and scared. Sometimes their lights, phone, or even water would be turned off because the bills hadn't been paid. Eventually, they had to move in with their grandmother, who lived in a different school district. Adrian wished his teachers knew what was going on at home, although he never had the courage to tell them.

Be prepared to meet basic needs. Many children of incarcerated parents may not have their basic needs (safety, security, food, shelter, clothing) met in the same way as they did before the incarceration. Therefore, consider keeping a change of clothes and granola bars or some other type of snack that can help students to regain focus at the beginning of their school days. This is true for the student mentioned in the previous vignette, who likely arrived at school hungry on several occasions.

Be honest. Students may sometimes ask educators difficult questions about their parent's incarceration, including inquiries about the reasons for incarceration, how it will change their lifestyle, or the well-being of the parent. The reason for incarceration can be explained in terms of relating it to the child's developmental level. For example, if the student correlates timeout with bad behavior, then incarceration can be explained as an extended timeout for adults. The lifestyle of parents in jail can be explained in terms of what they wear, where they live, and what resources they have in their rooms (cells) and on the premises ("yard" time, library, cafeteria, school, etc.). Children can begin to visualize their parent's lifestyle and learn of the differences and similarities, which may provide some comfort. In addition, children will want to know that the incarceration is not their fault, and it's important to make sure this is reinforced.

Before answering any questions, however, be sure to communicate with the current caregiver to ensure consistent messages. Importantly, misinforming or misleading a child about a parent's incarceration can lead to increased anxiety, fear, confusion, and mistrust. Be honest, accounting for the developmental level of the child, and answer questions as truthfully as possible. It's perfectly acceptable to defer questions to the existing caregiver if you feel uncomfortable. The link for *A Caregiver's Guide on How to Explain Jails and Prisons to Children* found at the end of the chapter will provide several examples of common questions with clear and concise answers addressing the student's concerns. Please note that these may differ based on the developmental stage of the child.

Reassure. Remind children that the parent did not leave because of them. Further, reassure them that you are always available to talk to them without judgment. It's also important to reassure students that you are there to listen to their experiences and how they are handling their parent's incarceration. Students, such as the one in the previous vignette, often wish teachers knew about their situation, although they do not voluntarily disclose the information on their own. These students are often missing a trusted adult to confide in at home.

Share the Bill of Rights for Children of Incarcerated Parents. The San Francisco Partnership for Incarcerated Parents offers a Bill of Rights[29] that can be shared with students to increase a sense of empowerment. The Bill of Rights includes:

1. I have the right to be kept safe and informed at the time of my parent's arrest.
2. I have the right to be heard when decisions are made about me.

3. I have the right to be considered when decisions are made about my parents.
4. I have the right to be well cared for in my parent's absence.
5. I have the right to speak with, see, and touch my parent.
6. I have the right to support as I struggle with my parent's incarceration.
7. I have the right not to be judged, blamed, or labeled because of my parent's incarceration.
8. I have the right to a lifelong relationship with my parent.

Create opportunities for students to connect with parents. Create a classroom discussion about people that students miss—it can be a family member or friend that lives far away, is deployed in the military, or is incarcerated. Encourage the students to talk about this person, their feelings, and how they maintain contact with the person (although do not force them to discuss it). Then have the students write a birthday card or letter to this person. Encourage them to include artwork or examples of their schoolwork. Not only is this beneficial for all students, but also it will encourage the students to maintain contact with their parent who is incarcerated. Activities such as journaling or drawing may also help students express themselves if they prefer not to talk about it.

Increase school connectedness. One mitigating factor for students with parents in prison is having a positive relationship with at least one caring adult.[30] Creating an environment that fosters positive student–educator relationships can help bolster academic, behavioral, and social-emotional outcomes for *all* students, including reduced violence, risk-taking behaviors, and school absenteeism.[31] This is particularly important for those students without as many opportunities for developing these relationships at home.

Focus on resilience and positive qualities. Children of incarcerated parents may lack opportunities to hear adults say positive things about them, particularly those that demonstrate increased externalizing problems following parental incarceration. Therefore, discuss difficult times in the past that have made students stronger and focus on their strengths rather than their detriments. In relation to the vignette from earlier, a teacher could praise the student for using candles or discuss how he and his brothers were able to continue showing up at school or finding ways to eat. This also opens up discussion for a future plan when another similar situation arises.

Maintain high expectations. Educators should recognize that students may have additional responsibilities placed on them in the absence of a parent or that financial difficulties from the loss of an income may make the home environment uncomfortable and not conducive to doing homework. In fact, over half of all incarcerated parents were the primary financial support for their children before going to prison. Educators should therefore remain flexible when these factors serve as barriers to completing assignments at home. However, educators should also maintain high expectations for hard work and learning. Offering flexible deadlines and varied ways to demonstrate mastery should not be confused with lowering standards.

Stay informed. If at all possible, be aware of what's going on at home with the students and any contact they may have with their incarcerated parent. If there is a weekly phone call or visit, note these dates and make sure you ask about the visit and be aware that the student may react differently in the classroom the next day. If the student is going for the first visit, consider preparing the student for what may occur—including possibly no opportunity for physical contact (hugging), a limited time to actually talk with the parent, dress codes, requirements to get on a visitation list prior to the visit, or age restrictions for visitors if the student plans to visit alone without an adult. Some parents may actually refuse to see their children out of shame or embarrassment.[32] Certain dates may also be important for educators to know that can trigger a reaction, including birthdays, important events the parent will miss (e.g., school play, sports game, family reunion), Father's Day or Mother's Day, anniversary of the arrest, and trial dates.

Encourage involvement. Students with incarcerated parents are more likely to lack proper supervision after school, which may contribute to the increased prevalence of criminality among these children. Therefore, these students may benefit from becoming involved in school-based activities after school, including sports teams, interest clubs, or even after-school tutoring programs. Such involvement may also foster increased connectedness with the school and other adults. Involvement in before- or after-school activities with other students may also increase peer relations and reduce social isolation.

Change stigma surrounding incarceration. Many people have preexisting notions about prison and inmates, which can lead to teasing and isolation for a student when the class knows about a parent's incarceration. Therefore, consider challenging some of these biases—discuss how many inmates receive high school equivalency or college degrees in prison, give back to the community as a part of their sentence, or make amends with victims of their crimes. Importantly, educators must first confront their own perceptions and biases about incarceration and prison.

Reach out to the existing caregiver(s). In the event of parental incarceration, many parents or caregivers are experiencing significant stresses themselves. Connect with them, and offer support. Develop a partnership in the interest of the student. As the remaining caregivers feel more connected with the school, they will increasingly support your efforts as an educator, and most important, the student will benefit.

Familiarize yourself with existing programs. Several parent–child visitation programs exist to help maintain or improve the relationship between incarcerated parents and their child(ren), such as the Girl Scouts Behind Bars Program,[33] which provides transportation to and from the prison, counseling, and community involvement with the Girl Scouts.

CONCLUSION

As a result of the immense number of parents currently incarcerated in state and federal prisons, children and adolescents face detrimental developmental and environmental impacts. In an attempt to alleviate these consequences at the school level, several classroom strategies and school-based interventions can be implemented to assist students with recovery. School-based interventions should be supplemented with external services at the community level to create an extended support network. Collaboration between the school and community can provide additional support for students to decrease any developmental or academic delays as a result of parental incarceration.

AUTHOR NOTE

Some information in this chapter was first published in Rossen, E. (2011). Supporting students with incarcerated parents. *Principle Leadership, 12*(3), 12–16. It has been adapted with permission by the National Association of Secondary School Principals. Copyright (2011). Retrieved from http://www.nasponline.org/resources/principals/Incarcerated_Parents_Nov2011.pdf

NOTES

1. Correctional Association of New York, 2009.
2. Glaze & Marushchak, 2010.
3. Mumola, 2000.
4. Glaze & Marushchak, 2010.
5. Mumola, 2000.
6. Glaze & Marushchak, 2010.
7. Phillips & Zhao, 2010.
8. Glaze & Marushchak, 2010.
9. Glaze & Marushchak, 2010.
10. Lopez & Bhat, 2007.
11. Herman-Stahl, Kan, & McKay, 2008.
12. University of Arizona, 2005.
13. Miller, 2006; Simmons, 2000.
14. Adalist-Estrin, n.d.
15. Glaze & Maruschak, 2010.
16. Glaze & Maruschak, 2010.
17. Glaze & Maruschak, 2010.
18. Herman-Stahl et al., 2008.
19. Simmons, 2000.
20. Lopez & Bhat, 2007.
21. U.S. Senate Report 106–404, 2001.

22. Parke & Clarke-Stewart, 2002.
23. Braman & Wood, 2003.
24. Harter, 1997; La Greca & Moore Harrison, 2005.
25. Johnson, 2006.
26. Parke & Clarke-Stewart, 2002.
27. Lopez & Bhat, 2007.
28. Eddy & Reid, 2001.
29. San Francisco Partnership for Incarcerated Parents, n.d.
30. Johnson, 2006.
31. Centers for Disease Control and Prevention, 2009.
32. Young & Smith, 2000.
33. The Girl Scouts Behind Bars Program can be found on the website for the Girl Scouts of the United States of America, at http://www.girlscouts.org/who_we_are/our_partners/government_grants/community/gsbb.asp

REFERENCES

Adalist-Estrin, A. (n.d.). Different children/behaviors. *Children of Prisoners Library.* Retrieved from www.fcnetwork.org/cpl/CPL304-Different.pdf

Braman, D., & Wood, J. (2003). From one generation to the next: How criminal sanctions are reshaping life in urban America. In J. Travis & M. Waul (Eds.), *Prisoners once removed: The impact of incarceration and reentry on children, families and communities* (pp.157–188). Washington, DC: Urban Institute.

Centers for Disease Control and Prevention. (2009). *School connectedness: Strategies for increasing protective factors among youth.* Atlanta, GA: U.S. Department of Health and Human Services.

Correctional Association of New York. (2009). *Imprisonment and families fact sheet.* Retrieved from http://prisonpolicy.org/scans/Families_Fact_Sheet_2009_FINAL.pdf

Eddy, J. M., & Reid, J. B. (2001, December 1). *The antisocial behavior of the adolescent children of incarcerated parents: A developmental perspective.* From Prison to Home Conference, hosted by the U.S. Department of Health and Human Services at the National Institutes of Health. Retrieved from http://aspe.hhs.gov/hsp/prison2home02/eddy.htm

Glaze, L. E., & Marushchak, L. M. (2010). *Parents in prison and their minor children.* Bureau of Justice Statistics Special Report. Washington, DC: U.S. Department of Justice, Office of Justice Programs, NCJ 222984. Retrieved from http://bjs.ojp.usdoj.gov/content/pub/pdf/pptmc.pdf

Harter, S. (1997). The development of self-representations. In W. Damon (Series Ed.) & N. Eisenberg (Vol. Ed.), *Handbook of child psychology* (5th ed., Vol. III). New York, NY: Wiley.

Herman-Stahl, M., Kan, M. L., & McKay, T. (2008). *Incarceration and the family.* Research Triangle Park, NC: RTI International.

Johnson, E. I. (2006). Youth with incarcerated parents: An introduction to the issues. *The Prevention Researcher, 13*(2), 3–6.

La Greca, A. M., & Moore Harrison, H. (2005). Adolescent peer relations, friendships, and romantic relationships: Do they predict social anxiety and depression? *Journal of Clinical Child & Adolescent Psychology, 34,* 49–61.

Lopez, C., & Bhat, C. S. (2007). Supporting students with incarcerated parents in schools: A group intervention. *The Journal for Specialists in Group Work, 32,* 139–153.

Miller, K. (2006). The impact of parental incarceration on children: An emerging need for effective interventions. *Child and Adolescent Social Work Journal, 23*(4), 472–486.

Mumola, C. (2000). *Incarcerated parents and their children.* Bureau of Justice Statistics Special Report. Washington, DC: Bureau of Justice Statistics.

Parke, R., & Clarke-Stewart, K. A. (2002, January 30). *Effects of parental incarceration on young children.* From Prison to Home Conference, hosted by the U.S. Department of Health and Human Services at the National Institutes of Health. Retrieved from http://aspe.hhs.gov/hsp/prison2home02/parke-stewart.htm

Phillips, S. D., & Zhao, J. (2010). The relationship between witnessing arrests and elevated symptoms of posttraumatic stress: Findings from a national study of children involved in the child welfare system. *Children and Youth Services Review, 32,* 1246–1254.

San Francisco Partnership for Incarcerated Parents. (n.d.). *Children of incarcerated parents bill of rights.* Retrieved from http://www.sfcipp.org/

Simmons, C. W. (2000). Children of incarcerated parents. *California Research Bureau, 7*(2), 1–11. Retrieved from http://www.library.ca.gov/crb/00/notes/v7n2.pdf

U.S. Senate Report 106–404: Departments of Commerce, Justice, and State, the Judiciary, and Related Agencies Appropriation Bill, 2001. Retrieved from http://www.gpo.gov/fdsys/pkg/CRPT-106srpt404/pdf/CRPT-106srpt404.pdf

University of Arizona. (2005). *Students with incarcerated parents/caretakers.* Tucson, AZ: Tucson LINKS.

Young, D. S., & Smith, C. J. (2000). When moms are incarcerated: The need of children, mothers, and caregivers. *Families in Society: The Journal of Contemporary Human Services, 81*(2), 130–141.

WEB RESOURCES

- Arizona Stars: http://www.starsmp.org/
- *A Caregiver's Guide on How to Explain Jails and Prisons to Children*: http://www.starsmp.org/PDFs/explaining_prison_final.pdf
- Family and Corrections Network (FCN): http://fcnetwork.org/
- Family to Family, California: http://www.f2f.ca.gov/res-YouthParents.htm
- The Osborne Association: http://www.osborneny.org
- Project Resilience: http://www.projectresilience.com/tgintro.htm

SELECTED CHILDREN'S LITERATURE (LIST FROM PARENTING INSIDE OUT[34]):

- Bender, J. M. (2003). *My daddy is in jail: Story, discussion guide, and small group activities for grades K-5.* Chapin, SC: Youthlight.

---

[1] http://www.parentinginsideout.org/resources

- Brisson, P. (2004). *Mama loves me from away.* Honesdale, PA: Boyds Mill Press.
- Gesme, C. (1993). *Help for kids: Understanding your feelings about having a parent in prison or jail.* Asheville, NC: Pine Tree Press.
- Hickman, M. W. (1990). *When Andy's father went to prison.* Niles, IL: Albert Whitman.
- Holeyfield, M. (2008). *Letters from prison.* Chapin, SC: Youthlight.
- Holmes, M. M. (2000). *A terrible thing happened—A story for children who have witnessed violence or trauma.* Washington, DC: Magination Press.
- Nelson, J. (2006). *Families change: A book for children experiencing termination of parental rights (Kids Are Important Series).* Minneapolis, MN: Free Spirit Publishing.
- Paterson, K. (2002). *The same stuff as stars.* New York, NY: Clarion Books.
- Stanglin, J. A. (2006). *What is jail, mommy?* Centennial, CO: Lifevest Publishing.
- Stauffacher, S. (2007). *Harry Sue.* New York, NY: Yearling.
- Woodson, J. (2002). *Visiting day.* New York, NY: Scholastic Press.

8

Students With Parents Involved in Substance Abuse or Dependence

BRIAN R. DEVINE ∎

INTRODUCTION

Research unequivocally demonstrates the negative effects of parental substance abuse or dependency on their children. For example, children of alcoholics demonstrate higher rates of substance abuse, behavioral problems, aggression, internalizing disorders (e.g., anxiety or depression), attention deficit/hyperactivity disorder (ADHD), and psychiatric distress than their nonaffected peers, and they tend to have lower academic achievement and verbal ability.[1] The most serious threat, however, is to younger children whose fathers are drug abusers and live in the household; in contrast, those with fathers who do not abuse substances have the lowest rates of clinical symptoms.[2]

The National Survey on Drug Use and Health found that between 2002 and 2007, more than 8.3 million children younger than age 18 (11. 9%) lived with at least one parent who was dependent on or abused alcohol or illegal drugs during the preceding year, although parental dependence or abuse of alcohol was significantly more common.[3] Parental substance dependency or abuse occurred most frequently among children age 5 years or younger (14%), followed by children ages 6 to 11 (12%), and then ages 12 to 17 (10%). More recent estimates suggest that one out of every six school-aged children experiences parental substance abuse or dependency.[4] Thus, it is likely that most teachers interact with students affected by parental substance abuse on a daily basis.

Substance abuse or dependency is twice as common among fathers when compared to mothers and occurs more frequently among parents with mental health problems or psychiatric disorders. The rate of parental abuse or dependency was 12.8% for two-parent households, compared with 16.1% for children living with only a father and 8.4% for those living with only a mother. Children with both parents abusing alcohol or other substances are at particular risk without another adult in the home to serve as a buffer between the child and an alcohol- or drug-abusing parent.[5]

Importantly, substance use occurs on a continuum from use, to abuse, to depen- dence. Not all those using substances are addicted. Abuse refers to recurrent use despite persistent problems (e.g., in school, at work, or socially). Dependence, or addiction, may be psychological (perceived need to function or feel better) or physical (symptoms of tolerance or withdrawal) and often is associated with failed attempts to reduce use.[6] For the purposes of this chapter, we focus prima- rily on abuse and dependence.

Impact on Students

The impact of parental substance abuse on children's school performance may vary widely, with the age of the child as a significant factor. Younger children, who have fewer coping skills and strategies, might withdraw or be inappropri- ately aggressive. Older children and teens may have developed coping skills that are manifested in certain characteristic patterns—for example, some may try to get straight A's as part of an effort to control the drinking or drug use going on at home; others may seek key positions in school activities, using friends as a buffer for their problems at home. In these cases, it may not be apparent to school staff that there is an issue with the student.

Despite the ability of some affected students to compensate adaptively, children of substance-abusing parents do have a higher incidence of edu- cational problems than their nonaffected peers, including grade retention, school mobility, truancy, reduced ability to concentrate on work, difficulty maintaining friendships, and placement in special education.[7] They are also at increased risk for exposure to violence (see chapter 6) and child maltreat- ment (see chapters 13, 14, and 15) as their needs take a backseat to the parent's activities.[8] The stresses and demands of their situation can make school suc- cess seem unattainable or irrelevant for many of these children, much like in the case of Anthony (see vignette).

VIGNETTE—ANTHONY

Anthony, a 12-year-old sixth grader, has recently begun realizing that his mother has been drinking more and more in the evenings, which would lead to either her falling asleep on the sofa or her becoming violent toward his father. At times, she would scream at his dad or even punch or throw things at him. One time Anthony's dad took him and his brother out of the house so they wouldn't have to see it, but his mother ended up driving and wrecking the car. When his mother became drunk, Anthony would usually hide out in his room, although he found it difficult to concentrate when she became belligerent, let alone ask for help on any assignments. Sometimes she would keep him up at night, making him tired in school the next day. He knew his mother cared about him, and she often helped him get ready for school in the morning— sometimes it seemed like she didn't even remember what happened the night before. Anthony once asked her to not drink, but she said it helped her "feel better" so he hasn't said anything since.

A parent who is addicted or who is abusing alcohol or drugs is often impaired and unable to take proper care of a child,[9] which may lead to a student's unkempt appearance, tardiness to school, falling asleep in class, or incomplete or missing homework (the case for Anthony in the vignette). Parents may drive their children while intoxicated or high. An affected child may have an advanced knowledge of alcohol or drugs, or there may be great discomfort when the subject is mentioned. These children may also get uncomfortable when the topic of parents is discussed, given the potential for feelings of guilt or shame. Other indications may be that the parent is never involved in any of the child's activities or that the student partakes in various after-school activities as an attempt to avoid having to go home.

DEVELOPMENTAL CONSIDERATIONS

Substance abuse or dependency from a parent can impact children throughout various stages of development. Mothers using alcohol or illicit drugs during pregnancy increase the risk of premature birth, miscarriage, low birth weight, birth defects, growth deficiencies, cognitive delays, small head and brain, and impaired development and are at increased risk for requiring intensive medical services after delivery.[10] Further, substance use during pregnancy may impact the child throughout his or her life with an increased risk of inattention, behavioral problems, and irritability. Unfortunately, 11.6% of mothers reportedly consume alcohol during pregnancy, and another 5.2% use an illicit drug during pregnancy—leaving an estimated 550,000 to 750,000 newborns exposed to drugs or alcohol in utero each year.[11]

For school-aged children, substance abuse can lead to disruptions in the bonding process. Parents abusing or dependent upon substances may have delayed reaction time to respond to their child's needs, may be unable to meet the financial demands of providing for a child, or may simply not be physically or emotionally present to develop a bond. This may lead to impaired social-emotional functioning and, once the child is in school, impaired academic performance.

Students with a substance-abusing parent may have little supervision at home, leading to lack of curfews, few rules to abide by, and possible increased exposure to other dangers in the community. These students may be less inclined to follow rules and understand boundaries in the classroom without having to abide by a set of rules at home.

Older students may have to accept caregiver responsibilities for younger siblings or other members of the family. These students have to balance their schoolwork with the responsibilities of helping support the family. This can lead to increased anxiety, stress, lack of focus on schoolwork, and often few opportunities to complete homework or study. These students may also place an undue burden upon themselves to put an end to the parental substance abuse. Adolescents with parents abusing or dependent upon substances are at increased risk for substance abuse themselves, which may serve as a coping mechanism for the distress associated with parental substance abuse.[12]

CULTURAL AND RELIGIOUS CONSIDERATIONS

Cultural sensitivity and awareness are critical in the attempts of schools to be supportive of students dealing with parental substance abuse, particularly given that racial and ethnic minorities tend to underreport problems at home and deny discomfort.[13] Meanwhile, the experiences of immigration and assimilating to our culture are often accompanied by an increase in substance abuse, perhaps as a way to cope with the associated stresses.[14] Substance abuse has been described as an "equal opportunity disease" given that it exists among all races, ethnicities, and socioeconomic groups[15]; however, some groups may be at increased risk for substance use and dependence yet less likely to seek support. Thus, it is important to recognize the warning signs listed previously and not expect students to discuss or initiate a conversation about their parent's substance or alcohol abuse.

Some beliefs, customs, and values specific to certain cultural and religious groups may have an impact on how a student may view issues surrounding alcohol and other drugs.[16] For example, the legal drinking age ranges across various countries around the world from having no laws, to teenage years (i.e., age 16 to 18 years) in parts of Europe, to age 25 years in some areas of India, to completely illegal in other countries such as Saudi Arabia and other Muslim countries. Some cultural and religious groups may see substance abuse as a reflection of a weak character, mental illness, sinful behavior, or supernatural influence. Conversely, others may see substance use as a normal and acceptable way of dealing with the stresses of life or as a sensible way to cope with psychological pain. It is not uncommon to see depictions of substance use or abuse suggested as an acceptable response to stress in movies or on television. Further, some cultures or religions may even view drug use as a religious, medicinal, or social practice—for example, the Native American Church uses peyote for religious purposes, and cannabis is used regularly within certain areas of India and the Hindu society, whereas alcohol use is looked down upon as taboo.

Knowing the various ways that cultures and religions view substance use and abuse gives teachers clues on how to support students and families and may also help determine whether the student or family will even see the need for help or assistance. Perhaps more important for teachers is recognizing that some children come from families that model substance abuse, and perhaps even encourage it, requiring that the strategies used to address it be modified.

STRATEGIES TO SUPPORT STUDENTS

Regardless of the level of special programming available in a given school, there are steps any concerned educator can take to be supportive of children with substance-abusing parents.

Don't be afraid to ask questions. It can often be uncomfortable to ask questions about a student's personal life. As noted earlier, certain racial and ethnic minority groups may have particular difficulty discussing their personal problems. However, asking the right questions can help develop a relationship, demonstrate to the student that you care, and immediately develop a safe place for the student to discuss concerns in the future, even if he or she does not disclose any information the first time. Importantly, the primary purpose of asking questions is to help meet the needs of the student by offering an opportunity to talk and identifying the need for support, rather than playing detective. Consider asking simple questions such as:

- I've noticed you coming late a lot and looking tired or dazed. Are there any problems at home that might be keeping you up at night?
- I've noticed you have not done your work—what's the problem?
- How can I help?
- How are things?
- Tell me about a typical day after school.
- Tell me about your family.

Think practically. Work with students to think of places and times to complete homework, or have them make a list of contacts (e.g., neighbors, relatives) to call if needed after school hours, such as if the parent forgets to pick them up. Even if students never use these ideas, they will know that they have someone at school they can rely on and will feel safer with a backup plan.

Meet students' basic needs. Given the increased potential for neglect and the financial burden of substance abuse and addiction, students' basic needs for safety, hunger, and warmth may not be met at home. Thus, an educator can significantly improve a student's readiness to learn simply by providing snacks, an extra set of clothing, or school supplies. This can often be a whole-school effort rather than having educators supply these materials on their own.

Don't keep it a secret. After learning about parental substance abuse (or even a suspicion), write down the conversation and share with others in your school such as the guidance counselor, school psychologist, school social worker, administrator, and other teachers. Discuss a course of action, and consider including the student depending on his or her developmental age.

Know the law. Most states, but not all, have some laws in place that address parents who abuse substances in the home with children present. In fact, many states consider parental substance abuse as a form of child abuse or neglect.[17] Complying with the law and reporting suspicions, even if unsubstantiated, can help protect the student and yourself. The Child Welfare Information Gateway[18] provides more information on state statutes related to parental substance abuse.

Develop trust. Some children of substance-abusing parents have difficulty developing trust.[19] Trust can best be built through establishing consistent boundaries with clear expectations, requirements, and consequences. Maintaining consistent classroom policies is more relevant to establishing a productive relationship with students than being personally liked by them. Further, self-esteem can be fostered by respectful treatment, acknowledgement of positive behaviors and successes, and use of positive reinforcement instead of criticism as much as possible. Taking time to listen respectfully to a student's thoughts and interests can do a great deal toward building a positive and trusting relationship.

Know what to say. Once trust has been developed, educators may find themselves in a position where they are asked to discuss the substance abuse or dependency. Some potential comments to make may include[20]:

- Addiction is a disease. Your parent is not a bad person, although people do things they wouldn't otherwise do when they are drinking alcohol or using drugs.
- You did not cause this, and you are not responsible for curing it.
- You are not alone. There are millions of other students like you, and there are adults in the building you can talk to.

Become a source of information. Children of substance-abusing parents need and deserve accurate and age-appropriate information from their teachers. The confusion that such children experience based on their home lives can be a source of fear, confusion, and misunderstanding, sometimes leading to self-blame. Teachers can help students learn about alcoholism and drug abuse and can encourage students to accept help and to have hope. Educational materials, including classroom kits, posters, lesson plans, and pamphlets, are available from organizations such as the National Association for Children of Alcoholics, the American Council for Drug Education, and Al Anon. A full list of organizations and resources is available at the end of the chapter. Several of these organizations have affiliates in communities across the nation, with a listing of local resources available for educators, families, and youth.

Classroom teachers can infuse education about alcoholism and drug abuse across the curriculum. In science classes, there can be discussion of the physiological effects of alcohol and drugs on the body and brain. Health classes can cover the effects of these substances and their potential impact on one's life. A story or book could be read in English class in which parental alcohol or drug abuse was a theme (see resources at the end of the chapter for a list of books). When reading a book in class on this topic, consider discussing the use of the book with the identified student beforehand to see if he or she is comfortable with reading about the topic. The student may prefer to read the book independently for a book report or assignment instead.

In all classes, educators can emphasize that students facing problems with alcohol or drugs—whether with their own use or the use of others in their lives—should feel they can ask for help from any member of the staff. This is particularly important given that children with parents abusing alcohol or drugs are at greater risk themselves for substance use and abuse.

Be flexible. Allowing students to get some of their work done at school to reduce the load of homework could be beneficial and help set them up for success. In a chaotic home environment, it may be difficult or nearly impossible to find a quiet, safe, secure place to think and complete homework.

Connect with parents and other family members—even the substance-abusing ones. When teachers meet with parents, an opportunity arises for the teacher to make a positive connection that could be helpful in cases of parental substance abuse. Communication in such situations has the potential to be volatile, and the teacher can best deal with this possibility by engaging in active listening, assertive expression, and problem solving. Educators may also consider bringing other stakeholders that know the student to the meeting for support, including other family members given that they can mitigate the effects of parental substance abuse and dependency.[21] In cases of families of diverse cultural backgrounds, educators can stay sensitive to other cultures by being aware of family dynamics, understanding who the key decision makers are, and possibly drawing on colleagues with more experience in such cases.

Establishing any type of partnership with parents requires a positive relationship, and this is no less true of parents who are involved in substance abuse. Such parents may volunteer information about past struggles with substance abuse and express concern about how their child might be affected, or a parent not involved in substance abuse may express concern about a spouse who is involved in it. Helping such parents feel that they are part of a real partnership means responding to any expressions of need for support or help, offering them choices for available resources, and helping them connect with individuals or agencies they may need to contact without imposing judgment. Some substance-abusing parents may actually be actively seeking help with their addictions; therefore, educators should be ready to assist with providing resources or referrals in the community.

Familiarize yourself with evidence-based interventions. Teachers can bring hope and encouragement to families by knowing that some new interventions are highly effective. Often the parents are looking for support for their child but do not know where to turn. Being able to refer parents to various programs can be invaluable. For example, one promising intervention is the Stress Management and Alcohol Awareness Program (SMAPP),[22] which is an 8-week school-based intervention program designed for children with alcoholic parents. A related program is the school-based support group for students with addicted parents.[23]

CONCLUSION

It is clear that the problem of parental substance abuse is widespread and poses serious challenges to children and adolescents, putting them at risk for a host of problems. It is also clear that many of the solutions to these problems lie outside the reach of educators in schools. Nevertheless, there are strategies that any educator can employ to engage these students more successfully, to provide them with the optimum learning environment, and to support their efforts to meet the challenges with which they are faced. With this understanding in mind, educators can be better prepared to help these students, who are always present in their classrooms and whose success depends on an informed and caring dedication on the part of those who teach them.

NOTES

1. Clark et al., 1997; Osborne & Berger, 2009; Sher, Walitzer, Wood, & Brent, 1991.
2. Fals-Stewart, Kelley, Fincham, Golden, & Logsdon, 2004.
3. Substance Abuse and Mental Health Services Administration (SAMHSA), 2009.
4. Davies, 2010.
5. SAMHSA, 2009.
6. Breshears, Yeh, & Young, 2004.
7. McKellar, 2011.
8. ICF International, 2009; McKellar, 2011.
9. Domestic Violence/Substance Abuse Interdisciplinary Task Force, 2005.
10. ICF International, 2009.
11. ICF International, 2009.
12. Kilpatrick, Acierno, Saunders, Resnick, & Best, 2000.
13. Farmer, Donders, & Warschausky, 2006.
14. Warner, Fishbein, & Krebs, 2010.
15. Breshears et al., 2004.
16. Straussner, 2001.
17. Child Welfare Information Gateway, 2008.
18. Child Welfare Information Gateway, 2009.
19. Breshears et al., 2004.
20. Breshears et al., 2004.

21. ICF International, 2009.
22. Emshoff & Price, 1999.
23. Gance-Cleveland, 2004.

REFERENCES

Breshears, E. M., Yeh, S., & Young, N. K. (2004). *Understanding substance abuse and facilitating recovery: A guide for child welfare workers*. U.S. Department of Health and Human Services. Rockville, MD: Substance Abuse and Mental Health Services Administration.

Child Welfare Information Gateway. (2008). *What is child abuse and neglect?* U.S. Department of Health and Human Services. Retrieved from http://www.childwelfare.gov/pubs/factsheets/whatiscan.pdf

Child Welfare Information Gateway. (2009). *Parental drug use as child abuse: Summary of state laws*. Retrieved from http://www.childwelfare.gov/systemwide/laws_policies/statutes/drugexposed.pdf

Clark, D. B., Moss, H. B., Kirisci, L, Mezzich, A. C., Miles, R., & Ott, P. (1997). Psychopathology in preadolescent sons of fathers with substance use disorders. *Journal of the American Academy of Child and Adolescent Psychiatry, 36*(4), 495–502.

Davies, L. (2010). Guide to children affected by parental drug abuse. *Education Digest: Essential Readings Condensed for Quick Review, 75*, 62–64.

Domestic Violence/Substance Abuse Task Force. (2005). *Safety and sobriety: Best practices in domestic violence and substance abuse*. Springfield, IL: Illinois Department of Human Services.

Emshoff, J. G., & Price, A. W. (1999). Prevention and intervention strategies with children of alcoholics. *Pediatrics, 103*(5), 1112–1121.

Fals-Stewart, W., Kelley, M. L., Fincham, F. D., Golden, J., & Logsdon, T. (2004). Emotional and behavioral problems of children living with drug-abusing fathers: Comparisons with children living with alcohol-abusing and non-substance-abusing fathers. *Journal of Family Psychology, 18*(2), 319–330.

Farmer, J. E., Donders, J., & Warschausky, J. (2006). *Treating neurodevelopmental disabilities: Clinical research and practice*. New York, NY: Guilford Press.

Gance-Cleveland, B. (2004). Qualitative evaluation of a school-based support group for adolescents with an addicted parent. *Nursing Research, 53*(6), 379–386.

ICF International. (2009). *Protecting children in families affected by substance use disorders*. Retrieved from http://www.childwelfare.gov/pubs/usermanuals/substanceuse/substanceuse.pdf

Kilpatrick, D., Acierno, R., Saunders, B., Resnick, H., & Best, C. (2000). Risk factors for adolescent substance abuse and dependence: Data from a national sample. *Journal of Consulting and Clinical Psychology, 68*(1), 19–30.

McKellar, N. (2011). Parental drug abuse: Information for educators. In *Helping Children and Families III*. Washington, DC: National Association of School Psychologists.

Osborne, C., & Berger, L. (2009). Parental substance abuse and child well-being: A consideration of parents' gender and co residence. *Journal of Family Issues, 30*(3), 341–370.

Sher, K. J., Walitzer, K. S., Wood, P. K., & Brent, E. E. (1991). Characteristics of children of alcoholics: Putative risk factors, substance use and abuse, and psychopathology. *Journal of Abnormal Psychology, 100*(4), 427–448.

Straussner, S. L. A. (2001). Ethnocultural issues in substance abuse treatment: An overview. In S. L. A. Straussner (Ed.), *Ethnocultural factors in substance abuse treatment* (pp. 3–28). New York, NY: Guilford Press.

Substance Abuse and Mental Health Services Administration (SAMHSA). (2009). *The NSDUH report: Children living with substance-dependent or substance-abusing parents: 2002-2007.* Rockville, MD: Author.

Warner, T. D., Fishbein, D. H., & Krebs, C. P. (2010). The risk of assimilating? Alcohol use among immigrant and U. S.-born Mexican youth. *Social Science Research, 39*(1), 176–186.

WEB RESOURCES

- Al-Anon/Alateen: http://www.al-anon.alateen.org
- American Council for Drug Education: http://www.acde.org
- Center for Substance Abuse Treatment: http://www.samhsa.gov/about/csat.aspx
- Center on Addiction and the Family: http://www.coaf.org/
- Faces and Voices of Recovery: http://www.facesandvoicesofrecovery.org/
- National Association for Children of Alcoholics: http://www.nacoa.org
- National Center on Substance Abuse and Child Welfare: http://www.ncsacw.samhsa.gov
- National Council on Alcohol and Drug Dependence: http://www.ncadd.org
- National Institute on Alcohol Abuse and Alcoholism: http://www.niaaa.nih.gov
- National Institute on Drug Abuse: http://www.nida.nih.gov
- SAMHSA's publications ordering page: http://store.samhsa.gov/home
- SAMHSA's treatment program locator: http://www.findtreatment.samhsa.gov
- Talking With Kids About Tough Issues: http://www.talkingwithkids.org

SELECTED CHILDREN'S LITERATURE

- Black, C. (1997). *My dad loves me, my dad has a disease: A child's view: Living with addiction.* Denver, CO: MAC Publishing.
- Hastings, J. M., & Typpo, M. H. (1994). *An elephant in the living room—The children's book.* Center City, MN: Hazelden Foundation.
- Hornik-Beer, E. (2001). *For teenagers living with a parent who abuses alcohol/drugs.* Bloomington, IN; iUniverse, Inc.
- Sinberg, J., & Daley, D. (1989). *The I can talk about what hurts: A book for kids in homes where there's chemical dependency.* Center City, MN: Hazelden Publishing & Educational Services.
- Vigna, J. (1988). *I wish daddy didn't drink so much (An Albert Whitman Prairie Book).* Park Ridge, IL: Albert Whitman.

9

Students Exposed to Domestic Violence

DESERI A. BURGESS AND LISA WEED PHIFER ■

INTRODUCTION

Domestic violence refers to a pattern of assaultive and coercive behaviors that adults use against their intimate partners.[1] It has many different forms, ranging from physical to psychological abuse, and can be minor to severe in nature. Domestic violence occurs across all levels of socioeconomic status, race, ethnicity, culture, and religion; however, it typically co-occurs with other risk factors or stressors such as poverty, child abuse, parental substance abuse, unemployment, homelessness, and involvement in crime.[2]

More than half of women who have experienced domestic violence have children younger than the age of 12.[3] Taken further, approximately 40% to 50% of children from homes with domestic violence have reported witnessing the abuse.[4] Aside from the myriad consequences of witnessing domestic abuse, these children are also at greater risk of being neglected or abused themselves.[5] In fact, an estimated 45% to 70% of children who witness domestic abuse are also physically abused,[6] either by the abusive or the abused parent.

Dealing with the aftermath of domestic abuse can be devastating for children as they are left to deal with distressed parents, potential injuries, changes in their family system (e.g., living with extended family or foster care), and possibly parental incarceration. In addition, domestic violence can negatively impact parenting styles. For instance, the parent victim may be overly authoritarian (overly controlling) or, in contrast, overly permissive, afraid to discipline the child due to guilt for exposing the child to such abuse. The parent may also be burdened with psychological stress from the violence, leading to depression or mental or physical problems, thus reducing his or her capacities as a parent.[7] The effects of domestic violence can then trickle into the classroom—children may come to school hungry or tired and may not have their homework completed. They are also more likely to have attendance issues and academic difficulties and are more at risk for dropping out.[8] The vignette provides an example of a young student's experience with domestic abuse.

Vignette—Donald

Donald, an 8-year-old student in the second grade, lived in a very volatile household with his mother and stepfather. Some nights, when his step-father would come home from work, his stepfather would verbally and physically abuse his mother. When this occurred, Donald often hid in his room; otherwise, he was at risk of being berated as well. He would turn up the music or put his hands over his ears, although it was terribly difficult to concentrate on schoolwork, let alone get any rest. There were good days when his stepfather worked late, and even some days when his stepfather came home in a good mood. On these days, his mother would help him with his homework, play games, and even make him dinner. Other nights, however, Donald was on his own; he would not do his homework and sometimes did not have dinner, causing him to arrive at school the next day hungry and without his work.

Donald felt ashamed, sad, helpless, angry, and scared. Instead of crying, he would just hold his anger inside and explode when he got to school. His behaviors in school became increasingly unpredictable, and he sometimes became insubordinate or would lie when teachers confronted him about his missing homework. As each school day came to an end, Donald often wondered what the evening had in store for him.

The impact of domestic violence on children spreads along a continuum depending on many variables, including type of exposure, gender, age, developmental level, and resiliency factors. The child's enmeshment with the dysfunction of the household may impact the ability to cope. Some children witness the violence from afar or only hear about it, whereas others see it firsthand almost daily. Some children may try to intervene by protecting the other parent, whereas others are abused themselves. Similarly, some children are able to recover quickly from their exposure, while others struggle with the effects throughout adulthood. It is imperative that educators understand that not all children respond the same to witnessing domestic violence, and they should be prepared to deal with a variety of symptoms that may present in the classroom.

DEVELOPMENTAL CONSIDERATIONS

Attachment in children is developed over time through a pattern of responses from their caregivers. In homes affected by domestic violence, attachment between the parent and child can be significantly impacted. For instance, parent victims of domestic violence are more prone to having an insecure attachment style with their children.[9] A child's relationships with his or her parents are also influenced by the degree of the violence, whether he or she was also abused, and when it occurred.[10] Accordingly, the bonds developed between teachers and students throughout the year can help promote positive, secure attachments and social-emotional growth when such relationships are not available at home.

Not all children who witness domestic violence have attachment issues; however, many have difficulty understanding and processing what they have seen. As a result, they may internalize the experience.[11] Some young children, for example, may not understand the cause of the violence and may blame themselves, leading to feelings of guilt, worry, and anxiety. Younger children may not have the vocabulary to express their feelings, and therefore any distress will manifest as behaviors such as whining, clinginess, sleeping difficulties, anxiety, crying, physical complaints to escape situations, or difficulties paying attention.

Older children are better able to express their emotions; thus, while they may experience similar reactions as younger children, they are also more likely to withdraw from their peers, have lower self-esteem, or demonstrate externalizing behaviors such as aggression or rule breaking.[12] In fact, children and adolescents exposed to domestic violence and marital violence for 75% or more of their lives showed significantly more externalizing problems than nonexposed children or those exposed to less than that amount.[13] Research has shown that repeated exposure to domestic violence can also increase the risk of depressive symptoms later on in life.[14]

Teachers should also be aware of other potential consequences of domestic violence, including fear, guilt, separation, and regression of skills or behavior.[15] Research has shown that the impact of domestic violence can also spill over to peers in the classroom, impacting test scores and classroom behavior.[16]

CULTURAL CONSIDERATIONS

Domestic violence can occur in families of any culture, although the way families deal with the violence can be heavily impacted by their cultural background. Some parents are able to seek out support and are open to discussing problems with the school, whereas others are more secretive. Depending on their own beliefs, families may have difficulties reaching out for support as easily as others due to feelings of guilt, shame, language barriers, fear of ridicule, or the potential for police involvement. Other families may not view domestic violence as a problem in need of fixing, including those with a history of domestic abuse from previous generations.

When discussing culture and domestic violence, it is important to understand that culture is also influenced by religion, ethnicity, and socioeconomic status.[17] Victims' responses to domestic violence can be heavily dependent on their beliefs and existing roles in their communities. For women in particular, the ability to address domestic violence may be based on whether they believe they can put their own needs above their family's needs.[18] For instance, in patriarchal families, the man is in control of the household, leaving the woman more inferior. Women believe that it is their role to keep the family together.[19] This leads to a certain level of tolerance to violence because of their strong devotion to their family.[20] Domestic violence can also be associated with shame,[21] which may also lead to a greater level of tolerance of violence to avoid experiencing community shame and embarrassment. Certainly, it's also common for some individuals not to report domestic abuse simply out of fear of retaliation from the abusing partner. Educators should be aware that different families will respond to domestic violence in different ways.

STRATEGIES TO SUPPORT STUDENTS

Educators can provide significant support to students (and families) who have experienced domestic abuse, from offering stable adult relationships for the children to reporting the abuse to authorities if needed. The classroom can function as a safe haven where these children can develop resiliency, learn to express emotions in appropriate ways, and develop positive relationships with others. Unfortunately, educators often may not know if students have been exposed to domestic violence.

Be prepared for varied methods of disclosure. It is natural for students exposed to domestic violence to express what happened to them in indirect ways. Young children, for example, may draw pictures illustrating an event that went on at home or enact domestic violence during playtime. Others may disclose witnessing domestic violence through journals or conversations with other students. If this occurs, consider following up with the student with open-ended questions such as "Tell me more about that," or "What do you do when you see this happening?" or "When have you seen things like this?" Importantly, do not pressure the child to talk—follow the child's lead. Also, be sure not to offer advice or share personal experiences of your own; your objective is to listen and be attentive to the student's needs.

Consult with professionals in your school building. Consult with your guidance counselor, school social worker, school psychologist, and school administrator when a child discloses information about domestic violence. The majority of children speak the truth, especially when they are disclosing something scary or hurtful. However, it is possible for children to fabricate or elaborate on details.

As educators, students' safety comes first, but be careful not to jump to conclusions. Consulting with other professionals in the building will help you sort through the information and decide on the most appropriate steps to take to support the student.

Know the law. An educator must report any suspicion of child abuse, neglect, or maltreatment. Further, many states have enacted specific legislation protecting children from domestic abuse. Domestic violence can be reportable when the educator believes that it is compromising a student's level of care within the home. Some examples include physical marks, hunger, hygiene, or attendance. As a mandated reporter, you may be required to complete time-sensitive paperwork. Educators can visit the Child Welfare Information Gateway (http://www.childwelfare.gov) or Child Help (http://www.childhelp.org) for more information. Some basic facts regarding mandated reporting include:

- All school employees are required by law to report any child who is being abused or neglected or has been subjected to abuse or neglect.
- Specifics about reporting vary state to state, so educators must be aware of policies in their districts and the state they work in.
- Reports must be made immediately to your supervisor and/or to Child Protective Services.
- Laws protect anyone who reports suspected abuse or neglect in good faith.
- Educators who fail to report abuse could lose their credentials.

Be honest. When talking with students, be honest and tell them that you may need to discuss this information with the principal or other authorities, and discuss what they may expect (e.g., "Someone from Child Protective Services will come to school and ask you some questions. Just be honest—you are not in trouble."). This may be particularly important when a child asks you not to tell anyone—your honesty and willingness to take charge of the situation will be appreciated even if telling the authorities goes against the child's wishes.

Document, document, document. Always document all conversations or examples of evidence that suggest domestic violence. This will be important to protect yourself and the child if you must report the abuse to authorities.

Provide structure and a sense of security. Children living in domestically abusive homes yearn for safety, predictability, and structure. Many come to school worrying whether a parent is coming home that night, if they will be able to sleep, if members of their family will be safe, or in some cases whether they are going to be victimized themselves. To help establish feelings of security, a personalized safety plan can be created with the student, teacher, parent, and guidance counselor. The purpose of a safety plan is to identify strategies children can use to cope when they feel anxiety or stress. This may include determining individuals or hotlines they can call, places they can go, or activities they can do within their room.

Validate and reassure the student. Upon hearing of students' experiences at home, mention you are glad they told you about the situation. Validate feelings with statements such as "That must have been frightening," or "It must be difficult to see that happening." Assure students that the violence is not their fault, nobody deserves to be hurt, and that at least when in school or in your classroom, they are safe and will be taken care of.

Only make promises you can keep. While important to reassure a child's safety, be sure not to make promises about safety that cannot be kept, such as "I won't let anyone else hurt you again." Educators may feel compelled to say such things to make a child feel better; however, such promises, if unfulfilled, can lead to distrust, feelings of helplessness, and a reduced chance of the child talking to a trusted adult in the future.

Do not blame or criticize the abusing parent. Despite a child's anger toward an abusing parent, he or she may still maintain a family loyalty and a love for that parent. Such mixed feelings are quite common. Criticizing the abusing parent may cause the student to not feel comfortable disclosing family business to an educator in the future or to actually express anger toward you instead.

Know the triggers. Keep in mind that certain events in school such as fights, raised voices, loud noises, or even school programs that talk about violence can cause heightened levels of stress, resulting in negative behaviors, emotional outbursts, or even flashbacks of events experienced at home. If this occurs, consider removing the student from the situation to a calm, relaxing area with a trusted adult.

Use a daily check-in. Consider having a short meeting each morning to check in with students (can be with all students or only certain students), asking about how the previous evening went, if they got enough sleep, and if they had breakfast. This serves several purposes; first, a teacher can get an idea of how a student's behavior might be for the day; second, it allows the student an opportunity to talk with a trusted adult; and finally, it provides a foundation for a caring relationship between the child and another adult.

Teach problem-solving skills. Children, particularly younger children, learn how to solve problems and negotiate conflict by observing adults. Thus, when witnessing domestic abuse, children may view violence as a means of resolving conflict with others, which may lead to excessive aggression with peers at school. This may also lead to confusion as adults may be telling the child not to hit others while the child witnesses adults using aggression toward one another (i.e., "Do as I say, not as I do."). While educators may feel they are swimming upstream at times, it is important to help children consider other alternatives to addressing conflicts. Importantly, set clear limits and boundaries on what is acceptable behavior in school.

Monitor attendance. Students who have witnessed violence at home may be fearful of leaving their parent during the school day. Students may refuse to come to school or fake illnesses such as a headache, pain, or an upset stomach to avoid coming to school. Other students enjoy coming to school but are consistently tardy. These students may be tardy because they must get themselves to school with minimal parental support, or they may oversleep due to being kept awake the night before. Whatever the reason, it is imperative that teachers monitor and report any changes in attendance to other school members and parents. Even with knowledge of domestic abuse occurring at home, students should still be made aware of their expectations for attendance.

Communicate concerns with parents. As with all families, establish a positive relationship with parents before there is a problem in school. If possible, send positive notes home or have a conference with the parent at the beginning of the year to help build rapport with the family. If the parents view the school as supportive, they will be more cooperative when there is a problem. When talking to the parents, express your concerns as they relate to the student's progress in school and invite them to come to school to discuss the concerns. Remember, parents need safe environments to talk just as students do. Consider asking questions such as "Do you have any ideas why [name] may be acting this way?" or "Is there something at home that may be upsetting him/her?"

CONCLUSION

Domestic violence occurs between adults; however, children in the household are victims as well. Not only do these children often witness physical or psychological abuse of their parent, but also they are often neglected or abused themselves. Children often struggle with feelings of guilt, fear, or anger and learn inappropriate methods of dealing with stress and conflict. They are unable to control events in their home lives and as a result demonstrate challenging behaviors in the classroom. A child's ability to cope with domestic violence can impact his or her social-emotional functioning and academic functioning, as well as the academic performance of their peers.

Teachers are generally the first school staff to notice changes in behavior or decreased attendance or to have a student disclose violence to them through schoolwork, drawings, or conversation. Given that educators are sometimes the most trusted and respected adults in a child's life, particularly those witnessing domestic abuse at home, educators can and should be prepared to provide support to children witnessing domestic violence by following the recommendations within this chapter.

NOTES

1. Holden, 2003.
2. Buckley, Holt, & Whelan, 2007.

3. Catalano, 2007.
4. Edelson, 2003; Holden, 2003.
5. Chang, Theodore, Martin, & Runyan, 2008; Strauss, Gelles, & Smith, 1990.
6. Holt, Buckley, & Whelan, 2008.
7. Cunningham & Baker, 2007.
8. Volpe, 1996.
9. Rodriguez, 2006.
10. Sternberg, Lamb, Guterman, Abbott, & Dawud-Noursi, 2005.
11. Fantazzo & Mohr, 1999.
12. Volpe, 1996.
13. Gewirtz & Edelson, 2007.
14. Russell, Springer, & Greenfield, 2010.
15. Cohen & Knitzer, 2004.
16. Carrell & Hoekstra, 2010.
17. Bent-Goodley, 2005.
18. Yoshioka & Choi, 2005.
19. Robinson, 2003.
20. Bauer, Rodriguez, Quiroga, & Flores-Ortiz, 2000.
21. Bauer et al., 2000.

REFERENCES

Bauer, H., Rodriguez, M., Quiroga, S. S., & Flores-Ortiz, Y. (2000). Barriers to health care for abused Latina and Asian immigrant women. *Journal of Health Care for the Poor and Underserved, 11*, 33–44.

Bent-Goodley, T. (2005). Culture and domestic violence: Transforming knowledge development. *Journal of Interpersonal Violence, 20*, 195–203.

Buckley, H., Holt, S., & Whelan, S. (2007). Listen to me! Children's experiences of domestic violence. *Child Abuse Review, 16*, 296–310.

Carrell, S., & Hoekstra, M. (2010). Externalities in the classroom: How children exposed to domestic violence affect everyone's kids. *American Economic Journal: Applied Economics, American Economic Association, 2*, 211–28.

Catalano, S. (2007). *Intimate partner violence in the United States.* U.S. Department of Justice, Bureau of Justice Statistics. Retrieved from http://bjs.ojp.usdoj.gov/content/pub/pdf/ipvus.pdf

Chang, J., Theodore, A., Martin, S., & Runyan, D. (2008). Psychological abuse between parents: Associations with child maltreatment from a population-based sample. *Child Abuse & Neglect, 32*, 819–829.

Cohen, E., & Knitzer, J. (2004). *Young children living with domestic violence: The role of early childhood programs.* National Center for Children Exposed to Violence. Iowa City, IA: University of Iowa. Retrieved from http://www.nccev.org/pdfs/series_paper2.pdf

Cunningham, A., & Baker, L. (2007). *Little eyes, little ears: How violence against a mother shapes children as they grow.* Center for Children and Families in the Justice System. Retrieved from http://www.lfcc.on.ca/little_eyes_little_ears.html

Edelson, J. L. (2003). How children are involved in adult domestic violence. *Journal of Violence, 18*, 18–32.

Fantazzo, J., & Mohr, W. (1999). Prevalence and effects of children exposure to domestic violence. *The Future of Children, 9*, 21–32.

Gewirtz, A. H., & Edelson, J. L. (2007). Young children's exposure to intimate partner violence: Towards a developmental risk and resilience framework for research and intervention. *Journal of Family Violence, 22*, 151–163.

Holden, G. W. (2003). Children exposed to domestic violence and child abuse: Terminology and taxonomy. *Clinical Child and Family Psychology Review, 6*, 151–160.

Holt, S., Buckley, H., & Whelan, S. (2008). The impact of exposure to domestic violence on children and young people: A review of the literature. *Child Abuse and Neglect, 32*, 797–810.

Robinson, G. (2003). Current concepts in domestic violence. *Primary Psychiatry, 10*, 48–52.

Rodriguez, C. (2006). Emotional functioning, attachment style and attributions as predictors of child abuse potential in domestic violence victims. *Violence and Victims, 21*, 199–212.

Russell, D., Springer, K., & Greenfield, E. (2010). Witnessing domestic abuse in childhood as an independent risk for depressive symptoms in young adulthood. *Child Abuse & Neglect, 34*, 448–453.

Sternberg, K., Lamb, M., Guterman, E., Abbott, C., & Dawud-Noursi, S. (2005). Adolescents' perceptions of attachments to their mothers and fathers in families with histories of domestic violence: A longitudinal perspective. *Child Abuse & Neglect, 29*, 853–869.

Strauss, M. A., Gelles, R. J., & Smith, C. (1990). *Physical violence in American families: Risk factors and adaptations to violence in 8,145 families.* New Brunswick, NJ: Transaction Publishers.

Volpe, J. (1996). *Effects of domestic violence on children and adolescents: An overview.* Retrieved from http://www.aaets.org/arts/art8.htm

Yoshioka, M., & Choi, D. (2005). Culture and interpersonal violence research. *Journal of Interpersonal Violence, 20*, 513–519.

WEB RESOURCES

- Child Help: http://www.childhelp.org
- Child Welfare Information Gateway: http://www.childwelfare.gov
- Family Violence Prevention Fund: http://www.endabuse.com
- National Center for Children Exposed to Violence: http://www.nccev.org
- National Coalition against Domestic Violence: http://www.ncadv.org
- The National Domestic Abuse Hotline: http://www.thehotline.org
- The Safe Start Center: http://www.safestartcenter.org

SELECTED CHILDREN'S LITERATURE

- Bernstein, S. C. (1991). *A family that fights.* Morton Grove, IL: Albert Whitman.
- Holmes, M. (2000). *A terrible thing happened.* Washington, DC: American Psychological Association.

- Loftis, C. (1997). *The words hurt.* Far Hills, NJ: New Horizon Press.
- Parr, T. (2009). *The feel good book.* New York, NY: Little Brown Books for Young Readers.
- Poole, J. S. (2011). *The cryin' house: A story for children who witness family violence.* Clarksville, TN: Path Life Coaching.
- Watts, G. (2009). *Hear my roar: A story of family violence.* Buffalo, NY: Annick Press.
- See   http://www.mincava.umn.edu/documents/bibs/kearney2/kearney2.html   for additional resources.

10

Students Anticipating the Death of a Family Member or Loved One

JARENA G. FLEISCHMAN ■

INTRODUCTION

Experiencing loss through death is a natural part of living; adults know this, but some children do not. Unfortunately, many children each year must live through this experience, often resulting in symptoms of grief and trauma. The American Cancer Society estimates that about one-third of patients with cancer have school-aged or adolescent children,[1] and an estimated more than 2 million children and adolescents younger than 18 years have experienced the death of a parent.[2] Thus, educators frequently will encounter children who have experienced the death of an immediate family member. When this occurs, the child is forced to confront the concept of death. Surviving parents, extended family members, teachers, and school-based professionals are in a position to help the child navigate through the processes of bereavement, grief, and mourning.

It is important to differentiate between expected death (e.g., terminal illnesses such as cancer, which remains among the leading causes of death worldwide; coma from an automobile accident; terminal birth defect of a sibling) and unexpected death (e.g., fatal accident, homicide, suicide, heart attack; see chapter 11). Certainly some overlap exists between the two types relating to a child's developmental age and general reactions to death. However, in the case of sudden death, a child misses the opportunity to say goodbye, whereas with an expected death, a child often has the opportunity to say goodbye during the period leading up to the death. In this regard, it may seem that children would adapt more proactively to an expected death, although they may have had to endure weeks, months, and possibly even years of seeing their loved one suffer from an illness while also having their own needs put aside. As a result, the effects of awaiting a death could seriously disrupt children's emotional, academic, and cognitive development.[3]

Anticipatory Grief

Years can pass by from the time a diagnosis is made until the actual death. During this time, periods of improvement may be seen and new medications or treatments may be tried when others have failed, allowing loved ones to maintain hope of a healthy outcome. In spite of this hope, family members and loved ones often experience grief prior to the anticipated death, which is often referred to as *anticipatory grief*. Anticipatory grief is not a substitute for postdeath grieving, nor will it guarantee that postdeath grieving will be easier or less severe. In many cases the school has been informed, although in other cases school-based personnel are the last to find out and will often learn of the situation after noting sudden changes in a child's behavior and reaching out to the family.

The vignette provided is a real-life example of the academic, social, and emotional outcomes that occurred during and following an expected death in a child's life.

VIGNETTE—ALYSON

Alyson, a 10th grader, age 15, reflects back on her time of bereavement and mourning.

I remember the day they [her parents] brought us [Alyson and her sister] up to mom's room and they told us it was cancer. I was 7 years old. I always knew there was a possibility she could die but I would always push that thought out of my mind. I watched my mom get thinner and weaker for almost 3 years until she finally died. My parents kept us informed. When the treatments, surgeries, and medications didn't work and her cancer came back, my parents would order pizza and we would eat it together in the living room. We hoped it would be good news but it always wasn't. I used to dream of the day they'd order pizza and we would go in there and they would say the cancer is gone and everything was going to be OK. I always held onto hope that the doctors would find the right medication, but I also knew there were only so many things they could try.

My sense of hope stayed to the very end because I was a kid and I couldn't see my mom not being there. The person I was closest to was my mom, and I wasn't ready to let myself think about her not being there. To an extent in my 7-, 8-, and 9-year-old mind I believed if I thought about mom dying then I would jinx her and it might actually happen so I avoided thinking about her actually dying. The last few weeks before she died, when I would go into her room, I would break down because I knew she was dying and there was absolutely nothing I could do. I never really got to say good-bye because we never really knew exactly when it was going to happen. I just remember my dad coming into where my sister and I were and I could tell by the look on his face and the tears in his eyes that she was gone. We all hugged each other and then I went to my room. Later, grandpa came up and talked to me but I don't remember what he said or anything else about that day. I try not to remember that day—it hurts too much. I remember crying a lot of nights in my room.

If I needed to talk I knew I could always talk to my dad, my grandparents, my aunt and uncle, or my mom's best friend. I talked a lot to my counselor at school. She never forced me to talk about my mom unless I wanted to and I always knew she would listen to me and not judge me. Sometimes I would just go see her to get away from class and be in a quiet place away from everybody. I knew my teachers were there for me, too. I never talked to my friends about my mom's death until seventh grade. Now that 5 years have passed I can say that I'm not in constant turmoil anymore. I get really upset when my friends say their lives suck or they hate their moms. I know they don't mean it but if my mom were here right now I would never say that. I would give anything to have my mom here with me.

I feel like there were a lot of unsaid things that I should have said. I wish I would have gone in her room during those last weeks to see her more but I just couldn't because I couldn't maintain my composure. Instead, I was playing my stupid video games that 9-year-olds play and I should've been spending more time with her. I regret that a lot. I remember being an ignorant little child and I didn't give her the respect she deserved. I also think I gave her more crap then I should have. I remember being upset sometimes because she couldn't go outside and play with me. I knew she couldn't but I wanted her to anyway and this probably hurt her. I should have cut her a little more slack. I wish during those 3 years when I was 7, 8, and 9 years old that I would have been more aware, that I would have known what I know now, because I would have behaved differently.

This vignette portrays how one child navigated through this process. Interestingly, Alyson did not talk about the death much at school, and instead often withdrew from classes or preferred to talk to a trusted adult. Many students like Alyson will not talk about their experiences or are unable to express their emotions. This further supports the importance of not simply assuming a student's behavior is due to an underlying disability, problem with authority, or lack of motivation—instead, educators can benefit from understanding common reactions or signs of distress and using that to determine when to reach out to a student's family.

DEVELOPMENTAL CONSIDERATIONS

The death of a loved one can change much of what a child knew existed before the death, including trust and predictability about the future. The child is desperately trying to process and understand the concept and finality of death. The amount of information a child is able to comprehend depends on several factors, including developmental age, maturity level, and personality. Table 10.1 presents common reactions children may experience when faced with the anticipated death of a loved one.[4] However, it is important to acknowledge that children and adolescents react and grieve in their own unique way to an anticipated death.

FAMILY AND CULTURAL CONSIDERATIONS

Research has shown that the most important protective factor for children and adolescents who experience the loss of an immediate family member is how well the surviving parents attends to their own grief and to the grief of their children.[5] Healing occurs best when there are continuous positive interactions with family and others throughout the process of the family member's illness, death,

Table 10.1 COMMON REACTIONS WHILE ANTICIPATING A DEATH

Grade	Reactions
Preschool	• Ability to "sense" separation • Increase in irritability, especially if the primary caregiver is sad or unable to play with or care for them • Sleep disturbances • Sluggish demeanor • Decrease in activity level • Decrease in appetite • Above symptoms usually occur due to routine changes
Preschool–early elementary school	• May continue to have above-mentioned characteristics • Separation anxiety and clinginess • Somatic complaints that may be similar to the ill family member • Irritable and upset if ill family member can't interact with them in play such as throwing a ball (egocentric nature of this developmental stage) • Regressive behaviors (thumb sucking, baby talk) • Night terrors or nightmares • Increase in temper tantrums • Withdrawal from siblings and peers • Attention-seeking behaviors • Express distress through drawings, fantasy, or pretend play rather than through words
Elementary— middle school	• May continue to experience above-mentioned characteristics, particularly sleep disturbances, vivid dreams or nightmares about the loved one, appetite issues, and attention-seeking behaviors • Can anticipate a death and feel sad about the future loss

(continued)

Table 10.1 (CONTINUED)

Grade	Reactions
	• May focus on themselves and display an uncaring attitude toward the terminally ill family member (egocentric behavior)
	• Younger children in this stage may not confide in peers about the terminally ill family member's status
	• If the parent is ill, children may withdraw from the parent or both parents due to a desire for more independence yet may inwardly yearn for them
	• Avoidance of emotions by turning to school, peers, or sports
	• Drop in grades
	• Intense, increased emotions
	• Magical thinking (e.g., thinking the ill individual will magically get better)
	• A desire to know detailed information about the illness even though they may not be able to fully understand abstract concepts
Secondary school	• May continue to experience above-mentioned characteristics
	• May show more sophisticated understanding regarding the family member's illness than earlier stages
	• Show distress and grieve more like an adult would
	• Young teens may want to distance themselves due to natural developmental changes (desire for independence) yet struggle with the desire to want to remain engaged with the terminal individual
	• May try to hide feelings and emotions
	• Desire more privacy and alone time; may leave the room to cry
	• Depression
	• May desire to talk to their peers or other nonrelated adults (this can be difficult for parents to accept)
	• Younger teens may seem callous and lack empathy due to egocentric behavior
	• Avoidance of feelings by distracting themselves with schoolwork or other activities
	• Excessive interest in terminal illnesses and/or death
	• Increased externalizing behaviors (e.g., oppositional, argumentative, demanding, emotional withdrawal, anger, risk-taking behavior)
	• May seek out individuals who have gone through similar experiences (school grief groups)

*Note: Refer to Table 11.1 in chapter 11, which discusses a child's typical understanding and common reactions to death regardless of whether the death was anticipated or sudden.

and postdeath. The interactions during the illness should inform, prepare, and guide the child as the anticipated death approaches. Equally important are interactions that offer encouragement, support, solace, meaning, and value to the child's experience.[6] Not surprisingly, educators can provide significant support to their students in this regard.

During the anticipated death of a sibling, teachers should watch for signs of parents placing unfair expectations or responsibilities on the surviving children. Older children may be forced to help care for younger siblings or help earn money given the costs for medical care or the loss of income when the parent can no longer work. In addition, following a sibling's death, surviving children may feel a need to be like their deceased sibling in hopes of helping their parents feel better. If a teacher suspects either of these situations are occurring, then it would be in the child's best interest if the teacher discussed these concerns with the school counselor, school social worker, or school psychologist to determine if contact should be made with the parents.

Cultural aspects of death and grieving should also be taken into consideration. Rituals for grieving can vary considerably across cultures. For example, in parts of Asia and India, there is widespread belief that individuals diagnosed with a terminal illness, especially a minor or an elderly person, may place a great emotional burden on themselves, thus expediting the death. Therefore, in a situation in which absolute truth about a diagnosis may harm the receiver, some cultures prefer a pragmatic lie. Euthanasia, also called mercy killing, is another practice accepted by some religions, such as the Hindu sect of Jainism,[7] and refers to the voluntarily ending of one's life instead of allowing the individual to suffer from an incurable and often painful disease or illness. On the other hand, Confucianism beliefs include acceptance that pain is an essential part of life, a "trial" or a "sacrifice"; therefore, when an individual suffers with pain, he or she will often choose to endure the pain until it is unbearable before reporting it to a physician. In Japan, some religious rituals expect survivors to maintain contact with the deceased. Families may keep an altar in their homes that is dedicated to their lost loved ones; they may offer them food and talk to the altar as if they were talking to their deceased loved ones. In contrast, the Hopi (Native American tribe) fear the spirits of the deceased and try to quickly forget those who have died. Understanding the various cultural and religious rituals associated with death may help educators support their students and families—at the very least, educators can recognize that not all individuals grieve in similar ways. See Table 11.3 in chapter 11 for more information on cultural and religious differences.

STRATEGIES TO SUPPORT STUDENTS

What the School Can Do Before Learning of a Student's Grief

Schools should be prepared to educate and support teachers in their daily interactions with bereaved students. It is important to offer in-service training for staff on issues of loss and grief before it is needed. Teachers may feel unprepared to address death due to a lack of knowledge and skills or because of their own anxious feelings or previous experiences. Training in this sensitive area is crucial for teachers and school-based professionals as it enhances their ability to educate traumatized, grieving students effectively. Teachers need to feel comfortable with the topic of death and grief *before* they encounter a bereaved student. Unfortunately, a student's grief is often disclosed without prior warning.

Establish a bereavement fund for students and staff who experience the loss of an immediate family member. This money could be part of the school's budget or a collection from school staff and parents. Monies could be used to purchase flowers and cards to send to the funeral home or sympathy cards to send directly to the family or child. The bereavement fund could be used in a multitude of ways to allow the staff, teachers, and classmates a way to express their care and concern for the student, family, or staff member. (See chapter 11 for information regarding memorials.)

Use teachable moments to educate your class about death within the context of everyday instruction (e.g., death of a class pet, death of a character in a book). For example, one of your students entered your classroom upset about his 15-year-old dog that died peacefully in his sleep last night of "old age." This real-life example would afford the educator the opportunity to do a death education lesson on the cycle of life and to explain to the class that all living things—plants, animals, and people—have a life cycle. Two excellent books to incorporate into the lesson would be *Lifetimes* by Bryan Mellonie and *Saying Goodbye to Lulu* by Corinne Demas.

To some it may sound somewhat morbid to teach students about grief and death. The goal, however, is to allow students the freedom to think about and discuss death through a nonthreatening activity. It also gives teachers the chance to assess their students and gain knowledge into what experiences they may already have regarding loss through death.

During the Terminal Stage of the Illness

Being told your loved one has a terminal illness indicates physicians have diagnosed the individual with a disease that cannot be cured or adequately treated and there is a reasonable expectation the individual will experience death as a result of the disease. The final stage of terminal illness, called the *terminal stage*, reflects a time when the ill individual is expected to die soon, usually within 6 months. Research has shown the terminal stage is often the most difficult for school-aged children.[8]

Prepare for separation anxiety. Some children may become anxious when it is time to separate from their caregiver(s) when arriving at school. Separation anxiety can occur for many different reasons; one in particular is the fear of losing their caregiver while they are apart. See chapter 11 for specific strategies on addressing separation anxiety. While separation anxiety is often best dealt with by having the student stay in school as typically planned, be sure to respect the wishes of the family if they prefer to have the child spend more time with the ill family member.

Keep in close contact with the spokesperson for the family. The healthy caregiver, sometimes a grandparent or even a close family friend, is a great resource to keep current of how the ill family member is doing, because the child may not readily share this information. Let the spokesperson know you would like advanced notice if the child may have a difficult day at school due to what occurred at home or at the hospital the night before. This contact is equally important for the caregiver to let him or her know about any changes in behavior that may occur at school or to simply maintain the important relationship between school and home. This relationship also takes the burden off the child to be a source of information.

Maintain a predictable routine. Routine, structure, and knowing what to expect help provide a sense of security and control in school, unlike what may be experienced at home. Life at home can be stressful, frightening, and very unpredictable during the terminal stage, leaving some children feeling powerless and out of control. The ill family member may feel sick from radiation treatments, be angry or irritable because he or she does not feel well, or need to be rushed to the hospital in the middle of the night. It is ideal to continue with the same expectations (e.g., behavior, following classroom rules, spelling test every Friday) that were in place for the child before the family member became sick, thereby fostering a sense of normalcy, predictability, and security. However, it should be clearly articulated to the child and caregiver that reasonable modifications can be made if the student becomes overwhelmed. Allowing the student to have a voice and to be part of the decision-making process can help empower the child and create a sense of control over one aspect of his or her world.

Know the student's triggers and avoid them when possible. Sometimes children react in an unusual or profound way when something triggers a memory or reminds them of a scary or traumatic event or of their loved one who is ill. A trigger could be reviewing a topic in a class related to the loved one's illness (e.g., cancer), a friend asking the student about the family member, or school-wide events that typically encourage parental involvement. Sometimes it takes investigative action and frequent documentation from an educator to help the child discover what may be triggering emotions and reactions.

Encourage students to write or draw pictures in a journal, which can be very helpful and therapeutic for children and adolescents during this stage. The child may find it easier to express inner feelings through writing or drawing. Very young children could draw faces to show how they are feeling, whereas older children and teens may choose to write details depicting what is transpiring in their life at that moment in time. If the student chooses to share the journal, ask if it is okay to respond back either in writing or with conversation. Back-and-forth journaling can be a powerful way to make a positive impact. It can also help the student express feelings and emotions, release stress, and sort through emotional confusion.

Once the Anticipated Death Has Occurred

Following an actual death, children or adolescents may experience numbness and not be able to believe their loved one has actually died. This initial shock may soon give way and be replaced with waves of intense emotions such as sadness, loneliness, anger, confusion, fear, or an overwhelming sense of missing their loved one. Children may blame others, themselves, or a higher power for their loved one's death. It is not unusual for children to feel guilty, believing they should have been the one to die (especially so in the case of a sibling's death). They may feel guilt about times they disappointed or argued with the deceased loved one. Younger children may describe their painful feelings as being an "achy feeling" on the inside. Any response from crying to laughing is considered normal.

Some students may voice a sense of relief that their loved one has finally died and is no longer in pain. For example, a seventh-grade boy once revealed to this author, "It was more painful seeing my mom lying in bed, turning yellow and struggling for each breath then it is now seeing her laying peacefully in this casket. I know she is pain free and in a better place." Similarly, a sixth-grade girl voiced her relief shortly after her father's death by stating, "Maybe now my life will get back to normal." Understanding and listening to the deep feelings of children can be difficult. Think about how you would respond to Alyson (see vignette).

A common experience for most children, whether following the death of a parent or sibling, is survivor's guilt, especially if the predeath relationship was ambivalent. In the vignette, Alyson verbalizes feelings of guilt, wishing she would have visited her mother more during her last days even though seeing her mother in the state she was in was unbearable to her. She carries feelings of guilt about playing too many video games during the terminal stage of her mother's illness, not realizing the video games served as a coping strategy during this difficult time. She clearly remembers and harbors regret for what she believes are misbehaviors on her part, again not fully understanding that what she considers "giving her mom crap" was most likely typical childhood coping behaviors during an extremely stressful time in her life.

Offer reassurances. Surviving children may need someone to explain to them that when we have close, loving relationships with others, especially our family members, it is virtually impossible to not experience disagreements, arguments, and disappointment in those individuals, even those we love the most. Reassurance that this is normal can keep the child from clinging to unnecessary guilt about past behaviors and incidences that occurred with the deceased loved one.

Consistent reassurance also needs to be given to children that their thoughts, actions, or words had absolutely no bearing on their loved one's circumstances or outcomes. Finally, educators can reassure students' safety and that they will continue to be cared for by the adults in their lives, including the adults at school.

Make contact with the bereaved student and family before the child returns to school. Ask what information is to be shared or not shared with the affected student, other students in the class, and staff (e.g., cause of death, funeral arrangements). Be sensitive to the family's privacy and honor their wishes and directives. Consider collaborating with other educators and support personnel in the school building about how information should be shared with others. Also, while it may seem unimportant given the circumstances, discuss strategies for reintegrating the student into the curriculum.

Do not impose your own beliefs. While you may feel strongly about what happens after individuals pass away (e.g., go to heaven or hell), do not discuss or impose these beliefs on children without first consulting with parents. Even though you may believe your understanding can help children cope, if they receive conflicting messages from their parents they can feel confused, anxious, and less trusting of adults.

Consider attending the visitation or funeral. It is extremely painful for students to have the death of a family member ignored, especially by individuals who were aware of the child's situation and what the inevitable outcome was going to be. Your presence will send a loud and clear message to your student that you care. This is a powerful message for a educator to convey, both to the grieving child and to all other students.

Be flexible. After a death in the family has occurred, children and adolescents may be expected to take on additional responsibilities at home such as doing more chores, babysitting younger siblings while the surviving parent is working, or even getting a job to help provide financial support to the family. If this is the case, the school will need to determine how it can help the student continue to be academically successful.

Provide a means to communicate with the child's teacher(s) for the following year(s). Communicate need-to-know information with current and future teachers who will have contact with the child. Be sure to give a detailed progress report on the child's social, emotional, and academic well-being. Passing along important information to the next year's teachers allows them insight into what the child has gone through in previous school years, what strategies have worked well to help the child, and triggers the child may have and allows them to plan ahead to help support the student's needs.

Reconstitution Stage

The reconstitution stage describes the period after the death of a loved one in which the survivors reorganize the family and discover a "new normal."[9] After the death, the reconstitution, or restructuring of the individual and the family, begins to occur. The process of reestablishing relationships with each other and the world without the living presence of the parent or loved one who died is a critical period in the healing of grief. There is no time limit as to how long this process may take. This reconstitution phase can be complicated by factors such as a parent who isn't grieving well or a parent who begins another romantic relationship shortly after the death of the spouse.

Research has shown that the children who successfully make it through the reconstitution stage had caregivers that kept them informed about the family member's illness and treatment; had positive interactions with family members and others throughout the process of the illness, death, and reconstitution; were supported and validated by others; and had parents who attended to their own grief so they were able to attend to the grief of their children.[10] The children soon began to feel confident once the parent was able to show the ability to take care of them emotionally and physically.

Children who have difficulty navigating through the reconstitution stage usually have other stressors in their lives that typically are unrelated to the death of the loved one. Typical stressors include, but are not limited to, minimal or absent parenting or other preexisting problems such as a mental illness, poverty, or other ill family members that may reduce the supports available to the child.[11] Children who struggle to find their "new normal" and have limited supports could end up experiencing "complicated grief" (described in more detail below), posttraumatic stress disorder, or depression. Table 10.2 provides some basic guidelines for educators to follow when supporting students during the reconstitution stage.

SPECIAL ISSUE

Complicated Grief

The impact of grief on children varies from child to child just as children who witness the same traumatic event may have varied responses. This response variation tends to occur because children have unique ways of understanding traumatic events, making meaning of these events in relation to themselves, accessing familial and other forms of support, and integrating these events within themselves.[12]

Death, unfortunately, is a common occurrence people experience, and the majority of people, including children, are able to work through grief in an uncomplicated, or normal, manner. This process usually includes stages or

Table 10.2 RECOMMENDATIONS FOR SUPPORTING STUDENTS DURING THE
RECONSTITUTION STAGE

Do	Don't
Allow the child to talk about the loss.	Avoid the child or minimize the loss as if nothing happened.
Listen intently.	Make comments such as "It could have been worse," "I know how you feel," or "You'll be stronger because of this." Children have a difficult time understanding such comments, and they can be interpreted as dismissive.
Provide a safe environment for the child to express feelings.	Make children feel they are a burden to you if they become emotional or want to talk about the same thing over and over.
Designate a place the child can go to without needing to explain why in front of classmates (e.g., counselor's office, preferred adult in the building, special place in the classroom).	Expect the bereaved child to go through a short grieving process and quickly return to previous functioning.
Use correct language (death, dead, died).	Use phrases such as "gone away" or "left for a while." This is confusing to some children, particularly younger children, and may leave them with the expectation of the loved one returning.
Ease the child's worries about missed schoolwork; adjusting to life without the child's loved one is much more important right now.	Suggest the child has been sad long enough or has missed too many days of school and needs to move on.
Keep to a predictable class routine.	Significantly switch your class routine, structure, or expectations.
Continue to expect the child to function and perform at school but be ready to "lighten the load" on an as needed basis.	Expect the child to never daydream, cry, or be forgetful, preoccupied with other thoughts, or unprepared for class.
Continue to stay in contact with the child's caregiver and make referrals to outside agencies for additional support if needed.	Assume now that the funeral is over the remaining caregiver(s) and the household routine is "back to normal."

Table 10.3 SIGNS OF COMPLICATED GRIEF IN CHILDREN AND ADOLESCENTS

- Intense focus on the death and how much the individual is missed
- Continued problems accepting the death
- Withdrawal and detachment, especially from social activities and peers
- Preoccupation with sadness and grief
- Inability to find joy in life and/or move on with life
- Depression
- Difficulty carrying out normal routines
- Hopelessness as if life has no meaning or purpose
- Increased irritability
- Distrust of others
- Ruminating; mind seems stuck on a particular event(s) related to the illness or death of the loved one

periods of sadness or sorrow, numbness and shock, anger and even guilt. These feelings gradually fade as the individual accepts the loss and moves on with life.

Some people, however, do not experience normal grieving. Some people experience much more painful and debilitating grief, which is known as *complicated grief*. During the first few months following the death of a loved one many signs of normal grief and complicated grief may look the same. However, while normal grief symptoms gradually start to fade, those of complicated grief get worse or linger for months or even years. Complicated grief describes a longer, more pronounced state of mourning.[13]

During normal grieving, development and learning may briefly become interrupted for several months. However, during complicated grief, development and learning could be interrupted for much greater lengths of time. Complicated grief, if not treated, could have detrimental effects on a child's physical, emotional, social, and academic development. Table 10.3 lists the most common signs of complicated grief displayed by children and adolescents, which may persist for months or even years.[14]

CONCLUSION

Children as well as adults grieve from the death of a loved one in many different ways, and no specific time frame indicates when grieving should end. Nevertheless, some common reactions may be exhibited by children and adolescents who anticipate losing an immediate family member due to a terminal illness or other causes. Educators and the school play an important role in the lives of grieving children by providing emotional support and flexibility and recognizing normal responses to grief at the various stages of death (i.e., antici-patory grief, terminal stage, reconstitution stage) and how to react.

The degree to which the child adjusts to the loss of a parent (or sibling) may depend to a large extent on the surviving parent's own distress and adjustment to the death. Bereavement in children and the reconstitution of their lives are largely shaped by the surviving parent(s).[15] The surviving caregiver's ability to understand and respond to the child at different developmental stages can play a significant role in determining the child's ability to grieve and move forward in life. Therefore, educators are encouraged to support the surviving caregivers by being a source of information and staying in frequent contact. If children struggle with the grieving process, then complicated grief could develop along with other mental health concerns. Educators must know their own limits and when collaboration with other professionals in the school building or a referral to mental health professionals is necessary.

In times of crisis, school-based professionals must recognize the significance of their role in supporting children and working with surviving family members to help the child through this traumatic time. When the surviving parent isn't able to provide the support needed for the child due to his or her own grief, then the school must be able to recognize this and have a plan in place to give addi-tional support until the surviving parent or other caregiver is able to provide what the child needs.

NOTES

1. Curry, 2010.
2. Black, 2005.
3. Hope & Hodge, 2006.
4. Christ, 2000; National Institute for Trauma and Loss in Children, 2009.
5. Christ, 2000.
6. Christ, 2000.
7. Stephens, 2010.
8. Black, 2005; Christ, 2000.
9. Christ, 2000.
10. Christ, 2000.
11. Christ, 2000.
12. Cohen, Mannarino, & Deblinger, 2006.
13. Mayo Foundation for Medical Education and Research (MFMER), 2009.
14. MFMER, 2009.
15 Christ, 2000; Raveis, Karus, & Siegel, 1999.

REFERENCES

Black, S. (2005). When children grieve. *American School Board Journal, 192*, 28–30.
Christ, G. H. (2000). *Healing children's grief: Surviving a parent's death from cancer.* New York, NY: Oxford University Press.

Cohen, J. A., Mannarino, A. P., & Deblinger E. (2006). *Treating trauma and traumatic grief in children and adolescents*. New York, NY: Guilford Press.

Curry, P. (2010). *Telling your kids about your terminal illness*. Retrieved from http://www.bidmc.org/YourHealth/TherapeuticCenters/Leukemia.aspx?ChunkID=14350

Hope, R. M., & Hodge, D. M. (2006). Factors affecting children's adjustment to the death of a parent: The social work professional's viewpoint. *Child and Adolescent Social Work Journal, 23*, 107–126.

Mayo Foundation for Medical Education and Research (MFMER). (2009). *Complicated grief*. Retrieved from http://www.mayoclinic.com/health/complicated-grief/DS01023/DSECTION=symptoms

National Institute for Trauma and Loss in Children. (2009). *Infant and toddler grief*. Retrieved from http://www.tlcinst.org/toddlergrief.html

Raveis, V. H., Karus, D., & Siegel, K. (1999). Children's psychological distress following the death of a parent. *Journal of Youth and Adolescence, 28*, 165–180.

Stephens, L. (2010, January). *Voluntary death, euthanasia, and Indian ethics: A critique*. Retrieved from http://www.associatedcontent.com/article/2595823/voluntary_death_euthanasia_and_indian_pg8.html?cat=34

WEB RESOURCES

- The Children's Grief Education Association: http://www.childgrief.org/childrenandgrief.htm
- The Dougy Center: http://www.dougy.org
- Hospice: http://www.hospicenet.org/index.html
- The National Institute for Trauma and Loss in Children: http://http://tlcinstitute.org/PTRC.html

SELECTED CHILDREN'S LITERATURE

Elementary School

- Adams, J. (2007). *The dragonfly door*. Maple Plain, MN: Feather Rock Books.
- De Paola, T. (1973). *Nana upstairs, nana downstairs*. New York, NY: Penguin Group.
- Greenlee, S. (1992). *When someone dies*. Atlanta, GA: Peachtree Publishing.
- Mellonie, B., & Ingpen, R. (1983). *Lifetimes: A beautiful way to explain life and death to children*. New York, NY: Bantam Books.
- Mills, J. C. (2004). *Gentle willow: A story for children about dying*. Washington, DC: Magination Press.
- Olivieri, L. (2007). *Where are you? A child's book about loss*. Olivieri.
- Stickney, D. (1997). *Waterbugs and dragonflies: Explaining death to young children*. Cleveland, OH: Pilgrim Press.
- Varley, S. (1984). *Badger's parting gifts*. New York, NY: Lothrop, Lee, Shepard Books.
- Vigna, J. (1991). *Saying goodbye to daddy*. Morton Grove, IL: Albert Whitman.
- Viorst, J. (1971). *The tenth good thing about Barney*. New York, NY: Antheneum.

Middle School and Teen

- Bode, J. (1993). *Death is hard to live with*. New York, NY: Bantam Doubleday Dell Publishing.
- Fitzgerald, H. (2000). *The grieving teen: A guide for teenagers and their friends*. New York, NY: Fireside.
- Gootman, M. E. (1994). *When a friend dies: A book for teens about grieving and healing*. Minneapolis, MN: Free Spirit Publishing.
- Grollman, E. A. (1993). *Straight talk about death for teenagers: How to cope with losing someone you love*. Boston, MA: Beacon Press.
- Jaffe, S. E. (2003). *For the grieving child: An activities manual*. Charlestown, MA: Acme Bookbinding.
- Krements, J. (1981). *How it feels when a parent dies*. New York, NY: Alfred A. Knopf.
- Romain, T. (1999). *What on earth do you do when someone dies?* Minneapolis, MN: Free Spirit Publishing.
- Samuel-Traisman, E. (1992). *Fire in my heart, ice in my veins*. Omaha, NE: Centering Corporation.
- Smith, D. B. (1983). *A taste of blackberries*. New York, NY: HarperCollins.
- Wolfelt, A. D. (2001). *Healing your grieving heart for kids: 100 practical ideas*. Fort Collins, CO: Companion Press.
- Wolfelt, A. D. (2001). *Healing your grieving heart for teens: 100 practical ideas*. Fort Collins, CO: Companion Press.

11

Students Responding to the Unexpected Death of a Family Member or Loved One

ROBERT J. WINGFIELD AND SUSAN A. CRAFT ■

INTRODUCTION

Students and educators rely heavily on predictability and daily routines, both in school and at home.[1] Unfortunately, structure and predictability can be compromised by the unexpected death of an immediate family member or friend. Causes of unexpected death may include, but are not limited to, suicide, homicide, car accidents, and heart attacks. Unfortunately, such tragedies are likely to impact several students in any given school each year. For example, it is estimated that over 33,000 fatalities result from suicide each year, 18,000 from homicide,[2] over 34,000 from automobile accidents, and, perhaps most alarming, an estimated 935,000 deaths from heart attacks.[3] Thus, it is likely that all educators will encounter students with these experiences throughout their career.

Unexpected death of a family member or friend represents a profound psychological event that will likely interfere with everyday functioning, academic performance, and attendance and cause significant distress and impairment. The event itself is stressful, and its impact pervades most aspects of the student's life with symptoms including depression, disinterest in activities previously viewed as enjoyable, changes in appetite (e.g., overeating or loss of appetite), risk-taking behavior (e.g., drug and alcohol use), social withdrawal, problems sleeping at night, difficulties getting out of bed in the morning, and drops in academic performance.[4] The vignettes provided here exemplify the academic, social, and emotional outcomes that might occur following an unexpected death in a student's life.

Steven, 12 years old and in seventh grade, was a gifted student athlete at North Middle School. He consistently made the honor roll and excelled in soccer and baseball. Just 2 months into the school year, his mother experienced a severe brain aneurism and died instantly in her sleep. Steven went to his coach and asked to have a few weeks off to recoup. Without hesitation, Steven's coach told him to take all the time he needed to get himself together. During this period, Steven did not show up for school. Steven was the youngest of three. His 28-year-old brother lived four states away and his 22-year-old sister was desperately trying to finish her final year of college. Steven's parents had been divorced since he was 7, and although Steven's father readily allowed Steven to move in with him, he had a second family to take care of, causing Steven to feel detached and alone. Upon returning to school 3 weeks later, Steven appeared lethargic throughout the day and quit the soccer team. His teachers noted that his grades were slipping drastically.

Grief is a strange force that molds you as a person, and continues to influence your decisions throughout your life. As a young girl, I lost my father to a heart attack; he was 42 and I was 7. Returning home from playing with my neighbor, I saw my mother crying in the kitchen with her brothers and sisters surrounding her. I was told my father had passed away. "He was at work and just fell asleep and now is in heaven." Adults need to present the facts and not use fantasy-type statements describing death. Through the years I had a recurring dream about my father being in a store. I would try to reach him, but just as I got close, he would jump out of the window and run away. In my mind, he was out there: I was really too young to understand it all. I did not get to see my dad in his casket, which I believe also contributed to my dream—I never had closure.

Three and a half years later, when my brother was killed on his bicycle after being struck by a car (I was 10, he was 8), I experienced death in a different light. In those few years, I was able to grow and understand a little more about grief. I was able to share my thoughts regarding his death with anyone who would listen. My teachers were very good about listening to me and comforting me when I asked those difficult questions. They took extra time, even after school was done for the year, to check on me and my family and make offers to help any way they could. Over the years, because of the losses I endured, I struggled with my grief and the fear of death. I know it's not true, but in my mind anything bad that can happen is going to happen to me and my family! In middle school when kids my

age had little worries, I was making phone calls to try and see where my mom
was since she was not home at the minute she said she would be—total panic had
set in and I just knew she wasn't coming back.

Just like the two previous vignettes, students who deal with unexpected death will often experience grief as well as a change in lifestyle. Accordingly, developing effective interventions and strategies to help students who are traumatized by such an event is critical to academic engagement and success. In fact, academic success can give grieving students a renewed sense of control over their lives. Notably, although some similar responses may occur between unexpected death and imminent (or expected) death of a close family member (see chapter 10 and "Special Issues" section at bottom of this chapter), an unexpected death can trigger different emotions due to the inability to prepare, plan, and say goodbye. It is also important to recognize that responses to death often play out differently depending on individual circumstances and the developmental level of the student.

DEVELOPMENTAL CONSIDERATIONS

Children experience death differently than adults do, especially because of their less developed levels of cognitive, social, and emotional maturity. Therefore, students who experience death of a loved one will respond differently than adults do, even though many students in secondary school physically resemble adults. Additionally, students across developmental stages (e.g., kindergarten through high school) will have various ways of understanding death and coping in a healthy manner. Table 11.1 presents some perceptions of death relative to a student's age or developmental level, as well as common reactions to the death of a loved one. It is important to keep in mind that all students react differently to death, especially an unexpected one, so this table serves only as a reference.

FAMILY AND CULTURAL CONSIDERATIONS

Research has indicated that a strong attachment or relationship with a caregiver can be a protective factor against negative outcomes.[5] When students feel loved and supported, they are likely to be able to cope more healthfully with difficult situations. However, with the unexpected death of a loved one, a student's caregiver(s) may be unable to invest as much time to providing for the student's basic or emotional needs, especially if it is the other parent who has passed away. The other caregiver may also not have as strong of a relationship with the student, as was the case for Steven in the vignette. Educators should consider the ways in which the student's home life is disrupted: Are there changes in the

Table 11.1[a] Developmental Understanding and Reactions to Death

Developmental Age	Typical Understanding of Death	Common Reactions to Death
Prekindergarten (ages 3–5)	• Belief that the loved one is coming back • "Magical thinking," such as imagining the person back to life or planning what to do with the loved one upon return	• Sense of guilt or responsibility for the loved one's death • Regression in developmental behaviors (e.g., thumb sucking, bed wetting) • Clinginess to remaining family members • Repetitive questioning about death and, in particular, the loved one's death
School-age (6–12)	• May also engage in "magical thinking" • Think that people die because they deserved it (cause-and-effect thinking) • May think that people can avoid death • May need to be taught about the biological causes of death	• May also experience a regression in developmental behaviors • Sense of guilt or responsibility for the loved one's death • Short attention span in the classroom • Somatic complaints (e.g., stomachache, headache) • Worry about other loved ones • Fear of death or the death of remaining family members • Disruptive behavior in the classroom
Adolescence (12–18)	• May have a developed understanding of death (irreversibility, finality, inevitability, causality) • May see the world through "self-colored glasses" (i.e., they think about how the event has affected themselves first before others).[b] May feel as if they could have prevented the death, even if they understand the biological basis of death • May think about their own mortality	• Risk-taking behavior (e.g., drug and alcohol use, sexual promiscuity) • Aggression • Social withdrawal • Avoiding people, events, or situations that remind them of the traumatic event or the lost loved one • Sleep problems • Low self-esteem • Depression • Taking on too many "adult" responsibilities, such as dropping out of school to obtain a full-time job

[a] National Institute of Mental Health, 2009a; Noppe & Noppe, 1997; Willis, 2002.
[b] Johnson, 1998.

student's everyday routine? Is the surviving caregiver financially stable enough to meet the student's basic needs (food, clothing, shelter)? Is the caregiver currently working? How has the caregiver reacted to the death? Examining these areas can help educators better understand the student's situation. After examining the situation, the educator can confidentially present the case to the student support team to collaborate on ways that the school can assist the family.

It is also very important to be aware of cultural concerns during the grieving process. Although the power of cultural influence is different for each individual, families who are newer to the United States may be more likely to carry out rituals that are markedly different from contemporary American tradition. To better anticipate the response of the family, school personnel should know whether the family will be engaging in specific customs that affect normal routines. One of the best ways to be culturally competent is to ask questions, engage with the family, and be a good listener. Educators should also collaborate with the family by sending work home, if determined to be appropriate, and by providing the student opportunities to finish tests and assignments without penalty upon returning to school. Table 11.2 is designed to help educators better understand some of the traditions regarding death across various cultural and religious groups.

STRATEGIES TO SUPPORT STUDENTS

The student's return to school following the unexpected death of an immediate family member is generally the first action taken in returning to normalcy. Ideally, classrooms are designed to allow students to demonstrate competency and control over their lives, which facilitates the healing process. There is no one-size-fits-all solution to helping a student return to school successfully; however, some common reactions and teacher tips are provided.

Provide as much choice and autonomy as possible. The educator can help the student feel comfortable and in control by providing choices and autonomy when appropriate. Writing assignments are usually good opportunities to provide this autonomy. For example, the teacher can allow the student to choose his or her own book report topic (e.g., favorite athlete, dream career, personal hero). There are a number of books that deal with overcoming adversity that may be especially helpful for a grieving student who is interested in sports. For example, the book entitled *Running for My Life*[6] by NFL running back Warrick Dunn tells the incredibly inspirational story of courage and determination in the face of the unexpected loss of his mother when he was a teenager. Many children's books are available that can help generate discussion about death. Some titles can be found at the Sudden Unexplained Death in Childhood website (http://www.sudc.org), or see the list of web resources and books provided in chapter 10.

Make classroom life as predictable and safe as possible. Educators can help bereaved students by posting daily schedules in visible locations so that students know what to expect throughout the day. Similarly, a clock should be placed in

Table 11.2[a] COMMON CULTURAL AND RELIGIOUS BELIEFS, RITUALS, AND
PRACTICES FOLLOWING A DEATH

Cultural Groups

African American

- African American Christians often refer to the wake as the "Home-Going," which refers to reuniting with Jesus and other deceased family members and friends
- A gathering of family and friends is common to comfort one another during the grief process
- Often hold a wake with a variety of songs and music
- Those who were close to the deceased often join for a communal meal after the wake and funeral
- Burials are more common than cremation
- Memorial services with gifts are common
- May wear white to funerals to symbolize resurrection

Asian American

- The body should be respected, even after death
- Stoicism is favored over public grieving
- The elders in the family are often responsible for planning the funeral ceremony
- Open-casket ceremonies are common, and the deceased are sometimes buried with small items or food
- Music is typically played during the ceremony
- Those in attendance are invited to a communal meal out of respect for the deceased
- Pictures and items that remind the family of the deceased are sometimes kept on display

Caucasian

- Typically a "death-defying/-denying" culture in which people fear death
- After an announcement about the death, friends and family often gather to support one another
- Clergymen and the funeral director are relied upon for funeral preparations
- A visitation at a funeral home followed by a gravesite service is common
- Dark clothing is typically worn to funerals to symbolize grieving
- Often includes a gathering of family and friends after the funeral services with food and refreshments

Hispanic American

- For Hispanic American Christians, saying the rosary is common to commemorate the deceased
- Sometimes make promises to the deceased, which are taken very seriously
- The priest is highly involved in planning the funeral service
- Friends and family members are invited to the funeral service and sometimes the procession to the burial site
- Mass is typically included in the funeral services
- Sometimes monetary gifts are provided to the deceased's family to ameliorate expenses

(continued)

Table 11.2 (Continued)

Cultural Groups

Native American

(Note: There is large variety between Native American tribes, so only commonalities are highlighted)

- Some groups believe that the living and the dead coexist (their actions influence each other)
- Deceased ancestors are sometimes asked to join in death and bereavement traditions
- Burials often occur, and it is encouraged that the deceased are buried in their natural homeland
- Often wear red or black to funerals
- Bodies are expected to deteriorate naturally without any other processes such as embalming
- Friends and families often bury the deceased with symbolic or sentimental items that demonstrate they are still living (often items found in nature)

Religious Groups

Islam

- Death should not be questioned because it is an act of God
- The deceased's body should touch the earth
- Mourners are encouraged to grieve publicly
- Friends and family members often visit the house of the deceased to ask details about the death
- Family members of the deceased are not left alone for 7 days
- Friends cook for the deceased's family at this time, as family members are not supposed to do so
- Prayers occur on the 40th and 52nd days after the death of the loved one
- Funerals should be led by a Muslim
- The deceased should be buried in a cemetery for Muslims
- The body should be washed in a certain ritualistic way before it is buried
- Usually occurs at a mosque or at the hospital
- The body is buried in a white cloth without a coffin
- After meeting a family member of the deceased, it is common to start the conversation with this sentence: "May you be alive and may God's blessings be on him/her—the deceased"

Judaism

- Dismembering or embalming the deceased body is not common
- It is not common to have a viewing of the body
- Funerals generally do not occur on Saturdays or other religious holidays
- It is not encouraged for services to include music or flowers
- Rabbis, friends, and family often deliver eulogies at the funeral
- Family members and friends who go to the burial site are usually asked to contribute to the burial by placing a shovel of dirt on top of the casket

(*continued*)

Table 11.2 (Continued)

Religious Groups

- Mourning lasts for 1 year
- A 7-day mourning period ("sitting shiva") occurs after the burial. No one in the deceased's family is allowed to cook food during this time, and a candle is kept burning in the deceased person's honor. The Kaddish, a declaration of faith, is said each day
- Sometimes visitors are not allowed for 3 days
- After "sitting shiva," survivors of the deceased repeat the Kaddish twice a day for the next 30 days
- Torn garments are often worn to the funeral and for a short period afterward to symbolize grief
- Family members are often named after the deceased
- The tombstone of the deceased is unveiled on the 1-year anniversary of his or her death

Protestant Christianity
- Life does not end with death; the faithful go to Heaven and sinners/nonbelievers spend eternity in Hell
- Family gatherings before the funeral are common
- Open- or closed-casket services are typical, and memorial items are sometimes placed in the casket
- Black clothing is typically worn to the funeral
- Funeral services often include music and testimonials said by a religious leader, family members, and friends
- Flowers and donations are accepted as expressions of condolences
- Church members often assist in the funeral service or with family members' recovery process
- There is no formal process of observing the death each year, although graveside visits are common

Roman Catholicism
- Life does not end with death; the faithful go to Heaven and sinners/nonbelievers spend eternity in Hell
- The Sacraments of the Sick (confession and communion) are performed before a person dies
- It is typical for families to have a wake for the deceased
- Priests preside over the wake in the form of a complete religious service (mass) or by saying the rosary
- The casket is covered with a white cloth and sprinkled with holy water
- The gravesite is blessed by the priest
- Sometimes the 1-year anniversary of the death is celebrated by a mass with family and friends

[a] Gire, 2002; National Association of School Psychologists, 2003.

a noticeable location within the classroom so students can keep track of time. Sometimes a digital clock or timer can be helpful for younger students who cannot read analog clocks. These simple measures can make meaningful differences for bereaved students who initially feel that their lives are unpredictable.

Research indicates that educators should place great emphasis on creating a safe environment in two ways. First, for those with a traumatic past, educators filter out subjects and perspectives that are painful or offensive. Second, they create an environment where learners feel comfortable asking for clarification, taking chances, and making mistakes.[7] Therefore, always welcome and encourage participation and questions before, during, or after class.

Make sure all conversations are developmentally appropriate. Young students are generally unable to process the intricacies of violence in the same manner as adolescents. Therefore, educators should avoid engaging in complicated dialogue about death and tragic events with younger students. Educators should be aware that young students do react positively to plain assurances by adults and straightforward examples of school safety, such as reminding younger students about exterior doors being locked, child monitoring efforts on the playground, and emergency drills practiced during the school day. Other assurances may simply include saying, "You are safe in our classroom."

Adjust or modify work requirements as needed. Many students experience changes in their daily lives during the early months after the death of a parent. A common change may be an increase in the household tasks and chores they are required to do. In light of this, educators should consider adjusting homework requirements for the bereaved student. For example, the student should be allowed to answer fewer math problems to demonstrate mastery or be provided extra time to complete a classroom project. Educators should not feel guilty for altering homework requirements, as the diversity of family values, family priorities, and individual differences in bereaved students renders the one-size-fits-all homework plan virtually useless.[8]

Help the student find a safe haven. Provide the grieving student the opportunity to go to a specified location if needed. The specified location should always be a place where there will be guaranteed adult supervision available, but also a place that the student finds safe, relaxing, or comforting. The student should be instructed to do something productive such as write in a journal as a means of expressing feelings. This provision should not be taken advantage of, however.

Document, document, document. Document signs of distress and share these observations with the family, school counselor, and school psychologist. Signs of distress may include changes in appetite, restlessness, moodiness, irritability, withdrawal, difficulties concentrating, disorganized behaviors, and acting out.

Encourage return to normalcy. Encourage the student to return to his or her favorite extracurricular activities such as a sports team or music programs as soon as possible. If the student is not engaged in any of these activities, consider suggesting some that he or she may be successful at doing.

Don't make assumptions. Don't assume that the student is fine simply by looking at overt behaviors. Take note of even small changes that may be observed in the content of the student's writing (e.g., depressive themes, pessimistic outlook) and art (e.g., violence, dark images).

Limit exposure to media coverage. In the event of a tragic accident, repeatedly viewing or reading media updates of the event can increase adverse reactions. This is particularly true if the media displays graphic images.

Help find ways to let the student memorialize the deceased. A student may talk excessively about the loss to stay connected with his or her deceased family member. Students may even devote considerable energy to staying connected with the deceased loved one through dreams, frequently thinking about the deceased person, believing that the dead family member is watching, and keeping some belongings of the deceased close by. Such behaviors could be interpreted as an attempt either to keep the deceased person alive or to make the loss real.[9]

School personnel should demonstrate leniency if the bereaved student memorializes the deceased in ways that conflict with school rules, within reason. For example, Steven (in the first vignette) may find comfort in wearing a hat from his mother's favorite baseball team to school. In collaboration with the student's caregiver and school administration, the educator should help the student identify a covert long-term measure of commemorating his deceased mother since wearing a hat may be a distraction or policy violation. The student should be encouraged to wear something discreet such as a commemorative button or necklace. Similarly, a female student whose grandmother has died from a heart attack may take solace in wearing her grandmother's very expensive gold watch to school. As with the former example, the educator should help the student identify another gesture to commemorate the life of the grandmother since wearing expensive jewelry in school is usually problematic (e.g., jewelry might be stolen or damaged).

Provide ways to express emotion. Give students different ideas on how to express their feelings beyond talking (e.g., drawing, journaling, writing letters, writing songs, talking, making a collage or banner, etc.). The student can write a letter to the deceased or the family of the deceased, or write about the life story of the individual who passed away. Educators can also volunteer to help students make a memory book about a loved one or encourage them to share favorite memories with the class.

It is recommended that written products such as these be used exclusively as journaling activities that are not graded. However, if a written product like this is used as a graded assignment, the teacher should explicitly state that any points deducted are simply an indication of technical writing errors. This disclaimer will help prevent the student from feeling as if the teacher is being judgmental or insensitive. In addition to writing assignments, drawing or creative art activities may help the grieving student cope with the unexpected loss. Consider consulting with school support personnel such as the school psychologist or school counselor for other helpful suggestions.

Avoidance in talking about the deceased family member might protect the student from the pain and overpowering grief that may be attached to memories of the lost person. *The educator should not force the student to talk about the deceased family member.*

Prepare for separation anxiety (especially among younger students). Young children may be especially prone to experiencing symptoms of separation anxiety following the death of a parent.[10] Separation anxiety is the fear of being away from a main caregiver, most commonly, a student's mother. Students with separation anxiety become extremely upset when they have to separate from their main caregiver for any reason. There are many reasons for this behavior. In many cases it appears to be a fear that something terrible will happen to the surviving parent, and that they consequently will never see each other again, much like in the second vignette. The following strategies may help alleviate separation anxiety:

1. Have the parent or guardian arrive to school 30 minutes earlier than usual.
2. Have the parent, student, and classroom teacher interact together in the classroom prior to other students arriving (e.g., eat a morning snack, color, read a story).
3. Have the parent tell the student that he or she will be leaving in a few minutes for work.
4. Tell the student an approximate time for when he or she will be picked up.
5. Give the student a special object (e.g., button, ribbon, bracelet) that serves as a reminder that the parent will return at the end of the school day.
6. The parent should say goodbye.
7. If the student cries, an educator should console the student but the parent should continue to exit.
8. If the student's crying does not dissipate in a reasonable span of time, the student should be sent to the school counselor's office.
9. Develop a communication plan in which the student has a method to contact the parent when overwhelmed with anxiety. Set limits on time and number of calls.
10. Keep in mind that it is better for the student to be sent to the school counseling office to regroup than to be picked up early by the parent. Planning for the student to stay in school helps to dispel the faulty cognition that something bad will happen to the surviving parent. Conversely, sending the student home will reinforce the student's anxiety and maladaptive thought pattern.

Discussing Death With Students

When a loved one dies unexpectedly, adults often have difficulty explaining the death to children and adolescents. Sometimes the physical death may be too gruesome to discuss in detail, or the student may not seem capable of comprehending the situation. To follow are tips to help adults communicate simply and honestly with students about the death of a loved one.[11] As you read the tips, reflect on what might have been helpful for the student in the second vignette after her father's death, after her brother's death, and to assist with her fears as she moved through secondary school.

Present the facts. Avoid the use of idiomatic statements such as "Your loved one is sleeping" or "Your loved one is going away for a while." You are better off providing developmentally appropriate, honest information. If the student asks, repeat what you have confirmed is true about the death (i.e., do not play into the magical thinking about a loved one coming back or tales about how he or she died).

Coordinate with parents. Always coordinate with the student's parents about how they wish to present information. It can be confusing to students if they receive different messages from their educators and parents. Some parents may also be reluctant to share the information with others in the class or with other school personnel. Finally, do not create visual memorials or shrines on school property *without consent from the family.* Memorials should never be created in the case of a suicide.

Listen openly and attentively. Let the student know that you are available to talk and encourage the student to ask questions or talk to you when he or she is feeling sad. Give the student your undivided attention when that time arises, and try to find a quiet space, away from other distractions, to have the conversation. If this is not possible at the moment, you can suggest opportunities later in the day where you can give your full attention. Once you have the opportunity to talk with the student, allow him or her to talk about the deceased loved one. You can encourage this by asking questions such as "Tell me about _____," or "_____sounds like a wonderful person. Tell me about some of your favorite times with him/her."

Engage in a classroom discussion or lesson. Classroom discussions can include defining death, loss, or separation, *being sure not to describe religious aspects of death.* Ask if anyone in the class has had previous experiences with death that they would like to share (pet, relative, etc.). Even a brief classroom discussion will help create an environment where students are free to share things from outside school that may impact what happens in the classroom.

You may also wish to have more general classroom lessons that focus on different situations that may trigger different emotions, using examples such as getting presents, having someone make fun of you, or going through something significant like Hurricane Katrina. Ask the students to think about certain situations or triggers for emotions in their lives that may have caused them distress. Have students draw a picture that represents a trigger for that emotion (individual or in groups), or for older students, ask them to write a paragraph about it. Let students know that they will not be required to share with others. Educators then can model how they might react to different emotions (e.g., someone made fun of them so they became upset). Discuss how our emotions lead to different behaviors and reactions (e.g., cried and ran to the bathroom or talked to a friend) and how some strategies are more effective than others. Finally, ask students to brainstorm how they would deal with their selected emotion and how effective those strategies are. Students will be asked to volunteer to share and then the class can problem solve other methods. Even if a student who experienced death of a loved one recently does not participate, that student may find comfort in hearing other people experiencing other emotions and benefit from hearing some suggestions from others. Peer-generated examples are usually culturally appropriate, and in addition, they create a positive peer support network.[12]

Know when to refer to student support personnel. While children often grieve for a longer period of time than adults, intense symptoms (such as depression or physical pains) should last for no more than 2 to 3 weeks. The following list includes warning signs for when to contact your school psychologist, school social worker, or school counselor immediately[13]:

- Physical symptoms that persist without medical explanation
- Unusual fears about everyday activities, such as leaving the house
- Disturbed sleep or eating patterns
- Lack of energy for daily life
- Numbness or detachment from peers and close adults
- Overwhelming sadness
- Continued decreased school performance
- Expression of a hopeless or gloomy future without the loved one
- Expression of wanting to join the deceased (i.e., to die or take own life)
- *Perseveration* and *fixation* regarding the loss (i.e., the student frequently talks about the death of the family member in a traumatic fashion for several months after the loss)

SPECIAL ISSUES

Suicide

Death due to suicide has a separate set of reactions and rules concerning the school's response. Reactions may include shock, anger, blame, guilt, relief, or even envy. The American Association of Suicidology has a website that provides extensive suggestions and discusses common experiences and reactions of those who have lost a loved one to suicide. Educators can access this information at http://www.suicidology.org/web/guest/home. However, some general dos and don'ts are provided in Table 11.3.

Homicide

Severe responses may be observed with a student who lost his or her family member to homicide. Young people in the United States, especially in urban areas, continue to be exposed firsthand to increasing amounts of violence in their homes, neighborhoods, and schools.[14] Further, the long-term impact that the murder of a loved one has on a co-victim cannot be underestimated: "Traumatic events have primary effects not only on the psychological structures of the self but also on the systems of attachment and meaning that link the individual to community [school]."[15] Educators should be aware that a student who has witnessed the murder of a close family member or loved one might develop a hypersensitive startle reflex as a result of the incident. For more information on exposure to community violence, see chapter 6.

Table 11.3 RECOMMENDATIONS FOR SCHOOL RESPONSE TO STUDENT SUICIDE

Do	Don't
• Obtain permission from the family to discuss the death as a suicide	• Fly flags at half staff
• Discuss with other students in the class what to do with the student's desk	• Dedicate memorials, plaques, songs, or sporting events in memory of student
• Identify friends of the student or others who may be at risk for strong emotional reactions	• Close the school
• Expect and allow grieving	• Glorify the suicidal act
• Return to a normal schedule ASAP, but allow opportunities to talk or write about it as needed	• Encourage funeral attendance
• Talk to the class about the suicide and feel free to share your reactions	• Allow moments of silence
• Discuss alternative, more prosocial ways to handle grief	• Have a school assembly in memoriam
• Expect some more daydreaming, inattention, misbehavior, absenteeism, or physical complaints than usual	• Provide details to other students
• Take care of yourself!	• Change normal routines
	• Sweep it under the rug or ignore it

CONCLUSION

This chapter provided an overview of the common reactions exhibited by students who have lost an immediate family member to unexpected death, along with a number of strategies and interventions to help support these students. It is important to remember that everyone processes strong emotions differently. The way that a student reacts to the unexpected death of a loved one will vary due to several factors, including age, culture, family dynamics, cognitive ability, and current level of development. In some ways, unexpected death may be more difficult to manage than imminent death of a close family member due to the inability to plan, prepare, and say good-bye. Some students may talk openly about the loss, while others will need to respond through art, poetry, prayer, or physical activity. Many may tend to resort to less prosocial methods of coping.

Educators and other school personnel play a vital role in helping the bereaved student adjust to life after the loss of an immediate family member. Normal routines help establish a sense of calm and predictability, which is important for maintaining effective learning environments. Educators also help enhance the social-emotional functioning of bereaved students by maintaining safe and nonthreatening classroom environments and allowing the student to show competency and be successful. When school personnel collaborate to determine methods of supporting bereaved students, these efforts will enhance social-emotional functioning and subsequent academic performance.

APPENDIX A

INFORMAL ADJUSTMENT ASSESSMENT

To assess the quality of the bereaved student's adjustment, school staff can utilize the following interview protocol when working with middle school– to high school–age students. The purpose of the interview is to identify where the student falls along the adjustment spectrum. Important areas to investigate include community/church support, extended family support, private therapy, and fulfillment of basic needs.

INTERVIEW QUESTIONS

1. How have things changed since your family member died?
2. What people, places, or things have helped you during this trying time?
3. Have you received any counseling since the loss? If not, would you like me to help you find counseling?

4. What has been the hardest thing to deal with since the loss?
5. Have you noticed any changes in yourself since the loss (e.g., eating habits, sleep schedule, attention span, health, etc.)?
6. Have you been able to return to extracurricular activities and/or hobbies since the loss?
7. What can the school do to help you during this difficult time?

NOTES

1. Perry, 2004.
2. National Institutes of Mental Health, 2009b.
3. Fatality Reporting Analysis System, 2007.
4. Goenjian et al., 1997; Gurwitch, Pfefferbaum, & Leftwich, 2002; Harris, 1991.
5. Noppe & Noppe, 1997.
6. Dunn & Yaeger, 2008.
7. Roberts et al., 2004.
8. Vatterott, 2009.
9. Silverman & Worden, 1992.
10. Rapee, Spence, Cobham, & Wignall, 2000.
11. American Hospice Foundation, 2009; National Association of School Psychologists, 2003.
12. Brackett & Katulak, 2007.
13. Dillen, Fontaine, & Verhofstadt-Deneve, 2009.
14. Spungen, 1998, p. 192.
15. Herman, 1992, p. 51.

REFERENCES

American Hospice Foundation. (2004). *Guidelines for parents to help their children through grief.* Retrieved from http://www.americanhospice.org/index.php?option=com_content&task=view&id=61&Itemid=8

Brackett, M. A., & Katulak, N. (2007). The emotionally intelligent classroom: Skill-based training for teachers and students. In J. Ciarrochi & J. D. Mayer (Eds.), *Improving emotional intelligence: A practitioner's guide* (pp. 1–27). New York, NY: Psychology Press/Taylor & Francis.

Dillen, L., Fontaine, J. R., & Verhofstadt-Deneve, L. (2009). Confirming the distinctiveness of complicated grief from depression and anxiety among adolescents. *Death Studies, 33,* 437–461.

Dunn, W., & Yaeger, D. (2008). *Running for my life.* New York, NY: Harper Collins Publishers.

Fatality Analysis Reporting System (2007), *Web-based encyclopedia.* Retrieved from http://www-fars.nhtsa.dot.gov/Main/index.aspx

Gire, J. T. (2002). How death imitates life: Cultural influences on conceptions of death and dying. In W. J. Lonner, D. L. Dinnel, S. A. Hayes, & D. N. Sattler (Eds.),

Online readings in psychology and culture. Bellingham, WA: Western Washington University. Retrieved from http://www.wwu.edu/culture/gire.htm

Goenjian, A. K., Karayan, I., Pynoos, R. S., Minassian, D., Najarian, L. M., Steinberg, A. M., et al. (1997). Outcomes of psychotherapy among early-adolescents after trauma. *American Journal of Psychiatry, 154*, 536–542.

Gurtwitch, R. H., Pfefferbaum, B., & Leftwich, M. (2002). The impact of terrorism on children: Considerations for a new era. *Journal of Trauma Practice, 3*, 101–124.

Harris, E. (1991). Adolescent bereavement following the death of a parent: An exploratory study. *Child Psychiatry and Human Development, 21*, 267–281.

Herman, J. (1992). *Trauma and recovery.* New York, NY: Basic Books.

Johnson, K. (1998). *Trauma in the lives of children: Crisis and stress management techniques for counselors, teachers, and other professionals.* Alameda, CA: Hunter House Publishers.

National Association of School Psychologists. (2003). *Understanding cultural issues in death.* Retrieved from http://www.nasponline.org/resources/principals/culture_death.aspx

National Institute of Mental Health. (2009a). *Helping children and adolescents cope with violence and disasters: For teachers, clergy, and other adults in the community.* Retrieved from http://infocenter.nimh.nih.gov/pdf/helping-children-and-adolescents-cope-with-violence-and-disasters-what-community-members-can-do.pdf

National Institute of Mental Health. (2009b). *Web-based suicide in the United States: Statistics and prevention fact sheet.* Retrieved from http://nimh.nih.gov/health/publications/suicide-in-the-us-statistics-and-prevention/index.shtml

Noppe, I. C., & Noppe, L. D. (1997). Evolving meanings of death during early, middle, and later adolescence. *Death Studies, 21*, 253–275.

Perry, B. D. (2004). *Understanding traumatized and maltreated children: The core concepts.* The Child Trauma Academy. Retrieved from http://www.lfcc.on.ca/Perry_Core_Concepts_Violence_and_Childhood.pdf

Rapee, R. M., Spence, S. H., Cobham, V., & Wignall, A. (2000). *Helping your anxious child: A step-by-step guide for parents.* Oakland, CA: New Harbinger Publications.

Roberts, C., Baynham, M., Shrubshall, P., Barton, D. P., Chopra, P., Cooke, M., et al. (2004). *English for speakers of other languages (ESOL): Case studies of provision, learner's needs and resources.* London: National Research and Development Centre for Adult Literacy and Numeracy, University of London.

Silverman, P. R., & Worden, J. W. (1992). Children's reactions in the early months after the death of a parent. *American Journal of Orthopsychiatry, 62*, 92–104.

Spungen, D. (1998). *Homicide: The hidden victim: A guide for professionals. Volume 20 of interpersonal violence.* Thousand Oaks, CA: Sage Publications.

Vatterott, C. (2009). *Rethinking homework: Best practices that support diverse need.* Danvers, MA: Association for Supervision and Curriculum Development (ASCD).

Willis, C. A. (2002). The grieving process in children: Strategies for understanding, educating, and reconciling children's perceptions of death. *Early Childhood Education Journal, 29*(4), 221–226.

12

Students From Military Families

C O U R T N E Y   D .   C A R T E R ■

INTRODUCTION

Military families face unique challenges during the various stages of military deployment. Active-duty military members are expected to be on call at all times, and a sudden call to duty is generally nonnegotiable, can lead to placement in unsafe war zones, and can last for up to 2 years. To make matters worse, active-duty military may be deployed multiple times throughout their military career, leading to a potentially chronic state of stress and anxiety for the entire family. In fact, military children are twice as likely to report elevated anxiety when compared to nonmilitary children.[1] Such stress has serious implications for schools given that nearly 2 million children are estimated to have one or both parents in the military.[2] This makes up nearly 4% of the entire school population. Thus, it is likely that several students in each school building are from military families, many of which may require added support.

Anxiety experienced during anticipation of deployment is warranted; as of November 21, 2011, the Department of Defense reported that Operation Iraqi Freedom had seen a total of 4,421 U.S. deaths and close to 32,000 U.S. military wounded in action; and Operation Enduring Freedom in Afghanistan had 1,831 U.S. deaths and close to 15,000 more troops wounded in action.[3] An added stress results from frequent geographical moves for military families, causing education gaps for the student that can heighten academic struggles and create additional adjustment difficulties.[4] Frequent school changes put students at a higher risk for grade retention, disrupted development, and school dropout.[5]

A recent study[6] of over 307,000 children ages 5 to 17 years who had at least one active-duty parent and had received outpatient medical care revealed that 16.7% had been diagnosed with at least one mental health disorder. The most common among them were related to stress, anxiety, depression, behavioral problems, and sleep. Importantly, results also revealed that the risk of a mental health problem increased with longer parental deployments.

Certainly, many students are resilient, have strong support networks, and do not experience any significant negative outcomes resulting from a parent's military involvement. However, a recent study found that elementary school-aged children with deployed parents were more likely to experience mental health and behavioral problems.[7] In point of fact, outpatient mental health visits for children of active-duty military doubled from 1 million in 2003 to 2 million in 2008,[8] and mental health visits increased by 11% during a parent's deployment.[9] While symptoms vary, boys typically express anger and aggression, whereas girls more frequently experience somatic complaints and internalizing behaviors such as depression. In addition, some research suggests that female adolescents with military parents may increase engagement in risky sexual behaviors and self-inflicted wounds in an attempt to keep the military parent home.[10]

Negative Outcomes for Returning Military Parents

Given the large quantity of deployments, many children have had to learn to adapt to the chronic state of stress during predeployment and actual separation during deployment, while looking ahead to the eventual return during postdeployment. However, postdeployment has become particularly problematic given the increasing need for mental health services and prevalence of posttraumatic stress disorder (PTSD) in returning service members. In fact, it is estimated that approximately 30% to 50% of military members returning from combat report physical and psychological conditions, including brain injury and PTSD.[11] As of May 2010, the Defense and Veterans Brain Injury Center reported 178,876 total cases of traumatic brain injury[12] among returning service members. The debilitating effects of these conditions make it even more difficult for parents to resume their caregiver duties after they have returned. Perhaps more alarming is the rapid increase in suicide among active-duty military personnel, with an increase of 71% from 2001 to 2009. In fact, the number of deaths due to suicide among the military is nearly equal to the number of American military killed in combat in Afghanistan in 2009,[13] which increases the risk of suicide among those children.

Symptoms of PTSD, which may include intense fear, hopelessness, or horror, may occur for weeks, months, or even years following the incident. An individual with PTSD may replay the event over and over through nightmares and vivid memories that can be so real that a noise can trigger an intense emotional reaction. Unfortunately, these individuals may avoid people, places, or feelings that serve as reminders of the event. Consequently, these individuals may also spend less time with their children, develop short tempers, behave differently, be reluctant to travel with their family, and have difficulties reconnecting with their children. Many with PTSD face challenges resuming "normal" household and caregiving duties, as they often need someone to care for them as well.

VIGNETTE—JERON

Jeron, age 6 years, is in his first year of school. Dad drops off and picks him up every day at school, which is something his mother always did. She recently returned from a 12-month deployment in Afghanistan as a member of a Forward Surgical Team (FST). This is a group of specially trained medics, doctors, and nurses who operate on wounded soldiers, stabilize them, and prepare them for transport. While she was deployed Jeron would draw pictures of his mommy fixing soldiers. Now that she has returned, he keeps telling stories in class about his mommy screaming in the middle of the night and his father trying to calm her down, then hearing them cry. His "mommy is different" he says. "She doesn't play with me like she used to." A month goes by and the teacher notices that Jeron is starting to draw pictures with his mom off to the side and he and his father together.

National Guard and Reserve

Many students may rely on a network of support within their community, particularly those attending Department of Defense schools with peers experiencing similar circumstances. However, children with parents in the National Guard and Reserves attending public schools may be at a disadvantage in this regard as they may feel isolated. Further, given that only 1.4% of the 1.96 million children with military parents attended Department of Defense Educational Activity (DoDEA) schools in the United States in 2009, an overwhelming majority of military dependents likely attend U.S. public schools,[14] leaving a large responsibility on public school educators.

The National Guard and Reserve units, while representing a large proportion of military families, may also represent an often neglected group when considering mental health needs. In fact, suicides among National Guard and Reserve personnel increased 80% from 2009 to 2010 (from 80 to 145 victims), whereas suicides among active-duty military remained relatively stable during that same time period (162 in 2009 and 156 in 2010).

DEVELOPMENTAL CONSIDERATIONS

A child's conception of war, deployment, and a parent's absence is highly variable depending on his or her developmental level. As such, how a teacher supports and educates students with deployed caregivers depends largely on students' current developmental understanding and methods of expressing stress. Table 12.1 provides common signs and symptoms of stress for children of deployed military parent(s); some symptoms may occur across various developmental levels (see chapter 3 for more detailed information on developmental responses to trauma).

Table 12.1 DEVELOPMENTAL SIGNS AND SYMPTOMS OF STRESS AMONG STUDENTS
FROM MILITARY FAMILIES

Developmental Level	Signs and Symptoms of Stress
Infants and toddlers	• May frequently ask questions such as "Why is my daddy gone?" or "When is my daddy coming home?" as their concept of time is limited
Preschool	• May feel their behavior caused the parent to leave • More fearful/irritable
Elementary and middle school	• Decline in performance in school and on standardized tests, particularly during deployment[a] • Worrying about deployed parent's safety
High school	• Distancing themselves from deployed parent[b] • Feeling that they need to accept adult responsibilities to compensate for the absence of a parent (e.g., working) • May engage in risky behaviors to force the parent to stay home

[a] Engel, Gallagher, & Lyle, 2010.
[b] Huebner & Mancini, 2005.

FAMILY AND CULTURAL CONSIDERATIONS

Cultural diversity is an important consideration when interpreting the psychological effects of war, military deployments, and separations on children and families. Some cultures or communities may be more supportive of the country's military involvement, whereas others may express opposition. This may depend on various factors including socioeconomic status, region of the country, and political climate. It may be difficult to know every culture's or family's view on war, although it is helpful to be cognizant that views may vary, even among small communities.

STRATEGIES TO SUPPORT STUDENTS

Student reactions are dependent on several factors. Research has shown that most military children remain healthy or even develop positive skills from the experience; however, some groups are at increased risk for poor mental health and/or academic struggles, including young children, males, students with preexisting health or mental health problems, families with multiple deployments, single-parent families, and dual-military-parent families.[15] Another important factor that influences student reactions and subsequent teacher recommendations is the *stage of deployment*. Specifically, military deployment consists of three major stages, each of which has different challenges and stressors to overcome for children: (1) predeployment, (2) deployment, and (3) postdeployment, or reunion.

Stage 1: Predeployment

The predeployment stage occurs from the time military personnel first learn about their deployment to when they actually deploy, and can last for weeks to as little as just a few hours. Given the sometimes short notice, families may develop overwhelming concerns about finances, employment, childcare, or social support, creating a heightened level of stress in the home. Some children, depending on the family situation, may have to live with relatives or other guardians while their military parent deploys, which could mean that the student must change schools and leave friends. This stage causes higher levels of anxiety and concern due to facing the unknowns of the event. When educators are aware of the upcoming deployment, make an appointment to meet with the parents to discuss plans and identify specific needs and concerns. Ask the school nurse, student's teachers, school psychologist, and guidance counselor to attend this meeting.

Talk about it. Many teachers may feel uncomfortable talking about the topic of deployment when first hearing about it, although discussing the deployment with a student can be extremely helpful, including details about where the deployed parent is going and why he or she is leaving. Research shows that students who discussed the deployment with an adult experienced a better adjustment to the deployment.[16] The level of discussion should be relevant to the developmental level of the student. **Personal opinions and beliefs of the war or military should not be discussed with the student**. If negative topics come up in discussion, it is best to end on a positive note. See the "Frequently Asked Questions" section for some examples of common questions and sample responses.

Maintain frequent communication with the at-home caregiver. Research has shown that mental health and coping abilities of the at-home parent strongly impact child adjustment.[17] Thus, by supporting the parent, you are also supporting your student. At the beginning of the school year or new class, send home a parent contact form with your classroom management plan. On this parent contact form, have a section that details the parents' and/or caregivers' preferred form of communication to ensure that you are creating an optimal communication channel (e-mail, phone, written letter, communication through the student's agenda book, etc.). Some military personnel may also have some options for communication through e-mail, albeit limited, even if deployed to a war zone.

Stage 2: Deployment

The actual deployment can last from weeks to years. This stage can be broken into three time periods: the first month, the months following, and the month before reunion. During the first month, students often report mixed emotions, security issues, and sleep difficulties.[18] If these issues are evident in the classroom, take time to discuss them with the student and encourage healthy eating and physical activity, and inform the caregiver. After the first month, a new routine typically is established, therefore promoting independence and confidence. Routines and structure are important practicalities for educators to encourage as they promote resiliency and academic success for students.

During the deployment, the student may begin to feel isolated given irregular opportunities to communicate with the parent. The student may also worry about the parent's safety, especially with media coverage of the war and other issues regarding the military. Many signs of distress listed in Table 12.1 may begin to emerge during this stage if they didn't during the predeployment stage. If distress signs and symptoms persist over several weeks, it would be best to consult with or refer the student using your school's referral process to the school guidance counselor, school social worker, or school psychologist. The Educational Opportunities Directorate of the U.S. Department of Defense (EODDD) has identified nine specific behaviors that educators should be highly concerned with and need to have supporting documentation of:

1. Difficulty resuming normal classroom assignments and activities
2. Intense emotional reactions such as frequent crying and intense sadness
3. Depression, withdrawal, and being noncommunicative
4. Inattention and lack of concentration
5. Expression of violent or depressed feelings in "dark" drawings or writings
6. Self-injury or threats to others
7. Significant and rapid weight changes
8. Reduced self-care
9. Substance abuse[19]

Make a deployment countdown to the reunion with the deployed parent. Creating a countdown chart in the classroom will provide a constant reminder of the forthcoming reunion and, more important, of the school's support. This would be a great way to get the class involved and help to foster empathy.

Use teachable moments. Incorporate geographical or cultural information into your classroom curriculum about the area the parent is deployed to. There will be cases where the deployment location is classified, and in this circumstance, the last known place could be incorporated. Encourage the student to research the location where the parent could be deployed to; find out about the climate, culture, agriculture, history, and so forth. For example, a U.S. mission in Afghanistan is to build schools, roads, and water systems. Talk to the class about the schools the troops are building and the children the troops are helping. This could help the student to envision where the parent will be and what the living conditions may be like, especially through pictures. Importantly, ask the student if he or she wants the class to know about the parent. If the student wants to keep it a secret, honor that decision.

Maintain consistent expectations. While leniency and understanding are important, it's equally important to maintain high expectations for a student's academic performance. If a student begins failing to turn in assignments, rather than simply giving him or her no credit, discuss the situation and provide a temporary extension. Emphasize that you still expect the student to learn, and create a list of *reasonable* expectations (e.g., if a student is temporarily staying with a relative 1 hour farther away from school, expect less time to complete homework).

Provide appropriate class placement. As a result of frequent mobility, the student of a military family may have experienced different curricula across schools, leading to gaps in education. Consider meeting with teachers, a school counselor, the school psychologist, the student, and the family during any transitions to help assess previous knowledge and ensure proper placement.

Encourage the writing of letters or e-mails (or drawing for younger students) and pretend play. Encourage the student to write a letter or draft an e-mail to the deployed parent. You can easily make this into a classroom activity by setting up pen pals with military members for all of your students. Several websites (http://www.operationmilitarypride.org, http://www.emailourmilitary.com, and http://www.militarycity.com/letters) can help you set up these connections. Encourage younger children to use drawing, physical activity, or pretend games (e.g., toys, props, hand puppets) to express what they may not be able to put into words. The National Child Traumatic Stress Network (http://www.nctsnet.org) has a list of resources that are available for military families. These resources range from reading materials and videos to activities and games for children. For instance, there is a 48-page journal available called *My Life: A Kid's Journal Coloring Book* that helps children to make sense of their feelings with their parent is deployed.

Many fun games exist online that teach children about the military; for example, http://www.deploymentkids.com/playtime.html provides games to learn the military alphabet codes along with ranks and insignia. For children too young to write letters, drawing and play can be a great way to let them convey unspoken fears, anxieties, or guilt[20] and can provide an incredibly soothing outlet. A class project could be to send care packages to military members. This could be a student's parent, or the class could "adopt" a solider. For more information on sending care packages and other supportive troop measures, please visit http://operationmilitarypride.org/ and other professional sites for troop support.

Encourage journaling. Discussing the parent's deployment with a student can be easily incorporated into the classroom curriculum through journal or essay writing. When you read the journal or essay, provide written feedback. Be honest and positive with your feedback. You might say, "I get a little scared too, but when I do, I make a plan and I discuss that with someone I trust and love." Journaling allows the student to put down thoughts, fears, and anxieties in a safe place. Encourage students to share, although remind them that sharing is optional.

Utilize the experiences of military students. Military students obtain a set of skills and background experiences that are unique to most classrooms. Given experiences in other cultures or countries, they can help enrich the curriculum during classroom instruction. Drawing attention to these experiences in a positive way can help the student feel both valuable and connected to the school. In this way, consider the presence of military students as an advantage to the classroom and the school.

Support various creative outlets. Aside from journaling, students can often express themselves well through art, music, and poetry, or even creating skits or stories about their military parent. Some teachers may feel comfortable helping to make a video or set up a video chat with the parent; others may refer the student to someone in the building who is more technologically savvy.

Keep an eye out for signs of maltreatment. Child abuse and neglect may increase during parental deployment.[21] In this case, be prepared to contact your school administrator and local authorities.

Anticipate changes as deployment ends. The anticipation of homecoming sets in as the deployment nears an end. Students may exhibit bursts of energy, impulsivity, and indecisiveness. Address issues as they arise, stay abreast of the student's academic progress, and be attentive that the student may be taken out of school for the homecoming day and days following.

Stage 3: Reunion or Postdeployment

The return of the deployed parent is the most anticipated event of the deployment process for children. They may experience a variety of feelings as a deployed parent reunites with the family, including anxiety that arose during the deployment, concern about whether the parent will remember or love them, joy of seeing the parent, excitement to share news with the parent, and anticipation of the day. Further, discipline issues may arise around the time the parent returns from deployment.[22]

The postdeployment period is a time of adjustment (which may take up to 7 months). There are needs for personal space during this stage for the entire family, as well as shifts in existing family dynamics and routines that had been created in the parent's absence. This may lead to feelings of disappointment. Consider discussing family roles and how roles change with the student and with the parents.

Open lines of communication. Talk to the student prior to the homecoming about what the family has planned for homecoming day. If possible, allow time for the student to make a sign or card for the returning parent. Encourage students to communicate to the parents on how they are feeling and how much they have missed the deployed parent. As an educator, you can also help your students by providing resources to parents, such as sharing helpful websites (e.g., http://www.militarychild.org, http://www.militaryfamily.org, http://www.nasponline.org).

Programs like Operation Purple are also available to aid children in dealing with the stress of war and deployments.

Allow leniency with attendance. It will be normal for students to miss a day or two of school during this stage, especially on the actual day of the homecoming. More time may be needed for the military family to see and spend time with loved ones out of state. However, holding the student accountable for his or her work is important as well. If you know in advance that the returning parent is arriving during a week when there is a test or project due, communicate that with the parent and student and work together to create a plan.

Maintain routines and structure. If the service member returns due to injury, know that the injury may have led to physical and/or emotional symptoms. Thus, expect an adjustment period to the "new normal" for the family, which will likely carry over into the classroom. Your role is crucial as an educator to maintain consistency, predictability, and structure in the school environment.

Help students create new ways to reconnect and understand disabilities. If the deployed parent returned physically injured (e.g., missing a leg) and the student is worried about shared activities, work on making a list of fun things they can do together. Include activities in your classroom that can help students understand disabilities better. For example, the students could play a game together from the seat of their chairs without using their legs or feet, or attempt daily activities such as combing their hair with a blindfold on. More challenging are the disabilities that are not "visible" to the student (e.g., PTSD) and, depending on the developmental age, the student may be too young to understand. In this case, routines are increasingly important, along with frequent reminders that the child is safe and will be cared for. This would be particularly helpful for students like Jeron (see the vignette) who have difficulty reconnecting with the parent.

Encourage active participation. Encouraging a student to volunteer or give back to the community in some way is extremely helpful and meaningful to the student. For high school students, this can include working with organizations that support war veterans. Encourage students to continue activities that are relaxing, such as sports, school dances, or extracurricular activities. Emphasize that they should not feel guilty for having fun.

Teach life skills. Many schools provide classes that consistently teach life skills as part of the curriculum, and encouraging students to take these classes would be helpful. They could learn how to do laundry, cook, maintain the house, manage money, go grocery shopping, and so forth. This would be particularly helpful for older students who have taken on additional responsibility in the absence of a parent.

Document. One of the most important things an educator has to do is document. Noting when a behavior was seen, what was going on in the classroom, responses, and the calendar date is crucial to seeing a possible developing pattern and if the problem is getting worse. Having a special documentation notebook

set aside to keep a log of parental communication, school resource communication, behaviors, responses, interventions, and so forth, is essential.

FREQUENTLY ASKED QUESTIONS AND SPECIAL ISSUES

How do I answer difficult questions from students about the war and their parents? When students have questions, answer them honestly but simply, although not all details are necessary and should be left up to the parent(s). If you have not spoken to the at-home caregiver about what he or she wants shared with the student, explain you will try to find out and call the parent to discuss. In the meantime, you, as the educator, can ask what students think is happening and talk about their feelings. Here are some common questions you may encounter:

Q: "When is Dad coming home?" or "Why can't he come home now?"

Response: "Your dad will be home when his job is finished. He loves you very much and can't wait to be home again."

Q: "How come Mom has to go away again but my friend Alex's mother doesn't have to go away at all?"

Response: "Everyone has a different job; your mother's job is one that needs to be done in another country (or a place far away)."

Q: "Is Dad leaving because he is angry at me?"

Response: "No. Your Dad may be frustrated or tired, but he is not angry with you."

Q: "When will the war be over?"

Response: "I'm not sure. I know they want to make sure they finished their job before they leave."

Q: "Do you think my Dad will get hurt?"

Response: "He will do everything he can to not get hurt. The military trains their soldiers to protect and help each other."

Side note: This is an extremely sensitive subject that could easily incorpo
rate faith, religion, personal beliefs, and so forth. Keep the response simple and redirect the student.

Should I limit coverage of the war? What if I teach a current events class? You can incorporate world events into the curriculum, but do not bombard the student with magazines, Internet sites, articles, and newspapers that have extensive coverage of war or frightening events. Try to avoid discussions of injuries or death; instead, focus on the mission of the country and the goals of our military involvement.

What if my students hear people talking or read about people who disagree with the war? You can say something like, "There are always going to be differing views on subjects. Tell me what you think."

What if one of the students in the class questions the war? Give an educated, professional, and nonbiased response. You can ask the student to write down his or her questions, but emphasize that at the moment you need to focus on the objectives for the day.

Will emergency drills result in a negative reaction among students with deployed parents? It is possible that students with deployed parents may not respond as quickly to a drill, or the drill could trigger fear and anxiety that they may not be safe in the school. This is true even if the student has practiced the drill many times. If that happens, reassure the student that he or she will be protected at school. If possible, warn the student about practice drills beforehand, and reassure the student that the school is one of the safest places to be.

Is there training that would be beneficial for school staff members? There are a variety of beneficial professional development opportunities, both live and online, which can be found by visiting various websites (e.g., http://www.militarychild.org, http://www.deploymentpsych.org/training, and http://www.jhsph.edu/mci). Many services are also available to schools through the local military installation's Family Service Centers, which can be found through the local military base website. These centers can have educators come to the schools to provide the following:

- Awareness of stressors faced during deployment and deployment training
- Assistance with military contacts for consultations with school liaisons
- Evaluation, documentation, and intervention training
- Identification of potential resources
- Follow-up with referrals[23]

CONCLUSION

Students exposed to the demands and stressors of having a military parent, especially one deployed to a war zone, frequently endure many negative social-emotional and academic outcomes. Further, the specific details surrounding the war (e.g., level of violence, location, funding) will greatly impact the experience of the families involved. Educators maintain the responsibility to learn how to best meet all of their learning needs, including recognizing and addressing barriers to learning. Military children are unique from other children who have experienced trauma, although they share many qualities as well. Equipping yourself with valuable resources and educating yourself about the military lifestyle and its demands will ensure that you can support the military student in the classroom.

With the large number of military children and parents deploying, it is important for educators to understand the effects on military children through awareness of signs and symptoms of distress, and how to best assist in meeting their unique needs. Schools can be the one place that provides structure, consistency, and dependability for military children and be the anchor they need during deployments.

AUTHOR NOTE

Some information in this chapter was first published in Rossen, E., & Carter, C. D. (2011). Supporting students from military families. *Principle Leadership,* *11*(6), 14–18. It has been adapted with permission by the National Association of Secondary School Principals. Copyright (2011). Retrieved from http://www. nasponline.org/resources/principals/Military_Families_Feb11_NASSP.pdf

NOTES

1. RAND, n.d.
2. Chandra, Lara-Cinisomo, et al., 2010.
3. Department of Defense, n.d.
4. Bradshaw, Sudhinaraset, Mmari, & Blum, 2010.
5. Paik & Phillips, 2002.
6. Mansfield, Kaufman, Engel, & Gaynes, 2011.
7. Flake, Davis, & Johnson, 2009.
8. Hefling, 2009.
9. Gorman, Eide, & Hisle-Gorman, 2010.
10. Chandra, Martin, Hawkins, & Richardson, 2010.
11. Kaiser Daily Health Policy Report, 2007.
12. Defense and Veterans Brain Injury Center, n.d.
13. American Psychological Association, 2010.
14. U.S. Department of Defense Education Activity, n.d.
15. The National Child Traumatic Stress Network, n.d.
16. Huebner & Mancini, 2005.
17. Huebner & Mancini, 2005.
18. Fitzsimons & Krause-Parello, 2009.
19. U.S. Department of Defense, Educational Opportunities Directorate, n.d.
20. Malchiodi, 2001.

21. Chandra, Lara-Cinisomo, et al., 2010; Rentz et al., 2007.
22. Fitzsimons & Krause-Parello, 2009.
23. U.S. Department of Defense, Educational Opportunities Directorate, n.d.

REFERENCES

American Psychological Association. (2010). Military suicides continue to climb. *Monitor on Psychology, 41,* 11.

Bradshaw, C. P., Sudhinaraset, M., Mmari, K., & Blum, R. W. (2010). School transitions among military adolescents: A qualitative study of stress and coping. *School Psychology Review, 39,* 84–105.

Chandra, A., Lara-Cinisomo, S., Jaycox, L. H., Tanielian, T., Burns, R. M., Ruder, T., et al. (2010). Children on the homefront: The experiences of children from military families. *Pediatrics, 125,* 16–25.

Chandra, A., Martin, L. T., Hawkins, S. A., & Richardson, A. (2010). The impact of parental deployment on child social and emotional functioning: Perspectives of school staff. *Journal of Adolescent Health, 46,* 218–223.

Defense and Veterans Brain Injury Center. (n.d.). *Department of Defense numbers of traumatic brain injury.* Retrieved from http://www.dvbic.org/TBI-Numbers.aspx

Department of Defense. (n.d.) *Defense casualty report.* Retrieved from http://www.defense.gov/news/casualty.pdf

Engel, R. C., Gallagher, L. B., & Lyle, D. S. (2010). Military deployments and children's academic achievement: Evidence from Department of Defense education activity schools. *Economics of Education Review, 29,* 73–82.

Fitzsimons, V. M., & Krause-Parello, C. A. (2009). Military children when parents are deployed overseas. *Journal of School Nursing, 25*(1), 40–47.

Flake, E., Davis, B. E., & Johnson, P. L. (2009). The psychosocial effects of deployment on military children. *Journal of Developmental & Behavioral Pediatrics, 30,* 271–278.

Gorman, G. H., Eide, M., & Hisle-Gorman, E. (2010). Wartime military deployment and increased pediatric mental and behavioral health complaints. *Pediatrics, 126,* doi:10.1542/peds.2009-2856

Hefling, K. (2009, July 7). More military children seeking mental care. *The Marine Corps Times.* Retrieved from http://www.marinecorpstimes.com/news/2009/07/ap_children_mental_health_070709/

Huebner, A. J., & Mancini, J. A. (2005, June). *Adjustment among adolescents in military families when a parent is deployed: A final report submitted to the Military Family Research Institute and the Department of Defense Quality of Life Office.* Falls Church, VA: Virginia Tech, Department of Human Development.

Kaiser Daily Health Policy Report. (2007, July 13). *Capitol Hill watch: Pentagon official urges improvements in mental health care for service members.* Retrieved from http://www.kaisernetwork.org/daily_reports/rep_index.cfm?hint=3&DR_ID=46212

Malchiodi, C. A. (2001). Using drawing as intervention with traumatized children. *Trauma and Loss: Research and Interventions, 1*(1), 15–22.

Mansfield, A. J., Kaufman, J. S., Engel, C. C., & Gaynes, B. N. (2011). Deployment and mental health diagnoses among children of US Army personnel. *Archives of Pediatrics and Adolescent Medicine.* doi:10.1001/archpediatrics.123

The National Child Traumatic Stress Network. (n.d.) *Military children and families.* Retrieved from http://www.nctsnet.org/nccts/nav.do?pid=ctr_top_military

Paik, S. Z., & Phillips, R. (2002). Student mobility in rural communities: What are the implications for student achievement? *Education Policy.* Retrieved from http://www. ncrel.org/policy/pubs/html/rmobile/effect.htm

RAND. (n.d.). *Viewed through a different lens: The effects of deployment on military children.* Retrieved from http://www.rand.org/congress/newsletters/child/2010/04/

Rentz, E. D., Marshall, S. W., Loomis, D., Casteel, C., Martin, S. L., & Gibbs, D. A. (2007). Effect of deployment on the occurrence of child maltreatment in military and nonmilitary families. *American Journal of Epidemiology, 165,* 1199–1206.

U.S. Department of Defense Education Activity. (n.d.). *DoDEA data center.* Arlington, VA: Author. Retrieved from http://www.dodea.edu/datacenter/enrollment.cfm

U.S. Department of Defense, Educational Opportunities Directorate. (n.d.). *Educator's guide to the military child during deployment.* Retrieved from http://www2.ed.gov/ about/offices/list/os/homefront/homefront.pdf

WEB RESOURCES

- Deployment Kids: http://www.deploymentkids.com
- Helping Children Cope with Deployment: http://www.usuhs.mil/psy/ CTChildrenCopeDuringDeployment.pdf
- Military Family books: http://www.militaryfamilybooks.com
- Military Families Resource Center: http://www.aacap.org/cs/ MilitaryFamilies.ResourceCenter
- National Military Family Association: http://www.nmfa.org

SELECTED CHILDREN'S LITERATURE

- Bunting, E. (2005). *My red balloon.* Honesdale, PA: Boyds Mills Press.
- Edlick, K. (2008). *We serve too! A child's deployment book.* Wee the People Publishing.
- Ehrmantraut, B. (2005). *Night catch.* Aberdeen, SD: Bubble Gum Press.
- Ferguston-Cohen, M. (2002). *Daddy, you're my hero! and Mommy, you're my hero!* Little Redhaired Girl Publishing.
- Hilbrecht, K., & Hilbrecht, S. (2000). *My daddy is a soldier.* Rossville, GA: New Canaan Publishing.
- McElroy, L. T. (2005). *Love, Lizzie: Letters to a military mom.* Park Ridge, IL: Albert Whitman.
- Pelton, M. L. (2004). *When dad's at sea.* Park Ridge, IL: Albert Whitman.
- Sederman, M., & Epstein, S. (2002). *The magic box: When parents can't be there to tuck you in.* Washington, DC: Magination Press.
- Sportelli-Rehak, A. (2004). *Uncle Sam's kids: When duty calls.* Island Heights, NJ: Abidenme Books.
- Tomp, S. W. (2005). *Red, white, and blue good-bye.* New York, NY: Walker Books.

13

Students Affected by Sexual Abuse

DELPHINE COLLIN-VÉZINA ■

INTRODUCTION

Child sexual abuse (CSA) is a form of maltreatment that provokes reactions of indignation and incomprehensibility across all cultures. Although CSA is recognized as a serious violation of human well-being and of the law, no community has yet developed mechanisms that ensure that none of its children will be sexually abused. Child sexual abuse is an international problem.[1] In fact, children of virtually all ages, sexes, races, cultures, ethnicities, and socioeconomic classes are at risk of being sexually abused. As such, educators are likely to have several victims of sexual abuse in their schools and classrooms every year.[2]

Until recently, there was much disagreement as to what should be included in the definition of CSA. In some past definitions, only contact abuse was included, such as penetration, fondling, kissing, and touching. Noncontact sexual abuse such as exhibitionism and voyeurism were not always considered abusive. It is now agreed that CSA comprises any sexual activity perpetrated against a minor by threat, force, intimidation, or manipulation. The array of sexual activities include fondling, inviting a child to touch or be touched sexually, intercourse, rape, incest, sodomy, exhibitionism, voyeurism, or involving a child in prostitution or pornography.[3] Child sexual abuse is contingent upon a relationship between a child and a person in a position of power, and is defined as sexual acts perpetrated on another without consent, without equality, or as a result of coercion.[4] As such, CSA is not exclusively linked to sexual contact between an adult and a child. Although sexual activity between children and youth has long been thought to be harmless, child-on-child sexual abuse experiences are becoming increasingly recognized to be as detrimental for the emotional well-being of children and youth as adult-on-child sexual abuse.[5]

The magnitude of the problem of CSA is difficult to approximate given differences in the data collection systems across areas, including variations in definitions and screening processes.[6] Approximately 66,000 reports of sexual abuse were made in the United States in 2009, which constitutes 9.5% of all reported maltreatment cases.[7] However, it is well acknowledged that many CSA victims continue to be unknown; in fact, only about half of victims disclose CSA to *anyone,* and the majority of youth do not reveal CSA during childhood.[8] Further, research findings clearly demonstrate a major lack of congruence between the low number of official reports of CSA to authorities and the high rates of CSA that youth and adults self-report retrospectively (often as adults). Indeed, a recent comprehensive meta-analysis that combined estimations of CSA in 217 publications published between 1980 and 2008 showed the rates of CSA to be more than 30 times higher in self-report studies (127/1,000, or 12.7%) than in official-report inquiries (4/1,000, or 0.4%).[9] Based on self-report measures, which include both disclosed and unreported occurrences, CSA is clearly a widespread problem, with more than one out of eight people reporting this experience.

Although females are about two times more likely to be CSA victims than males,[10] several authors point out that there is a strong likelihood that boys are more frequently abused than the ratio of reported cases would suggest given their probable reluctance to report the abuse.[11] A recent study confirmed this assumption by showing that among CSA survivors, 16% of female victims had never disclosed the abuse, whereas this proportion rose to 30% for male victims.[12] School-aged children and adolescents are most vulnerable to CSA, though about one-quarter of CSA survivors report they were first abused before age 6 years.[13]

Educators' Knowledge of CSA and Perceived Confidence in Ability to Intervene

School personnel are increasingly seen as key figures in detecting sexual victimization in students. Educators can play important roles by identifying signs and symptoms of CSA, responding appropriately to disclosures, and reporting abuse (suspected or disclosed).[14] Most school professionals will have to report some form of abuse, including CSA, at some point in their career.

An interesting study that speaks to educators' attitudes and beliefs toward CSA disclosures was conducted among primary school teachers.[15] It found that most teachers were reasonably well informed; however, female teachers were significantly more accurately informed than male teachers and were also significantly more likely than males to believe a child's disclosure. Female teachers also had a greater inclination to put the child's word before that of the parent. Interestingly, over half the teachers denied there was ever a child in their school who was sexually abused, and a substantial number said they would hesitate to report if they suspected it—which perhaps explains the case of Tonya (see the vignette). Two-thirds of the teachers feared being sued if a child disclosed to them.

Vignette—Tonya

Tonya is a 12-year-old girl who is one of four children. Her stepfather, who moved into the house about 3 years ago, has sexually abused Tonya and her other sister, whereas he leaves her brothers alone. Tonya's mother is passive, such that despite having suspicions of abuse, she has remained silent. Tonya's two brothers have also not told anyone out of fear of the stepfather, who has threatened them both on several occasions. Tonya comes home from school feeling fearful and has recently begun acting differently at school. She has thought about telling someone, but she is afraid it might break up the family and thinks her mother would be heart-broken if she knew. In this regard, Tonya feels that she must be strong. Tonya has begun acting overtly sexual toward other boys in her grade and has been found in the boys' locker room on three separate occasions. While her teachers have noticed some differences in her behavior, her grades have remained fairly stable, so they have not pursued their concerns any further.

Despite the knowledge that school personnel have regarding CSA, scholars in the field wonder whether educators receive the appropriate training that is required to intervene on behalf of students.[16] The decision of an educator to report to Child Protective Services seems to be informed by several different factors. In one study, Crenshaw, Crenshaw, and Lichtenberg[17] did not find a relationship between reporting tendency and gender of the victim or respondent. However, certain factors distinguished reporters from nonreporters, such as the possibility that reporting may damage the relationship between the educator and the family, fear of parental reaction and concern for the educator's relationship with the student, the view that the school should not be the first line of defense for students, and concern that there is not enough evidence to support reporting. In that vein, Tite[18] found that educators were reluctant to be bound by the definitions of the legal acts when it came to reporting CSA. Educators preferred to intervene with the problem informally at the school level as opposed to formal reporting. According to this study, the reporting of CSA by educators is often complicated by their disciplinary role, concerns that they establish reasonable grounds, and a belief that it can be better handled by the school than by Child Protective Services.

Although the disclosure experience is stressful for the child and the reporting process can be quite stressful for educators, it is worth highlighting that several countries, and all 50 states in the United States, possess mandatory reporting requirements of some sort, which infers that all suspected CSA cases must be brought to the attention of the authorities. Beyond these legal principles, it should not be forgotten that sexual victimization can be of a shockingly long duration, and that reporting can be a powerful means to put an end to an abusive situation that may, otherwise, last for months or years.

Reporting can also lead to early assessment and treatment, which may off-set the exacerbation and continuation of negative mental health outcomes.[19] Disclosure of CSA soon after its occurrence reduces the risk of negative outcomes when compared to delaying disclosure. With this in mind, it is quite unfortunate that a majority of CSA victims delay disclosure until adulthood and that those who try to disclose in childhood often first attempt disclosure through behavior and other indirect ways.[20] Moreover, adolescents are likely to take more time to disclose than younger children, which could be partly explained by their fear of negative consequences and their feelings of being responsible for the abuse.[21]

School-Related and Mental Health Outcomes of CSA

The Four-Factor Traumagenics Model[22] suggests that CSA alters a child's cognitive and emotional orientation to the world and causes trauma by distorting his or her self-concept or affective capacities. The unique nature of CSA as a form of maltreatment is highlighted by the four trauma-causing factors that victims may experience, which are traumatic sexualization, betrayal, stigmatization, and powerlessness. This model underscores the issues of trust and intimacy that are particularly pronounced among victims of CSA, which require heightened sensitivity on the part of professionals who work with them.[23]

Child sexual abuse is a substantial risk factor in the development of a host of negative consequences in both childhood and adulthood. Posttraumatic stress disorder and dissociation symptoms are more common among CSA victims than nonabused children in the preschool years,[24] in the school years,[25] and in adolescence.[26] Mood disorders, such as major depressive episodes, as well as sleeping disturbances, eating problems, and regressive behaviors (e.g., thumb sucking) have also been strongly associated with CSA across the lifespan.[27] In school-aged children, CSA outcomes can manifest in behavioral problems, such as inappropriate sexualized behaviors.[28] In the teenage years, victims have been shown to present more conduct problems, at-risk sexual behaviors, substance abuse, fear, anxiety, withdrawal, and self-harming behaviors.[29] These mental health outcomes are likely to continue into adulthood given the demonstrated link between CSA and lifetime psychopathology.[30] Even more worrisome is the fact that CSA victims are more at risk than non-CSA youth to experience violence in their early romantic relationships.[31] In a 10-year review of CSA studies, Putnam[32] found that the majority of CSA victims are moderately to seriously symptomatic and may present with more than one psychiatric diagnosis. Considering that several genetic and environmental factors can contribute to the occurrence of the aforementioned mental health and behavioral issues, it was recently suggested to consider CSA as a general, nonspecific risk factor for psychopathology.[33]

More specific to school-related issues, the role of CSA on academic performance and school dropout has not been fully studied and has led to inconclusive results thus far. One study[34] highlighted four different academic profiles of CSA female victims. The girls in the *Academic-specific* cluster made up 15% of the sample and were characterized by severe and long-lasting academic problems, whereas their social and emotional functioning was rated within the average range. The *Acting out/withdrawn* cluster (16% of the sample) comprised girls likely to function at an average level academically, socially accepted by their peers, but perceived to externalize their negative feelings by expressing anger, breaking rules, or withdrawing socially. In the third cluster, *Polyclinical* (22% of the sample), girls were distinguishable from the other clusters by their social problems, such as peer rejection or bullying, and clingy and suspicious behavior. They also had decreased academic performance and displayed withdrawal and externalizing behaviors. The last cluster, *Resilient* (47% of the sample), stood on its own in many ways, as girls were rated as best adjusted in all spheres of competence and they obtained scores comparable to what would be expected of a nonsexually abused comparison group.

In light of this, despite overwhelming evidence of the deleterious impacts of CSA, some studies suggest that not all victims show symptoms. About one-third of victims may not manifest any clinical symptoms at the time the abuse is disclosed.[35] This can be explained, in part, by the extremely diverse characteristics of CSA, which lead to a wide range of potential outcomes. Sexual victimization is a complex life experience where victims form a heterogeneous group for which no generalizations can be made. Also, students are not equally equipped with personal, familial, and environmental resources that can help them cope with the abuse. Among an array of factors potentially influencing the resilience capacities of CSA victims, students who receive support from their nonoffending parents or other trusting adults and those who have not experienced prior abuses seem to fare better in spite of the sexual abuse adversity.[36]

DEVELOPMENTAL CONSIDERATIONS

Many factors are likely to contribute to symptoms displayed by victims, including personal factors (e.g., age, gender), familial factors (e.g., family structure, family stress), and abuse-specific factors (e.g., duration, relationship between victim and perpetrator), yet more research is warranted to clarify their impact.[37] For instance, the impact of CSA has been hypothesized to vary with the developmental stage at which the abuse occurs—and more specifically to vary depending on CSA being perpetrated at prepubertal or pubertal stages—though research has produced conflicting results to date. There are many studies showing that CSA at a younger age is predictive of greater deleterious outcomes, whereas others suggest that teenagers are more negatively impacted by the abuse.[38]

Overall, CSA seems to produce negative outcomes in a majority of victims regardless of the developmental stage at which the abuse occurs. That being said, the effects of CSA can be manifested in different ways that relate to the areas of the victim's psychological development.[39] For instance, CSA in prepubescent students may result in self-degradation and decreased self-esteem, whereas pubescent students may manifest difficulties in engaging in healthy intimate relationships following the abuse.

CULTURAL CONSIDERATIONS

While low socioeconomic status is a significant risk factor for physical abuse (chapter 15) and neglect (chapter 14), it has much less impact on CSA.[40] The faulty belief that CSA occurs more frequently among underprivileged families may be the product of the disproportionate number of CSA cases reported to Child Protective Services that come from lower socioeconomic classes.[41] In that vein, some populations of students have been overrepresented in research that focused on vulnerable populations, such as students from low-socioeconomic-status families, which may have created an erroneous belief that race and ethnicity are risk factors for CSA.[42]

Certain aspects of various cultures may impact how students disclose, cope, and process CSA experiences. For example, individuals from various minority groups may distrust police and law enforcement, resulting in fewer disclosures to authorities. As a more specific example of cultural differences in reporting, Latino women have described themselves as strong, resilient, and even secretive, leading this culture to also be less inclined to disclose CSA experiences.[43] Further, Latino women have noted that the main reason for not reporting CSA was fear of not being believed by others, being blamed, stigmatization, getting in trouble, or even being physically harmed.[44] Interestingly, Latina and Black women have described children's behaviors (e.g., withdrawal, excessive crying) as the most likely way to detect CSA, as opposed to direct disclosure.[45] One study found that Hispanic girls experienced more CSA yet waited longer to disclose when compared to Black girls.[46]

Other cultural explanations for differences in disclosure include shame; taboo and modesty (e.g., Arab and Spanish cultures dissuade discussion of sexual experiences and sex education[47]); the importance of virginity among some cultures (e.g., Muslim and Arab); fear of sparking retaliation from family members; and honor and respect for male elders (e.g., Latino and some Asian cultures).[48] It is also possible that cultural differences in reporting may be a result of actual cultural differences in the experiences of CSA. For example, Hispanic girls tend to experience more CSA by their fathers or stepfathers than other groups.[49] Taken further, various religious ideals may also impact disclosure and how individuals process CSA.

SCHOOL-BASED PREVENTION PROGRAMS

As pointed out by Wurtele,[50] current rates of school-based program implementation are unknown, and it is likely that attention to CSA prevention diminished during the mid- to late 1990s as other social problems of students gained awareness. In addition, these programs have been critiqued for focusing on concepts and skills too complex for students to learn, for increasing anxiety in students, and, more important, for not actually preventing CSA from happening in the first place.[51] Although there is little evidence that primary prevention programs do *prevent* CSA,[52] several systematic reviews showed that the implementation of prevention programs increases students' safety knowledge and enhances appropriate attitudes toward CSA victims and disclosure processes.[53] In cases where parents and educators were involved, child abuse prevention programs led to significant gains in knowledge for these participants as well.[54]

In light of this, prevention programs should be conceptualized in terms of "reducing risk factors and building protective factors in the potential perpetrator, potential victim and his or her family, and in the environment in which they all exist."[55] At an organizational level, school-based policies can be implemented such as developing CSA screening techniques and providing school personnel with guidelines for intervening appropriately when disclosure and reporting situations happen. Schools should explore possibilities of offering their staff web-based educational programs as opposed to workshop trainings, as it could alleviate some of the challenges and constraints that educators experience, such as lack of time, problems in scheduling, and scarce resources.[56]

RECOMMENDATIONS FOR EDUCATORS

Respond to disclosures with empathy and without judgment. Some students will directly disclose their experience to an educator. In order to do so, they need to feel that they are in a safe place and that the expectation is that they will be believed.[57] Further, the response of the adult to the disclosure has an impact on the student.[58] One study found that students might disclose bits of information to gauge the adult's response; if the reaction is positive and caring, the student may disclose more.[59] When it appears to students that they are not believed or taken seriously or if child services and the police are called in without warning, they may not talk again.

Disclosure is a challenging and delicate process and needs to be handled with empathy and sensitivity, particularly given the tremendous risk the student is taking by disclosing.[60] Positive and supportive professionals who acknowledge and validate the abuse mitigate the negative effects of the abuse.[61] In contrast, unsupportive professionals who minimize the abuse or disbelieve it may exacerbate the negative effects of the abuse.

Make school-based support personnel known to all students. A variety of professional supports are available in most schools, including school counselors, school psychologists, school nurses, and school social workers. Aside from providing a range of supports to all students, they may also increase the likelihood of disclosure of CSA. Some studies showed that fewer students disclosed to a teacher with whom they had an ongoing relationship than to other adults in the building.[62] Some students may feel less hesitant to disclose the abuse to an outsider with whom they have not been much in contact with, and with whom they may have little contact afterward. Therefore, students should be well informed of the different professionals who work within their school as to expand the range of adults they may feel trustworthy enough to confide in.

Help locate any needed medical attention. Some student victims of CSA may require a medical evaluation depending on the nature of the abuse. Educators who become aware of CSA should help connect the student with medical resources—the school nurse is a great place to start.

Stay attuned to hints of sexual abuse. CSA is often disclosed through hints rather than direct disclosure.[63] Some examples may include statements such as "I couldn't sleep last night," or "I don't like going to my uncle's house." Other signs may include somatic complaints, withdrawal or crying a lot, sexualized behavior toward others, bloodied or stained clothing, or even contraction of a sexually transmitted disease.

Follow legal and ethical obligations when responding to disclosure. Educators should be very clear and honest with students making a disclosure that they cannot keep it a secret, while reassuring the students that they did the right thing by disclosing. There is no need to question the veracity of the allegations or confirm the abuse, as it is only necessary to have a *suspicion* to report CSA cases. Students should not be asked leading questions; using leading or suggestive interview techniques (e.g., "Did he touch you on your private parts?" while the child did not mention being touched) could hinder the legal process at a later date and could place them in even further emotional and physical jeopardy. Avoid telling them everything will be all right because the outcome is unknown, although educators should emphasize that the abuse is not their fault and that other people will be called to put a plan in place to protect them.

FORENSIC PROTOCOLS AND TREATMENT STRATEGIES

Although forensic assessment protocols and treatment programs are usually neither located in nor subsidized by the school system, educators are likely to collaborate with other organizations when CSA cases are disclosed and reported to the authorities. If educators are aware of best practices in interviewing and investigating, they can provide better support to investigative agencies.

When it comes to forensic assessment (e.g., interviewing) protocols, there are two models that have undergone considerable evaluation. These are the National Institute of Child Health and Human Development (NICHD) Structured Interview Protocol[64] and the Sexual Assault Nurse Examiner (SANE) model.[65] In terms of treatment, trauma-focused cognitive-behavioral therapy (TF-CBT) is the most established treatment for students who have experienced CSA and present with posttraumatic stress disorder symptoms.[66] It is a psychosocial treatment model designed to treat posttraumatic stress and related emotional and behavioral problems in children and adolescents. The components of the treatment model include psychoeducation and parenting skills, relaxation skills, affect expression and regulation skills, cognitive coping skills and processing, trauma narrative, in vivo exposure, conjoint parent–child sessions, and enhancing safety and future development. Trauma-focused cognitive-behavioral therapy is generally delivered in 12 to 16 sessions of individual and parent–child therapy, although it may be provided in the context of a longer term treatment process or in a group therapy format. This treatment has demonstrated effectiveness in improving participant symptoms as well as parenting skills and students' personal safety skills, even when the duration of the program was as short as 8 weeks.[67] Information on TF-CBT, including free resources and online training modules, can be found at http://tfcbt.musc.edu/

CONCLUSION

Child sexual abuse is a widespread problem that affects an estimated one out of eight people. This alarming rate clearly calls for extensive and powerful policy and practice efforts. While the effects of CSA may not always be visible, victims still carry the threat to their well-being. The traumatic experience of CSA is one major risk factor in the development of school-related and mental health problems. Considering that many victims continue to be unknown, the roots of these mental health problems may also be undetected. In an effort to provide effective services to all victims, we should prioritize the development of strategies to address the barriers to disclosure and reporting. Although the taboo of CSA might not be as prominent as a few decades ago when CSA was rarely spoken of, veiled issues may still prevent victims from reaching out to authorities or even trusted adults to reveal the abuse they suffer. Educators can, and should, play a pivotal role in providing the victims a nonjudgmental, supportive setting that facilitates and promotes the disclosure of CSA experiences.

NOTES

1. Finkelhor, 1994.
2. Hinkelman & Bruno, 2008.
3. Putnam, 2003.
4. National Task Force on Juvenile Sexual Offending, 1993; Webster, 2001.
5. Shaw, Lewis, Loeb, Rosado, & Rodriguez, 2000.
6. Johnson, 2008.
7. U.S. Department of Health and Human Services, Administration for Children and Families, Administration on Children, Youth and Families, Children's Bureau, 2010.
8. Finkelhor, 1994; Fontes & Plummer, 2010; Putnam, 2003.
9. Stoltenborgh, van IJzendoorn, Euser, & Bakermans-Kranenburg, 2011.
10. Stoltenborgh et al., 2011.
11. O'Leary & Barber, 2008.
12. Hébert, Tourigny, Cyr, McDuff, & Joly, 2009.

13. Putnam, 2003.
14. Wurtele, 2009.
15. Lawlor, 1993.
16. Goldman & Padayachi, 2002; Hinkelham & Bruno, 2008.
17. Crenshaw, Crenshaw & Lichtenberg, 1995.
18. Tite, 1993.
19. Briere & Elliott, 1994.
20. Alaggia, 2005.
21. Goodman-Brown, Edelstein, Goodman, Jones, & Gordon, 2003.
22. Finkelhor & Browne, 1985.
23. Baker, Curtis, & Papa-Lentini, 2006.
24. Bernier, Hébert, Collin-Vézina, 2011.
25. Collin-Vézina & Hébert, 2005.
26. Kilpatrick et al., 2003.
27. American Psychological Association, 2011; Sadowski et al., 2003; Spataro, Mullen, Burgess, Wells, & Moss, 2004.
28. Friedrich, 1991.
29. Brezo et al., 2007; Danielson et al., 2010; Kilpatrick, Acierno, Saunders, Resnick, Best, & Schnurr, 2000; Lalor & McElvaney, 2010; Shin, Eswards, & Heeren, 2010; Wright, Friedrich, Cinq-Mars, Cyr, & McDuff, 2004.
30. MacMillan et al., 2001.
31. Vezina & Hébert, 2007.
32. Putnam, 2003.
33. Maniglio, 2009.
34. Daignault & Hébert, 2009.
35. Kendall-Tackett, Meyer-Williams, & Finkelhor, 1993.
36. Elliott & Carnes, 2001; Hébert, Collin-Vézina, Daigneault, Parent, & Tremblay, 2006.
37. Yancey & Hansen, 2010.
38. Downs, 1993; Yancey & Hansen, 2010.
39. Trickett & Putnam, 1993.
40. Putnam, 2003.
41. Finkelhor, 1993.
42. Kenny & McEachern, 2000.
43. Ligiéro, Fassinger, McCauley, Moore, & Lyytinen, 2009.
44. Ligiéro et al., 2009.
45. Fontes, Cruz, & Tabachnik, 2001.
46. Shaw et al., 2000.
47. Gilligan & Akhtar, 2006.
48. Fontes & Plummer, 2010.
49. Fontes & Plummer, 2010.
50. Wurtele, 2009.
51. See Wurtele, 2009.
52. Finkelhor, 2009.
53. Kenny, Capri, Thakkar-Kolar, Ryan, & Runyon, 2008; MacIntyre & Carr, 1999; Topping & Barron, 2009; Zwi et al., 2007.
54. MacInyre & Carr, 1999.

55. Wurtele, 2009, p. 7.
56. Wurtele, 2009.
57. Goldman & Padayachi, 2002.
58. Goodman-Brown et al., 2003; Ullman, 2003.
59. Goldman & Padayachi, 2002.
60. Webster & Hall, 2004.
61. Denov, 2003.
62. see Topping & Barron, 2009.
63. Fontes & Plummer, 2010.
64. See Lamb et al., 2009.
65. See Campbell, Patterson, & Lichty, 2005.
66. Cohen, Deblinger, Mannarino, & Steer, 2004.
67. Deblinger, Mannarino, Cohen, Runyon, & Steer, 2011.

REFERENCES

Alaggia, R. (2005). Disclosing the trauma of child sexual abuse: A gender analysis. *Journal of Loss and Trauma, 10,* 453–470.

American Psychological Association. (2011). *Understanding child sexual abuse: Education, prevention, and recovery.* Retrieved from http://www.apa.org/pubs/info/brochures/sex-abuse.aspx

Baker, A. J. L., Curtis, P. A., & Papa-Lentini, C. (2006). Sexual abuse histories of youth in child welfare residential treatment centers: Analysis of the Odyssey Project Population. *Journal of Child Sexual Abuse, 15,* 29–49.

Bernier, M. J., Hébert, M., & Collin-Vézina, D. (2011). *Evolution of dissociation symptoms over a year in a sample of sexually abused preschoolers.* Paper presented at the 28th Annual Conference of the International Society for the Study of Trauma and Dissociation, Montreal, QC, Canada.

Brezo, J., Paris, J., Tremblay, R., Vitaro, F., Hébert, M., & Turecki, G. (2007). Identifying correlates of suicide attempts in suicidal ideators: A population-based study. *Psychological Medicine: A Journal of Research in Psychiatry and the Allied Sciences, 31,* 1551–1562.

Briere, J., & Elliott, D. M. (1994). Immediate and long-term impacts of child sexual abuse. *The Future of Children, 4,* 54–69.

Campbell, R., Patterson, D., & Lichty, L. (2005). The effectiveness of sexual assault nurse examiner (SANE) programs: A review of psychological, medical, legal, and community outcomes. *Trauma, Violence, & Abuse, 6,* 313–329.

Cohen, J. A., Deblinger, E., Mannarino, A. P., & Steer, R. A. (2004). A multisite, randomized controlled trial for children with sexual abuse-related PTSD symptoms. *Journal of the American Academy of Child & Adolescent Psychiatry, 43,* 393–402.

Collin-Vézina, D., & Hébert, M. (2005). Comparing dissociation and PTSD in sexually abused school-aged girls. *Journal of Nervous Mental Disorders, 193,* 47–52.

Crenshaw, W., Crenshaw, L., & Lichtenberg, J. (1995). When educators confront child abuse: An analysis of the decision to report. *Child Abuse & Neglect, 19,* 1095–1113.

Daignault, I., & Hébert, M. (2009). Profiles of school adaptation: Social, behavioral and academic functioning in sexually abused girls. *Child Abuse & Neglect, 33,* 102–115.

Danielson, C. K., Macdonald, A., Amstadter, A. B., Hanson, R., de Arellano, M. A., Saunders, B. E., et al. (2010). Risky behaviors and depression in conjunction with—or in the absence of—lifetime history of PTSD among sexually abused adolescents. *Child Maltreatment, 15,* 101–107.

Deblinger, E., Mannarino, A. P., Cohen, J. A., Runyon, M. K., & Steer, R. A. (2011). Trauma-focused cognitive behavioral therapy for children: Impact of the trauma narrative and treatment length. *Depression and Anxiety, 28,* 67–75.

Denov, M. S. (2003). To a safer place? Victims of sexual abuse by females and their disclosures to professionals. *Child Abuse & Neglect, 27,* 47–61.

Downs, W. R. (1993). Developmental considerations for the effects of childhood sexual abuse. *Journal of Interpersonal Violence, 8,* 331–345.

Elliott, A. N., & Carnes, C. N. (2001). Reactions of nonoffending parents to the sexual abuse of their child: A review of the literature. *Child Maltreatment, 6,* 314–341.

Finkelhor, D. (1993). Epidemiological factors in the clinical identification of child sexual abuse. *Child Abuse and Neglect, 17,* 67–70.

Finkelhor, D. (1994). Current information on the scope and nature of child sexual abuse. *Sexual Abuse of Children, 4,* 31–53.

Finkelhor, D. (2009). The prevention of childhood sexual abuse. *The Future of Children, 19,* 169–194.

Finkelhor, D., & Browne, A. (1985). The traumatic impact of child sexual abuse: A conceptualization. *American Journal of Orthopsychiatry, 55,* 530–541.

Fontes, L. A., & Plummer, C. (2010). Cultural issues in disclosures of child sexual abuse. *Journal of Child Sexual Abuse, 19,* 491–578.

Fontes, L. A., Cruz, M., & Tabachnick, J. (2001). Views of child sexual abuse in two cultural communities: An exploratory study with Latinos and African Americans. *Child Maltreatment, 6,* 103–117.

Friedrich, W. N. (1991). *Assessing sexual behavior in sexually abused children: Parents and self-report.* Paper presented at the Annual Meeting of the International Academy of Sex Research, Barrie, Ontario, Canada.

Gilligan, P., & Akhtar, S. (2006). Cultural barriers to the disclosure of child sexual abuse in Asian communities: Listening to what women say. *British Journal of Social Work, 36,* 1361–1377.

Goldman, J. D., & Padayachi, U. K. (2002). School counsellors' attitudes and beliefs about child sexual abuse. *Journal of Family Studies, 8,* 53–73.

Goodman-Brown, T. B., Edelstein, R. S., Goodman, G. S., Jones, D. P., & Gordon, D. S. (2003). Why children tell: A model of children's disclosure of sexual abuse. *Child Abuse & Neglect, 27,* 525–540.

Hébert, M., Collin-Vézina, D., Daigneault, I., Parent, N., & Tremblay, C. (2006). Factors linked to outcomes in sexually abused girls: A regression tree analysis. *Comprehensive Psychiatry, 47,* 443–455.

Hébert, M., Tourigny, M., Cyr, M., McDuff, P., & Joly, J. (2009). Prevalence of childhood sexual abuse and timing of disclosure in a representative sample of adults from Quebec. *Canadian Journal of Psychiatry, 54,* 631–636.

Hinkelman, L., & Bruno, M. (2008). Identification and reporting of child sexual abuse: The role of elementary school professionals. *The Elementary School Journal, 108,* 376–391.

Johnson, R. J. (2008). Advances in understanding and treating childhood sexual abuse: Implications for research and policy. *Family & Community Health, 31*(Suppl 1), S24–S34.

Kendall-Tackett, K., Meyer-Williams, L., & Finkelhor, D. (1993). Impact of sexual abuse on children: A review and synthesis of recent empirical studies. *Psychological Bulletin, 113,* 164–180.

Kenny, M. C., Capri, V., Thakkar-Kolar, R. R., Ryan, E. E., & Runyon, M. K. (2008). Child sexual abuse: From prevention to self-protection. *Child Abuse Review, 17,* 36–54.

Kenny, M. C., & McEachern, A. G. (2000). Racial, ethnic, and cultural factors of childhood sexual abuse: A selected review of the literature. *Clinical Psychology Review, 20,* 905–922.

Kilpatrick, D. G., Acierno, R., Saunders, B. E., Resnick, H. S., & Best, C. L. (2000). Risk factors for adolescent substance abuse and dependence: Data from a national sample. *Journal of Consulting and Clinical Psychology, 68,* 19–30.

Kilpatrick, D. G., Ruggerio, J. J., Aciemo, R., Saunders, B. E., Resnick, H. S., & Best, C. L. (2003). Violence and risk for PTSD, major depression, substance abuse/ dependence, and comorbidity: Results from the National Survey of Adolescents. *Journal of Consulting and Clinical Psychology, 71,* 692–700.

Lalor, K., & McElvaney, R. (2010). Child sexual abuse, links to later sexual exploitation/ high-risk sexual behavior, and prevention/treatment programs. *Trauma, Violence, & Abuse, 11,* 159–177.

Lamb, M. E., Orbach, Y., Sternberg, K. L., Aldridge, J., Pearson, S., Stewart, H. L., et al. (2009). Use of a structured investigative protocol enhances the quality of investigative interviews with alleged victims of child sexual abuse in Britain. *Applied Cognitive Psychology, 23,* 449–467.

Lawlor, M. (1993). Assessment of the likelihood of primary school teachers believing children's disclosures of sexual abuse. *Child Abuse Review, 2,* 174–184.

Ligiér, D. P., Fassinger, R., McCauley, M., Moore, J., & Lyytinen, N. (2009). Childhood sexual abuse, culture, and coping: A qualitative study of Latinas. *Psychology of Women Quarterly, 33,* 67–80.

MacIntyre, D., & Carr, A. (1999). Helping children to the other side of silence: A study of the impact of the stay safe programme on Irish children's disclosures of sexual victimization. *Child Abuse & Neglect, 23,* 1327–1340.

MacMillan, H. L., Fleming, J. E., Streiner, D. L., Lin, E., Boyle, M. H., Jamieson, E., et al. (2001). Childhood abuse and lifetime psychopathology in a community sample. *American Journal of Psychiatry, 158,* 1878–1883.

Maniglio, R. (2009). The impact of child sexual abuse on health: A systematic review of reviews. *Clinical Psychology Review, 29,* 647–657.

National Task Force on Juvenile Sexual Offending. (1993). National adolescent perpetrator network revised report. *Juvenile & Family Court Journal, 44*(Suppl 4), 3–108.

O'Leary, P. J., & Barber, J. (2008). Gender differences in silencing following childhood sexual abuse. *Journal of Child Sexual Abuse, 17,* 133–143.

Putnam, F. W. (2003). Ten-year research update review: Child sexual abuse. *Journal of the American Academy of Child & Adolescent Psychiatry, 42,* 269–278.

Sadowski, H., Trowell, J., Kolvin, I., Weeramanthri, T., Berelowitz, N., & Gilbert, L. H. (2003). Sexually abused girls: Patterns of psychopathology and exploration of risk factors. *European Child and Adolescent Psychiatry, 12,* 221–230.

Shaw, J. A., Lewis, J. E., Loeb, A., Rosado, J., & Rodriguez, R. A. (2000). Child on child sexual abuse: Psychological perspectives. *Child Abuse & Neglect, 24,* 1591–1600.

Shin, S. H., Edwards, E. M., & Heeren, T. (2010). Child abuse and neglect: Relations to adolescent binge drinking in the national longitudinal study of Adolescent Health (AddHealth) Study. *Addiction Behaviors, 34,* 277–280.

Spataro, J., Mullen, P. E., Burgess, P. M., Wells, D. L., & Moss, S. A. (2004). Impact of child sexual abuse on mental health: Prospective study in males and females. *British Journal of Psychiatry, 184,* 416–421.

Stoltenborgh, M., van IJzendoorn, M. H., Euser, E. M., & Bakermans-Kranenburg, M. J. (2011). A global perspective on child sexual abuse: Meta-analysis of prevalence around the world. *Child Maltreatment, 16,* 79–101.

Tite, R. (1993). How teachers define and respond to child abuse: The distinction between theoretical and reportable cases. *Child Abuse & Neglect, 17,* 591–603.

Topping, K. J., & Barron, I. G. (2009). School-based child sexual abuse prevention programs: A review of effectiveness. *Review of Educational Research, 79,* 431–463.

Trickett, P. K., & Putnam, F. W. (1993). Impact of child sexual abuse on females: Toward a developmental, psychobiological integration. *Psychological Science, 4,* 81–87.

Ullman, S. E. (2003). Social reactions to child sexual abuse disclosures: A critical review. *Journal of Child Sexual Abuse: Research, Treatment, & Program Innovations for Victims, Survivors, & Offenders, 12,* 89–121.

U.S. Department of Health and Human Services, Administration for Children and Families, Administration on Children, Youth and Families, Children's Bureau. (2010). *Child maltreatment 2009.* Retrieved from http://www.acf.hhs.gov/programs/cb/stats__research/index.htm##can

Vezina, J., & Hébert, M. (2007). Risk factors for victimization in romantic relationships of young women: A review of empirical studies and implications for prevention. *Trauma, Violence, & Abuse, 8,* 33–66.

Webster, R. E. (2001). Symptoms and long-term outcomes for children who have been sexually assaulted. *Psychology in the Schools, 38,* 533–547.

Webster, R. E., & Hall, C. W. (2004). School-based responses to children who have been sexually assaulted. *Education & Treatment of Children, 27,* 64–81.

Wright, J., Friedrich, W. N., Cinq-Mars, C., Cyr, M., & McDuff, P. (2004). Self-destructive and delinquent behaviors of adolescent female victims of child sexual abuse: Rates and covariates in clinical and nonclinical samples. *Violence & Victims, 19,* 627–643.

Wurtele, S. K. (2009). Preventing sexual abuse of children in the twenty-first century: Preparing for challenges and opportunities. *Journal of Child Sexual Abuse, 18,* 1–18.

Yancey, C. T., & Hansen, D. J. (2010). Relationship of personal, familial, and abuse-specific factors with outcome following childhood sexual abuse. *Aggression and Violent Behavior, 15,* 410–421.

Zwi, K., Woolfenden, S., Wheeler, D. M., O'Brien, T., Tait, P., & Williams, K. J. (2007). School-based education programmes for the prevention of child sexual abuse. *Cochrane Database of Systematic Reviews,* (3), CD004380. doi:10.1002/14651858.CD004380.pub2

WEB RESOURCES

- American Humane Association: http://www.americanhumane.org/
- American Professional Society on the Abuse of Children: http://www.apsac.org/
- Child Help Lines:
  - U.S. (ChildHelp Hotline): http://www.childhelp.org or 11-800-4-A-CHILD
  - Canada (Kids Help Phone): http://www.kidshelpphone.ca or 11-800-688-6868
  - United Kingdom (Child Line): http://www.childline.org.uk or 08000 1111
- From Darkness to Light: http://www.d2l.org/
- METRAC: What It Is Project: http://www.metrac.org/whatitis.htm
- National Sexual Violence Resource Center: http://www.nsvrc.org
- Prevent Child Abuse America: http://www.preventchildabuse.org
- Safe Kids British Columbia: http://www.safekidsbc.ca/links.htm
- Stop It Now: http://www.stopitnow.org/
- U.S. Department of Justice, Office of Juvenile Justice and Delinquency Prevention: http://www.ojjdp.gov/

SELECTED CHILDREN'S LITERATURE

Elementary School-Aged Children

- Federico, J. K. (2009). *Some parts are not for sharing.* Mustang, OK: Tate Publishing.
- Hansen, D. (2004). *Those are MY private parts.* Redondo Beach, CA: Empowerment Productions.
- King, K. (2008). *I said no!! A kid-to-kid guide to keeping your private parts private.* Weaverville, CA: Boulden Publishing.
- Kleven, S. (1998). *The right touch: A read-aloud story to help prevent child sexual abuse.* Bellevue, WA: Illumination Arts Publishing.
- Ottenweller, J. (1991). *Please tell!!: A child's story about sexual abuse (early steps).* Center City, MN: Hazeldon Publishing.
- Spelman, C. M. (1997). *Your body belongs to you.* Marton Grove, IL: Albert Whitman.
- Starishevsky, J. (2009). *My body belongs to me.* New York, NY: Safety Star Media.

Adolescents

- Carter, W. L. (2002). *It happened to me: A teen's guide to overcoming sexual abuse.* Oakland, CA: New Harbinger Publications.

- Daugherty, L. (2004). *Why me? Help for victims of child sexual abuse (even if they are adults now)* (4th ed.). Roswell, NM: Cleanan Press.
- Mather, C. L. (2004). *How long does it hurt: A guide to recovering from incest and sexual abuse for teenagers, their friends, and their families* (rev. ed.). San Francisco, CA: Jossey-Bass.
- Riskin, K., & Munson, L. (1995). *In their own words: A sexual abuse workbook for teenage girls*. Washington, DC: CWLA Press (Child Welfare League of America).

14

Students Affected by Neglect

MARDI BERNARD AND ELIZABETH POPARD NEWELL ■

INTRODUCTION

There is no universally accepted definition of what constitutes child neglect as definitions vary based on state laws and reporting mandates.[1] State laws and definitions are all generally guided by a minimum standard set at the federal level through the Federal Child Abuse Prevention and Treatment Act (CAPTA), which was later amended by the Keeping Children and Families Safe Act of 2003. This law defines neglect as an act or an omission on the part of a parent, guardian, or caretaker to provide for the basic needs of a child, which results in actual harm or creates a risk for harm.[2]

Attempts to further categorize types of neglect have resulted in four main classifications, although not all states adopt these definitions:

- *Physical neglect* involves acts of omission related to a child's health or physical well-being and might include a failure to provide basic needs such as food, clothing, or shelter or to provide adequate supervision (also called *supervisory neglect*).
- *Educational neglect* includes the failure of a caregiver to provide an appropriate education or promote school attendance. Examples include not registering a child in school or failing to attend to special education needs.
- *Emotional neglect* results from a caregiver failing to meet a child's emotional needs, which may include withholding love and attention or permitting substance use.
- *Medical neglect* might include a failure to access adequate medical or mental health care for a child or a failure to follow the directions of a health care provider.

Difficulties in creating a clear and universal definition of child neglect have resulted in inconsistencies in the protection of children, as various jurisdictions define neglect using different terms. Further, because child neglect is more common in families living in poverty, it is important to differentiate whether omissions of care to children are due to families lacking the necessary resources or families choosing not to act. For instance, a family who is unable to afford a set of eyeglasses for a visually impaired child might be viewed differently from a family who *could* buy the glasses but chose not to.

Educators may be surprised to learn that the consequences of neglect can be as severe as, if not more severe than, those consequences of other forms of maltreatment (i.e., physical and psychological/emotional, and sexual abuse — see chapters 15 and 13, respectively). Childhood neglect is the most frequently reported form of maltreatment, and children are more likely to die from the experience of chronic neglect than they are from single incidents of other types of maltreatment.[3] According to the U.S. Department of Health and Human Services, Administration on Children, Youth and Families,[4] in 2009 more than three-quarters of the reported victims of all childhood maltreatment types had experienced neglect either in isolation or along with other forms of maltreatment. In that same year, neglect exclusively accounted for 35.8% of fatalities related to all forms of child maltreatment. Similarly, the Canadian Incidence Study of Reported Child Abuse and Neglect (CIS-2003) notes that neglect is the most frequently investigated category of maltreatment in Canada, with nearly one-third of maltreatment cases involving neglect as the primary category.[5] Neglected students experience more severe cognitive deficits, have greater difficulties in achieving school success, are more socially withdrawn, and demonstrate more internalizing behavioral problems than do those who are victimized by other means, including physical abuse.[6]

Risk and Protective Factors

School personnel may not always have confirmation that a child's difficulties are related to the experience of child neglect. Often, there can be no verification of the age that neglect occurred, nor the severity or duration. However, some specific factors may suggest that a child is more likely to have this adverse experience. When neglect is suspected, the educator's intentional consideration of risk factors for neglect may be useful, including:

1. A history of disruptive home environments that result from multiple placements in foster care or exposure to domestic violence[7]
2. Environmental factors including poverty, living in a dangerous community, and having few social supports available in that community[8]
3. Family characteristics including having high levels of stress, large numbers of children living in the home, parental substance abuse, parental mental health issues, and parents who are less well informed about growth and development in children[9]

4. Individual child characteristics including having been born prematurely, being younger than the age of 3, and having a difficult temperament or special needs

Educators should be mindful not to accuse families in these situations of being neglectful—instead, these merely serve as risk indicators for neglect.

Likewise, community, family, and individual child characteristics have been identified that may protect children from the possibility of being neglected. These include:

1. Families who have multiple and strong support systems including extended family, neighbors, schools, and religious institutions
2. Employed parents
3. Individual child characteristics including possessing good health, an easy temperament, good social skills, a lack of self-blame, and above-average intelligence[10]

CULTURAL CONSIDERATIONS

Educators are encouraged to view the context of neglect through a cultural lens. Cultural standards of caring for children can be remarkably different from one region or population to another. For instance, families who move from reservations to urban centers may find some difficulty adapting to the level of supervision expected in the community. Many families report that while on reservations, children roam freely in the community, and all residents are involved in their supervision and caretaking. When families relocate to large urban centers, the practice of allowing young children to play outdoors in high-traffic areas without supervision is considered to be neglectful and can result in the involvement of Child Protective Services. Similarly, some cultures might choose to keep an older child home from school to care for a sick family member or serve as a translator within the community, unaware that this practice, although part of their cultural belief system about family obligation, is considered educational neglect within some societies. Another example relates to disciplinary practices of some Asian cultures that emphasize shame as a punishment; educators may have difficulty determining whether this constitutes emotional neglect or standard cultural child-rearing practices.[11]

To further complicate matters, what constitutes neglect has also changed over time. Whereas we might now consider it to be neglectful to hold an infant on our lap during a car ride, only a few short decades ago, this was standard practice. Likewise, several North American cities have now passed laws against smoking in motor vehicles with children inside. Parents who choose to violate these laws might now be seen as being neglectful of their child's health or well-being, whereas this would not have been considered neglect just one generation earlier.

DEVELOPMENTAL CONSIDERATIONS

The impact of neglect is thought to be the result of multiple mechanisms. The specific outcomes of neglect for a child will depend on the timing, nature, and duration of the neglect as well as the remediation and experiences provided after the neglect occurs. Neglect that occurs during early childhood is thought to result in the most profound problems, presumably due to the importance of this critical period in developing secure attachments, forming relationships, building trust of others, and developing socially and emotionally, and because it is a time when the brain is rapidly developing.[12]

Cicchetti[13] posits that disruptions in the normal course of development will have a ripple effect on later development. Others note that the impact of neglect on future development is cumulative over time.[14] During early childhood and the school-aged years, the most detrimental impacts occur from a lack of physical contact and negative effects on cognitive, language, and social development. As students who have experienced childhood neglect age through adolescence and into adulthood, they exhibit more internalizing problems (e.g., depression and anxiety) and social withdrawal when compared to other nonneglected students, as well as increased risk for criminal behavior, substance use, and personality disorders.[15]

THE IMPACT OF NEGLECT IN THE CLASSROOM

VIGNETTE—TYLER

Tyler is 7 years old and in the second grade, attending an elementary school in a middle-class urban neighborhood. His parents are divorced, and while he lives with his father, the current court order allows Tyler unsupervised visitations with his mother on weekends. His mother has a diagnosis of schizophrenia but has not used medication consistently to manage symptoms. Tyler's father works in the construction industry and his mother is supported through welfare services. While the school staff are generally aware of these circumstances, Tyler avoids talking about his home life with others out of shame and embarrassment.

Tyler attends after-school care in a building near his school. His father picks him up after he has finished work for the day, usually around 6 p.m. Tyler is often the last child to leave the center.

When they arrive home to their apartment, Tyler's father immediately goes to the fridge for a beer, sometimes the first of many over the course of an evening. His father knows that his limited income in the construction industry means that they are unlikely to be able to move out of this area of the city, although it would be nice to be closer to work.

*There are many nights when Tyler has to ask his father to make their sup-
per. Frequently, both become immersed in a video game and forget about the
time. It isn't unusual for the two to finally eat at 8:30 or 9:00 p.m. By this time
Tyler's dad may be too tired or intoxicated to care about the nutritional value
of the food, and they frequently eat foods such as potato chips and hot dogs.
Tyler will often stay up late after his father passes out, sometimes to watch TV
and other times because his stomach hurts.*

*The current court order allows Tyler to visit his mother each weekend, from
Friday evening until Sunday afternoon at her home in another area of the
city. Tyler's mom was diagnosed with schizophrenia before he was born, and
although she tried to be compliant with medications in the beginning, she hasn't
seen a psychiatrist in years and does not take medications now. She isn't working and receives a disability pension. Her home is full of cats and often is dirty.*

*Tyler doesn't have his own bedroom at his mother's home; he sleeps on the
living room couch instead. As she frequently has male friends visiting, he often
does not get to sleep until the early hours of the morning. Nevertheless, he is
likely to be up hours earlier than his mother and frequently fends for himself to
find breakfast and lunch items. He used to stand outside of her bedroom door
crying when this occurred, but when this had little effect, he returned to sitting
quietly on the couch watching the television. Now that the weather is nicer, he
sometimes opens the front door and plays across the street with other children.
He often gets into trouble with these children, however, as he doesn't share well
and he's sometimes been aggressive with them. When the other children return
to their homes for lunch, he walks back across the street and resumes his post
on the couch watching television. Most of the time, he's returned home before
his mother or her visitors have discovered that he's gone.*

*Tyler has never been to a dentist and has only seen doctors when his fre-
quent ear infections have occurred. When he has needed antibiotics for the
infections, his father has sometimes been very angry and has lamented loudly
that having children is very expensive and he'd be better off without Tyler.
Sometimes Tyler has had to wait many days before his dad bought the medicine. Tyler's back teeth sometimes hurt, but he doesn't want to complain about
them, because he doesn't want his father to be angry.*

Educators describe students who are known to have experienced neglect as being
anxious, inattentive, slow learners, and highly dependent on classroom teachers for approval, encouragement, and assistance.[16] In more extreme cases, students who have been neglected may present as aggressive and even cruel toward
animals or small children and may appear to lack empathy or to feel remorse.[17]
Seasoned educators will recognize, however, that this list of behaviors could easily be mistaken for other identifiable disabilities such as attention deficit/hyper-
activity disorder (ADHD), emotional disturbance, or a learning disability. These
factors make recognition somewhat difficult without prior knowledge or suspicion of neglect.

Cognitive Impact of Neglect

Current evidence suggests that neglected students are at increased risk to have significant deficits in the function of their prefrontal cortex, the brain area responsible for what is commonly known as the executive functions.[18] The executive functions include the skills necessary to plan behaviors, attend and focus, problem solve, and utilize working memory—all critical prerequisite skills for learning in the classroom. It is believed that the development of this area of the brain is altered when chemicals such as cortisol are generated in massive quantities and for long durations of time as a result of neglect. This creates an overdevelopment of the "survival" areas of the brain, including the hippocampus and amygdala.[19] This change to the architecture of the brain is the neurobiological root to the cognitive, behavioral, social, and emotional challenges that educators observe at school among neglected students.

Cells in the brain develop and make connections to other cells based on their use. When the needs of young children are not met, the brain cells related to survival are used most frequently, and therefore, these "stress cells" become the most fully developed and numerous. This comes at the expense of the cells that are not being used frequently, such as those related to higher level thinking, planning, and organizing. As a result, when children grow older, their ability to regulate their own stress response can be impaired and they can develop a persistent hyperreactive response to stress.[20] This also leads to a pattern of predictable behavior—the typical anxious behavioral response may escalate from simply crying to temper tantrums, since crying did not elicit a response from the caregiver, and then to aggressive behaviors or inattention and withdrawal, all in an effort to engage the caregiver. The child might also then become psychologically disengaged, resulting in apathy or excessive daydreaming in an attempt to "run away" from the stress of a neglectful caregiver.[21] While this reaction is presumed to be functional for immediate survival, the same behavior becomes harmful when transferred to school settings.

It is important to remember that the various subtypes of child neglect can impede specific areas of cognitive functioning and, similarly, learning. For instance, if the childhood neglect included nutritional neglect, then the brain may not have received the necessary nutrients for growth and development to occur. Parental supervisory neglect could result in fewer opportunities to engage in stimulating activities during critical periods of early childhood. Neglect of medical needs could result in illnesses or injuries going undetected and untreated, thus altering the brain's developmental trajectory.

Neglected students may present in the classroom with foundational learning deficits that are therefore best understood as being brain based. They may have difficulty initiating and sustaining attention and holding information in their working memory for a functional length of time, and may then struggle with such foundational tasks as copying notes from the white board. It is essential that educators recognize that the root of such barriers to learning are not necessarily based in behavioral opposition, but rather are reflective of the direct effects of neglect on cognitive and brain development.

Social and Emotional Impact of Neglect

When children lack early attachments to sensitive and caring individuals, their ability to build social relationships may be compromised. Educators report that students who have experienced neglect may be more socially withdrawn and tend to have greater social difficulties than their nonneglected peers.[22] Neglected students may exhibit poor impulse control and poor communication skills and experience sudden temper outbursts.[23] They may perceive that they have very little control over events in their life; therefore, they may attempt to exert control in ways that are dysfunctional—for instance, they may be bossy to their peers or may refuse to complete academic tasks. Given that the ability to effectively attach to adults in school affects academic motivation and that a student's relationships with peers considerably impacts learning and development in school, difficulties developing attachments can result in significant social-emotional and learning problems.

The experience of childhood neglect also impacts the ability to manage emotions and to accurately and quickly perceive the emotions of others, even more so than physical abuse.[24] De Bellis et al.[25] suggest that the brain area responsible for a student's ability to quickly and accurately process information such as facial expression is biologically altered by the experience of neglect.

In contrast to physically abused children, there tends to be a noted increase in internalizing behaviors for children of neglect, including anxiety and depression.[26] While physically abused students might interpret the world as being full of danger and imminent threats, neglected students may respond with internalized emotions including a sense of shame, self-blame, and isolation.[27]

Behavioral Impact of Neglect

The altered development of the brain's executive functions related to neglect is likely to affect the ability to plan, make decisions, and inhibit impulsive reactions.[28] It is likely that this brain change is at least partly responsible for behavioral challenges experienced by neglected students. In the past decade, research has found that the behaviors of students who have been neglected differ from the behavior of students who have experienced other forms of maltreatment. When young children perceived a lack of early affection, later social problems were reported by the parents, and later externalizing behaviors were reported by the children.[29] Further, when a lack of maternal support was reported by the children, parents reported both externalizing and internalizing problems 4 years later.

Students experiencing neglect may also exhibit behaviors as a direct result of the neglect, such as fatigue, lack of focus or poor concentration, and physical complaints. For example, Tyler from the vignette would likely have difficulty concentrating if his tooth hurt, or he may experience pain when eating certain foods in the cafeteria.

STRATEGIES TO SUPPORT STUDENTS

Don't be afraid to report a suspicion of neglect. Research suggests that educators generally lack the attitudes and awareness necessary to protect students by making reports of general child abuse and maltreatment, including neglect.[30] A range of factors appear to influence the process of making a professional decision of whether to report incidents of child neglect, including the perception of what compromises acts of child neglect, the perception of the educator's professional role, and the views of professional colleagues.[31]

Educators and other school personnel are considered *mandatory* reporters of child neglect, and most states impose penalties upon mandated reporters who fail to report such suspicions. It is not the educator's job to substantiate the suspicion of neglect, only to report it. Educators are protected when making such reports by "good faith" provisions, which assume that reports are being made in good faith out of concern for the child. Teachers should therefore be aware of indicators of possible neglect, know who to call in their geographical area, and know what information will be asked of them during the report. Generally, those reporting suspicions of child neglect to authorities will be asked for the child's name, age, date of birth, grade, and school name. In addition, educators making the reports will be asked to describe the physical, behavioral, emotional, or developmental indicators of neglect they have observed. It might be useful to have notes prepared to ensure that your report is comprehensive. Be sure to inform other stakeholders in the school about your report, including direct supervisors, school administrators, and the school social worker. Notably, most states explicitly protect the identity of the reporter.

Following the report, the child protective agency will follow the legislated protocol for assessing the child and family situation. This may include phone calls to parents or the school, home visits, or other assessment strategies. As noted previously, families who provide ineffective and neglectful parenting often have predisposing risk factors including parental mental illness or substance abuse, and these issues may need to be dealt with first in order to protect the student from further neglect. Sometimes, children who are being severely neglected are removed from their home for a period of time, and they may or may not end up remaining in your classroom, depending on the policies in your jurisdiction. If the child is required to attend a different school or classroom, consider preparing a folder detailing the work the student did to help with the transition.

Talk to the student about your concerns. Conversations with students about sus-picions of neglectful parenting can be among the most difficult that educators will have. Strategies that may be helpful include:

1. Ensure that the staff member who will have the conversation is some-one the student trusts. Consult with the colleagues in your building to make this decision.
2. Ensure that the conversation is held in private.
3. Let the student know that although the conversation is a private one, when parents are not able to take care of their children, educators need to contact Child Protective Services. Make this clear at the outset of the conversation.
4. Use language that the child will understand.
5. Tell the student that you are worried about him or her, and reassure the student that he or she is not in trouble.
6. Don't outwardly show shock or negative judgment of the actions of the parents. It is possible that the neglect is not intentional.

Reconsider the use of suspension or expulsion for discipline. The behavioral manifestations of neglect may include disruptive behaviors that can sometimes result in harsh disciplinary action. Despite the lack of support for zero toler-ance and harsh punitive discipline policies, many schools continue to use sus-pensions or expulsions as punishment for inappropriate behavior. There may be a mistaken assumption that parents will be available to provide support and supervision during the imposed exclusion from school, although this is often an unlikely situation in neglectful families. The lack of supervision during suspen-sion or expulsion may increase the likelihood of the student engaging in risky or antisocial behavior.[32] Thus, educators should advocate for alternative methods of discipline that include teaching the desired behavior, implementing positive behavioral supports, and structured interventions aimed at addressing student academic and behavioral needs. Consider calling on fellow educators and school support personnel to consider available options.

Meet basic needs. Students experiencing ongoing neglect may come to school without having their basic needs met, and therefore may be at a disadvantage when it comes to learning. Neglected students may not have eaten, slept, or bathed; may not be receiving needed medical or mental health care; and may have had to find their own way to school in the morning. Therefore, to learn in school they may need to be fed, use school locker rooms to shower, see the school nurse, or even be provided with an inexpensive alarm clock to help them get to school on time. Some students may benefit from learning independent adaptive skills and how to be home alone safely (e.g., reviewing emergency phone num-bers and how to get to school alone, finding after-school employment for adoles-cents). While these activities may take away from time in direct instruction, they are necessary measures to help prepare the student for learning. These measures are short term and temporary, and the school's support staff (e.g., school social worker) as well as child protection agencies may need to be engaged to provide longer term and more intensive support for the child and family.

Engage with the parent or caregiver. Teachers often need to speak with parents about a student's classroom performance, including any pressing concerns about learning or behavior. Conversations with parents in these situations include describing the student's behavior or performance and problem solving with the parent. As with any other parent, your goal in this conversation is to work together to help understand and support the student and develop a partnership in helping the child succeed. Strong social support networks, including school–family partnerships, can serve as protective factors for neglected students. Describe your concerns honestly, and ask open-ended, nonaccusatory questions, such as "I've noticed Tyler falls asleep at his desk many mornings. What is his behavior like at home?" or "Tyler has complained about some pain with one of his teeth. Has he mentioned this to you at all?" Be sure to describe all of the available support services in the school and within the community.

Know your limits. Caring educators who suspect neglect may feel inclined to take students home with them after school or bring them food on a daily basis. These actions, while possibly necessary and well intentioned, should also be considered as a short-term solution. Educators, despite their compassionate actions, may in fact be considered in violation of mandatory reporting laws, or the chronic nature of the neglect will be allowed to continue by helping the student independently. If a student is not being cared for properly, call Child Protective Services and share your concerns with other necessary stakeholders in the school.

Learn to manage your own emotions. Neglected students have difficulty perceiving others' emotions and may respond to nonverbal cues (e.g., tone of voice, body language) as inherently rejecting or threatening, even if the message itself was nonthreatening. This response can impact both behavior and learning given that students learn most easily when their brain is in a state of calm. Thus, it remains important for educators to pay attention to their own emotional state and nonverbal cues. Many novice teachers are asked to film themselves teaching a class; this may serve as a good opportunity to self-evaluate.

Maintain predictable and consistent routines and expectations. Provide and maintain clear expectations and guidelines for classroom behavior, and perhaps more important, be consistent in reinforcing those expectations. This provides a contrasting experience for students whose caregivers' expectations tend to vacillate based on their moods or level of engagement. Expectations should be positively and simply stated with a focus on what to do, rather than focused on what not to do (e.g., "Raise your hand to speak," which is stated positively, vs. "Don't speak unless called upon," which is stated negatively). Students can help to develop these classroom expectations and are more likely to be successful in adhering to the rules if they have had input into them.

When students do make mistakes and fail to successfully follow the agreed upon classroom rules, the consequences need to be predictable. Children and youth who have been neglected may rarely receive consequences for misbehavior, or conversely may receive punishment that is disproportionate to the misbehavior. Perhaps more important, educators should consider these mistakes as learning opportunities and teachable moments.

Provide direct social skills instruction. Neglected students may not have had opportunities to develop social skills through rich, quality interactions with caregivers, and so they may not be able to use social language effectively in the classroom or in social situations. These language deficits may extend to an inability to use "procedural self-talk" for behavior management and academic success.[33] These students may subsequently present with socially maladaptive behaviors such as meltdowns, tantrums, or passive withdrawal when they become overwhelmed with academic or social demands. Given the social nature of a typical classroom, these weaknesses can impede learning and cause isolation and withdrawal. Therefore, educators should provide direct, intentional social skills instruction, such as accurate expression and interpretation of verbal and nonverbal social cues, or appropriate play skills for younger children such as sportsmanship and inviting, joining, and ending play. This can also be done within the context of the classroom by rewarding positive interactions, modeling proper etiquette, problem solving peer disputes, and processing through negative interactions.

While these classroom activities may be targeting certain students, it is likely that most students in the class will benefit from this instruction. Educators should consider calling on other experts in the building to support these efforts, including school psychologists, speech and language pathologists, and school counselors. Ideas for school-based activities that promote social and emotional learning can be found on the Collaborative for Academic, Social, and Emotional Learning website (http://www.casel.org).

Intentionally create opportunities for positive peer interaction. As noted earlier, neglected students may have difficulties developing appropriate peer relationships and may sometimes present as isolated and withdrawn while at other times being aggressive or even hostile. When these children present to school with dirty clothing or poor hygiene or underdeveloped emotional regulation skills, they may be rejected by peers. To ensure that these students have ample opportunity to practice and hone social skills, designated recess times might include the intentional pairing of students with the task of playing together, developing small teams for various games, or simply actively encouraging peers to include the student in play activities. Neglected students in secondary schools may benefit from pairings with other students for classroom projects or assignments or study groups, or encouragement to engage in after-school groups or activities.

Educators should also do what they can to ensure that neglected students do not become victims of bullying in their school. Potential language difficulties, social skills deficits, emotional regulation challenges, and potential hygiene problems can make them prime targets for ridicule, teasing, and harassment. Bullying behavior on the part of peers will serve to create an unsafe school environment for these students, possibly mirroring their family experiences and triggering negative reactions, thereby negatively impacting the conditions for learning.

CONCLUSION

Childhood neglect can be devastating for a student's development. The experience can change the architecture of the brain and leave the student at increased risk for a variety of difficulties that can impact cognitive, academic, emotional, and social functioning and learning. Although classrooms are generally not designed to provide therapy to heal these brain changes, all educators can employ strategies to support success in the classroom. To most effectively support neglected students, school staff should develop awareness of the myriad factors that contribute to neglect and the impacts that neglect has on students, and use this knowledge to develop a compassionate classroom. All school staff should also familiarize themselves with the mandated reporting laws in their state and the proper procedures to report a suspicion of neglect to Child Protective Services.

Educators can best serve students by intentionally reminding themselves that the students they serve are part of family, community, and other formal systems, including the education system, each possessing risk and protective factors related to that individual. Families may live in poverty, communities may be unsafe, and schools may be overcrowded and lack resources. None of these factors alone will directly cause either parental child neglect or systemic child neglect, but each has the potential to have an impact in either a positive or a negative way. Although schools are not likely to be able to easily or effectively remove these risk factors, it is well within the school's realm of control to build on protective factors.

NOTES

1. Review state laws and policies at http://www.childwelfare.gov/systemwide/laws_policies/
2. Child Welfare Information Gateway, 2008.
3. Berry, Charlson, & Dawson, 2003.
4. U.S. Department of Health and Human Services, Administration for Children and Families, Administration on Children, Youth and Families, Children's Bureau, 2010.
5. Roy, Black, Trocmé, MacLaurin, & Fallon, 2005.
6. Hildyard & Wolfe, 2002.
7. Wilkerson, Johnson, & Johnson, 2008, p. 346.
8. DePanfilis, 2006.
9. Daniel, Taylor, & Scott, 2010; Slack, Holl, McDaniel, Yoo, & Bolger, 2004.
10. DePanfilis, 2006.

11. Tower, 1996.
12. Perry, Colwell, & Schick, 2002.
13. Cicchetti, 1989.
14. Hildyard & Wolfe, 2002.
15. Hildyard & Wolfe, 2002.
16. Tyler, Allison, & Winsler, 2006.
17. Perry, 2001.
18. De Bellis, 2005.
19. De Bellis, 2005.
20. Neigh, Gillespie, & Nemeroff, 2009.
21. American Academy of Pediatrics, Committee on Early Childhood, Adoption and Dependent Care, 2000.
22. Hildyard & Wolfe, 2002.
23. O'Neill, Guenette, & Kitchenham, 2010; Wilkerson et al., 2008.
24. Sullivan, Carmody, & Lewis, 2010.
25. De Bellis, Hooper, Spratt, & Woolley, 2009.
26. Hildyard & Wolfe, 2002.
27. Kinniburgh, Blaustein, & Spinazzola, 2005.
28. De Bellis, 2005.
29. Dubowitz et al., 2005.
30. Kenny, 2004.
31. Horwath, 2007.
32. Aizer, 2004.
33. Cole et al., 2005.

REFERENCES

Aizer, A. (2004). Home alone: Supervision after school and child behavior. *Journal of Public Economics, 88*, 1835–1848.

American Academy of Pediatrics, Committee on Early Childhood, Adoption and Dependent Care. (2000). Developmental issues for young children in foster care. *Pediatrics, 106*, 1145–1150.

Berry, M., Charlson, R., & Dawson, K. (2003). Promising practices in understanding and treating child neglect. *Child and Family Social Work, 8*, 13–24.

Child Welfare Information Gateway. (2008). *What is child abuse and neglect?* U.S. Department of Health and Human Services. Retrieved from http://www.childwelfare.gov/pubs/factsheets/whatiscan.pdf

Cicchetti, D. (1989). How research on child maltreatment has informed the study of child development: Perspectives from developmental psychopathology. In D. Cicchetti & V. Carlson (Eds.), *Child maltreatment: Theory and research on the causes and consequences of child maltreatment and neglect* (pp. 377–431). Cambridge, UK: Cambridge University Press.

Cole, J. D., O'Brien, J. G., Gadd, M. G., Ristuccia, J., Wallace, D. L., & Gregory, M. (2005). *Helping traumatized children learn: Supportive school environments for children traumatized by family violence.* Boston, MA: Massachusetts Advocates for Children: Trauma and Learning Policy Initiative.

Daniel, B., Taylor, J., & Scott, J. (2010). Recognition of neglect and early response: Overview of a systematic review of the literature. *Child and Family Social Work, 15,* 248–257.

De Bellis, M. D. (2005). The psychobiology of neglect. *Child Maltreatment, 10,* 150–172.

De Bellis, M. D., Hooper, S. R., Spratt, E. G., & Woolley, D. P. (2009). Neuropsychological findings in childhood neglect and their relationships to pediatric PTSD. *Journal of the International Neuropsychological Society, 15,* 868–878.

DePanfilis, D. (2006). *Child neglect: A guide for prevention, assessment, and intervention.* Washington, DC: U.S. Department of Health and Human Services, Administration on Children and Families, Administration for Children, Youth, and Families, Children's Bureau, Office on Child Abuse and Neglect.

Dubowitz, H., Newton, R., Litrownik, A. J., Lewis, T., Briggs, E. C., Thompson, R., et al. (2005). Examination of a conceptual model of child neglect. *Child Maltreatment, 10,* 173–188.

Hildyard, K. L., & Wolfe, D. A. (2002). Child neglect: Developmental issues and outcomes. *Child Abuse and Neglect, 26,* 679–695.

Horwath, J. (2007). The missing assessment domain: Personal, professional and organizational factors influencing professional judgments when identifying and referring child neglect. *British Journal of Social Work, 37*(8), 1285–1303.

Kenny, M. C. (2004). Teachers' attitudes toward and knowledge of child maltreatment. *Child Abuse and Neglect, 28,* 1311–1319.

Kinniburgh, K. J., Blaustein, M., & Spinazzola, J. (2005). Attachment, self-regulation and competency. *Psychiatric Annals, 35,* 424–430.

Neigh, G. N., Gillespie, C. F., & Nemeroff, C. B. (2009). The neurobiological toll of child abuse and neglect. *Trauma, Violence and Abuse, 10,* 389–410.

O'Neill, L., Guenette, F., & Kitchenham, A. (2010). "Am I safe here and do you like me?" Understanding complex trauma and attachment disruption in the classroom. *British Journal of Special Education, 37,* 190–196.

Perry, B. (2001). *Bonding and attachment in maltreated children: Consequences of emotional neglect in childhood.* Retrieved from http://www.childtrauma.org/images/stories/Articles/attcar4_03_v2_r.pdf

Perry, B. D., Colwell, K., & Schick, S. (2002). Child neglect. In D. Lavinson (Ed.), *Encyclopedia of crime and punishment* (pp. 1992–1996). Thousand Oaks, CA: Sage Publications.

Roy, C., Black, T., Trocmé, N., MacLaurin, B., & Fallon, B. (2005). *Child neglect in Canada.* CECW Information Sheet #27E, CIS Series. Montreal, QC, Canada: McGill University, School of Social Work.

Slack, K. S., Holl, J., McDaniel, M., Yoo, J., & Bolger, K. (2004). Understanding the risks of child neglect: An exploration of poverty and parenting characteristics. *Child Maltreatment, 9,* 395–408.

Sullivan, M. W., Carmody, D. P., & Lewis, M. (2010). How neglect and punitiveness influence emotion knowledge. *Child Psychiatry and Human Development, 41,* 285–298.

Tower, C. (1996). *Child abuse and neglect.* Boston, MA: Allyn & Bacon.

Tyler, S., Allison, K., & Winsler, A. (2006). Child neglect: Developmental consequences, intervention and policy implications. *Child and Youth Care Forum, 35,* 2–20.

U.S. Department of Health and Human Services, Administration for Children and Families, Administration on Children, Youth and Families, Children's Bureau. (2010). *Child maltreatment 2009.* Retrieved from http://www.acf.hhs.gov/programs/cb/stats_research/index.htm#can

Wilkerson, D., Johnson, G., & Johnson, R. (2008). Children of neglect with attachment and time perception deficits: Strategies and interventions. *Education, 129*, 343–352.

WEB RESOURCES

- American Humane Association: http://www.americanhumane.org
- Child Welfare Information Gateway: http://www.childwelfare.gov/
- Child Welfare League of America: http://www.cwla.org
- National Resource Center for Child Protective Services: http://www.nrc cps.org
- Prevent Child Abuse, America: http://http://www.preventchildabuse.org/
- U.S. Department of Health and Human Services, Administration for Children and Families: http://www.acf.hhs.gov/

SELECTED CHILDREN'S LITERATURE

- Cassidy, C. (2006). *Indigo blue.* New York, NY: Puffin.
- Connor, L. (2008). *Waiting for normal.* New York, NY: Harper Collins.
- Grove, V. (2000). *Reaching Dustin.* New York, NY: G. P. Putnam and Sons.
- Lisle, J. T. (2012). *Afternoon of the elves.* London: Orchard Books.

15

Students Affected by Physical and Emotional Abuse

LISA WEGMAN AND A. MICHELLE O'BANION ■

INTRODUCTION

Among all substantiated reports from Child Protective Services for all types of child maltreatment, 17.8% were for physical abuse and 7.6% for emotional abuse.[1] An estimated 1,770 fatalities resulted from all forms of child maltreatment in 2009 nationally, most of which occurred among children aged 3 years or younger (80.8%). Among child fatalities from maltreatment, 23.2% were attributed exclusively to physical abuse, whereas virtually no deaths were exclusively attributed to emotional or psychological abuse. The majority of fatalities were attributed to multiple maltreatment types or child neglect.

Physical abuse refers to purposeful, physical acts that can result in injury or harm. Emotional or psychological abuse refers to "acts or omissions, other than physical abuse or sexual abuse that caused, or could have caused, conduct, cognitive, affective, or other mental disorders and includes emotional neglect, psychological abuse, and mental injury."[2] Emotional abuse may include verbal abuse or excessive and unreasonable demands on a child. Characteristics of emotional abuse may include persistent hostility, failure to respond to a child's needs, unrealistic expectations, inappropriate exposure to sexuality and aggression, and inconsistent care.[3] Emotional abuse could also include making degrading remarks, isolating the child from others, exploiting, or even exposing the child to family violence.

Lowenthal[4] and Iwaniec et al.,[5] both summarized how physical and emotional abuse can impact school performance (see Table 15.1), including impacts on general cognitive functioning, lower school achievement, lower self-esteem and motivation, and higher rates of school dropout.

Table 15.1 IMPACT OF PHYSICAL AND EMOTIONAL ABUSE

Neurological Effects	Psychological and Behavioral Effects	Cognitive and Learning Effects	Physical and Health Effects
Increased levels of cortisol, which cause the death of brain cells and reduction in number of synapses	Avoidance of or difficulty developing close relationships	Difficulty learning	Smaller in stature
Shrinkage in areas of brain associated with memory, learning, and regulation of affect	Provocative behaviors that include aggression, agitating others, and inflicting harm on others	Deficits in basic skills in the areas of reading, math, and written language	Developmental delays/failure to thrive
Reduced brain size	Attachment problems impact ability to tolerate stress, regulate emotions, and benefit from social supports	Lack of motivation, hope, optimism, and aspirations	Lower weight
Sleep disturbances	View the world as a dangerous, unpredictable place	More disorganized and distractible	
Constant state of alertness leads to disorganization of the brain, which leads to delayed response time	More vulnerable to stress	Higher rates of special education referral, grade failure, and dropout	
Disassociation (i.e., separating experiences from conscious awareness)	Increased substance abuse and delinquency		
	Anxiety and other mood disorders		

Risk and Protective Factors

Factors that increase a student's risk for experiencing physical and emotional abuse, as well as factors that may help protect students from experiencing negative effects from it, can be broken down into several categories, including parent or caregiver factors, child factors, and environmental factors.

Parent/caregiver factors. Severe mental health disorders among parents/caregivers who abuse their children are rare, although some parent/caregiver risk factors for abuse include low self-esteem, low impulse control, antisocial behavior, a history of maltreatment, family stress (e.g., financial), single parenthood, teenage parenthood, and anxiety or depression when compared to nonabusing caregivers.[6] Notably, positive experiences and attachments with caregivers can serve as a protective factor against the effects of abuse.[7]

Child factors. Risk factors include youth (age 4 or younger), having a disability, and exhibiting behavioral problems such as inattention and aggression. Children who attribute the abuse to external factors (e.g., the abuser is drunk, angry, confused) tend to fare better than those who attribute the abuse to themselves (e.g., "I deserve the abuse").

Environmental factors. Various environmental factors may increase the risk of abuse, including poverty and unemployment, social isolation, and living within violent communities. The school environment plays an important role in how a child responds to abuse. On one hand, "school can provide an opportunity for maltreated children to gain the social and practical support they need."[8] On the other hand, difficulties with learning and schoolwork can worsen the impacts of abuse. The presence of proper emotional and social support, including school connectedness and positive relationships, has consistently emerged as one of the most powerful protective factors against maltreatment.

DEVELOPMENTAL CONSIDERATIONS

The nature, frequency, intensity, duration, and timing of abuse can impact a child's response. For example, research suggests that when physical or psychological abuse ends early in a child's life, associated negative outcomes diminish over time.[9] In contrast, children who are exposed to continuous abuse or who first experience abuse during adolescence do not experience such reductions in negative outcomes. Despite this finding, some research suggests that early exposure can lead to worse outcomes due to the lack of existing coping mechanisms and the critical brain growth that occurs during this period.

Depending on the child's age, level of functioning, and developmental stage, behavior can be an indication that a child is being physically or emotionally abused. Table 15.2 lists some of the behavioral and social indicators within the classroom that may suggest possible abuse. Educators should note when a variety of these factors are occurring, as well as other more obvious signs of abuse (e.g., physical bruises or lacerations).

CULTURAL CONSIDERATIONS

In a country as diverse as the United States, culture should be taken into account when considering how to respond to physical and emotional abuse. As an example, many immigrants are given little to no information about the written and unwritten rules regarding parenting, and therefore will continue their existing

Table 15.2 DEVELOPMENTAL IMPACT OF PHYSICAL AND EMOTIONAL ABUSE

Early Childhood	Elementary School	Secondary School
Developmental delays	Academic delays	Excessive absence or truancy
Lack of attachment to caregivers	Withdrawal, fearful or anxious about doing something wrong or making mistakes	Inability to form friendships
Fear or discomfort with physical contact	Impulsivity	Distrustful and suspicious of others
Lack of curiosity or interest in exploring	Irritability	Substance abuse
Afraid to go home	Difficulty with peer and adult relationships	Aggression and conduct problems
Overly aggressive	Extremely passive or aggressive	
Anxious, stressed, and fearful behavior around adults of authority	Low self-esteem	

disciplinary and parenting practices just as they did in their country, even if those strategies are problematic in the United States.[10] In some cases, actions that are considered abusive in the United States are based on long-standing, rich cultural traditions—for example, a folk medicine used by some Southeast Asian cultures involves rubbing oils on a child's body with a coin's edge and is considered medicinal, yet this practice may leave marks or bruises on the skin.[11] In other cases, children are physically disciplined in various cultures in such ways that would be considered abusive in the United States (e.g., striking with belt, punching, kicking, flogging). While the American courts generally rely on American statutory standards to define abuse, it remains important to have an understanding of differing opinions on parenting and discipline across cultures and maintain sensitivity to these differences. This may help in both the response and identification of abusive practices that may harm students.

Cultural beliefs may also impact the nature of emotional abuse given stated gender roles and responsibilities within a household, how people relate to each other, or how resources are distributed among siblings in a family. Some cultures are less permissive of even expressing emotions, whereas some cultures are more nurturing than others.[12]

As for racial differences in child maltreatment, the National Incidence Study of Child Abuse and Neglect (NIS)[13] revealed that Black children experienced significantly higher amounts of physical abuse than White and Hispanic children, a difference that was largely due to differences in income or socioeconomic status (SES). In other words, when comparing White and Black children from similarly low-SES households, the differences were minimal or nonexistent. Black children also experienced significantly higher levels of emotional abuse when compared to White children, and Hispanic children had significantly lower rates of emotional abuse than both racial groups. Other research has found that Black children are similarly overrepresented among those experiencing physical or emotional abuse, although one large study of adolescents found the highest lifetime prevalence of child physical abuse among Hispanic youth.[14] Some have suggested that such racial differences, as well as inconsistencies in the research, may be due to differences in reporting rates and research methodology.

STRATEGIES TO SUPPORT STUDENTS

Report suspected abuse. Each state has statutes defining the process of reporting suspected abuse. Generally speaking, when an individual has reasonable cause to believe or knows that a child is being maltreated, he or she is *obligated or mandated* by law to report. Even if educators have a mild suspicion, they are required to report and are typically immune from civil or criminal liability if the report is made in good faith. The educator typically contacts the appropriate agency to file a report and then the agency determines the measures that are taken next. The reporter's name may or may not be kept confidential depending on the circumstances and the statutes of that particular state. Educators should always clarify with their administration the recommended procedure for filing a child abuse report, as there are often school or district procedures and forms to complete as well.

States vary to some degree in their legislation regarding the reporting of suspected abuse and neglect. Details about individual state laws can be found by visiting the Child Welfare Information Gateway (http://www.childwelfare.gov/systemwide/laws_policies/state/can/) or FindLaw (http://law.findlaw.com/state-laws/child-abuse/). Know that as a reporter, you may be asked a variety of questions about the abuse and may eventually be asked to testify if the case goes to trial.

If students ask what might happen next, be as honest as possible. Depending on the age and development level of the students, describe that some authorities or Child Protective Services will work to make sure they remain safe, and that might mean that someone might ask them some other questions about what happened. Reinforce their safety at the school, and that they did the right thing by telling an adult. Also reinforce that while you will keep this confidential from other peers or students, you may need to share some information with those authorities.

Shift thinking about causes of behavior. A shift in thinking is sometimes needed to educate students who have been physically or emotionally abused. Consider the vignette about Erika.

While Erika's behavior and academic difficulties could be perceived as a possible learning disability or even attention deficit/hyperactivity disorder (ADHD),

VIGNETTE—ERIKA

The first 5 years of Erika's life were relatively peaceful. Her mother was able to get off of welfare, complete her cosmetology license, secure a full-time job, and get married. Erika's half brother was born when she was 5. Erika's stepfather did not want to formally adopt her and her older sister now that he had a child of his own, and he also did not want to be responsible for disciplining or financially supporting them. When her mother would ask for more grocery money or money for clothes, his typical response was, "Those are your kids; you take care of them." He routinely spent time with his son while he asked the girls to stay home and do extra chores. Erika's teachers commented that she was an easygoing child, got along well with others, and enjoyed school. She had the tendency to take more time than other students to complete her work, but she had passing marks at the end of the school year.

When Erika was around the age of 10 years, Erika's mother and stepfather began having marital problems, and he soon moved into an apartment nearby. Erika's mother returned to college to become a nurse, thus leaving Erika's older sister as the default caretaker of the younger children. When Erika's sister became frustrated she would scream obscenities at her and sometimes slap or punch her. When Erika would complain to her mother about how her sister treated her, her mother would tell Erika that she didn't have the time or energy to deal with their arguing. Erika felt isolated and constantly lived in a state of fear. The stability of her world depended on her mother's and her sister's moods each day. Erika would sometimes avoid coming home after school and would crawl back into her room through a window she left unlocked or stay the night at her friend's house down the street just to avoid interacting with them. This trend at home continued, although she decided not to tell anyone at school because her sister threatened her into not "snitching."

Erika's teachers began to see a marked decline in her behavior and grades at school. Her teachers commented that the work that Erika turned in was satisfactory, but that they observed her constantly erasing her work and starting over. Many times she would become so frustrated that she would just put her head down and refuse to work anymore. By the end of her eighth-grade year she had passing marks in only two of her eight classes. She had been recommended for a remedial reading class and was being referred for evaluation to determine her eligibility for special education services.

her difficulties were likely heavily influenced by abuse. The combination of physical abuse and emotional abuse from her family led to excessive stress and multiple learning problems. When students begin to experience difficulties in school, educators frequently ask themselves, "What is wrong with this student?" However, educators may be more equipped to meet their students' needs when also considering, "What experiences are impacting this student's behavior and learning?" Acknowledging that Erika is not at fault for the abuse and using the classroom to counterbalance her experiences at home are both critical in providing a safe and enriching learning environment. Cole and colleagues[15] remind us that "when we believe an individual has complete control over his or her behavior, we are more likely to be angry when that behavior is inappropriate. But if we recognize the factors that shape a child's behavior and compromise self-control, we are more likely to attempt to ease the child's plight."

Model emotional control. Children identify with their parents or caregivers, even when they are abusive. Thus, the aggressive treatment they are subject to at home carries over into the classroom. Erika's sister hit Erika when she became frustrated. Erika learned that it was acceptable, or perhaps even preferable, to hit others when she became frustrated. Educators are similarly powerful models of behavior and can model appropriate ways to work through difficult emotions and situations. There will be instances when educators experience anger, sadness, frustration, and disappointment in front of their students. These times should be used as teachable moments to model emotional control.

Shift students' beliefs about the world. Students experiencing physical or emotional abuse are at increased risk for depression, persistent pessimism, and hopelessness.[16] Such pessimism and hopelessness can impact behavior and learning in school. As one strategy to challenge this belief, ask the student or the entire class to write down what they think will happen during the school day on the left-hand side of a piece of paper. At the end of the day ask the students to take their piece of paper from the morning and describe what really happened. This helps them to see in black-and-white terms the problems with their "glass half empty" mentality. Many times the outcome will not be nearly as bad as what they projected it to be. This activity may also serve as an academic writing activity. Other resources to help shift students' beliefs about the world and improve positive thinking may include the Fishful Thinking website (http://www.fishful-thinking.com) and the University of Pennsylvania's Positive Psychology Center, which includes educational programs and resources for teachers (http://www.ppc.sas.upenn.edu).

Offer choices. Students' behavior, particularly those experiencing physical or emotional abuse, is often motivated by a desire to gain control over the situation. One effective method of increasing a sense of control is offering choices rather than making explicit demands. For example, rather than demanding that students stop talking in class, a teacher may offer them the choice to write down their ideas, raise their hand, or wait until after class to converse with a peer. Also, consider ways to offer choices on how to demonstrate mastery of a skill, such as completing an exam, writing a paper, or doing some other kind of creative project.

Provide frequent opportunities for success. Students experiencing abuse, particularly emotional abuse, may frequently have their personal attributes attacked and ridiculed. As a result, these same students may be less inclined to take risks in the classroom (e.g., raising their hand to answer a question) due to a fear of failure. They may make statements such as "I can't do it" before even making an attempt. On the opposite end of the spectrum is the perfectionist student who will try everything, yet rarely finish anything because nothing is good enough to turn in. Both behaviors impede learning and academic success. Educators who offer frequent opportunities for success (behaviorally and academically) can improve a student's desire to take academic risks and feel comfortable learning without the prospect of ridicule. Consider warm-up activities that the student is comfortable with, preparing him or her for a question or activity that you plan to present to the class, offering the student opportunities to correct work until it is right rather than giving a grade for the first assignment turned in, and frequently praising the student for desired behaviors, including effort and persistence, rather than having praise contingent on correct responses to questions.

CONCLUSION

According to Zimrin,[17] abused children who grew up to be healthy, nonabusing adults knew an adult during their childhood who treated them with kindness, respect, empathy, and encouragement. School-based professionals are listed in Zimrin's research as one of the major supports in these children's lives. Importantly, this type of support does not require extra time, just sincerity and confidence in the student. Keep in mind that small successes are important for all students, but especially for those students who have been abused. Many abused students are afraid to hope or do not know what success looks like, so they sabotage their own efforts out of fear or frustration or they refuse to try in order to avoid failure. While this can be very challenging for educators, considering the factors that play into the student's behavior and academic performance and providing the supports suggested in this chapter can not only help mitigate the negative effects of abuse but also make the student feel empowered to achieve and succeed.

NOTES

1. U.S. Department of Health and Human Services, Administration for Children and Families, Administration on Children, Youth and Families, Children's Bureau, 2010.
2. U.S. Department of Health and Human Services, Administration for Children and Families, Administration on Children, Youth and Families, Children's Bureau, 2010, p. 127.
3. Mitchell, 2005.
4. Lowenthal, 2000.
5. Iwaniec, Larkin, & Higgins, 2006.
6. Goldman, Salus, Wolcott, & Kennedy, 2003.
7. Iwaniec et al., 2006.
8. Iwaniec et al., 2006, p. 79.

9. Thornberry, Ireland, & Smith, 2001.
10. Renteln, 2010.
11. Renteln, 2010.
12. Ferrari, 2002.
13. Sedlak, McPherson, & Das, 2010.
14. e.g., Hawkins et al., 2010.
15. Cole et al., 2005, p. 13.
16. Courtney, Kushwaha, & Johnson, 2008; Hanley & Gibb, 2011; Logan, Leeb, & Barker, 2009.
17. Zimrin, 1986.

REFERENCES

Cole, S. F., O'Brien, J. G., Gadd, M. G., Ristuccia, J., Wallace, D. L., & Gregory, M. (2005). *Helping traumatized children learn: Supportive school environments for children traumatized by family violence.* Boston, MA: Massachusetts Advocates for Children.

Courtney, E. A., Kushwaha, M., & Johnson, J. G. (2008). Childhood emotional abuse and risk for hopelessness and depressive symptoms during adolescence. *Journal of Emotional Abuse, 8,* 281–293.

Ferrari, A. M. (2002). The impact of culture upon child rearing practices and definitions of maltreatment. *Child Abuse and Neglect, 26,* 793–813.

Goldman, J., Salus, M. K., Wolcott, D., & Kennedy, K. Y. (2003). *A coordinated response to child abuse and neglect: The foundation for practice.* Child Abuse and Neglect User Manual Series. Washington, DC: Government Printing Office. Retrieved from http://www.childwelfare.gov/pubs/usermanuals/foundation/foundation.pdf

Hanley, A. J., & Gibb, B. E. (2011). Verbal victimization and changes in hopelessness among elementary school children. *Journal of Clinical Child and Adolescent Psychology, 40,* 772–776.

Hawkins, A. O., Danielson, C. K., de Arellano, M. A., Hanson, R. F., Ruggiero, K. J., Smith, D. W., et al. (2010). Ethnic racial differences in the prevalence of injurious spanking and other child physical abuse in a national survey of adolescents. *Child Maltreatment, 15,* 242–249.

Iwaniec, D., Larkin, E., & Higgins, S. (2006). Research review: Risk and resilience in cases of emotional abuse. *Child and Family Social Work, 11,* 73–82.

Logan, J. E., Leeb, R. T., & Barker, L. E. (2009). Gender-specific mental and behavioral outcomes among physically abused high-risk seventh-grade youths. *Public Health Reports, 124,* 234–245.

Lowenthal, B. (2000). Child maltreatment: Effects on development and learning. In *Issues in early childhood education: Curriculum, teacher education, & dissemination of information. Proceedings of the Lilian Katz Symposium* (pp. 365–371). Retrieved from http://ceep.crc.uiuc.edu/pubs/katzsym/lowenthal.html

Mitchell, G. (2005). Emotional abuse and neglect: An overview. Part II. *Representing Children, 17,* 252–262.

Renteln, A. D. (2010). Corporal punishment and the cultural defense. *Law and Contemporary Problems, 73,* 253–279.

Sedlak, A., McPherson, K., & Das, B. (2010). *Supplementary analyses of race differences in child maltreatment rates in the NIS-4*. U.S. Department of Health and Human Services, Administration on Children, Youth and Families. Retrieved from http://www.acf.hhs.gov/programs/opre/abuse_neglect/natl_incid/reports/supp_analysis/nis4_supp_analysis_race_diff_mar2010.pdf

Thornberry, R. P., Ireland, T. O., & Smith, C. A. (2001). The importance of timing: The varying impact of childhood and adolescent maltreatment on multiple problem outcomes. *Development and Psychopathology, 13*, 957–979.

U.S. Department of Health and Human Services, Administration for Children and Families, Administration on Children, Youth and Families, Children's Bureau. (2010). *Child maltreatment 2009*. Retrieved from http://www.acf.hhs.gov/programs/cb/pubs/cm09/cm09.pdf

Zimrin, H. (1986). A profile of survival. *Child Abuse & Neglect, 10*, 339–349.

WEB RESOURCES

- American Professional Society on the Abuse of Children: http://www.apsac.org/
- Bridging Refugee Youth & Children's Services: http://www.brycs.org/
- Child Abuse National Hotline: 1–800–4-A-CHILD
- Child Welfare Information Gateway: http://www.childwelfare.gov/
- ChildHelp: http://www.childhelp.org/
- International Society for Prevention of Child Abuse and Neglect: http://www.ispcan.org/
- National Children's Advocacy Center: http://www.nationalcac.org/
- National Children's Alliance: http://www.nationalchildrensalliance.org/
- Prevent Child Abuse America: http://www.preventchildabuse.org/

SELECTED CHILDREN'S LITERATURE

- Copen, L. M., & Pucci, L. M. (2000). *Finding your way: What happens when you tell about abuse*. Thousand Oaks, CA: Sage Publications.
- Loftis, C. (1995). *The words hurt: Helping children cope with verbal abuse*. Far Hills, NJ: New Horizon Press.
- Patterson, S. (1987). *I wish the hitting would stop: A workbook for children living in violent homes*. Fargo, ND: Rape & Abuse Crisis Center.
- Wilson, J. (2010). *Cookie*. New York, NY: Roaring Book Press.

16

Students Responding to Natural Disasters and Terrorism

RYAN P. KILMER, VIRGINIA GIL-RIVAS, AND
STEVEN J. HARDY ∎

INTRODUCTION

The last decade has seen significant large-scale traumas, including the tragedy of September 11, 2001, the most deadly and damaging terrorist act on U.S. soil, as well as the immense damage wrought by 2005's Hurricane Katrina and its aftermath, regarded as the most severe and costly natural disaster in U.S. history. In fact, the last 10 years have included 8 of the 10 most costly documented U.S. hurricanes,[1] the deadly Super Tuesday tornado outbreak in 2008 as well as the tornadoes of April 2011, the October 2007 California wildfires, and other major events that have affected children, youth, and families from all reaches of the nation, both directly and indirectly. According to the Federal Emergency Management Agency (FEMA),[2] the United States experienced 560 federally declared disasters between January 2000 and January 2010.

Natural disasters and terrorist acts, while distinct in many ways (e.g., hurricanes or tsunamis can sometimes be predicted ahead of time, in contrast to acts of terrorism), share the fact that they can impact multiple levels of a young person's life.[3] For instance, depending on the nature and magnitude of the event, a youngster's home may be damaged, his or her neighborhood may be destroyed, and/or his or her social network may be shattered. Moreover, a parent's place of employment may have been destroyed, leading to financial concerns, or worse, a loved one may have been seriously injured or killed. Such events can disrupt children's beliefs about safety, predictability, and protection from harm, contributing to the loss of one's known routines and experiences and even lost trust or faith.[4]

Schools can serve a critical role in responding comprehensively to these children's needs. Schools are a core element of a community's fabric, serving as a source of continuity and structure, facilitating connections between community members, and providing stability during difficult times.[5] Schools can help children and families reclaim normalcy, reestablish routines, and rebuild a sense of safety and security.[6] In this regard, schools possess many characteristics that can facilitate recovery for children, families, and the community at large.

Given the magnitude and far-reaching effects of mass traumas, teachers and other school professionals are often affected themselves. In other instances, even when an educator's community is not impacted directly, one still needs to be aware of and responsive to the experiences of those who did experience the adverse event. As one case in point, Hurricane Katrina initially displaced roughly 1 to 1.3 million residents of the Gulf Coast, including an estimated 372,000 school children, and many children and families had to move several times.[7] These youth and families faced multiple challenges (e.g., learning expectations at the new school, adapting to the new community), as did their teachers and schools, particularly those enrolling high numbers of evacuees.[8] In the latter circumstance, schools faced issues of overcrowding and struggled to meet the needs of the relocated students.

EFFECTS OF NATURAL DISASTERS AND TERRORISM ON SCHOOL CHILDREN

Almost all youngsters evidence acute distress after trauma.[9] Although most return to prior levels of functioning over time with proper support, noteworthy proportions of youngsters exhibit a range of negative mental health consequences[10] that may require more intensive services. A child's ability to return to prior functioning may vary based on individual factors (e.g., temperament, coping competence, cognitive abilities), the nature of the event, the degree of exposure, the number of additional risks and adversities experienced, the nurturance and support received after the trauma, and the degree to which a youngster's day-to-day routine or basic views about how the world works have been disrupted. In addition, the effects of trauma vary for children and youth of different ages and developmental levels (see later in this chapter for more detail). Table 16.1 summarizes a number of common reactions observed across age/grade levels.

Overall, school personnel need to be prepared to identify common signs of distress in their students, which may include acting out (e.g., aggression, defiance), as well as other concerns such as anxiety, sadness, fear for personal safety and that of others, withdrawal, and somatic complaints (e.g., headaches, stomachaches).[11] Beyond those initial reactions, in the longer term, negative effects may reflect posttraumatic stress symptoms (PTSS) and other problems related to anxiety, depressive symptoms, behavioral problems, withdrawal, sleep difficulties, and suicidality.[12] These various effects can contribute to difficulty with attention and concentration and, in turn, with learning.

Table 16.1 AGE-RELATED INITIAL EFFECTS OF NATURAL DISASTERS AND
TERRORISM[a]

Age Level	Initial Effects of Disasters and Terrorism
Preschool	Behavioral • Regression to simpler speech or may become mute • Regression to infant-like behavior (e.g., bed-wetting, thumb sucking) • Irritability, tantrums, crying, or difficulty calming • Clinginess; difficulty separating from parents or teachers • Become attached to a place where they feel safe • Difficulty falling or staying asleep; nightmares or night terrors • Reenactment of the event through play • Exaggerated startle response Cognitive/emotional • Fear of the dark, strangers, animals, or "monsters" • Worry about safety of self, siblings, or caregivers • Feelings of self-blame or confusion Somatic • Decreased appetite • Vomiting, constipation, diarrhea
Elementary school	Academic • Declines in academic performance • School avoidance and increased school absences Behavioral • Irritability, aggression, or anger • Persistent talking or asking of questions about the event • Clinginess to parents or teachers • Difficulty falling or staying asleep; nightmares or night terrors • Withdrawal from activities, groups, and friends • Regression to behaviors more typical of younger child (e.g., asking to be fed, baby talk, wanting to carry a teddy bear or blanket) • Re-enactment of the event through play • Decreased interest in peers, hobbies, or school Cognitive/emotional • Focus on specific details of the tragedy and on personal safety • Difficulties with attention and concentration, confusion, or forgetfulness • Worry about innocent people being injured or killed Somatic • Physical complaints (e.g., stomachaches, headaches, dizziness)

(*continued*)

Table 16.1 (CONTINUED)

Age Level	Initial Effects of Disasters and Terrorism
Middle school	**Academic** • Declines in academic performance • Increased school absences **Behavioral** • Self-destructive, reckless, or risk-taking behaviors (e.g., experimenting with alcohol or drug use) • Disruptive behaviors • Withdrawal or increased irritability • Increased conflicts with peers, teachers, or administrators • Sleep difficulties • Vigorously competing for teachers' attention **Cognitive/emotional** • Feeling self-conscious about their emotional responses to the event • Feelings of shame or guilt • Fantasizing about revenge and retribution • Easily distracted, difficulty concentrating, or forgetful **Somatic** • Changes in eating habits • Physical complaints (e.g., stomachaches, headaches, dizziness)
High school	**Academic** • Declines in academic performance • Increased school absences **Behavioral** • Denial or minimizing of emotional reactions • Self-destructive, reckless, or risk-taking behaviors (e.g., experimenting with alcohol or drug use) • Increased conflicts with peers, teachers, or administrators • Decreased interest in social activities, peers, hobbies, or school **Cognitive/emotional** • Feeling self-conscious about their emotional responses to the event • Feelings of shame or guilt • Fantasizing about revenge and retribution • Easily distracted, difficulty concentrating, or forgetful **Somatic** • Changes in eating habits • Physical complaints (e.g., stomachaches, headaches, dizziness)

[a] See, e.g., Beauchesne, Kelley, Patsdaughter, & Pickard, 2002; Berger et al., 2007; Joshi & O'Donnell, 2003; Lazarus et al., 2003b; NCTSN, n.d.-a, n.d.- b; Usofsky et al., 2007; SAMHSA, 2005; SAMHSA, n.d.-c.

Posttraumatic Growth

In addition to these responses to trauma, an emerging literature indicates that, as a result of their struggle with trauma and its aftermath, some children and youth perceive positive changes in themselves, a phenomenon known as post-traumatic growth.[13] This construct emphasizes the potential for transformation as a result of one's efforts to understand the trauma and cope in its aftermath, including growth in one's sense of personal strength, faith or spiritual beliefs, views about relationships and relating to others, and other areas, including val-ues.[14] It is important to note that the distress that emerges as youth struggle with traumatic experiences appears to be a necessary element for the development of posttraumatic growth. The implications of this growth for long-term adjust-ment, however, are unclear.

DEVELOPMENTAL CONSIDERATIONS

Reactions and responses to trauma vary based on a student's developmental level—they are tied to children's cognitive, emotional, and behavioral capaci-ties.[15] Of particular importance, varying cognitive capabilities may influence many elements of posttrauma response, including one's appraisal and under-standing of the trauma, coping strategies and ability to organize and utilize available resources, and capacity to attend to and express emotions and internal experiences.[16] From about age 6 or 7 years on, many school-aged children become better able to manage their trauma-related thoughts and emotions, including the abilities to reframe or reappraise a difficult situation.[17] Roughly between ages 6 and 9, children begin to exhibit more realistic expectations about what they can and cannot control and how to cope with controllable and uncontrollable situ-ations.[18] Awareness of and sensitivity to such differences, a strength for teach-ers and other school personnel, can help determine how to talk with students, respond to questions, and decide when and how supports should be provided.

FAMILY AND SOCIAL FACTORS

Beyond broad developmental considerations, youths' reactions and behavior following a major trauma vary according to their family, ethnic, cultural, and religious background; personal history; and socioeconomic status. For instance, aspects of the parent–child relationship, including the quality of the relation-ship (i.e., perceived warmth, conflict), parental responsiveness to their children's emotional states, and parenting behaviors, are associated with children's adjust-ment.[19] In particular, caregivers can create a supportive family environment that contributes to positive adjustment.

Disaster and terrorism, however, can also affect parents, which may compromise their ability to support and guide their children. In a study of adolescents indirectly exposed to the attacks of September 11, parental PTSS were associated with higher trauma-related symptoms 7 months following the attacks.[20] Large-scale trauma also can contribute to negative parent–child interactions that may be detrimental to children's long-term adjustment. For example, parent–child conflict is associated with more severe PTSS among youth exposed to terrorism[21] and natural disasters.[22] Furthermore, children may also be concerned about their parents' well-being, which can compromise their feelings of safety and willingness to seek help. Indeed, children's perceptions of caregiver distress and their caregivers' availability to talk with them about their feelings and concerns appear to contribute to greater PTSS[23] and psychological distress.[24]

Support from larger social networks may be particularly important following trauma. For example, following Hurricane Katrina, family support from friends, parents' co-workers, church members, and professionals (including teachers) was associated with lower levels of PTSS among children, while support from family members was not significantly related to children's symptoms.[25] Therefore, a supportive classroom may provide important resources for facilitating adaptive coping, particularly among children lacking a warm or stable home environment.

SOCIOCULTURAL FACTORS

Beyond the role of primary caregivers, a family's history, cultural values, and beliefs may influence the meaning given to traumas, the resulting distress, and the coping strategies used. Unfortunately, relatively few studies have examined differences in the rates of posttraumatic stress disorder (PTSD) and trauma-related symptoms among ethnically and culturally diverse samples of youths.[26] The available studies have yielded equivocal results. A study of elementary school children exposed to Hurricane Andrew did not find ethnic differences in PTSS.[27] However, a follow-up of this sample revealed that African American and Hispanic children demonstrated smaller reductions in symptoms over time compared to Caucasian children.[28] Similarly, a study of children indirectly exposed to the September 11 attacks found that African American children reported greater distress and avoidance symptoms compared to Caucasian children.[29] In contrast, another study of youngsters exposed to Hurricane Andrew did not find differences in PTSS between Caucasian and ethnic minority elementary- and middle-school children.[30] These mixed findings suggest that diverse factors in the lives of these children are likely salient contributors to their long-term adjustment.

It is possible that factors such as poverty, prior exposure to potentially traumatic events (e.g., community violence, domestic violence), beliefs about seeking psychological and social services, caregiver resources (i.e., education, support), and the social and financial resources available posttrauma may influence a student's adaptation more so than race or ethnicity. For example, children liv-ing in poverty frequently reside in areas that are geographically vulnerable to disaster and have limited access to resources that may buffer them against the negative effects of these events. Furthermore, prior adversity exposure may have affected children's internal (i.e., hope for the future, self-efficacy) and external (i.e., support from parents and friends) resources that could assist them in their efforts to cope.

RECOMMENDATIONS FOR TEACHERS

Large-scale traumas such as natural disasters or terrorist acts create unique posttrauma circumstances for teachers. For one, teachers typically must be available to support a substantial number of children affected by the event—sometimes everyone in a given class—as opposed to a single student or small group. In addition, because such events are often mass traumas, many teachers may have been affected directly themselves. Teachers could consider the follow-ing recommendations.

Focus on helping students reclaim normalcy. This is a crucial goal—some have referred to this as working to "restore equilibrium."[31] Doing so involves reestab-lishing classroom routines, normal patterns, and predictability.[32] During such a challenging time, the need for structure, consistency, and clarity is relevant for global classroom management as well—it is important to maintain expectations and standards for student behavior, although, given the context, balancing those expectations with compassion and empathy is a necessity.[33]

Stay calm and reinforce safety. Much like airplane passengers look to flight attendants during turbulence to help gauge whether to remain calm or become anxious, children look to adults for cues on how to react to confusing or ambig-uous situations. Remain calm and assure them that they are safe. To that end, engaging in appropriate self-care is critical. A teacher who is struggling will be less able to create an appropriate environment and help his or her students.[34]

Listen and observe actively. Follow your students' lead. If they have questions or want to talk, allow for or even create opportunities to do so. This can take many forms, from "just" talking to adapting lesson plans and curricula (see later for more). Being a careful listener is important, as is keeping an eye out for changes in children's behavior or school performance, or other potential reactions, such as those summarized in Table 16.1.[35]

Help identify susceptible students. Certain youngsters may be more vulnerable than others, including those who may have a missing, injured, or deceased fam-ily member as a result of the event (see chapter 11); those having experienced pre-vious disasters; children whose homes were destroyed; and those who may have a strong connection with certain aspects of the area affected (e.g., children who are particularly devastated by the destruction of their school, church, or temple).

Provide opportunities for sharing and expressing emotions. A number of groups have provided lists of questions that may serve to facilitate classroom discussion. For instance, the Substance Abuse and Mental Health Services Administration (SAMHSA) includes the following:

- Where were you and what were you doing when [the disaster] happened?
- What was your first thought when it happened?
- What reminds you of the disaster?
- How have you gotten through rough times before?[36]

As a caution, it is crucial that we do not force children to tell their stories or set up situations in which they have little or no choice or control[37]; rather, students are better served when we establish situations in which they feel comfortable and can choose whether to express themselves.[38]

Tools for generating discussion can take different forms (many caution against using media reports or video as a springboard for discussion—this can be too much for children) and may use different methods (including art, writing, circle-time discussions—see next recommendation for more). Importantly, any answers to children's questions should be targeted, factual, and developmentally appropriate.

Consider modifying your curriculum. On some level, this may reflect reconsidering the scheduling and pace at which you planned to cover particular content or lessons.[39] In other instances, it may involve activities or lessons in science, reading, writing, and art (and other subjects) that relate to some aspect of the trauma and can provide a means through which students can express themselves, process what happened, and attempt to make meaning of the event(s) and what has happened since.[40] While some teachers employ such methods as part of a curriculum that emerges from student interest, others may be hesitant to broach such material or to integrate elements of the trauma (e.g., teaching about hurricanes or earthquakes) into their curriculum because of their desire not to upset or elicit distress in the children; still others limit their roles because they are not aware of developmentally appropriate lessons and activities that might be of benefit.[41]

The University of Illinois Extension has developed a Disaster Resources page with curriculum guides and numerous examples of activities for youth of different ages to help facilitate the expression of feelings, educate children about disasters, and develop service project ideas.[42] Other sources[43] also provide suggestions for youngsters of varying ages (e.g., using puppets, making a collage, creating a skit or play), including many in which students do not have to talk about their experiences. Regardless of the modality, these kinds of activities can both yield rich academic experiences and provide a context through which teachers and students alike can address their reactions, responses, and feelings following adverse events.[44]

Provide caring support to students. Teachers are well positioned to be natural supports. Feel free, within appropriate boundaries, to empathize with students, acknowledge their feelings, and demonstrate caring.[45] This can help children feel more secure and contribute to fewer symptoms of traumatic stress, depression, or other anxiety-related concerns.[46] Particularly during trying times, it can be very important for children to have supports outside of their families.

Draw on students' past experiences or provide opportunities to demonstrate competence. Provide opportunities for students to demonstrate mastery and feel competent and efficacious. For instance, teachers can help students draw from their previous experiences of hardship and how they overcame them, or discuss with students how they think other communities have recovered from similar disasters. These exercises can help students maintain positive expectations and hope for their futures, facilitate their adaptive problem solving, and assist them as they try to make sense of what has happened.

Help your students help others. Develop classroom projects that involve teamwork and respectful connections with others, as well as ones focusing on assisting others affected by the event.[47] Examples of such activities include group activities to help their school (e.g., fundraising, beautifying school grounds), improve their neighborhood, or benefit others in the community (e.g., volunteering in shelters).[48] Such efforts can increase students' sense of community and connectedness and help them feel as though they are doing something actively to help.[49]

Draw attention to stories of compassion. Following mass trauma, stories of heroism, generosity, and humanity are frequently shared through the media. For example, in the aftermath of the 9/11 attacks, one could focus on the number of firefighters that volunteered their time and drove through the night across state lines to help others in need. Sharing such stories may help children feel that they live within a society that will support and protect them.

Communicate with parents. It can also be of benefit to extend support to parents and, at least, keep them informed. This is a difficult time for them as well and they may be struggling with questions of trust or worrying about the school's capacity to protect students.[50]

Recognize the importance of cultural values and beliefs. Acknowledge that there is considerable variability in the extent to which members of particular ethnic or racial groups adhere to specific cultural values and beliefs. Thus, it is important to take the time to learn about the unique experiences and history of children and families and the role that these factors may play in their responses to trauma and their willingness to seek and receive help.

RECOMMENDATIONS FOR SCHOOL MENTAL HEALTH PROFESSIONALS

Following large-scale traumas that may have affected a significant proportion if not all of a school's students, there are multiple necessary layers to school mental health professionals' responses. First, as would typically be the case for school psychologists, counselors, and social workers, they will provide individual support or counseling to youngsters in need. However, arguably the most critical component of their role in such circumstances is cast at a much broader level, reaching students beyond their one-on-one work. Several such steps fall under their purview.

Support teachers. School mental health professionals need to seek continuing education or specialized training in trauma mental health[51] and draw on this knowledge to help teachers understand children's reactions and responses to trauma, making sure they are vigilant for signs that may suggest that a child is struggling, and identify strategies for responding to their students' needs.[52] Some circumstances may warrant partnering with community-based organizations or aid/relief agencies for assistance in implementing necessary interventions, meeting the demand for referrals, or responding appropriately to the needs of a diverse student body (e.g., providing culturally competent services, serving those with special needs).[53]

Preparing information for parents is another way to support teachers. Parents are more likely to contact teachers as a first line of communication with the school, and reaching out and providing information proactively can enhance the relationship between the school and parent. Moreover, organizing materials to give parents can reduce the burden on teachers to respond individually to several parents with similar questions. In work conducted following Hurricane Katrina, teachers reported that they wanted information to share with parents.[54]

Develop an infrastructure to support students. Beyond the urgency to meet student and staff needs in trauma's aftermath, it is important for schools to implement plans for doing so in the longer term.[55] This may involve tapping into community-based supports[56]; identifying programmatic options (see "Evidence-Supported School-Based Interventions" later in the chapter); and considering approaches for screening, assessing, and referring children,[57] being sure to allow for self- or parental referral.[58]

RECOMMENDATIONS FOR PRINCIPALS AND ADMINISTRATORS

Administrators play a critical role before and after mass trauma. Prior to the event, principals can oversee crisis plans, establish and communicate with crisis response teams, put resources in place for response, and develop networks for communication in adverse circumstances. In fact, evidence suggests that such pre-event planning and capacity or infrastructure development can contribute meaningfully to efficient and well-targeted postevent responses.[59] After the event, principals' leadership is of tremendous importance, and flexible thinking is an asset. Administrators can communicate a philosophy to guide decisions and a strategy for action, serving "as rudders for their schools, helping to steer them in the desired direction."[60] These qualities were exemplified by Jacqueline

MacDonald, principal of Mayfair Elementary School, which reopened in East Baton Rouge Parish in Hurricane Katrina's aftermath.[61] MacDonald appropriately recognized the importance of focusing on students' emotional needs and families' resource and information needs, rather than retaining a primary and exclusive emphasis on academics.

Don't rush in—be a careful consumer. In the press to "do something," it is important not to rush decisions. Principals of schools impacted directly or in which a large proportion of students have been affected by disaster or terrorism will be approached by multiple organizations and entities who want to provide assistance, share an intervention program, and the like. While it certainly helps to do some legwork pre-event and evaluate the extant options carefully, the situation may feel more hectic after the event, and administrators may not feel as though they have time to weigh alternatives. A take-home point to inform those decisions: One size does not fit all. A program may have data to support its efficacy, and an organization may have a sound track record and good intentions; however, a central criterion is making sure they are a good fit for your community, your school, and your students. Then, be sure to weigh in with your school's mental health professionals or school crisis teams to guide decisions, particularly around programmatic or intervention options.

Think broadly in considering your school's role. At Mayfair Elementary School, MacDonald saw the instrumental role her school could play in her community and in the lives of her students and their families by becoming a key source of information and resources for parents. She worked to develop connections and a sense of community with parents and took steps to facilitate those relationships by hiring a full-time parent liaison who communicated with parents, surveyed their needs, and sought to increase their awareness of the services and supports available in the community.[62] Working with community partners, Mayfair also hosted a resource and informational fair for families.[63]

Support parents and teachers. It is important to be accessible to parents and provide opportunities for their voices to be heard, particularly around their child's needs. It can be helpful to provide means or settings that can help them connect with others—for example, the school could sponsor parent gatherings or organize activities or workshops intended to meet parental needs, provide information, and discuss their concerns.[64] In addition, school-sponsored meetings can provide information about common child reactions, services and supports provided at school, the school's safety/crisis plan, how to help their children, and other such topics.[65]

Following large-scale trauma, teachers and school staff will also likely benefit from extra support and resources, particularly since they may have been affected themselves. This support can help them address their own needs and identify strategies to assist their students or, in some cases, engage new (i.e., relocated) students.[66]

Prepare for the long haul. Following disasters or terrorism, efforts to meet the needs of children and families are typically fragmented, limited in scope, and focused on the immediate crisis response.[67] Following recent events, many schools were able to meet their students' needs in the immediate aftermath but struggled and often lacked the resources to provide necessary services in the longer term.[68] For instance, one study following Hurricane Katrina highlights that children continued to experience high levels of needs (including counseling, tutoring, or medical needs) and unmet service needs both 1 and 2 years after the hurricane.[69] Their caregivers also reported numerous significant needs, such as housing or financial assistance, medical needs, and counseling.[70]

EVIDENCE-SUPPORTED SCHOOL-BASED INTERVENTIONS: RESOURCES FOR FURTHER INFORMATION

It is difficult to do justice to the full range of considerations for meeting students' needs following a disaster or terrorist act. Chapters within the final section of this volume describe systemic school responses and school-wide interventions. However, in light of the growing literature on school-based interventions following disaster or terrorism, several programs warrant specific mention.

In this context, school-based interventions can be classified as those that primarily target children with trauma-related symptoms (i.e., PTSS, depression, anxiety, behavioral difficulties) and universal interventions that target all children regardless of symptoms. Furthermore, some interventions are designed to respond to the needs of children immediately after the disaster, while others focus on their long-term adjustment.

Psychological First Aid (PFA), developed by the National Child Traumatic Stress Network (NCTSN) and the National Center for PTSD,[71] is designed to address the needs of children, adults, and families immediately after disaster, terrorism, and other traumas. Mental health and other disaster first responders typically deliver the intervention in emergency settings (i.e., shelters, hospitals, schools). Recently, the U.S. Department of Homeland Security[72] released a manual that provides teacher guidelines for implementing PFA. Although PFA is widely employed, it is unclear to what extent it contributes to faster recovery or prevents the development of psychosocial difficulties.

Jaycox and her colleagues at RAND[73] developed a toolkit for schools that reviews a range of programs for children affected by trauma (including some that focus on a specific type of trauma such as disaster). Importantly, the authors provide school administrators and staff with suggestions on how to select programs to best meet the needs of children.

The Enhancing Resilience Among Students Experiencing Stress (ERASE-Stress) program[74] has shown promising results in reducing PTSS, depression, and bodily complaints and improving functioning among youth exposed to disasters, terrorism, and war. ERASE-Stress can be delivered by trained teachers, and sessions cover topics including identifying personal strengths and resources, learning about the body's responses to stress and how to manage and cope with those responses, identifying and expressing feelings, learning skills for strengthening relationships, identifying negative thinking and methods for reframing such thoughts, and exploring hopes for the future and how to make them a reality.

CONCLUSION

A large-scale trauma can have implications for students and school personnel alike, potentially disrupting teaching and learning.[75] Following such events, not only do schools often face increases in rates of student learning or socio-emotional problems, but also they encounter challenges related to the trauma's impact on the teachers and staff, the resource demands related to new students (e.g., because of relocation), and the global weight of meeting the needs of students, school personnel, and even the community.[76] At such times, schools—from administrators to teachers—may experience palpable tension between focusing on academics and their accountability for student progress (i.e., high-stakes testing), and helping address their students' emotional/psychological, as well as basic, needs.[77] In light of such demands, Mayfair Elementary School's Principal MacDonald sought to emphasize the "whole child" (i.e., mental health, social, and educational needs), with a clear primary objective of attending to psychological needs first, recognizing that, without doing so, it would be difficult to establish a productive learning environment.[78] That said, although the initial emphasis was on support and assessing and responding to student and family needs, the school did not "lose sight" of its educational mission.[79] Mayfair's approach was logical, sound, sensitive, and successful.

Our schools have a clear educational mission—and, each and every day, they increasingly face challenges in being able to reach their scholastic goals, meet the dynamic needs of their student bodies, prioritize often scarce resources, and prepare their students for positive scholastic trajectories. Many teachers, school mental health professionals, and administrators are invested and dedicated to helping their students follow a positive path in school and beyond, but they also must account for numerous obstacles along the way. The New Freedom Commission on Mental Health[80] asserted that "mental health is essential to learning as well as to social and emotional development. Because of this important interplay between emotional health and school success, schools must be partners in the mental health care of our children." That global notion holds true following natural disasters or terrorism.

Many sources have described schools as prime settings for assessment, intervention, and support following trauma—not only are they a structured context in which to establish the infrastructure for such steps, but also they are a natural environment for youth, one that may be less stigmatizing than a community-based agency and one in which support services can be incorporated into the school or classroom routines.[81] Indeed, as a "critical context for action, outreach, and support" following a disaster or terrorist act,[82] schools can be leaders in efforts to meet the needs of children and families and in establishing networks of supports, services, and resources. Such efforts will facilitate the well-being of those with whom they work and increase the likelihood that students, teachers, and schools will attain their academic goals.

NOTES

1. See, e.g., Blake, Rappaport, & Landsea, 2007.
2. http://www.gismaps.fema.gov/recent.pdf
3. Kilmer & Gil-Rivas, 2010b.
4. Klingman & Cohen, 2004; Lieberman & Van Horn, 2004.
5. Kilmer, Gil-Rivas, & MacDonald, 2010.
6. Klingman & Cohen, 2004; Osofsky, Osofsky, & Harris, 2007.
7. Louisiana Recovery Authority, 2007; Select Bipartisan Committee to Investigate the Preparation for and Response to Hurricane Katrina, 2006; U.S. Department of Education(DOE), 2005a.
8. Madrid, Grant, Reilly, & Redlener, 2006; see also Pane, McCaffrey, Tharp-Taylor, Asmus, & Stokes, 2006.
9. APA Presidential Task Force on PTSD and Trauma in Children and Adolescents [APA Presidential Task Force], n.d.
10. e.g., APA Presidential Task Force, n.d.; Hoven, Duarte, & Mandell, 2003; La Greca, Silverman, Vernberg, & Prinstein, 1996.
11. National Association of School Psychologists (NASP), 2002; National Child Traumatic Stress Network (NCTSN), n.d.-a, n.d.-b; Norris et al., 2002.
12. Hoven et al., 2003.
13. See, e.g., Kilmer & Gil-Rivas, 2010a; Kilmer et al., 2009; Laufer & Solomon, 2006.
14. See, e.g., Kilmer & Gil-Rivas, 2010a; Kilmer et al., 2009.
15. Shahinfar & Fox, 1997.
16. Kilmer & Gil-Rivas, 2010a; Osofsky, 2004; Shahinfar & Fox, 1997.
17. e.g., Salmon & Bryant, 2002.
18. Salmon & Bryant, 2002.
19. La Greca et al., 1996.
20. Gil-Rivas, Silver, Holman, McIntosh, & Poulin, 2007.
21. Gil-Rivas, Holman, & Silver, 2004.
22. Gil-Rivas, Kilmer, Hypes, & Roof, 2010.
23. Gil-Rivas et al., 2007.
24. Gil-Rivas et al., 2004.
25. Pina et al., 2008.
26. Rabalais, Ruggiero, & Scotti, 2002.
27. Vernberg, La Greca, Silverman, & Prinstein, 1996.
28. La Greca et al., 1996.
29. Lengua, Long, Smith, & Meltzoff, 2005.
30. Jones, Frary, Cunningham, Weddle, & Kaiser, 2001.

31. Center for Mental Health in Schools, University of California, Los Angeles [CMHS], n.d.

32. e.g., NCTSN, n.d.–c.

33. Kilmer et al., 2010.

34. Jaycox, Morse, Tanielian, & Stein, 2006; Lazarus, Jimerson, & Brock, 2003a; NCSTN, n.d.-c.

35. Lazarus et al., 2003a; Osofsky et al., 2007.

36. Substance Abuse and Mental Health Services Administration (SAMHSA), n.d.-a.

37. APA Presidential Task Force, n.d.

38. e.g., DOE, 2005b; Lazarus et al., 2003a; NCTSN, n.d.-b; Shen & Sink, 2002.

39. NCTSN, n.d.-c.

40. Buchanan, Casbergue, & Baumgartner, 2010; Lazarus et al., 2003a; SAMHSA, n.d.-b

41. Buchanan et al., 2010.

42. University of Illinois Extension Disaster Resources, n.d.; please see http://web. extension.illinois.edu/disaster/teacher/csndactx.html

43. SAMHSA, n.d.-b.

44. Buchanan et al., 2010.

45. DOE, 2005b.

46. Klingman & Cohen, 2004; La Greca et al., 1996.

47. American Psychological Association, n.d.; DOE, 2005b; SAMHSA, n.d.-b.

48. Buchanan et al., 2010.

49. NCTSN, n.d.-c.

50. Klingman & Cohen, 2004.

51. APA Presidential Task Force, n.d.; Evans & Oehler-Stinnett, 2006.

52. DOE, 2005b; Lazarus, Jimerson, & Brock, 2003b; Osofsky et al., 2007; Shen & Sink, 2002; see also Felix et al., 2010.

53. DOE, 2005b; Lazarus et al., 2003b.

54. Buchanan et al., 2010.

55. CMHS, 2006.

56. Kilmer et al., 2010.

57. See Jaycox et al., 2006.

58. Lazarus et al., 2003b.

59. CMHS, 2005; Kilmer et al., 2010.

60. Kilmer et al., 2010, p. 180.

61. Kilmer et al., 2010.

62. Kilmer et al., 2010.

63. Kilmer et al., 2010.

64. Klingman & Cohen, 2004; DOE, 2005b.

65. NCTSN, n.d.-d.

66. e.g., DOE, 2005b.

67. CMHS, 2006.

68. See, e.g., Jaycox et al., 2007.

69. Kilmer & Gil-Rivas, 2010c.

70. Kilmer & Gil-Rivas, 2010c.

71. NCTSN and National Center for PTSD, 2006; Vernberg et al., 2008.

72. U.S. Department of Homeland Security, 2006.

73. Jaycox et al., 2006.
74. Gelkopf & Berger, 2009.
75. NCTSN, n.d.-b.
76. CMHS, 2006; Jaycox et al., 2006, 2007; Klingman & Cohen, 2004.
77. Jaycox et al., 2007; Kilmer et al., 2010; Society for Community Research and Action Task Force for Disaster, Community Readiness, and Recovery, 2010.
78. See Kilmer et al., 2010.
79. Kilmer et al., 2010.
80. New Freedom Commission on Mental Health, 2003, p. 58.
81. Berger, Pat-Horenczyk, & Gelkopf, 2007; Klingman & Cohen, 2004; New Freedom Commission on Mental Health, 2003.
82. Kilmer et al., 2010, p. 171; see also Klingman & Cohen, 2004, for a detailed description of a systematic approach to postdisaster work.

REFERENCES

American Psychological Association. (n.d.). *Fact sheet: Fostering resilience in response to terrorism: For psychologists working with children.* Retrieved April 30, 2012, from http://www.deep.med.miami.edu/media/FostResilRspTerChildAPA.pdf

APA Presidential Task Force on PTSD and Trauma in Children and Adolescents. (n.d.). *Children and trauma: Tips for mental health professionals.* American Psychological Association. Flyer also accessible at http://www.apa.org/pi/families/resources/children-trauma-tips.aspx

Beauchesne, M. A., Kelley, B. R., Patsdaughter, C. A., & Pickard, J. (2002). Attack on America: Children's reactions and parents' responses. *Journal of Pediatric Health Care, 16*, 213–221.

Berger, R., Pat-Horenczyk, R., & Gelkopf, M. (2007). School-based intervention for prevention and treatment of elementary-students' terror-related distress in Israel: A quasi-randomized controlled trial. *Journal of Traumatic Stress, 20*, 541–551.

Blake, E. S., Rappaport, E. N., & Landsea, C. W. (2007). *The deadliest, costliest, and most intense United States tropical cyclones from 1851 to 2006 (and other frequently requested hurricane facts).* NOAA Technical Memorandum NWS TPC-5. Miami, FL: National Hurricane Center. Retrieved August 21, 2010, from http://www.nhc.noaa.gov/pdf/NWS-TPC-5.pdf

Buchanan, T. K., Casbergue, R. M., & Baumgartner, J. J. (2010). Consequences for classroom environments and school personnel: Evaluating Katrina's effect on schools and system response. In R. P. Kilmer, V. Gil-Rivas, R. G. Tedeschi, & L. G. Calhoun (Eds.), *Helping families and communities recover from disaster: Lessons learned from Hurricane Katrina and its aftermath* (pp. 117–139). Washington, DC: American Psychological Association.

Center for Mental Health in Schools, University of California, Los Angeles (CMHS). (2005). *Special ENEWS: Lessons learned so far (11/22/05) – Disaster aftermath.* Retrieved April 21, 2007, from http://smhp.psych.ucla.edu/pdfdocs/enews/ENEWS(11-22-05).pdf

Center for Mental Health in Schools, University of California, Los Angeles (CMHS). (2006, July 12). *End of the school year update on the aftermath of the hurricanes.*

Retrieved December 1, 2007, from http://smhp.psych.ucla.edu/pdfdocs/enews/enews%287-12–06%29.pdf

Center for Mental Health in Schools, University of California, Los Angeles (CMHS). (n.d.). *Responding to crises: A few general principles.* Retrieved September 6, 2010, from http://smhp.psych.ucla.edu/qf/crisis_qt/crisis_principles.pdf

Evans, L., & Oehler-Stinnett, J. (2006). Children and natural disasters: A primer for school psychologists. *School Psychology International, 27,* 33–55.

Felix, E., Vernberg, E. M., Pfefferbaum, R. L., Gill, D. C., Schorr, J., Boudreaux, A., et al. (2010). Schools in the shadow of terrorism: Psychosocial adjustment and interest in interventions following terror attacks. *Psychology in the Schools, 47,* 592–605.

Gelkopf, M., & Berger, R. (2009). A school-based, teacher-mediated prevention program (ERASE-Stress) for reducing terror-related traumatic reactions in Israeli youth: A quasi-randomized controlled trial. *Journal of Child Psychology and Psychiatry, 50,* 962–971.

Gil-Rivas, V., Holman, E. A., & Silver, R. C. (2004). Adolescent vulnerability following the September 11th terrorist attacks: A study of parents and their children. *Applied Developmental Science, 8,* 130–142.

Gil-Rivas, V., Kilmer, R. P., Hypes, A. W., & Roof, K. A. (2010). The caregiver-child relationship and children's adjustment post-Hurricane Katrina. In R. P. Kilmer, V. Gil-Rivas, R. G. Tedeschi, & L. G. Calhoun (Eds.), *Helping families and communities recover from disaster: Lessons learned from Hurricane Katrina and its aftermath* (pp. 55–76). Washington, DC: American Psychological Association.

Gil-Rivas, V., Silver, R. C., Holman, E. A., McIntosh, D. N., & Poulin, M. (2007). Parental responses and adolescent adjustment to the September 11, 2001 terrorist attacks. *Journal of Traumatic Stress, 20,* 1063–1068.

Hoven, C. W., Duarte, C. S., & Mandell, D. J. (2003). Children's mental health after disasters: The impact of the World Trade Center attack. *Current Psychiatry Reports, 5,* 101–107.

Jaycox, L. H., Morse, L. K., Tanielian, T., & Stein, B. D. (2006). *How schools can help students recover from traumatic experiences: A tool kit for supporting long-term recovery.* Technical Report 413. Rand Corporation. Retrieved April 3, 2007, from http://www.rand.org/pubs/technical_reports/2006/RAND_TR413.pdf

Jaycox, L. H., Tanielian, T. L., Sharma, P., Morse, L., Clum, G., & Stein, B. D. (2007). Schools' mental health responses following Hurricanes Katrina and Rita. *Psychiatric Services, 58,* 1339–1343.

Jones, R. T., Frary, R., Cunningham, P., Weddle, J. D., & Kaiser, L. (2001). The psychological effects of Hurricane Andrew on ethnic minority and Caucasian children and adolescents: A case study. *Cultural Diversity & Ethnic Minority Psychology, 7,* 103–108.

Joshi, P. T., & O'Donnell, D. A. (2003). Consequences of child exposure to war and terrorism. *Clinical Child and Family Psychology Review, 6,* 275–292.

Kilmer, R. P., & Gil-Rivas, V. (2010a). Exploring posttraumatic growth in children impacted by Hurricane Katrina: Correlates of the phenomenon and developmental considerations. *Child Development, 81,* 1211–1227.

Kilmer, R. P., & Gil-Rivas, V. (2010b). Introduction: Attending to ecology. In R. P. Kilmer, V. Gil-Rivas, R. G. Tedeschi, & L. G. Calhoun (Eds.), *Helping families and communities recover from disaster: Lessons learned from Hurricane Katrina and its aftermath* (pp. 3–24). Washington, DC: American Psychological Association.

Kilmer, R. P., & Gil-Rivas, V. (2010c). Responding to the needs of children and families after a disaster: Linkages between unmet needs and caregiver functioning. *American Journal of Orthopsychiatry, 80,* 135–142.

Kilmer, R. P., Gil-Rivas, V., & MacDonald, J. (2010). Implications of major disaster for educators and school-based mental health professionals: Needs, actions, and the example of Mayfair Elementary. In R. P. Kilmer, V. Gil-Rivas, R. G. Tedeschi, & L. G. Calhoun (Eds.), *Helping families and communities recover from disaster: Lessons learned from Hurricane Katrina and its aftermath* (pp. 167–191). Washington, DC: American Psychological Association.

Kilmer, R. P., Gil-Rivas, V., Tedeschi, R. G., Cann, A., Calhoun, L. G., Buchanan, T., et al. (2009). Use of the revised Posttraumatic Growth Inventory for Children (PTGI-C-R). *Journal of Traumatic Stress, 22,* 248–253.

Klingman, A., & Cohen, E. (2004). *School-based multisystemic interventions for mass trauma.* New York: Kluwer Academic/Plenum Publishers.

La Greca, A. M., Silverman, W. K., Vernberg, E. M., & Prinstein, M. J. (1996). Symptoms of posttraumatic stress in children after Hurricane Andrew: A prospective study. *Journal of Consulting and Clinical Psychology, 64,* 712–723.

Laufer, A., & Solomon, Z. (2006). Posttraumatic symptoms and posttraumatic growth among Israeli youth exposed to terror incidents. *Journal of Social and Clinical Psychology, 25,* 429–447.

Lazarus, P. J., Jimerson, S. R., & Brock, S. E. (2003a). *Helping children after a natural disaster: Information for parents and teachers.* National Association of School Psychologists Resources. Retrieved September 6, 2010, from http://www.nasponline.org/resources/crisis_safety/naturaldisaster_ho.aspx

Lazarus, P. J., Jimerson, S. R., & Brock, S. E. (2003b). *Responding to natural disasters: Helping children and families: Information for school crisis teams.* National Association of School Psychologists Resources. Retrieved September 6, 2010, from http://www.nasponline.org/resources/crisis_safety/naturaldisaster_teams_ho.aspx

Lengua, L. J., Long, A. C., Smith, K. I., & Meltzoff, A. N. (2005). Pre-attack symptomatology and temperament as predictors of children's responses to the September 11 terrorist attacks. *Journal of Child Psychology and Psychiatry, 46,* 631–645.

Lieberman, A. F., & Van Horn, P. (2004). Assessment and treatment of young children exposed to traumatic events. In J. D. Osofsky (Ed.), *Young children and trauma: Intervention and treatment* (pp. 111–138). New York: Guilford Press.

Louisiana Recovery Authority. (2007). *Moving beyond Katrina and Rita: Recovery data indicators for Louisiana.* Retrieved April 25, 2012, from http://lra.louisiana.gov/assets/docs/searchable/reports/Indicators082107.pdf

Madrid, P. A., Grant, R., Reilly, M. J., & Redlener, N. B. (2006). Challenges in meeting immediate emotional needs: Short-term impact of a major disaster on children's mental health: Building resiliency in the aftermath of Hurricane Katrina. *Pediatrics, 117,* S448–S453.

National Association of School Psychologists (NASP). (2002). *Children and fear of war and terrorism: Tips for parents and teachers.* Retrieved September 6, 2010, from http://www.nasponline.org/resources/crisis_safety/children_war_general.aspx

National Child Traumatic Stress Network (NCTSN). (n.d.-a). *Age-related reactions to a traumatic event.* Retrieved April 9, 2009, from http://www.nctsnet.org/nctsn_assets/pdfs/age_related_reactions.pdf

National Child Traumatic Stress Network (NCTSN). (n.d.-b). *The effects of trauma on schools and learning*. Retrieved September 6, 2010, from http://www.nctsnet.org/nccts/nav.do?pid=ctr_aud_schl_Effects

National Child Traumatic Stress Network (NCTSN). (n.d.-c). *Teacher guidelines for helping students after a hurricane*. Retrieved April 9, 2009, from http://www.nctsnet.org/nctsn_assets/pdfs/teachers_guidelines_talk_children_hurricanes.pdf

National Child Traumatic Stress Network (NCTSN). (n.d.-d). *Response: When a crisis occurs*. Retrieved September 6, 2010, from http://www.nctsnet.org/nccts/nav.do?pid=ctr_aud_schl_3rs_response&Type=3rs&navPid=ctr_aud_schl_3rs_desc

National Child Traumatic Stress Network and National Center for PTSD. (2006). *Psychological first aid: Field operations guide, 2nd ed.* Retrieved April 19, 2012, fromhttp://www.nctsnet.org/sites/default/files/pfa/english/1-psyfirstaid_final_complete_manual.pdf

New Freedom Commission on Mental Health. (2003). *Achieving the promise: Transforming mental health care in America. Final Report.* DHHS Pub. No. SMA-03-3832. Rockville, MD: U.S. Department of Health and Human Services.

Norris, F., Friedman, M., Watson, P., Byrne, C., Diaz, E., & Kaniasty, K. (2002). 60,000 disaster victims speak, part I: An empirical review of the empirical literature, 1981–2001. *Psychiatry, 65,* 207–239.

Osofsky, J. D. (2004). Different ways of understanding young children and trauma. In J. D. Osofsky (Ed.), *Young children and trauma: Intervention and treatment* (pp. 3–9). New York, NY: Guilford Press.

Osofsky, J. D., Osofsky, H. J., & Harris, W. W. (2007). Katrina's children: Social policy considerations for children in disasters. *Society for Research in Child Development Social Policy Report, 21,* 1–18.

Pane, J. F., McCaffrey, D. F., Tharp-Taylor, S., Asmus, G. J., & Stokes, B. R. (2006). *Student displacement in Louisiana after the hurricanes of 2005: Experiences of public schools and their students. Technical Report 430.* Santa Monica, CA: Rand Gulf States Policy Institute, Rand Corporation.

Pina, A. A., Villalta, I. K., Ortiz, C. D., Gottschall, A. C., Costa, N. M., & Weems, C. F. (2008). Social support, discrimination, and coping as predictors of posttraumatic stress reactions in youth survivors of Hurricane Katrina. *Journal of Clinical Child & Adolescent Psychology, 37,* 564–574.

Rabalais, A. E., Ruggiero, K. J., & Scotti, J. R. (2002). Multicultural issues in the response of children to disasters. In A. M. La Greca, W. K. Silverman, E. M. Vernberg, & M. C. Roberts (Eds.), *Helping children cope with disasters and terrorism* (pp. 73–100). Washington, DC: American Psychological Association.

Salmon, K., & Bryant, R. A. (2002). Posttraumatic stress disorder in children: The influence of developmental factors. *Clinical Psychology Review, 22,* 163–188.

Select Bipartisan Committee to Investigate the Preparation for and Response to Hurricane Katrina. (2006). *A failure of initiative: Final report of the select bipartisan committee to investigate the preparation for and response to Hurricane Katrina* (U.S. House of Representatives). Retrieved November 22, 2007, from http://www.gpoaccess.gov/katrinareport/mainreport.pdf

Shahinfar, A., & Fox, N. A. (1997). The effects of trauma on children: Conceptual and methodological issues. In D. Cicchetti and S. L. Toth (Eds.), *Rochester symposium* on *developmental psychopathology (Vol. 8): Developmental perspectives on trauma: Theory, research, and intervention* (pp. 115–139). Rochester, NY: University of Rochester Press.

Shen, Y-J., & Sink, C. A. (2002). Helping elementary-age children cope with disasters. *Professional Counseling, 5,* 322–330.

Society for Community Research and Action Task Force for Disaster, Community Readiness, and Recovery. (2010). *How to help your community following disaster: A manual for planning and action.* Society for Community Research and Action. Retrieved August 21, 2010, from http://www.scra27.org/disaster_recovery_manual

Substance Abuse and Mental Health Services Administration (SAMHSA). (2005). *Tips for talking to children after a disaster: A guide for parents and teachers.* Retrieved April 21, 2012, from http://store.samhsa.gov/shin/content/KEN01-0093/KEN01-0093.pdf

Substance Abuse and Mental Health Services Administration (SAMHSA). (n.d.-a). *Emergency mental health and traumatic stress: Tips for teachers: Questions to help children talk about a disaster.* Retrieved September 6, 2010, from http://mentalhealth.samhsa.gov/cmhs/EmergencyServices/questions.asp

Substance Abuse and Mental Health Services Administration (SAMHSA). (n.d.-b). *Emergency mental health and traumatic stress: Tips for teachers: When talking doesn't help: Other ways to help children express their feelings following a disaster.* Retrieved September 6, 2010, from http://mentalhealth.samhsa.gov/cmhs/EmergencyServices/otherways.asp

Substance Abuse and Mental Health Services Administration (SAMHSA). (n.d.-c). *Coping with traumatic events: Tips for talking about traumatic events.* Retrieved September 12, 2010, from http://mentalhealth.samhsa.gov/cmhs/TraumaticEvents/tips.asp

U.S. Department of Education (DOE). (2005a). *New support for families and areas affected by Hurricane Katrina.* Retrieved April 25, 2012, from http://www2.ed.gov/katrina/0916-factsheet.pdf

U.S. Department of Education (DOE). (2005b). *Tips for helping students recovering from traumatic events.* Retrieved September 5, 2010, from http://www.ed.gov/parents/academic/help/recovering/recovering.pdf

U.S. Department of Homeland Security. (2006). *Listen, protect, and connect – Model & teach: Psychological First Aid for students and teachers: Helping you help your students in times of disaster, school crisis, or emergencies.* Retrieved September 9, 2010, from http://www.listo.gov/ninos/_downloads/PFA_SchoolCrisis.pdf

University of Illinois Extension Disaster Resources. (n.d.). *Children, stress, and natural disasters: School activities for children.* Retrieved September 5, 2010, from http://web.extension.uiuc.edu/disaster/teacher/csndactx.html

Vernberg, A. M., Steinberg, A. M., Jacobs, A. K., Brymer, M. J., Watson, P. J., Osofsky, J. D., et al. (2008). Innovations in disaster mental health: Psychological First Aid. *Professional Psychology: Research and Practice, 39,* 381–388.

Vernberg, E. M., La Greca, A. M., Silverman, W. K., & Prinstein, M. J. (1996). Prediction of posttraumatic stress symptoms in children after Hurricane Andrew. *Journal of Abnormal Psychology, 105,* 237–248.

WEB RESOURCES

- American Psychological Association
  - Report of the Task Force on PTSD and Trauma in Children & Adolescents: http://apa.org/pi/families/resources/task-force/child-trauma.aspx
- Centers for Disease Control and Prevention
  - Coping With a Disaster or Traumatic Event: http://www.bt.cdc.gov/mentalhealth/
- Department of Education
  - Tips for Helping Students Recovering From Traumatic Events: http://www2.ed.gov/parents/academic/help/recovering/index.html
  - Crisis Planning: http://www2.ed.gov/admins/lead/safety/crisisplanning.html
- Federal Emergency Management Agency
  - Ready Kids: http://www.ready.gov/kids/
  - FEMA Kids: http://www.fema.gov/kids/
- National Association of School Psychologists
  - Natural Disasters, School Violence, War/Terrorism: http://www.nasponline.org/resources/crisis_safety/
- National Center for Crisis Management: http://www.schoolcrisisresponse.com
- National Child Traumatic Stress Network
  - School Violence and Crises: http://www.nctsnet.org/nccts/nav.do?pid=ctr_aud_schl
  - Responding to a School Crisis: http://www.nctsn.org/resources/audiences/school-personnel/crisis-situation
  - Natural Disasters: http://www.nctsnet.org/nccts/nav.do?pid=typ_nd
- RAND Corporation: http://www.rand.org/pubs/technical_reports/2006/RAND_TR413.pdf
- Substance Abuse and Mental Health Services Administration (SAMHSA)
  - Coping with Violence and Traumatic Events: http://www.samhsa.gov/trauma/?from=carousel&position=1&date=04162012
  - Multiple Resources for Schools: http://www.samhsa.gov/trauma/?from=carousel&position=1&date=04162012#schools
  - Oil Spill Distress Resources: http://oilspillstress.promoteprevent.org/
  - Tips for Talking About Traumatic Events: A Guide for Parents and Educators: http://store.samhsa.gov/shin/content//KEN01–0093R/KEN01–0093R.pdf
- UCLA School Mental Health Project
  - Center for Mental Health in Schools: http://smhp.psych.ucla.edu/crisisresp.htm

SELECTED CHILDREN'S LITERATURE

- Griffey, H. (2010). *Earthquakes and other natural disasters.* New York, NY: DK Children.
- Mark, B. S., & Layton, A. (1997). *I'll know what to do: A kid's guide to natural disasters.* Washington, DC: Magination Press.
- Substance Abuse and Mental Health Services Administration (SAMHSA). *Children and youth resource collection: Annotated bibliography.* http://www.samhsa.gov/dtac/dbhis/dbhis_children_bib.asp
- University of Illinois Extension Disaster Resources. *Children's literature on floods and natural disasters.* http://web.extension.illinois.edu/disaster/teacher/floodbib.html

Administrative and Policy Considerations: Fostering Resiliency

17

Creating Safe and Supportive Schools for Students Impacted by Traumatic Experience

JOEL M. RISTUCCIA ■

INTRODUCTION

The impact of traumatic experiences on children's learning is far more significant than initially thought by most educators. In the Adverse Childhood Experiences (ACE) study,[1] which looked at a limited number of categories (not including homelessness, neglect, and neighborhood violence), over half of all children and youth had experienced a traumatic experience within at least one adversity category. As this book has clearly described, such traumatic experiences place school children and youth at significant risk for a host of social, emotional, academic, and cognitive impairments, and these impairments may create barriers to learning that lead to difficulties in school, risk-taking behaviors, and long-term social, occupational, and health issues.

Aside from ongoing support from a student's educators, successfully addressing these barriers to learning also requires school-wide initiatives. Students learn best when they feel safe, when they feel connected and supported by school staff, and when their social, emotional, and physical/health needs are met, goals that are best met through a whole-school approach. We refer to such environments that foster this culture and promote the conditions for learning as safe and supportive schools. Definitions of safe and supportive schools have focused on the integration of academic competency, social and emotional functioning, healthy relationships, physical safety, and student health/well-being to foster positive learning environments for *all* students; this is particularly true for those with trauma histories.

Developing safe and supportive schools can often effectively improve outcomes for traumatized students. For example, a traumatized student may respond to normal stresses (tests, in-class participation, presentations, homework, etc.) as if they were significant stressors, overreacting in a way that triggers basic survival responses and makes them unavailable to focus and learn.[2] However, increasing students' sense of safety and connectedness reduces the stress response, making them more available to learn and more likely to adopt prosocial and proacademic norms.[3] This cycle of creating a sense of safety, connectedness, reduced stress response, and enhanced student learning leads to a positive learning environment that cannot be duplicated by individual student interventions alone, no matter how well intentioned or implemented.

The creation of a safe and supportive school environment for students impacted by traumatic experience also enhances the learning environment for all students. When we create safe and supportive school communities, the benefits to all children are significant and include enhanced achievement, engagement, improved attendance and graduation rates, and increased resilience,[4] regardless of exposure to trauma. For many of our students, the school is the most significant community in their lives, outside of their family, and as such has a marked influence on who they are and who they aspire to be. Safe and supportive schools provide students with the opportunity to freely participate in the community and learn the skills necessary to be engaged and contributing members of school and society, all while offering a secure place to make mistakes and learn from them. In this regard, the creation of safe and supportive school environments serves students and the community and is an investment in our nation's future.

TRAUMA-SENSITIVE SCHOOLS

A trauma-sensitive school ecology supports the learning of students impacted by traumatic experience by helping them develop relationships, learn to regulate emotions and behavior, maintain healthy lifestyles, and achieve academically. More specifically, trauma-sensitive school ecologies possess the following characteristics (as developed by the Trauma Learning Policy Initiative (TLPI)):

1. Provide all students with a safe school environment (socially, emotionally, academically, and physically)
2. Increase staff understanding of and ability to mitigate the potential impacts of traumatic experiences on students' learning and behavior
3. Encourage *all* school staff to work together to meet the needs of students in the school
4. Address student needs in relationship development, self regulation, academic competency, and health and well-being
5. Ensure that all students are included in and connected to the school community

6. Adapt school planning and operations to the ever-changing needs/demands of the students
7. Include community resources and parents in the support network in addressing student needs

Safe and supportive schools develop this trauma-sensitive ecology/environment as opposed to identifying needy subgroups and targeting services exclusively to them. In this way, the school is aligned with the needs of all its students, reducing the need for referrals to mental health professionals within the community or costly programs targeting a small handful of students. The importance of school ecology/environment to learning is demonstrated by a recent study[5] within the Montgomery County Public Schools in Maryland, the 16th largest district in the nation, which found that students from low-income families performed better when placed in more affluent schools when compared to similar students placed in lower performing school environments, despite the lower performing schools having more funds targeting individual interventions and supports. Such a study highlights the prevailing importance of the school environment and its potential for improved impact when compared to expensive interventions targeting specific students. In short, meeting the needs of students is first addressed by school ecology, and it is within this safe and supportive ecology that individual supports can be developed as needed.

Developing a Trauma-Sensitive Ecology Using the Flexible Framework

The Flexible Framework (FF) is a systemic overview of school operations and provides a process for reviewing a school's impact on student success.[6] As such, the FF is a process, not a program to be used today and replaced tomorrow, wherein a school community can review its operations to identify where it could make coordinated and integrated changes to enhance the safe and supportive nature of the school. The key functions of the FF are threefold:

1. Make sure that identified initiatives are executed effectively (e.g., if we want to use morning meetings, let's make sure we have sufficient training in their utilization and that the schedule will allow for the time needed to use them)
2. Integrate all the individual action steps that make up an initiative to make sure they are all working in harmony
3. Ensure that all initiatives undertaken are working together to create a trauma-sensitive school ecology

As a community-wide process, teachers cannot do this alone. To be sure, teachers are important as they are often the primary contacts with students in the school; however, the support of everyone is critical in the building of safe and supportive school ecologies, including teachers, administrators, paraprofessionals, support personnel (e.g., school psychologists, school counselors, school social workers, school nurses), cafeteria workers, custodial staff, bus drivers, and volunteers. The six components of the Flexible Framework, described in more detail in the following paragraphs, each contribute to creating a safe and supportive school ecology:

1. Infrastructure and leadership
2. Professional development
3. Role of mental health (internal and external)
4. Classroom-based academic strategies
5. Nonacademic strategies
6. Policies, procedures, and protocols

Infrastructure and leadership. Administration's commitment to the process of creating a safe and supportive trauma-sensitive environment is vital. Direct engagement from administrators is central to commitment (rather than simply assigning a task force or workgroup) and includes direct participation in strategic planning, working with staff to identify needs and opportunities for growth, and keeping the vision of a safe and supportive school alive within the hectic day-to-day work of a school. In fact, principal leadership has been noted as the single most important predictor of quality implementation for whole-school reform.[7]

Making safe and supportive practices a part of the school's daily operations and infrastructure is central to supporting a trauma-sensitive ecology, which may include creating and regularly using a planning/design group within the school to guide the process, assessing staff training needs, conducting a confidential review of individual cases, and establishing a community liaison team. Additionally, having feedback structures and evaluation metrics in place will also guide efforts based on objective outcome data as opposed to anecdotal information—for example, schools may anonymously survey students' perceptions of personal safety in school or the quality of teacher–student relationships before and after implementing safe and supportive school initiatives. The Safe and Supportive Schools Technical Assistance Center (http:// safesupportiveschools. ed.gov) has compiled a list of student, staff, and family surveys that can be used to assess various aspects of the school climate. Regardless of the method used, school programs with a more structured and planned approach are typically more effective than those without as much formal structure.

Invariably, barriers to incorporating trauma-sensitive approaches into the school infrastructure will arise and should be addressed with input from all stakeholders in the school community. The solution to such barriers may vary depending on the context and the existing school community, although all barriers are best addressed through acknowledgment and collaborative problem solving that includes administrative leaders. See Table 17.1 for examples of barriers to developing a safe and supportive school and associated perceptions that may perpetuate or refute those barriers.

Table 17.1 ADDRESSING BARRIERS TO SAFE AND SUPPORTIVE SCHOOLS

Barriers to Developing a Safe and Supportive School	Educators' Perceptions That Perpetuate Barriers	Perceptions That Refute Barriers
Personal impact on staff	"This is hard work, and I am already stressed and overwhelmed."	"Developing a trauma-sensitive environment may lead to student outcomes that will actually help reduce my stress level."
Balancing individual student needs with those of the class	"Why should I make so many changes just to help the students that give me the hardest time?"	"The entire class can benefit from improving the school ecology, including my more challenging students, leaving more time to devote to learning rather than discipline."
Lack of skills to address social, emotional, and academic learning in the school	"I was trained to teach students about science, not how to make friends."	"By teaching students how to cooperate, compromise, respect one another, problem solve, and self-regulate, I can teach them how to use peers as learning supports, become active and engaged learners, and become better human beings."
Tendency to view trauma as a home issue and not a school issue	"Dealing with my student's home situation is not in my job description. Isn't that the school psychologist's/counselor's/social worker's job?"	"If I want all students to learn, I have to teach who I have in my class/school—not who I wish I had in my class."

Professional development. Staff training in safe and supportive schools should cover three primary areas. The first is strengthening relationships between children and adults, with an emphasis on the vital role that staff can play as caring adults in the child's life. This may include during school or after-school events that foster a sense of community and connectedness among students and staff. School faculty should consistently rethink their roles under the doctrine of *in loco parentis*, which places teachers in the role of both teacher and caretaker during the school day—this role defines them beyond a teacher of specific content (e.g., science, calculus) and includes the role of teaching students how to live and function as members of society.

The second area of need for professional development includes developing skills and sharing strategies among educators to help students modulate their emotions and gain social and academic competence. This can include building on existing competencies and resources among the staff in supporting traumatized students, frequently reviewing behavior management strategies, regularly reviewing expectations for discipline, and identifying and understanding the roles of teachers and mental health professionals within the school. Some workshop topics may include:

1. Helping students regulate emotions and behavior
2. Helping children feel safe
3. Setting limits and clear boundaries
4. Reducing bullying and harassment
5. Understanding the connection between emotion and behavior
6. Building on student strengths
7. Identifying positive behavior supports

The third area should focus on identifying and using outside supports to help students become successful and see the value in school (e.g., tutoring, after-school activities, employment). This may include partnering with outside agencies or simply with parents and caregivers. Professional development can also focus on understanding the cycle of family and community violence and its effects on learning, for example, or improving communication strategies when working with diverse cultures and communities.

Consider contacting the Safe and Supportive Schools Technical Assistance Center (http://safesupportiveschools.ed.gov) for resources or to request training in your district. Organizations such as the Collaborative for Academic, Social, and Emotional Learning (CASEL), the National Child Traumatic Stress Network (NCTSN), and the National Association of School Psychologists (NASP) provide resources, materials, and strategies for school staff and parents. In addition, the National Center for Mental Health Promotion and Youth Violence Prevention at the Education Development Center (EDC) also provides technical assistance as well as a free guide titled *Realizing the Promise of a Whole-School Approach to Children's Mental Health: A Practical Guide for Schools.*[8]

Linking with mental health professionals. Mental health professionals within the school (e.g., school psychologists, school counselors, school social workers, school nurses) can be a valuable resource. They can provide consultations; help locate resources; assess student needs; participate in intervention efforts; support data collection, analysis, and progress monitoring; and provide staff training in several areas described earlier. They may also offer confidential case discussions, share strategies for reacting to antisocial student behavior, develop classroom structures and rules that enhance self-regulation, and help identify when more intense intervention or outside resources are required. Notably, "at a minimum, school psychologists should be involved in the interface between community mental health and the schools" given that outside providers have less knowledge of school culture, classroom management, curriculum, consultation, and special education.[9]

Classroom-based academic strategies for traumatized students. Many believe that the primary goal for students within school is to master the academic curriculum. Unfortunately, many students experience adverse experiences that may inhibit their academic mastery, and recognizing these situations is often paramount in providing the support required. However, students impacted by traumatic experience may be difficult to identify as many have learning profiles that are similar to students with disabilities (e.g., learning disabilities, attention deficit/hyperactivity disorder [ADHD], emotional disturbance), while some exhibit no discernible issues in the classroom. This highlights the importance of creating a safe learning environment for *all* students, one that supports social skills development and enhances self-regulation.[10]

Rather than trying to identify the key instructional strategy needed for specific students, recent research identifies the importance of explicit instruction of social and emotional skills to support learning and making this learning a part of the structured classroom experience for every student. This learning can be fostered through enhancing *safety* (e.g., clear, consistent, fair, and predictable rules and boundaries; consistent transition processes; and visible schedules); *self-awareness and self-regulation* (e.g., building an emotional vocabulary, helping students be self-aware, identifying and processing feelings, teaching relaxation techniques); and *quality instruction* through varied academic teaching strategies (e.g., multimodel instruction, reinforcing cause–effect relationships, addressing sequential memory skills by repeating and emphasizing sequences of events in learned materials, and focusing on student areas of strength).

Nonacademic strategies. For many students impacted by traumatic experiences, a caring relationship with even one adult in school can foster a sense of safety, improve student engagement and social success, and increase student attention and achievement. Often these relationships are easier built around nonacademic issues, as often the child impacted by traumatic experience will struggle to be successful with academic material and associate academics with negative emotions. Further, engaging students in nonacademic activity–based learning increases the opportunity to engage them in their areas of competence and provides a common ground between student and staff for discussion and relationship building. For example, having teachers as coaches and activity leaders can provide an opportunity for teachers to work with students in their area of strength and can help draw attention to mutual interests outside of school.

The importance of a whole-school approach to working with students impacted by traumatic experience is probably best leveraged in this area, as the larger the group of engaged adults, the higher the likelihood of finding a staff member with common interests to the students, be it athletic, vocational, artistic, or leisure activities. Many schools have developed mentorship or advisory programs where all faculty members are assigned mentees or advisees from different grade levels at the beginning of the school year.

Policies, procedures, and protocols. A school's culture is best observed through its policies, procedures, and protocols. It is imperative that these be reviewed as part of creating a trauma-sensitive school for students. One of the most significant of these can be the discipline policy of the school.

Discipline systems that rely on punitive responses to student behavior assume that students will "learn" to use more appropriate behavior as a result of their punitive exclusion. This premise is based on two false assumptions. First, it is assumed that students actually have more appropriate responses to the situations that confront them in their behavioral repertoire. Without educators working to proactively teach these responses/skills, it is unclear if students impacted by traumatic experience actually have alternative responses they can use that the leadership would find more appropriate. The second false assumption is that punitive responses/exclusion will actually produce the desired response in our students in the future (i.e., that students will work hard to change their behavior to meet expectations and avoid future punishment). Punitive and exclusionary environments actually create distance, intolerance, and disconnection,[11] just the opposite of what we are trying to nourish. These types of reactive school environments may actually increase the frequency of problematic behavior.

These issues of disconnection and intolerance are exacerbated by "zero tolerance" policies that attempt to create safe environments by enforcing predetermined, harsh consequences (i.e., suspension or expulsion) for behavior. Despite being favored by many educators and administrators as quick interventions that serve to remove difficult students from school, the research has generally found such policies to be ineffective.[12] Additionally, the utilization of these policies all but precludes the integration of students learning from their mistakes and often accelerates student disconnection from the school community.

Students need to be accountable for their behavior; there is no argument on this point. However, schools must proactively address student needs/learning in the relational and self-regulatory domains as opposed to merely punishing them when their behavior conflicts with existing rules for behavior. We cannot simply assume that all students possess the skills needed to meet school-based expectations or that they are simply choosing to disobey school rules. Instead, we need to address these needs just as we would academic difficulties—by reteaching skills and providing more opportunities for practice and mastery. Punitive models do not work in teaching students to read, write, and do math; and there is similarly no compelling evidence that they would help students develop skills in self-regulation and relationships.

Successful discipline policies view maladaptive behaviors as an opportunity to teach more adaptive behaviors rather than simply an opportunity to remove students from the environment for a few days. The discipline moment is a learning moment. Policies that take advantage of this moment to teach the student the explicit connection between his or her behavior and the outcome and look for skill deficits that need to be addressed also provide a safe and supportive environment for all students—one in which they are accountable for their behavior, yet accepted as valuable members of the school community.

In addition to discipline and standards of behavior, there are a number of policies, procedures, and protocols that would benefit from review with all staff. Some examples include:

- Communication
  - Addressing confidentiality regarding students and families
  - Communicating with families of traumatized students or other diverse backgrounds
  - Responding to emergencies
  - Filing abuse and neglect reports
- Compliance
  - Disclosing student record information
  - Transferring records safely
  - Supporting court orders
    - Obtaining copies of orders
    - Informing relevant personnel
    - Responding to violations
    - Cooperating with law enforcement
    - Notifying caregiver of violations
- Collaboration with the community
  - Connecting families to community resources
  - Appointing a liaison to coordinate collaboration with community resources and public policymakers

CONCLUSION

A significant number of our students are impacted by traumatic experiences and come to school with social, emotional, and learning deficits. While they often can present as defiant and disruptive, they also can present with learning issues, ADHD symptoms, and social-emotional concerns, and still others just blend in unnoticed. Thus, the best way to ensure that traumatized students receive the support they need is to improve the conditions for learning for every student in the school through safe and supportive trauma-sensitive school ecologies that enhance academic, social, emotional, and physical health/well-being.

Schools that are narrowly focused on academic achievement and student behavioral control to achieve safety and order do not provide a safe and supportive school, but instead have created an intolerant school culture.[13] This punitive environment leads to reduced school attachment and connectedness and lowered achievement.[14] In contrast, a safe and supportive trauma-sensitive school addresses student learning in the areas of academic, social, emotional, and physical health, and in so doing improves the ability of students to profit from instruction. These schools also provide a receptive learning community for students impacted by traumatic experience as well as all other students in the school. The process for achieving this trauma sensitive school ecology is contained in the Flexible Framework, which provides a method for schools to review their operations in a systemic fashion to identify areas of improvement in meeting student needs.

NOTES

1. Anda & Filletti, 1998.
2. Nemeroff, 2004.
3. Collaborative for Academic, Social, and Emotional Learning, 2008.
4. e.g., Klem & Connell, 2004; Centers for Disease Control and Prevention, 2009.
5. Schwartz, 2010.
6. Cole et al., 2005.
7. Devaney, O'Brien, Resnik, Kesiter, & Weissberg, 2006.
8. http://www.promoteprevent.org/webfm_send/2102
9. Furlong, Paige, & Osher, 2003, p. 451.
10. Durlak, Weissberg, Dymnicki, Taylor, & Schellinger, 2011.
11. Noguera, 2003.
12. Skiba, 2000, 2004.
13. Osher, Woodruff, & Sims, 2002; Skiba, Michael, Nardo, & Peterson, 2000.
14. Noguera, 2003; Osher et al., 2008.

REFERENCES

Anda, R. F., & Feletti, V. J. (1998). The relationship of adult health status to childhood abuse and household dysfunction. *American Journal of Preventive Medicine, 14,* 245–258.

Centers for Disease Control and Prevention. (2009). *School connectedness: Strategies for increasing protective factors among youth.* Atlanta, GA: U.S. Department of Health and Human Services.

Cole, S. F., O'Brien, J. G., Gadd, M. G., Ristuccia, J., Wallace, D. L., & Gregory, M. (2005). *Helping traumatized children learn.* Boston, MA: Massachusetts Advocates for Children.

Collaborative for Academic, Social, and Emotional Learning. (2008). *Social and emotional learning and student benefits: Implications for the Safe Schools/Healthy Students core elements.* Washington, DC: National Center for Mental Health Promotion and Youth Violence Prevention, Education Development Center.

Devaney, E., O'Brien, M. U., Resnik, H., Kesiter, S., & Weissberg, R. P. (2006). *Sustainable schoolwide social and emotional learning (SEL) (implementation guide and toolkit).* Chicago, IL: Collaborative for Academic, Social, and Emotional Learning.

Durlak, J. A., Weissberg, R. P., Dymnicki, A. B., Taylor, R. D., & Schellinger, K. B. (2011). The impact of enhancing students' social and emotional learning: A meta-analysis of school-based universal interventions. *Child Development, 82,* 405–432

Furlong, M., Paige, L. Z., & Osher, D. (2003). The safe schools/healthy students (SS/HS) initiative: Lessons learned from implementing comprehensive youth development programs. *Psychology in the Schools, 40,* 447–456.

Klem, A, M., & Connell, J. P. (2004). Relationships matter: Linking teacher support to student engagement and achievement. *Journal of School Health, 74,* 262–273.

Nemeroff, C. B. (2004). Neurobiological consequences of childhood trauma. *Journal of Clinical Psychiatry, 65,* 18–28.

Noguera, P. (2003). *City schools and the American dream: Reclaiming the promise of public education.* New York, NY: Teachers College Press.

Osher, D., Sprague, J., Weissberg, R. P., Axelrod, J., Keenan, S., Kendziora, K., et al. (2008). A comprehensive approach to promoting social, emotional, and academic growth in contemporary schools. In A. Thomas & J. Grimes (Eds.), *Best practices in school psychology V* (Vol. 4, pp. 1263–1278). Bethesda, MD: National Association of School Psychologists.

Osher, D., Woodruff, D., & Sims, A. (2002). Schools make a difference: The relationship between education services for African American children and youth and their overrepresentation in the juvenile justice system. In D. Losen (Ed.), *Minority issues in special education* (pp. 93–116). Cambridge, MA: The Civil Rights Project, Harvard University and the Harvard Education Publishing Group.

Schwartz, H. (2010). *Housing policy is school policy: Economically integrative housing promotes academic success in Montgomery County, Maryland.* The Century Foundation. Retrieved from http://www.inhousing.org/PDFs/HeatherSchwartzArticle.pdf

Skiba, R. (2000). *Zero tolerance, zero evidence: An analysis of school disciplinary practice* (Policy Research Report #SRS2). Bloomington, IN: Indiana Education Policy Center. Retrieved from http://www.indiana.edu/~safeschl/ztze.pdf

Skiba, R. (2004). Zero tolerance: The assumptions and the facts. *Education Policy Briefs, 2,* 1–8.

Skiba, R. J., Michael, R. S., Nardo, A. C., & Peterson, R. (2000). The color of discipline: Sources of racial and gender disproportionality in school punishment. *Urban Review, 34,* 317–342.

18

Addressing Trauma and Other Barriers to Learning and Teaching: Developing a Comprehensive System of Intervention

HOWARD S. ADELMAN AND LINDA TAYLOR ■

INTRODUCTION

No one doubts the importance of helping students with trauma histories. Schools have a clear stake in this since traumatized students often manifest learning and behavioral problems at school. The chapters in this book add considerably to the discussion of how all educators within the school can help provide support and encourage learning. This chapter, specifically, clarifies why efforts to address problems related to trauma in schools need to go well beyond just enhancing availability and access to individual, *clinically oriented* mental health services. From this perspective, we emphasize that trauma and all other student learning, behavioral, and emotional problems can and should be approached within the context of a comprehensive system of intervention within schools and school districts.

First, we start with two realities:

- Schools are not in the mental health business; their mission is to educate.
- Accomplishing their mission requires that schools play comprehensive and effective roles in dealing with the broad range of psychosocial and mental health concerns that affect learning. In other words, addressing interfering factors (both internal and external) is essential for *enabling* learning.

It is the need to deal with such psychosocial and mental health issues that makes the discussion of trauma so relevant to schools. However, acknowledging and appreciating the complex nature and scope of the many barriers to learning and teaching (the effects of which are exacerbated when students are traumatized) underscores the need to place that discussion into a broad context. With all this in mind, this chapter highlights (1) the need to expand the focus of mental health in schools, (2) the importance of embedding mental health interventions into a comprehensive and multifaceted systemic approach for addressing barriers to learning and teaching and re-engaging disconnected students, and (3) blueprints for such an approach. Then, with these matters as background and context, (4) we make recommendations for addressing trauma in schools.

EXPANDING MENTAL HEALTH IN SCHOOLS: JUST ANOTHER INITIATIVE?

Schools are constantly confronted with new initiatives (e.g., another project, another program) aimed at addressing a specific learning, behavioral, or emotional problem—making schools safe, improving crisis response, and so forth. Schools are stretched thin by the many programs already in play. As a result, a common reaction of principals and teachers is: *Enough! We can't take on another thing!*

Perhaps more alarming is the trend for proposed initiatives and existing interventions not to be conceived as part of a comprehensive system; rather, each is proposed and implemented as a separate entity with sparse resources and inadequate interconnectivity. Take, for example, the history of mental health services available in the District of Columbia Public School (DCPS) system, which is outlined in a report from George Washington University's Center for Health and Health Care in Schools.[1] During their evaluation, they discovered at least 12 different mental health programs within the school system, many of which did not coordinate with each other or outside agencies. This trend was not exclusive to this school system. The piecemeal, underfunded nature of the enterprise contributes to widespread counterproductive competition for resources, compromises effectiveness, and works against efforts to take projects, pilots, and programs to scale. All school stakeholders need to understand this state of affairs and take steps to fix it.

Fragmentation

Currently, most districts offer a range of programs and services oriented to students' needs and problems, including those with trauma histories. Some interventions are funded through district and school budgets, while others are provided through community agencies and usually are linked to targeted schools. The interventions may be for all students in a school, for those in specified grades, for those identified as "at risk," or for those in need of compensatory interventions or special education.

Looked at as a whole, a considerable amount of activity is taking place and substantial resources are being expended. Many programs and services are generated by special initiatives, short-term grants, and projects, including initiatives for positive behavioral supports, violence prevention, and safe and drug-free schools; efforts to address bilingual, cultural, and other diversity concerns; compensatory and special education programs; the mandates stemming from the No Child Left Behind Act and the Individuals with Disabilities Education Act (IDEA); and many more.

The effectiveness of many of these programs is supported by research. However, it is widely recognized that interventions are often highly fragmented with little or no coordination or integration of efforts.[2] For example, in many school districts, the local departments of mental health or other outside agencies provide mental health therapists for the school. However, in some programs, the therapists can *only* work with students in special education, whereas in others they can *only* work with general education students. This is usually due to each program having very specific goals, such as decreasing nonpublic placement of special education students or primary prevention of mental health problems among the general population. Objectively, it seems to make the most sense to provide services to any student who requires it. However, services for all those in need are less likely to occur with fragmented programs designed to separately address specific populations.

Furthermore, in every facet of a district's operations, an unproductive separation usually exists between "instructional staff" (e.g., teachers) and "support staff" (e.g., counselors, school psychologists). Teachers are often unaware of the various mental health programs occurring in their schools or how they operate. Further, few programs are designed to incorporate mental health within the classroom context, and instead pull identified students out of class individually or in small groups. It is not surprising, then, how often efforts to address barriers to learning and teaching are planned, implemented, and evaluated in a fragmented, piecemeal manner. And, given the fragmentation, it is commonplace for those staffing the various efforts to function in relative isolation of each other and other stakeholders, with an overreliance on specialized services for individuals and small groups.[3] For example, in some schools, we have found that individual students identified as having three different problems (i.e., misbehavior, substance use, and at risk for dropping out) were being seen by a different staff member for each problem. This substantiates the foundation of this book, which emphasizes that the supports needed by students can and should be provided by all educators in a school building as part of a larger framework that supports all students.

Schools confronted with a large number of students experiencing barriers to learning pay dearly for fragmented interventions. Moreover, such schools are frequently underfunded and therefore cannot afford fragmented delivery of interventions. For these schools in particular, the reality is that test score averages are unlikely to increase adequately until student and learning supports are rethought and redesigned. This is particularly the case for low-performing schools designated for a "turnaround,"[4] which tend to experience a higher incidence of students with trauma histories.

Coordination: Necessary but Not Sufficient

One response to the fragmentation has been the call to enhance coordination among programs and service providers. Clearly, schools are enmeshed in many overlapping programs, services, and initiatives designed to address barriers to learning and promote healthy development. Certainly, a more unified and cohesive approach is needed. However, the emphasis on enhancing coordination is insufficient for dealing with the core problem, which is the *marginalization of efforts to address barriers to learning and teaching* in school improvement policy, planning, and practices. Marginalization refers to the general finding that supports for addressing barriers to learning are viewed as less important than academic supports. It is evident, for example, that mental health problems among students affect their readiness to learn, thereby creating a barrier to the learning process; yet the importance of providing supports to students with such problems is given short shrift in discussions of school improvement.

Evidence of the degree to which this is the case is readily seen in school improvement planning guides and school governance.[5] The marginalization is a major factor contributing to and maintaining fragmented planning, implementation, and evaluation.[6] The following sections provide blueprint frameworks that have been adopted in states such as Louisiana and Iowa in order to end the marginalization and resulting fragmentation of student and learning supports.[7]

A COMPREHENSIVE AND MULTIFACETED SYSTEMIC APPROACH TO UNIFYING STUDENT AND LEARNING SUPPORTS

Analyses of prevailing policy and practice raise concerns about the question: *What systemic changes are needed to end the marginalization and fragmentation of student and learning supports?* First and foremost, there is a need to adopt a unifying concept that provides an umbrella for the wide range of initiatives, programs, and services (see Figure 18.1). Such an umbrella provides a context into which all mental health concerns, including dealing with trauma, can be readily embedded.[8]

As illustrated in Figure 18.1, the term *addressing barriers to learning and teaching* increasingly is being recognized as an umbrella concept. In our work, we operationalize this concept as an *enabling* or *learning supports component*.[9]

A. Current School Improvement Planning

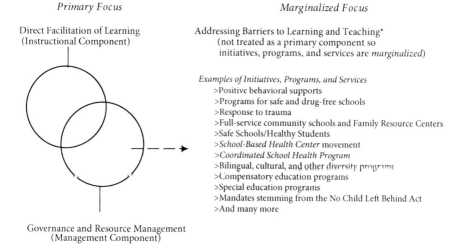

Primary Focus   *Marginalized Focus*

Direct Facilitation of Learning   Addressing Barriers to Learning and Teaching*
(Instructional Component)   (not treated as a primary component so
                                                          initiatives, programs, and services are *marginalized*)

Examples of Initiatives, Programs, and Services
  >Positive behavioral supports
  >Programs for safe and drug-free schools
  >Response to trauma
  >Full-service community schools and Family Resource Centers
  >Safe Schools/Healthy Students
  >*School-Based Health Center* movement
  >*Coordinated School Health Program*
  >Bilingual, cultural, and other diversity programs
  >Compensatory education programs
  >Special education programs
  >Mandates stemming from the No Child Left Behind Act
  >And many more

Governance and Resource Management
(Management Component)

*While not treated as a primary and essential component, schools generally offer some amount of school-owned student "support services" — some of which link with community-owned resources. Many types of student support personnel staff the interventions (e.g., school counselors, psychologists, social workers, nurses, etc.). Schools have been reaching out to community agencies to add a few more services. All of this, however, remains marginalized and fragmented in policy and practice.

B. Needed: Revised Policy to Establish an Umbrella for School Improvement Planning Related to Addressing Barriers to Learning and Promoting Healthy Development

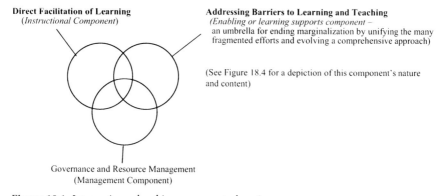

Direct Facilitation of Learning   **Addressing Barriers to Learning and Teaching**
(*Instructional Component*)   (*Enabling or learning supports component –*
                                                          an umbrella for ending marginalization by unifying the many
                                                          fragmented efforts and evolving a comprehensive approach)

                                                      (See Figure 18.4 for a depiction of this component's nature
                                                      and content)

Governance and Resource Management
(Management Component)

Figure 18.1 Improving school improvement planning.

An enabling or learning supports component focuses on collaborative approaches that maximize learning and, in the process, strengthen the well-being of students, families, schools, and neighborhoods. For individual students, this means preventing and minimizing the impact of as many problems as is feasible, and doing so in ways that maximize school engagement, productive learning, and positive development. For the school and community as a whole, the intent is to produce a safe, healthy, nurturing environment characterized by respect for differences, trust, caring, support, social justice, and high expectations for cognitive and social-emotional learning.

All this, of course, requires major systemic changes that address the complications stemming from the scale of public education. That is, changes must be based on frameworks and procedures that can be adapted to fit every school in a district and modified for small and large urban, rural, and suburban settings.

Toward Operationalizing an Enabling or Learning Supports Component

Given the current state of school resources, efforts to establish and institutionalize an enabling or learning supports component clearly must be accomplished by rethinking how existing resources are used. Such efforts require weaving school-owned resources and community-owned resources together to develop comprehensive and cohesive approaches. The work also must take advantage of the natural opportunities at schools and in classrooms for addressing learning, behavioral, and emotional problems and promoting personal and social growth—a large component of this book.

In short, the ideal is to install a well-designed, nonfragmented, and non-marginalized component for addressing barriers to learning and promoting healthy development at every school. This encompasses a commitment to fostering staff and student competence, as well as self-determination; promoting staff and student well-being; and creating an atmosphere that encourages mutual support, caring, resilience and growth, and a sense of community. Staff *and* students must feel good about themselves and feel supported if they are to cope with challenges proactively and effectively. Properly implemented, such a component can foster smooth transitions, enable positive formal and informal social interactions and functioning, facilitate social and learning supports, and provide opportunities for learning how to function effectively in the school culture. School-wide strategies for welcoming and supporting staff, students, and families at school *every day* are part of creating a safe, supportive, healthy, caring school—one where all stakeholders interact positively with each other and identify with the school and its goals. All this has fundamental implications for promoting mental health, improving achievement test scores, *and* allaying the impact of traumatic events.

As illustrated in Figure 18.2, an enabling component involves first addressing interfering factors and then re-engaging students in classroom instruction. The reality is that interventions that do not include an emphasis on ensuring that students are engaged meaningfully in classroom learning generally are insufficient in sustaining, over time, student involvement, good behavior, and effective learning at school. Specifically, traumatized students are less likely to take positive risks in classrooms, participate in classroom discussion, maintain attention and focus, and remain engaged in traditional instruction. As a result, teaching content alone without addressing mental health and other barriers to learning

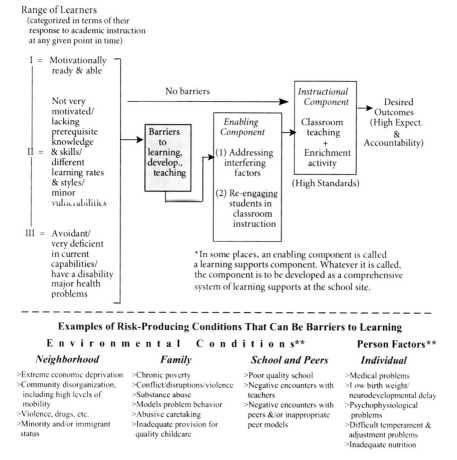

Figure 18.2 An enabling or learning supports component to address barriers and re-engage students in classroom instruction.*

will likely lead to decreased learning and increased frustration for both the student and teacher. Many of the strategies in this book are designed to increase student engagement and create an emotionally and socially inviting classroom that enables learning.

Various states and localities are moving in the direction of the three-component approach for school improvement illustrated in Figure 18.1.[10] In doing so, they are adopting different labels for the component for addressing barriers to learning and teaching. For example, the state education agencies in California, Iowa, and Louisiana and various districts across the country have adopted the term *learning supports*. Some places use the term *supportive learning environment*. The Hawaii Department of Education calls it a *Comprehensive Student Support System* (CSSS). Whatever it is called, the important point is that a component for addressing barriers to learning is seen as necessary and viewed as just as important as the instructional component (complementing and overlapping it).

A Continuum of Interventions to Meet the Needs of All Children and Youth

By viewing programs, services, projects, and initiatives along a continuum of interventions, schools and communities are more likely to provide the right interventions for the right students at the right time. As illustrated in Figure 18.3, such a continuum encompasses efforts to positively affect a full spectrum of learning, physical, social-emotional, and behavioral problems in every school and community by:

- Promoting healthy development and preventing problems
- Intervening as early after the onset of problems as is feasible
- Providing special assistance for severe and chronic problems

Note in Figure 18.3 that, unlike the trend to describe the continuum simply in terms of tiers, the effectiveness of such a continuum depends on *systemic* design. That is, at each level the emphasis is on not just having an initiative or program

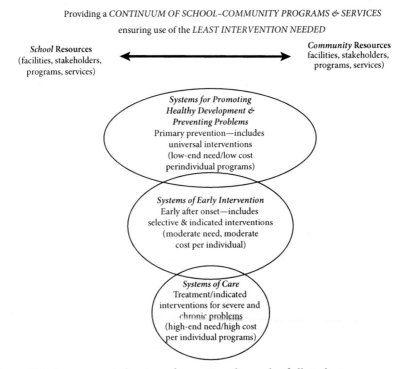

Providing a *CONTINUUM OF SCHOOL–COMMUNITY PROGRAMS & SERVICES*

ensuring use of the *LEAST INTERVENTION NEEDED*

School **Resources**
(facilities, stakeholders,
programs, services)

Community **Resources**
facilities, stakeholders,
programs, services)

*Systems for Promoting
Healthy Development &
Preventing Problems*
Primary prevention—includes
universal interventions
(low-end need/low cost
perindividual programs)

Systems of Early Intervention
Early after onset—includes
selective & indicated interventions
(moderate need, moderate
cost per individual)

Systems of Care
Treatment/indicated
interventions for severe and
chronic problems
(high-end need/high cost
per individual programs)

Figure 18.3 Interconnected systems for meeting the needs of all students.

for that specific tier, but on developing a unified and comprehensive system by weaving together school and community. Moreover, through effective collaboration, all levels need to be interconnected systemically to ensure success. The collaboration involves complete restructuring of programs and services (1) within jurisdictions, school districts, and community agencies (e.g., among departments, divisions, units, schools, and clusters of schools) and (2) between jurisdictions, school districts, and community agencies, public and private sectors; among schools; and among community agencies.

Such a continuum encompasses efforts to enable academic, social, emotional, and physical development and address learning, behavioral, and emotional problems at every school, regardless of the size of the school or district. As suggested earlier, most schools have some programs and services that fit along the entire continuum. However, the tendency to focus mostly on the most severe problems (e.g., diagnosable pathology such as learning disabilities, attention deficit/hyperactivity disorder, posttraumatic stress disorder) has skewed things so that too little is done to prevent and intervene early after the onset or awareness of a problem. As a result, the whole enterprise has been characterized as reactive, not cost effective, and as waiting for the worst to happen.

With respect to comprehensiveness, the school and community examples highlight that many problems must be addressed holistically and developmentally and with a range of programs, with some focused on individuals, their families, and the contexts in which they live, work, and play, and some focused on mental and physical health, education, and social services. With respect to concerns about integrating programs, the systemic emphasis underscores the need for linkages between (and within) programs, and for those linkages to be maintained over extended periods of time. The continuum also provides a basis for adhering to the principle of using the least restrictive and nonintrusive forms of intervention needed to appropriately respond to problems and accommodate diversity.

Moreover, given the likelihood that many problems are interrelated, the continuum is designed to address root causes (e.g., factors undermining motivation for school engagement such as child maltreatment, chronic exposure to community violence, etc.), thereby minimizing tendencies to develop separate programs for each observed problem or outcome, such as low academic achievement, aggression, substance abuse, suicide prevention, and so forth. In turn, this enables increased coordination and integration of resources, which can increase impact and cost effectiveness.

As graphically illustrated by the tapering of the three levels of intervention and prevention in Figure 18.3, development of a fully integrated continuum of interventions is meant to reduce the number of individuals who require specialized supports. For example, with respect to trauma, the aim is to prevent the majority of symptoms/problems by developing skills within students that make them better equipped to deal with future traumatic events, providing interventions and supports as soon after onset of an adverse event as is feasible, and ending up with relatively few students needing specialized assistance and other intensive and costly interventions.

Framing the Content of Learning Supports

Schools, districts, and state education agencies have operationalized the content of an enabling or learning supports component into programmatic arenas. In effect, they have moved from a "laundry list" of programs, services, and activities to a defined content or "curriculum" framework that outlines a set of components that are critical in addressing barriers to learning.

As outlined in Exhibit 18.1, the learning supports content arenas involve:

- *Enhancing supports in regular classrooms to enable learning* (e.g., improving instruction and bringing into the classroom other interventions for students with mild to moderate learning and behavioral problems and for re-engaging those who have become disengaged from learning at school)
- *Supporting transitions* (e.g., assisting students and families as they negotiate many daily and school-year transitions, e.g., school and grade changes; to and from school; periods before school, during lunch, and after school; summer; attendance problems)
- *Increasing home and school connections* (e.g., addressing specific support and learning needs for families; enhancing communication with the home; involving homes with school decision making; recruiting families to strengthen the school)
- *Responding to and, where feasible, preventing school and personal crises and traumatic events* (e.g., crisis planning, response, and follow-up; violence and bullying prevention; substance abuse prevention)
- *Increasing community involvement and support* (e.g., outreach to recruit a wide range of community resources, including enhanced use of volunteers and mentors; connecting school and community to promote child well-being)
- *Facilitating student and family access to effective services and special assistance as needed* (e.g., health and social services; personalized academic and career counseling; dropout outreach)

EXHIBIT 18.1

EXAMPLES OF "CONTENT" ARENAS FOR A COMPONENT TO ADDRESS BARRIERS TO LEARNING*

(1) Classroom-Based Approaches
- Opening the classroom door to bring available supports in (e g , peer tutors, volunteers, aides trained to work with students in need; resource teachers and student support staff work in the classroom as part of the teaching team)

- Redesigning classroom approaches to enhance teacher capability to prevent and handle problems and reduce need for out-of-class referrals (e.g., personalized instruction; special assistance as necessary; developing small group and independent learning options; reducing negative interactions and overreliance on social control; expanding the range of curricular and instructional options and choices; systematic use of pre-referral interventions)
- Enhancing and personalizing professional development (e.g., creating a Learning Community for teachers; ensuring opportunities to learn through coteaching, team teaching, and mentoring; teaching intrinsic motivation concepts and their application to schooling)
- Curricular enrichment and adjunct programs (e.g., varied enrichment activities that are not tied to reinforcement schedules; visiting scholars from the community)
- Classroom and school-wide approaches used to create and maintain a caring and supportive climate

(2) Support for Transitions
- Welcoming and social support programs for newcomers (e.g., welcoming signs, materials, and initial receptions; peer buddy programs for students, families, staff, volunteers)
- Daily transition programs (e.g., before school, breaks, lunch, after school)
- Articulation programs (e.g., grade to grade—new classrooms, new teachers; elementary to middle school; middle to high school; in and out of special education programs)
- Summer or intersession programs (e.g., catch-up, recreation, and enrichment programs)
- School-to-career/higher education (e.g., counseling, pathway, and mentor programs):
- Broad involvement of stakeholders in planning for transitions (e.g., students, staff, home, police, faith groups, recreation, business, higher education)
- Capacity building to enhance transition programs and activities

(3) Home Involvement and Engagement in Schooling
- Addressing specific support and learning needs of family (e.g., support services for those in the home to assist in addressing basic survival needs and obligations to the children; adult education classes to enhance literacy, job skills, English as a second language, citizenship preparation)
- Improving mechanisms for communication and connecting school and home (e.g., opportunities at school for family networking and mutual support, learning, recreation, and enrichment, and for family members to receive special assistance and to volunteer to help; phone calls and/or e-mail from teacher and other staff with good news; frequent and balanced

conferences—student led when feasible; outreach to attract hard-to-reach families—including student dropouts)
- Involving homes in student decision making (e.g., families prepared for involvement in program planning and problem solving)
- Enhancing home support for learning and development (e.g., family literacy; family homework projects; family field trips)
- Recruiting families to strengthen school and community (e.g., volunteers to welcome and support new families and help in various capacities; families prepared for involvement in school governance)
- Capacity building to enhance home involvement

(4) Community Outreach for Involvement and Collaborative Support
- Planning and implementing outreach to recruit a wide range of community resources (e.g., public and private agencies; colleges and universities; local residents; artists and cultural institutions, businesses and professional organizations; service, volunteer, and faith-based organizations; community policy and decision makers)
- Systems to recruit, screen, prepare, and maintain community resource involvement (e.g., mechanisms to orient and welcome, enhance the volunteer pool, maintain current involvements, enhance a sense of community)
- Reaching out to students and families who don't come to school regularly—including truants and dropouts
- Connecting school and community efforts to promote child and youth development and a sense of community
- Capacity building to enhance community involvement and support (e.g., policies and mechanisms to enhance and sustain school–community involvement; staff/stakeholder development on the value of community involvement; "social marketing")

(5) Crisis Assistance and Prevention
- Ensuring immediate assistance in emergencies so students can resume learning
- Providing follow-up care as necessary (e.g., brief and longer term monitoring)
- Forming a school-focused crisis team to formulate a response plan and take leadership for developing prevention programs
- Mobilizing staff, students, and families to anticipate response plans and recovery efforts
- Creating a caring and safe learning environment (e.g., developing systems to promote healthy development and prevent problems; bullying and harassment abatement programs)
- Working with neighborhood schools and community to integrate planning for response and prevention
- Capacity building to enhance crisis response and prevention (e.g., staff and stakeholder development; enhancing a caring and safe learning environment)

(6) Student and Family Assistance

- Providing extra support as soon as a need is recognized and doing so in the least disruptive ways (e.g., prereferral interventions in classrooms; problem-solving conferences with parents; open access to school, district, and community support programs)
- Timely referral interventions for students and families with problems based on response to extra support (e.g., identification/screening processes, assessment, referrals, and follow-up—school based, school linked)
- Enhancing access to direct interventions for health, mental health, and economic assistance (e.g., school-based, school-linked, and community-based programs and services)
- Care monitoring, management, information sharing, and follow-up assessment to coordinate individual interventions and check whether referrals and services are adequate and effective
- Mechanisms for *resource* coordination and integration to avoid duplication, fill gaps, garner economies of scale, and enhance effectiveness (e.g., braiding resources from school-based and linked interveners, feeder pattern/family of schools, community-based programs; linking with community providers to fill gaps)
- Enhancing stakeholder awareness of programs and services
- Capacity building to enhance student and family assistance systems, programs, and services

---

*In each arena, there is broad involvement of stakeholders in planning the system and building capacity. Emphasis at all times in the classroom and school-wide is on enhancing feelings of competence, self-determination, and relatedness to others at school and reducing threats to such feelings because this is essential to engagement and re-engagement and creating and maintaining a caring, supportive climate.

Matrix Framework: What's Being Done? What's Missing?

Combining the continuum of interventions with these six content arenas provides a "big picture" of *a unified and comprehensive approach*. The resulting matrix creates an umbrella framework to guide rethinking and restructuring the daily work of all staff at a school (see Figure 18.4). The matrix can be used to guide mapping and analysis of resources and identifying gaps and redundancies, thus increasing effectiveness and efficiency of the supports to learning. Educators and administrators across the country report that such a matrix is extremely helpful in enhancing school improvement planning.

With specific respect to addressing concerns about trauma, the central focus is on the content arena designated as *crisis/emergency assistance and prevention* (i.e., responding to, and where feasible, preventing school and personal crises). The emphasis is on weaving together a significant range of school and

Figure 18.4 Matrix for reviewing scope and content of a component to address barriers to learning.*

community resources to deal with the concerns. We will discuss addressing trauma in schools in the context of this arena after briefly noting the need for reworking school leadership and infrastructure to increase the emphasis on developing a unified and comprehensive system of learning supports as a critical and fully integrated facet of school improvement plans.

---

*General initiatives and specific school-wide and classroom-based programs and services can be embedded into the matrix. Think about those related to positive behavioral supports; programs for safe and drug-free schools; full-service community schools and Family Resource Centers; special project initiatives such as the *School-Based Health Center* movement, the *Safe Schools/Healthy Students* projects, and the *Coordinated School Health Program*; efforts to address bilingual, cultural, and other diversity concerns; compensatory and special education programs; and the mandates stemming from the No Child Left Behind Act.

A Few Comments About Leadership and Infrastructure

It is clear that building an enabling or learning supports component requires strong leadership and new positions to help steer systemic changes and construct the necessary infrastructure.[11] Establishment and maintenance of the component requires continuous, proactive, and effective teaming, organization, and accountability.

Administrative leadership *at every level* is key to the success of any systemic change initiative in schools. Given that an enabling or learning supports component is one of the primary and essential components of school improvement, it is imperative to have designated administrative and staff leadership for this component at school and district levels. Everyone at the school site should be aware of who in the school district provides leadership in, promotes, and is accountable for the development of the component. It is imperative that there is an administrative leader whose job description makes him or her accountable for developing a comprehensive and cohesive component and who is at a high enough level to be at key decision-making tables when budget and other fundamental decisions are discussed.

At the school level, an administrative leader for the component may be created by redefining a percentage (e.g., 50%) of an assistant principal's day. Or, in schools that only have one administrator, the principal might delegate some administrative responsibilities to a coordinator (e.g., Title I coordinator or a center coordinator at schools with a Family or Parent Center). The designated administrative leader must sit on a resource-oriented learning supports leadership team and represent and advocate team recommendations at administrative and governance body meetings.

The administrative leader must also guide and be accountable for daily implementation, monitoring, and problem solving. This individual is the natural link to component leaders in a family of schools (e.g., a feeder pattern) and at the district level and should be a vital force for outreach to engage the community.

There is also the need for a staff lead to address daily operational matters. This may be one of the learning supports staff (e.g., a school counselor, school psychologist, social worker, school nurse) or a Title I coordinator, or a teacher with special interest in learning supports. In general, these leaders, along with other key staff, embody the vision for the component. Their job descriptions should be reframed to delineate specific functions related to their new roles, responsibilities, and accountabilities.[12]

The long-range aim is to weave all resources together into the fabric of every school and evolve a comprehensive component that effectively addresses barriers to development, learning, and teaching. As leaders and policymakers recognize the essential nature of such a component, it will be easier to integrate resources to address all barriers, including responding to school- and community-wide traumatic events. In turn, this will enhance efforts to foster healthy development and improve academic outcomes.

PLANNING FOR ADDRESSING TRAUMA IN SCHOOLS

Each year many children and adolescents experience events that can traumatize them (e.g., disrupt their sense of safety, security, and well-being) from such events as school and community shootings, natural disasters, death of a family member or a friend, maltreatment, and abandonment and neglect. Resulting trauma may be acute or chronic and manifested in a variety of ways, such as anxiety, sadness, withdrawal, disturbed sleep, difficulty paying attention, anger, irritability, repeated and intrusive thoughts, depression, and a variety of behavioral problems. And, of course, the trauma can significantly disrupt learning and neurological development.

Addressing trauma in schools is a natural facet of crisis/emergency response and prevention, which is highlighted in Exhibit 18.1 as one of the six major content arenas of a comprehensive system for addressing barriers to learning and teaching and re-engaging disconnected students. Moreover, while the tendency often is to focus on trauma only as an aftermath concern (and sometimes not until a youngster is clinically diagnosed as having posttraumatic stress disorder), schools are in a good position to plan with a full continuum of interventions in mind (again see Figures 18.3 and 18.4). Traumatic events for which schools must plan can be grouped as (1) school-wide or community crises (e.g., major community-wide disaster such as a hurricane, flood, earthquake, terrorist attack; fire in building; sniper on campus), (2) small group crises (e.g., minor community disruption such as an earth tremor, death of a shared acquaintance), and (3) individual crises, which may be short lived or repeated over time (e.g., student has experienced a divorce in the family, separation from a parent, serious illness, physical and/or sexual abuse, or domestic violence, and students who migrate after natural disasters or who come from war zones). In some schools, a significant number of children have experienced a variety of crises over an extended period of time.

Extensive resources and references related to crisis and trauma are available (see Notes section at end of chapter). A few have focused specifically on the role schools can play.[13] As with other areas of child mental health practices in schools, the emphasis is often on finding ways to offer clinically oriented individual and group practices provided by highly qualified professionals (which are in short supply). And because strong empirical support for effectiveness is sparse, most of these are viewed mainly as promising and best practices. Generally missing from proposals for what schools should do is how the work can appropriately be embedded as part of an overall system for addressing barriers to learning and teaching.

Key Concerns in Planning Responses to Potentially Trauma-Producing Events

Major disasters tend to show the gaps in planning for emergencies. Exhibit 18.2 provides an example of some lessons learned from the 2005 Gulf Coast hurricanes and flooding.

EXHIBIT 18.2

SOME LESSONS LEARNED FROM THE GULF COAST DISASTER

Following the 2005 Gulf Coast disaster, there was an outpouring of resources and talented people who expressed a desire to help those affected. One focus was the schools. From the various accounts, a significant proportion of those ready to volunteer did actually attempt to help initially. However, in many cases, the mechanisms for linking people and resources to where they were needed often weren't in place. Here are a few lessons learned.

1. The focus seems to have been mainly on using sparse resources to provide clinical services (e.g., triage and counseling) to individual students, but the numbers in need far outweighed the available clinical services.
2. In some (but not enough) situations, school districts and specific schools did move quickly to develop systemic plans and implement broad-band programs to address the needs of the many displaced students and families. These districts seemed to have leadership and staff with a breadth of understanding about how to go beyond immediate crisis responses to attend to the multifaceted and ongoing needs of students, families, and staff.
3. Those schools where crisis response planning and training had been done effectively in recent years apparently were able to respond better than those without such preparation. A few districts and schools did the type of systemic planning and responding necessary to effectively (a) address the transition needs of many students, families, and staff who had to move into new schools (often in new states) and (b) deal with the longer term psychological and social aftermath effects continuing to interfere with students learning and teachers teaching.
4. In all cases, a major burden fell on a relatively few people, and they continued over the longer term to bear the responsibility and often overwhelming stress. Their plight underscores the need for systemic changes that enhance how school and community resources are woven together to broaden the base of support and provide support for those bearing the brunt of helping others.
5. In some places the response was particularly bad. One volunteer reported feeling that "The bottom line [was] ... NO ONE was prepared!" Another emphasized there was no effective coordination. The situation was described in the feedback as the "disaster within the disaster."

The extent of crisis or trauma from an event often is in the eye of the beholder (i.e., is dependent on personal perception). Thus, there can be wide variability at a school with respect to whether an event is labeled as potentially trauma producing. In planning, then, decisions must be made about when an event should be designated as warranting a crisis response. After deciding on this, the dilemma in planning and decision making is that of establishing a set of checks and balances to ensure potentially trauma-producing events are not ignored *and* that there is not an overreaction to events that should not be treated as such. Given the inevitability of differences regarding how an event is perceived, efforts to formulate criteria probably should focus on delineating an expedient *process* for deciding rather than the more difficult task of detailing what is and isn't likely to produce a traumatic response.

For example, we have seen schools develop a process whereby each member of its crisis team is encouraged to take the initiative of contacting another team member whenever an event (e.g., a drive-by shooting in the neighborhood) might warrant a response. If the contacted team member agrees a response is needed, the rest of the crisis team is immediately mobilized to see if the majority concurs that the event is potentially traumatizing for students at the school. Then, appropriate responses are implemented. These may range from a school-wide response to an intervention focused on a specific classroom or on a small group or individual. Importantly, these interventions are delivered collaboratively through a planned, team-based approach rather than relying exclusively on external sources or fragmented intervention programs. For example, such planning encourages school administrators, teachers, and other school support staff to develop plans and deliver essential supports in classrooms rather than having outside providers deliver isolated services.

Obviously, some staff, because of their roles, are critical to the success of crisis response (e.g., school nurses, psychologists, specific administrators, teachers, office staff). In addition, others have relevant interests and special abilities (e.g., first aid and counseling skills). And some events require mobilization of off-campus resources. Planning involves identifying available resources and clarifying steps by which such resources will be mobilized as needed. Planning also must account for the ongoing staff development for all educators and staff in the building to ensure continuous support throughout the school day.[14]

In brief, for schools, the immediate concern in planning responses to any crisis is how to ensure the school is safe and how to restore a sense of equilibrium. A second concern is to provide psychological first aid.[15] A third emphasis is moving traumatized students and staff from feeling like victims to developing a sense of control, including empowering all educators to provide supports even if they are not of a therapeutic nature. A fourth involves planning ways to connect students with immediate social support, such as peer buddies, other staff, family, and community agencies.

Finally, schools need to plan for aftermath support, guidance, and other forms of assistance, including how they will handle referrals for those who need more intensive interventions. Such planning must account for the special needs of specific subgroups, school staff, and those who have the added stress of implementing response plans. Aftermath planning for classroom activities center around enabling students to express and discuss feelings about the crisis event, which are available throughout this book as well as through the Center for Mental Health in Schools' website (http://smhp.psych.ucla.edu/). And, when a traumatic event includes death and other forms of loss, schools must be prepared to address grief reactions (see chapters 10 and 11, as well as *Practice Notes on Grief and Loss*[16]).

When decisions are made to include psychotherapy or behavior change interventions, special attention is given to empirically supported treatments (for a list of empirically supported interventions, visit http://smhp.psych.ucla.edu/qf/ests. htm). A special focus throughout involves planning for language and relevant cultural considerations—a topic addressed throughout this book.

At an appropriate time after a crisis, a debriefing analysis of the quality of the response should be made to identify the need for system improvements and additional training. To maintain a big-picture focus, such an analysis should be done by the team responsible for developing the school's comprehensive and cohesive system of learning supports.

CONCLUSION

Schools clearly need to focus on how to help students, families, and staff with respect to trauma. At the same time, the emphasis should not be on responding to trauma as another ad hoc mental health agenda item. Instead, we suggest broadly conceiving the work as that of addressing barriers to learning and teaching and re-engaging disconnected students (including a full range of psychosocial and mental health concerns). Concerns for trauma fit well into such a unifying concept.

As indicated in Figure 18.3, we conceive three overlapping *systems* that encompass a continuum of caring. These systems are designed to do the following:

- Promote health and prevent problems
- Intervene as early after onset of a problem as is feasible
- Treat severe, pervasive, and chronic problems

The comprehensive nature of such a continuum requires concerted efforts to coordinate interventions and supports at any given time as well as over the span of time that students and their families are being assisted.

Given this perspective, the call is for policy decision makers and school improvement leaders to move beyond "another initiative" and modest tinkering in enhancing supports for students. The need is to transform public education to ensure all students have an equal opportunity to succeed at school and beyond. Such a transformation requires drawing on well-conceived, broad frameworks and the best available information and scholarship and calls for weaving together school-owned resources and community and family resources. To do less is to maintain a very unsatisfactory status quo.

NOTES

1. Price & Lear, 2008.
2. Adelman & Taylor, 1997, 2010; Marx & Wooley, 1998; Price & Lear, 2008.

3. Adelman & Taylor, 1997.

4. Center for Mental Health in Schools, 2010.

5. See Center for Mental Health in Schools, 2005a.

6. Adelman & Taylor, 1997, 2000, 2006, 2007, 2009, 2010; Taylor & Adelman, 2000.

7. Iowa Department of Education with the Iowa Collaboration for Youth Development, 2004; Louisiana Department of Education, 2009.

8. Center for Mental Health in Schools, 2005b.

9. Adelman & Taylor, 2000, 2006, 2010.

10. See Center for Mental Health in Schools, 2007a.

11. Adelman & Taylor, 2006, 2008, 2010; Center for Mental Health in Schools, 2007b.

12. Prototype job descriptions have been developed and are online at http://smhp. psych.ucla.edu/pdfdocs/studentsupport/toolkit/aidd.pdf

13. Auger, Seymour, & Roberts, Jr., 2004; Cole et al., 2005; Horenstein, 2002; Jaycox,2004; Jimerson, Brock, & Pletcher, 2005; National Child Traumatic Stress Network, n.d.

14. Center for Mental Health in Schools, 2008.

15. National Child Traumatic Stress Network and National Center for PTSD, 2009; National Institute of Mental Health, 2000; Saltzman, Steinberg, Layne, Aisenberg, & Pynoos, 2001.

16. http://smhp.psych.ucla.edu/pdfdocs/practicenotes/grief.pdf

REFERENCES

Adelman, H. S., & Taylor, L. (1997). Addressing barriers to learning: Beyond school-linked services and full service schools. *American Journal of Orthopsychiatry, 67,* 408–421.

Adelman, H. S., & Taylor, L. (2000). Looking at school health and school reform policy through the lens of addressing barriers to learning. *Children Services: Social Policy, Research, and Practice, 3,* 117–132.

Adelman, H. S., & Taylor, L. (2006). *The school leader's guide to student learning supports: New directions for addressing barriers to learning.* Thousand Oaks, CA: Corwin Press.

Adelman, H. S., & Taylor, L. (2007). School improvement: A systemic view of what's missing and what to do about it. In B. Despres (Ed.), *Systems thinkers in action: A field guide for effective change leadership in education.* New York, NY: Rowman & Littlefield.

Adelman, H. S., & Taylor, L. (2008). *Rebuilding for learning: Addressing barriers to learning and teaching and re-engaging students.* New York, NY: Scholastic.

Adelman, H. S., & Taylor, L. (2009). Ending the marginalization of mental health in schools: A comprehensive approach. In R. Christner & R. Mennuti (Eds.), *School-based mental health: A practitioner's guide to comparative practices.* New York, NY: Routledge Publishing.

Adelman, H. S., & Taylor, L. (2010). *Mental health in schools: Engaging learners, preventing problems, and improving schools.* Thousand Oaks, CA: Corwin Press.

Auger, R., Seymour, J., & Roberts, Jr., W. (2004). Responding to terror: The impact of September 11 on K-12 schools' responses. *Professional School Counseling, 7,* 222–230.

Center for Mental Health in Schools. (2005a). *School improvement planning: What's missing?* Los Angeles, CA: Author. Retrieved from http://smhp.psych.ucla.edu/whatsmissing.htm

Center for Mental Health in Schools. (2005b). *Another initiative? Where does it fit? A unifying framework and an integrated infrastructure for schools to address barriers to learning and promote healthy development.* Los Angeles, CA: Author. Retrieved from http://smhp.psych.ucla.edu/pdfdocs/infrastructure/anotherinitiative-exec.pdf

Center for Mental Health in Schools. (2007a). *Where's it happening? Examples of new directions for student support & lessons learned.* Los Angeles, CA: Author. Retrieved from http://smhp.psych.ucla.edu/summit2002/wheresithappening.htm

Center for Mental Health in Schools. (2007b). *Toward a school district infrastructure that more effectively addresses barriers to learning and teaching.* Los Angeles, CA: Author. Retrieved from http://smhp.psych.ucla.edu/pdfdocs/briefs/toward%20a%20school%20district%20infrastructure.pdf

Center for Mental Health in Schools. (2008). *Responding to crisis at a school.* Los Angeles, CA: Author. Retrieved from http://smhp.psych.ucla.edu/pdfdocs/crisis/crisis.pdf

Center for Mental Health in Schools. (2010). *Turning around, transforming, and continuously improving schools: Federal proposals are still based on a two- rather than a three-component blueprint.* Los Angeles, CA: Author. Retrieved from http://smhp.psych.ucla.edu/pdfdocs/turning.pdf

Cole, S. F., O'Brien, J. G., Gadd, M. G., Ristuccia, J., Wallace, D. L., & Gregory, M. (2005). *Helping traumatized children learn, a report and policy agenda: Supportive school environments for children traumatized by family violence.* Boston, MA: Massachusetts Advocates for Children.

Horenstein, J. (2002). Provision of trauma services to school populations and faculty. In M. Williams & J. Sommer, Jr. (Eds.), *Simple and complex post-traumatic stress disorder: Strategies for comprehensive treatment in clinical practice* (pp. 241–260). Binghamton, NY: Haworth Maltreatment and Trauma Press/Haworth Press.

Iowa Department of Education with the Iowa Collaboration for Youth Development. (2004). *Enhancing Iowa's systems of supports for development and learning.* Des Moines, IA: Author. Retrieved from http://smhp.psych.ucla.edu/pdfdocs/iowasystemofsupport.pdf

Jaycox, L. (2004). *Cognitive behavioral intervention for trauma in schools (CBITS).* Longmont, CO: SoprisWest.

Jimerson, S., Brock, S., & Pletcher, S. (2005). An integrated model of school crisis preparedness and intervention—A shared foundation to facilitate international crisis intervention. *School Psychology International, 26,* 275–296.

Louisiana Department of Education. (2009). *Louisiana's comprehensive learning supports system: The design document for addressing internal and external barriers to learning and teaching.* Baton Rouge, LA: Author. Retrieved from http://www.doe.state.la.us/lde/uploads/15044.pdf

Marx, E., & Wooley, S., with Northrop, D. (Eds.). (1998). *Health is academic: A guide to coordinated school health programs.* New York, NY: Teachers College Record.

National Child Traumatic Stress Network and National Center for PTSD. (2009). *Psychological first aid: Field operations guide (2nd ed.).* Retrieved from http://www.nctsnet.org/nccts/nav.do?pid=typ_terr_resources_pfa

National Child Traumatic Stress Network. (n.d.). *Resources for school personnel.* Retrieved from http://www.nctsnet.org/nccts/nav.do?pid=ctr_aud_schl

National Institute of Mental Health. (2000). *Children and violence.* Retrieved from http://www.nimh.nih.gov/publicat/violence.cfm

Price, O. A., & Lear, J. G. (2008). *School mental health services for the 21st century: Lessons from the District of Columbia School Mental Health Program.* Retrieved from http://www.healthinschools.org/~/media/Files/PDF/92ECED7541B34498949 D03E692EAA4F1.ashx

Saltzman, W. R., Steinberg, A. M., Layne, C. M., Aisenberg, E., & Pynoos, R. S. (2001). A developmental approach to school-based treatment of adolescents exposed to trauma and traumatic loss. *Journal of Child and Adolescent Group Therapy, 11,* 43–56.

Taylor, L., & Adelman, H. S. (2000). Toward ending the marginalization of mental health in schools. *Journal of School Health, 70,* 210–215.

WEB RESOURCES

Rather than make an extensive list here, you can obtain a sense of the nature and scope of what is easily accessible by starting with our Center for Mental Health in Schools' online clearinghouse. See in particular the Quick Find Topics:

1. *Crisis Prevention and Response:* http://smhp.psych.ucla.edu/qf/ p2107_01.htm
2. *Post-Traumatic Stress:* http://smhp.psych.ucla.edu/qf/ptsd.htm
3. *Grief and Bereavement:* http://smhp.psych.ucla.edu/qf/p3003_01.htm

Each Quick Find provides links to resource materials from our center and links to other centers that offer a variety of resources and references. Also, for immediate aids in an emergency, click on the icon labeled *Responding to a Crisis* on our center's homepage (http://smhp.psych.ucla.edu/).

19

Lessons for Developing Resilience

GEORGE S. EVERLY, JR., AND RACHEL M. FIRESTONE ■

INTRODUCTION

The stress and degree of pressure inherent in the lives of children is at an all-time high. As a brief example, approximately 700 children were hit by gunfire last year on the south side of Chicago.[1] This amounts to an average of nearly two children being shot *every day*. Further, suicide is the third leading cause of death among adolescents and is at its highest level in 15 years among preteen and teen-age girls.[2] Therefore, it is with great empathy, generosity of spirit, and kindness that an educator must come to the table when educating children who have lived through adversity and who have and may continue to live through traumatic experiences. For these children, critical incidents can challenge their ability to cope and may cause acute impairment and dysfunction.

Educators know that learning is a lot harder to accomplish for students who do not have coping strategies and adaptive skills. Effective educators model and teach these coping strategies to children (consciously or unconsciously), which in turn facilitates the ability to "rebound" after trauma and to develop a greater sense of personal effectiveness—all components of *resiliency*. Resiliency is and should be viewed as a life skill, one that is developed through actions and behaviors.

It is not easy to educate children who have undergone trauma. Many may be hesitant and unwilling to move forward. Symptoms of traumatic stress may make them unavailable for learning and in turn hinder their academic functioning. However, there are some well-documented strategies and resources to help alleviate these barriers to learning that can be implemented in schools. This concluding chapter seeks to further define resilience while also delving into the nature of psychological trauma. Most important, this chapter will introduce a model of resilience and seven skills necessary to cope with stress and to build resiliency among children. Though this chapter is at the close of your text, it is hoped that the preceding chapters will connect to these invaluable lessons.

THE NATURE OF PSYCHOLOGICAL TRAUMA: A WORLDVIEW PERSPECTIVE

To understand the repercussions of critical incidents for children, it is imperative to grasp the psychological mechanisms that impact the symptoms of traumatic stress. As an educator, it is helpful to understand what is going on in the minds of students, considering behavioral, psychological, and physiological mechanisms of action and the extent to which they play a role in the development of resiliency.

The automatic cognitive actions (thoughts) of individuals differ in the face of adversity or trauma. Children react differently depending on the way their minds interpret their surroundings. In addition, cognitive appraisal plays a large role in the response to trauma, which "...refers to the process of cognitive interpretation, that is, the meaning that we assign to the world as it unfolds before us."[3] Our cognitions help us to derive meaning from potentially traumatic experiences. It can therefore be said that cognitive appraisal, in combination with the emotional reaction, results in how a traumatic event is perceived. Every individual interprets critical incidents and then attaches meaning to them in unique ways.

Children can be taught that their minds innately process information in certain ways, and that these processes of cognitive appraisal and emotional reactions are integral in the face of future traumatic experiences. Individuals can become more aware of their emotional reactions in order to more effectively cope with traumatic experiences in the future. Students should be taught about cognitive appraisal, the objective interpretation of the event, and the corresponding emotions, as they may very well determine the likelihood of the development of resiliency.

Cognitive appraisal and emotional reactions are in many ways tied to the values that we hold as individuals. Values may include beliefs about norms and rules, treatment of other individuals, or self-reliance. Each student holds a unique set of values, though not completely developed. Most classrooms can also probably find similarities in the values they hold as a group. To get an idea of the values contained within classrooms, teachers can brainstorm and post classroom values and core beliefs about the world. Aside from offering many benefits to a classroom under normal circumstances, individual and universal values are helpful in understanding why some experiences are deemed to be traumatic by some individuals while others are not.

Jellinek, Patel, and Froehle[4] found that mentally healthy students maintain a sense of security and trust in the world. However, by definition, a critical incident may become debilitating and can cause dysfunction when it causes a "contradiction to some deeply held cognitive schema, assumption about the world."[5]

Students may have had a traumatic experience that violated a core belief. They may ask questions such as "Is this world safe?" or "Is this going to happen again?" or "I thought my parents are supposed to care for me, so why are they never around?" All of these questions show the contradictions that children may grapple with. Educators can answer their questions through reflection of the experiences and through probing further to get to the positive aspects of these situations: Have these situations made students stronger? Do they feel safe now? In what situations do they feel most safe? In which environments do they continue to thrive?

It has been noted that "leading a successful life, even surviving, depends on the ability to predict future events from present ones, or at least the belief that one can do so. ... [T]he need to make sense of events is as fundamental as the need for food and water."[6] When children cannot make sense of their experiences, psychotraumagenesis—psychological disturbance due to trauma—may develop. Educators can help children rebuild stable core beliefs about their world and make sense of their experiences.

There are some specific core beliefs that are relevant to this discussion; such core beliefs include the need for attachment to and trust in others, the need for a positive self-identity, view of oneself (self-esteem and self-efficacy), the belief in a fair and just world, the need for physical safety, and the belief in some over-arching order to life (e.g., spirituality, or faith in a defining order, unifying paradigm, etc.).[7] An experience is considered to be traumatic when one of these beliefs is threatened, violated, or destroyed. Most classrooms have many students whose physical safety was jeopardized, whose trust was broken, or whose self-esteem was greatly diminished. The key in working with these children is to restore their "dysfunctional" beliefs back to feeling like *functional* beliefs. There are two ways of achieving this goal.

First, when appropriate, have children understand that the critical incident(s) was an exception to the rule.[8] They must gain a sense that the event was a single occurrence among others that do not violate their core belief. This allows children to understand that their beliefs about their world have not disappeared or been taken from them, and that they can be restored and kept in their belief system. It should be noted that the reality is that some critical incidents are not exceptions to the rule and may pervade the life of a child. In this case, it may be detrimental to present them as rare or one-time events, and reliance on the other strategies in this chapter is critical.

The second approach is to help children understand that the experience did not actually violate the core belief. They may feel that the situation was awful, but in the grand scheme of their other life experiences they are able to see that their core belief was not shattered. These two approaches are very similar, yet distinct, and are quite effective in approaching children's feelings. By restoring core beliefs, children can rebound and thus work toward building resiliency.

Depending on the classroom or learning environment, discussion of core beliefs can be quite helpful to your students. Additionally, do not underestimate the power of characters in literature as means of addressing the diminishing and restoring of these beliefs. At the elementary, middle, and high school levels these characters can be discussed in great length for their ambition to overcome challenges, their reliance (or lack of reliance) on support systems, individual coping mechanisms, and overall outcomes.

DEFINING RESILIENCE: THE MODEL OF HUMAN RESISTANCE, RESILIENCY, AND RECOVERY

Resilience has been defined as "the ability to withstand or rebound from extreme challenges or adversity."[9] The most important word from this definition is "rebound." Data cited in earlier chapters indicate that most, if not all, classrooms contain children who may be experiencing high levels of distress, lacking energy, having trouble sleeping, and even having suicidal thoughts and the loss of hope and future orientation. Additionally, children who have experienced trauma often act out behaviorally. Chronic irritability, poor academic performance, verbal altercations, physical violence, and even self-medication may be commonplace.[10] It is with these symptoms in mind and the children who embody them that resiliency, and the ability to rebound, must be fostered.

Resiliency can be described within a three-point continuum: resistance, resiliency, and recovery. Each notion along this continuum is connected with a very specific meaning. To begin, *resistance* is the existence of immunity. Just as our bodies must build immunity against bacteria and others pathogens, our minds must build up immunity against the traumatic experiences often inherent in life. As stated previously, *resiliency* is connected with the ability to rebound from adverse situations. Lastly, *recovery* refers to the ability to return to previous levels of adaptability and function, both psychologically and behaviorally, following critical incidents. Recovery often deals with specific collaborative efforts between educators and family members following trauma. This model, referred to as the Johns Hopkins University Model of Human Resistance, Resiliency, and Recovery, is broken down into a four-pronged strategic foundation, consisting of (1) providing realistic expectations, (2) fostering group cohesion and social support, (3) fostering positive cognitions, and (d) building self-efficacy and hardiness.[11]

Providing realistic expectations refers to helping a child develop reasonable expectations and coping skills prior to the occurrence of a potentially traumatic experience. If a child is better able to predict or imagine what an event or experience may look, sound, and feel like, he or she will most likely be able to rebound more readily.

Fostering group cohesion and social support refers to the power of social support (e.g., family, friends, educators, mentors) to buffer stress.[12] Communication with these significant individuals should include providing honest and accurate information, reassurance, direction, motivation, and a sense of connectedness. Each of these specific forms of communication should be integrated into the way that the school staff interacts with students and in turn the way they interact with one another.

Research has even shown that sharing meals and eating together on a fairly regular basis can serve to build important bonds for children.[13] Lunchtime meals spent together can be opportunities to promote these types of communication with students. Book talks and thematic discussions can take part during lunch at school or through an after-school club.

Fostering positive cognitions refers to positive and optimistic thinking, versus that of negative and more pessimistic thought processes. Research has shown that positive cognitions deter excessive stress and foster resilience.[14] Examples of positive cognitions are positive memories from the past that may connect to the critical incident or lead to generally optimistic thoughts about the future.

Self-efficacy and hardiness, though connected, are distinct terms. Self-efficacy is defined as the belief in one's ability to organize and execute the courses of action required to achieve necessary and desired goals.[15] Hardiness refers to the belief in one's own self-efficacy, the tendency to see stressful events as challenges to be overcome and opportunities for growth, and a strong commitment and sense of purpose.[16]

Let's take a closer look at both of these constructs as they relate to building resiliency among children who have experienced trauma. Self-efficacy, in the life of a child, will play out in peer interactions, academic success or failure, and just about every realm of life. If children can develop a deep sense of self-efficacy, they will take on challenges and push themselves in positive directions. Children who have high levels of self-efficacy tend to develop hobbies, engage in social interactions more frequently, and have a greater curiosity about the world—even in the face of adversity.

According to Bandura,[17] self-efficacy is developed through performance, vicarious experiences (e.g., surrounding oneself with others who achieve and work hard, or visualizing others performing successfully), and verbal persuasion and support (self-talk and motivational speech). More specifically, successes and positive performances help children build greater self-efficacy and actually allow for failures to feel less important or significant. If an event is considered to be a success to a child, optimism is built. We must set students up for opportunities for success and teach them how to view experiences in their daily lives as learning experiences and successes, when appropriate.

Self-efficacy is further developed through successfully managing physiological and affective arousal. Relaxation practices, which can be integrated into a general classroom setting, can aid children in stabilizing physiological and affective arousal, thereby increasing self-efficacy. As mentioned earlier, resiliency and its components are life skills that require time and energy to develop.

We should be aware that some of the experiences children have dealt with are not one-time occurrences. These may be pervasive experiences that reoccur for many years. It is how we prepare these children for such events that will dictate their cognitive understandings, emotional reactions, and ultimately, their physical and psychological health. The Model of Human Resistance, Resiliency, and Recovery can help educators understand the components of resiliency in the face of trauma and can be used to teach children how to build resistance and resiliency against adverse experiences in their lives.

DEFINING THE CORE ELEMENTS OF RESILIENCE—*THE RESILIENT CHILD*

To truly aid children who have experienced trauma, honing in on essential life skills, such as optimism, responsibility, and the development of friendships with peers and other support networks, helps to provide a framework within which they can function more productively and in a psychologically healthy state. Importantly, there is a fine balance to be struck between allowing children to make their own mistakes and discoveries about the ways of the world and teaching these life skills, which will help to guide them through daily life and post-trauma recovery. Given that children are the most precious commodity in our society, it is our responsibility to make sure they learn these lessons and not simply hope they acquire these understandings along the way on their own. This is not an easy feat, however, and requires patience and persistence.

There are specific actions, thoughts, and behaviors that can be used to develop and enhance resiliency among children. In the classroom these lessons can be engrained, discreetly or overtly, in daily instruction, in classroom discussions, and through other educational endeavors. The following seven lessons are critical in fostering resiliency among children[18]:

- Valuing friends, mentors, and the support of others
- Making the three most difficult decisions (decisions regarding conflicts with other people, when to be loyal, and how to navigate levels of control in decision making)
- Taking responsibility for one's actions
- Investing in personal health
- Learning the power of optimism
- Learning the importance of faith
- Cultivating integrity

Educators are frequently asked to create a classroom climate engrained with aspects of collaboration, trust, growth, and a focus on fostering needed emotional and academic strength. This is quite a balancing act. Given the pressure of standardized testing in many school settings, instituting some of these lessons may seem like a divergence from your initial focus. However, teaching many of these lessons is in fact what will empower your students to succeed on these mandated tests. In this regard, these lessons are not tangents from your already planned goals, and instead will supplement them in leading to student success. While each lesson carries its own utility, it is believed that through an understanding and development of *all seven lessons*, resiliency has the greatest likelihood of being fostered.

Value friends, mentors, and the support of others. Valuing others is critical to the development of resiliency. Research has consistently shown that the support of family, friends, and peers is critical in enhancing resilience in stressful situations.[19]

Learning occurs most in an environment where friends and other supportive individuals are part of the learning experience. This can be facilitated by allowing students to work in cooperative groups and on teams. Children thrive when given a purpose, and group work often promotes leadership and the need to develop relationships within the classroom. When children learn to rely on themselves *and on others* to complete assignments and projects, a trust in themselves and those around them is fostered. Additionally, students can learn to problem solve and think critically through struggles related to working together. In this vein, students can be asked to reflect in writing or verbally about their own and their group's performance—this can be related to listening skills, openness to new ideas, flexibility, teamwork, and a general ability to work together toward a common goal. Students can also be placed in groups, if possible, with those of varying levels of academic abilities—heterogeneous groups. Lower performing students are then challenged by their peers and higher performing students are able to teach and break down tasks into manageable steps.

Children, especially those who have experienced trauma and may be dealing with the associated psychological ramifications, must have mentors they can look to for inspiration and optimism. Teaching incorporates many of the same characteristics of mentoring; in fact, simply showing up each day and teaching students provides an example of many appropriate behaviors. Additionally, students can find and connect with mentors and role models in literature. For instance, many books that are appropriate for use in the classroom have characters that portray varying levels of empathy, emotion, optimism, and self-efficacy. *Feelings* is a book full of pictures, poems, and stories that portray various emotions such as anger, fear, and joy.[20] Also appropriate for lower elementary school students is *Mr. Magnolia*, a story of optimism in the face of adversity,[21] and *What If? And The Short Tree and the Bird That Could Not Sing*, which focuses on the importance of optimism, empathy, and emotion regulation in the development of resiliency.[22]

Mentors can be found in many places. Individuals from the community who show leadership and qualities of resilience are often willing to come speak to students. Within the school, older students can be mentors to younger students with projects or through such activities as after-school tutoring. Encourage students to reflect on who the mentors and role models are in their lives. Do they have mentors at home? Who are the people they view as mentors at school? Do not forget that students also have the capacity to be mentors themselves. Allow students to share their experiences with others and to reflect upon how they have grown, become more optimistic, and made important decisions.

Make decisions related to conflicts with other people, decisions related to when to be loyal, and those related to the issue of control. We can help foster resilience by teaching students about difficult decisions and in turn teaching them the tools to handle them when they arise, thus allowing for more fluid and productive decision making. When dealing with conflicts with other people, children can learn to always seek out a conclusion that leads to a win-win for both parties—this often comes out of negotiation and compromise. When dealing with decisions of loyalty, children must learn to identify when loyalty is warranted or when loyalty should be broken. The three greatest challenges to loyalty include loyalty to one friend versus another, loyalty to friends versus parents, and issues of authority and right and wrong.[23] Finally, children can learn to recognize and accept the things in their lives over which they have little to no control. Being present and available to your students is critical, such that when such conflicts arise, educators can assist in the problem-solving process.

Teach children to take responsibility for their actions. When a person takes responsibility for his or her actions, self-esteem is affected.[24] While lowered self-esteem is not enjoyable, it is an inevitable part of a healthy life. In the short run, a child may experience lowered self-esteem as a result of taking responsibility for an action that he or she is not particularly proud of, but that child benefits in the long run. Children can build their self-esteem if they consistently take responsibility for their actions and if they receive feedback that promotes this process.

Invest in one's health. Some educators have found success beginning class with 10 minutes of mindfulness meditation and yoga. These 10 minutes can be effective in lowering anxiety levels and calming minds, and in turn increasing academic engagement. Thich Nhat Hahn, a Vietnamese and Buddhist teacher, states, "By bringing one's body and mind together in the present moment, we can experience peace and a unity with humanity and with all of life."[25]

Investment in one's health should be viewed as a preventative medicine and consists of encouraging (1) a positive attitude, (2) sleep/rest, (3) nutrition, and (4) exercise.[26] Beginning with attitude, and remembering that attitudes are an important component to behavioral change, each component provides a building block to promote general physical health. Students' level of physical wellness is closely tied to their ability to focus on schoolwork and for their brains to function at optimal levels. So, why not tie the promotion of physical health into a daily routine? Who says this is only the job of the physical education teachers or coaches? Stretching and allowing students time to be out of their seats are simple, effective strategies that fall into this category. *The Resilient Child*[27] offers specific classroom strategies to help students invest in their own health.

Learn the power of optimism. For an educator, this means learning to teach students how to be optimistic. Optimism is defined as taking the most positive or hopeful view of life. Optimistic people are actually more resilient than pessimistic people, and optimism offers a psychological immunity to some symptoms of traumatic stress. Additionally, optimistic people get depressed less often, they tend to be higher achievers, and on average they are physically healthier than pessimistic people.[28] In classrooms, having students write about the pros and cons of specific situations can help develop optimism. Teaching children to pick out the positive components, in even the most difficult of situations, is essential in building optimism and in turn resiliency. One of the best ways to teach optimism to students is for adults to model optimistic behavior.

According to Seligman, optimistic people tend to expect positive outcomes and see problems as temporary rather than chronic, specific, and somewhat limited in scope, and that some happenings in life are out of their control.[29] Encourage students, through educational activities and exercises, to frame some of their thoughts through these optimistic lenses. Certainly, it would be naïve to think that good is going to be found in everything your students experience or have experienced in their lives; however, it is in the present and future moments that optimism can be fostered.

Learn the importance of faith. It should be noted that faith, in this context, does not refer to religious faith. Rather, faith is viewed as an expectation or belief in something for which we might have no tangible, objective evidence. It's a form of psychological glue that holds all of our experiences together and puts them into context, allowing children and adults to derive a sense of order in the world. Faith fuels optimism and allows individuals to accept the things they cannot understand.[30] Much of this belief deals with teaching children to try to let go of what is out of their control and instead to focus on what is in fact within their control.

Having faith also encompasses accepting that there are gray areas with regard to why situations occur. Encourage students to ask questions and to reflect upon their experiences. Let them know that it is all right not to come to concrete, black-and-white answers.

Cultivate integrity. Lastly, we must hone in on teaching children to follow a moral compass and to cultivate integrity. It is clear that without such guidelines, all of the aforementioned lessons have little to stand on. In educational environments, integrity must be explicitly discussed. Offer students a metaphorical compass with four points: honesty, virtue, self-discipline, and reflection. Teach students to practice random acts of kindness. Educators have the power to change the way that students view themselves, and the actions of others, as they navigate the world around them.

Importantly, children (and educators) should be aware that they do not need to develop these skills all at once. If overwhelmed by a plethora of lessons, children may reject these lessons entirely. Instead, this is a life list—teach children to hone in on as many of these lessons as possible as they navigate social situations, family dynamics, and academic settings. When children embody these lessons and live by them, they are able to develop a sense of self and more positive self-esteem and self-efficacy—all important aspects of resiliency.

CONCLUSION

Why do some children show resiliency in the face of adversity while others do not? As noted throughout the chapter, how children appraise, interpret, and react to potentially traumatic experiences is unique based on a variety of individual and environmental factors. Generally, contradictions between experiences and core beliefs can result in traumatic stress. Resiliency, and the ability to withstand and rebound from adversity, can be viewed as a life skill—one that can be developed through actions and behaviors. Most children demonstrating resilience employ some combination of the aforementioned lessons.

Building resiliency is a constant and dynamic process and is integral to preventative mental health care.[31] We have a responsibility to help children build resiliency through education. We must work as a "village" of educators to build resilience among our youth—regardless of socioeconomic background, race, and family structure. As the Hoving Effect demonstrates, "a single, crucial event that shatters the routine of childhood or adolescent life—for better or worse—can markedly alter pessimism or optimism by changing the child's theory of who he is and what he is worth."[32] With children who have experienced trauma, we must legitimize the experiences and their effects while continuing to push children forward. The seven lessons provided in this chapter can aid educators in doing so.

NOTES

1. Schaper & Corley, 2011.
2. Everly, 2009.
3. Everly & Lating, 2002, p. 26.
4. Jellinek, Patel, & Froehle, 2002.
5. Everly & Lating, 2005, p. 266.
6. Frank & Frank, 1991, p. 24.
7. Everly & Lating, 2005.
8. Kaminsky, McCabe, Langlieb, & Everly, 2007.
9. Kaminsky et al., 2007, p. 3.
10. Kaminsky et al., 2007.
11. Nucifora, Langlieb, Siegal, Everly, & Kaminsky, 2007.
12. Flannery, 1990.
13. Eisenberg, Olson, Neumark-Sztainer, Story, & Bearinger, 2004.
14. Affleck & Tennen, 1996; Meichenbaum, 1985; Taylor, 1983; Tedeschi & Calhoun, 1996.
15. Bandura, 1997.
16. Kobasa, Maddi, & Kahn, 1982.
17. Bandura, 1982, 1997.
18. Everly, 2009.
19. e.g., Delmonico, 1997; Ozbay, Fitterling, Charney, & Southwick, 2008; Rosario, Salzinger, Feldman, & Ng-Mak, 2008.

20. Brandenberg,1984.
21. Blake, 2010.
22. Foon, 1991.
23. Everly, 2009.
24. Everly, 2009.
25. Hahn, 2008, p. 57.
26. Everly, 2009.
27. Everly, 2009.
28. Seligman, 2006.
29. Gillham & Reivich, 2004; Seligman, 1995.
30. Everly, 2009.
31. Bonnano, 2004.
32. Seligman, 1995, p. 100.

REFERENCES

Affleck, G., & Tennen, H. (1996). Construing benefits from adversity: Adaptational significance and dispositional underpinnings. *Journal of Personality, 64*, 822–899.

Bandura, A. (1982). The self and mechanisms of agency. In J. Suls (Ed.), *Psychological perspectives on the self* (pp. 3–39). Hillsdale, NJ: Erlbaum.

Bandura, A. (1997). *Self-efficacy: The exercise of control*. New York, NY: Freeman.

Blake, Q. (2010). *Mr. Magnolia*. London, Great Britain: Red Fox.

Bonanno, G. A. (2004). Loss, trauma, and human resilience: Have we underestimated the human capacity to thrive after extremely adverse events? *American Psychologist, 59*(1), 20–28.

Brandenberg, A. (1984). *Feelings*. New York, NY: Muberry Books.

Delmonico, L. (1997). *Stressful life events and resiliency: Coping responses, social support resources, hardiness, and perceived childhood family relationships in adult children of alcoholics* (doctoral dissertation). Retrieved from Dissertation Abstracts International.

Eisenberg, M. E., Olson, R. E., Neumark-Sztainer, D., Story, M., & Bearinger, L. H. (2004). Correlations between family meals and psychosocial well-being among adolescents. *Archives of Pediatrics & Adolescent Medicine, 158*, 792–796.

Everly, G. S., Jr. (2009). *The resilient child: Seven essential lessons for your child's happiness and success*. New York, NY: DiaMedica Publishing.

Everly, G. S., Jr., & Lating, J. M. (2002). *A clinical guide to the treatment of the human stress response* (rev. ed.). New York, NY: Plenum.

Everly, G. S., Jr., & Lating, J. M. (2005). Integration of cognitive and personality-based conceptualization and treatment of psychological trauma. *International Journal of Emergency Mental Health, 7*, 263–276.

Flannery, R. B., Jr. (1990). Social support and psychological trauma: A methodological review. *Journal of Traumatic Stress, 3*, 593–612.

Foon, D. (1991). *What if? And the short tree and the bird that could not sing*. Tonawanda, NY: Firefly Books.

Frank, J. D., & Frank, J. B. (1991). *Persuasion and healing: A comparative study of psychotherapy*. Baltimore, MD: Johns Hopkins University Press.

Gillham, J., & Reivich, K. (2004). Cultivating optimism in childhood and adolescence. *The Annals of the American Academy of Political and Social Science, 591,* 146–163.

Hahn, T. N. (2008). *Mindful movements: Ten exercises for well-being.* Berkeley, CA: Parallax Press.

Jellinek, M., Patel, P., & Froehle, M. C. (Eds.). (2002). *Bright futures in practice: Mental health.* Washington, DC: National Center for Education in Maternal and Child Health at Georgetown University.

Kaminsky, M. J., McCabe, O. L., Langlieb, A., & Everly, G. S., Jr. (2007). An evidence informed model of human resistance, resilience, & recovery: The Johns Hopkins outcome driven, paradigm for disaster mental health services. *Brief Therapy and Crisis Intervention, 7,* 1–11.

Kobasa, S. C., Maddi, S. R., & Kahn, S. (1982). Hardiness and health: A prospective study. *Journal of Personality and Social Psychology, 42,* 168–177.

Meichenbaum, D. (1985). *Stress inoculation training.* New York, NY: Pergamon.

Nucifora, F., Jr., Langlieb, A., Siegal, E., Everly, G. S., Jr., & Kaminsky, M. J. (2007). Building resistance, resilience, and recovery in the wake of school and workplace violence. *Disaster Medicine and Public Health Preparedness, 1,* 33–37.

Ozbay, F., Fitterling, H., Charney, D., & Southwick, S. (2008). Social support and resilience to stress across the lifespan: A neurobiologic framework. *Current Psychiatry Reports, 10,* 304–310.

Rosario, M., Salzinger, S., Feldman, R. S., & Ng-Mak, D. S. (2008). Intervening processes between youths' exposure to community violence and internalizing symptoms over time: The roles of social support and coping. *American Journal of Community Psychology, 41,* 43–62.

Schaper, D., & Corley, C. (2011, March 21). Chicago's schools, police work to stem violence. *National Public Radio.* Retrieved from www.npr.org

Seligman, M. E. P. (1995). *The optimistic child: A proven program to safeguard children against depression and build lifelong resilience.* New York, NY: Houghton Mifflin Company.

Seligman, M. E. P. (2006). *Learned optimism: How to change your mind and your life.* New York, NY: Vintage Books.

Taylor, S. E. (1983). Adjustment to threatening events: A theory of cognitive adaptation. *American Psychologist, 38,* 1161–1173.

Tedeschi, R. G., & Calhoun, L. G. (1996). The post-traumatic growth inventory. *Journal of Traumatic Stress, 9,* 455–471.

CPSIA information can be obtained at www.ICGtesting.com
Printed in the USA
BVOW010604050213

312416BV00002B/5/P

9 780199 766529